Decorating with
F·A·B·R·I·C

Decorating with
F·A·B·R·I·C

A Design Workbook with More than 200 Beautiful Projects to Sew for Your Home

By Donna Lang and Lucretia Robertson

Photographs by Michael Datoli

Illustrations by Dolores R. Santoliquido

Clarkson N. Potter, Inc./Publishers

DEDICATED TO

Dee and Irene

for even though life has been full of those things we dreamed of, nothing we've found has touched us more profoundly or offered us more than has the love of beauty and the joy of handicraft we learned from you.

Published by Clarkson N. Potter, Inc., 201 East 50th Street, New York, New York 10022. Member of the Crown Publishing Group.

Originally published in hardcover by Clarkson N. Potter, Inc., in 1986.

CLARKSON N. POTTER, POTTER and colophon are trademarks of Clarkson N. Potter, Inc.

Manufactured in Japan

Library of Congress Cataloging-in-Publication Data

Lang, Donna.
   Decorating with fabric.

   Includes index.
   1. Sewing.   2. House furnishings.   3. Interior decoration—Amateurs' manuals.   4. Textile fabrics.
I. Robertson, Lucretia.   II. Title.
TX715.L266   1986   646.2′1   85-28180
ISBN 0-517-57378-4
10 9 8 7 6 5 4

Acknowledgments

Writing a book as complicated as this one requires the concerted efforts and the support of many people. The authors are grateful to them all, especially the following:

Michael Datoli for his talent and undaunted good humor; Nancy Novogrod for signing us up, Carolyn Hart Gavin, Kathy Powell, and Pam Krauss for seeing us through, and Steven Martindale for making it legal; Gael Dillon, Juanita Dugdale, and Gigi Knoll for their design skill and good taste, and Dolores Santoliquido for her charming yet technical art; Judy Petersen for the endless hours behind her sewing machine and her steady belief that it could all be done, and done well, and Mavis Brown for her masterful slipcovers; Nancy Work for her constant support, hard work, and sweet friendship; Mary Havlicek for her careful research and assistance; Nancy Caparullo for her nimble fingers and efficient intelligence; Jim Williams for all the bouquets delivered without fail by 6:00 A.M.; the many manufacturers, companies, and fabric shops whose interest and support were crucial to this effort, especially the McCall Pattern Company; all the clients and friends who cordially opened their homes to us, especially Mr. and Mrs. Joel Simon, Mr. and Mrs. Norman Polonofsky, Mr. and Mrs. Lawrence Senn, Mr. and Mrs. Barry Simon, Mr. and Mrs. Joseph Stuhlman, Mr. and Mrs. H. Peter Lorentzen, Mr. and Mrs. Ian Hooper, and Mr. and Mrs. Michael Gregory; Carolyn Sollis for all she's done for us, and Ralph Timm for the years of outspoken belief in us; Dick Rogers for believing in the concept of sewing for the home, both corporately and personally; Peter Garland for his guidance all those years ago and whose courageous spirit inspires us now; Russ Norris, who was one of the most exceptional people we have ever known and whose kind example and extraordinary good taste will never leave us; Lou and Irene and Emma Speziale, and Bill and Dee Flynt, who brought us up and saw us through and were always there for an emotional refueling along the way; Bill Robertson and Joe Lang for far more than we can ever say; and Evan, Ian, Wes, and Keith for waiting patiently for Mommy to read, or play, or button, or to just come home, and still loving us. We thank you, one and all.

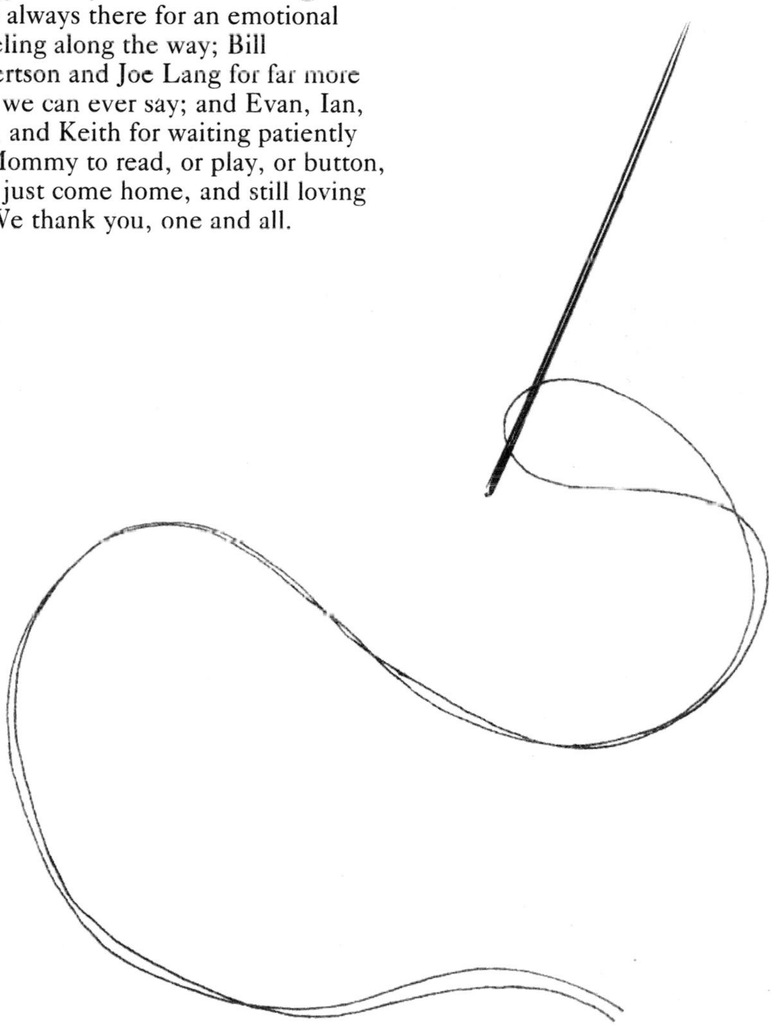

Contents

Preface

Every August I can remember, my mother and I would scour Charleston, West Virginia, looking for the best fabrics for my back-to-school clothes. Since there was always a strict budget, half of the job was finding things we both loved at prices we could afford, but the challenge of getting the absolute most for our money was a big part of the fun. We spent a lot of time downtown at Woolworth's where there was the best selection of good basics like corduroy, piqué, organdy, and those dark ground cotton prints we all wore then for fall. We had some great tricks, my mother and I. We'd recycle my father's suits into beautiful spring coats by opening the seams, laundering the wool serge or gabardine, and recutting them. And every spring and fall I'd use dye to turn my sweaters into brand-new colors. The white one I got at Christmas became spring's pink, next autumn's rose, then spring's deep red, and finally, autumn's purple before it was retired to the Goodwill bag. I never really thought of it as a matter of economy. Making something beautiful from practically nothing was immensely gratifying, and it was something my mother and I did as a team —a creative and exciting gesture. I've still got a silly picture taken of me when I was in the first grade, grinning that toothless six-year-old grin, dressed in the favorite ensemble of my first grade year—a pale blue pinwale corduroy suit with a cunning little beanie hat, cut from the same cloth and decorated with a single white feather. To this day, I <u>love</u> that hat! It was my pride and joy.

Donna F. Lang

—Donna Lang

By the time I met Donna, the hat was a chinchilla beret, and the dress was a Vogue Couturier Pattern she'd whipped up over the weekend. Those childhood experiments with remnants and Rit dye had blossomed into a remarkable talent and a real delight in the creative process. Figuring out just how things are done—sewn, glued, cut, stapled, draped—and then doing them very well on her own was Donna's most satisfying pastime. That was in New York in 1968 and we were both working at Vogue/Butterick Patterns. What we didn't realize then was that we shared a great deal more than the excitement of our jobs in the fashion industry. It wasn't until seven years later, when we shifted our careers from fashion to decorating and began our interior design partnership, that we discovered that there were great similarities in our backgrounds.

I was born and brought up in a little town called Carnegie, about eight miles to the southwest of Pittsburgh, Pennsylvania. My grandfather had been a tailor in the court of Franz Josef, King of Austria, and when he emigrated to the United States he brought little more than his extraordinary talent with him. He settled in Carnegie, started a small tailoring business, married, and had a family. My mother was the oldest daughter. He taught her early and well; by the age of twelve she was helping out at the shop after school and on weekends. She loved to sew—so much so that when I came along some twenty years later, the only child and a daughter, to boot, the little dresses, suits, coats, and hats fairly flew from her machine. My childhood and adolescence were punctuated by the seasonal ritual of standing on the kitchen table, staring down at Mummy's head as she busily marked and pinned hems, racing against the limits of my ability to stand still. I hated to sew. I had little patience with the process of cutting and pinning and stitching. But I loved to concoct outfits, pick fabrics, play with color, and to wear what my mother sewed for me—now *that* was exciting! My First Communion dress with hundreds of yards of white ruffles, a red Valentine's Day dress I promised I'd never outgrow (but did), my first long dress for the eighth grade Christmas dance, my wedding gown, copied exactly from the exorbitant original my mother made sketches of on the back of an envelope when the salesgirl left the room—these are memories as sweet and dear to me as those of my mother herself. She was a wizard, a magician with a needle and thread, and dressing up in something she had made was an event that left a tingling, somewhat giddy feeling of being different, special. Oh, the glorious uniqueness those wardrobes bestowed!

When Donna and I settled in New York after college, it was perhaps inevitable that each of us would choose a fashion career. Equally inevitable was the migration of fabrics and trimmings from our professional sources into our first apartments. Neither of us can really remember the first time the fabrics came off the kitchen table or out of the scrap box to be used in our apartments, but soon they were transformed into pillows, bed throws and quilts, pasted onto hatboxes, pinned into slipcovers or stitched over wooden

hangers. On our own, but with those lessons of suitability, practicality, and ingenuity well learned, we quickly and inexpensively transformed those cubicles into spaces so personal, so uniquely our own, that coming home at the end of the day was truly coming *home*. The joy and love of creating, that special gift from our individual pasts, had permeated our personal and professional lives.

We began our interior design partnership in the winter of 1976, each of us drawing from our fashion and fabric heritage and experience, and each committed to excellence. Pragmatics and professionalism cause us to begin every project with the basics of space, plan, and budget, but the real excitement for us comes when the fabrics are finally pulled out, and we get down to the business we love. A new trim application that delineates a floral chintz at the windows; a lace that can be beautifully mitered for an effective finish at the bottom of a tablerunner, a new technique that turns a slipcover from serviceable to beautiful—these are the cookies and ice cream for Lang and Robertson.

Now it's time to share our thoughts, our experience, and our expertise with you, a reader who, like us, believes that a beautiful living space is both a desirable and obtainable goal, limited only by the boundaries of imagination and the creative energy each of us directs. Sewing is among the most practical of the creative arts, and sewing for the home is certainly one of the most gratifying and rewarding of cre-

ative experiences. To those of our fellow interior designers who have asked us why we are writing this book, rather than a slick, photographic record of our design work, we've answered without hesitation: *Decorating with Fabric* is a book we've been writing, consciously and unconsciously, separately and together, nearly all of our lives. Quite simply, we're writing about sewing because we love it, and because it reminds us both of home.

Lucretia Robertson
New York, New York
September 1985

Introduction

Pamela and her husband have a lovely old Victorian house, two children, a dog, and no draperies. Her friends advise her to call in the local upholsterer. But Pamela is a crack seamstress. She has even tried sewing from her own patterns, made from newspaper. She would love to sew for her home, but no one makes patterns for her unusual windows, and the handbooks she has seen confuse her or, worse, bore her. So Pamela keeps the lights low and does nothing.

Mary has just sent her youngest child off to college. The crafts projects she has done for years really don't fill up her day, and Mary keeps gazing into Jeff's now-vacant bedroom. She wishes she could get up the courage to upholster the walls, sew up a canopy for a guest bed, and, in short, lavish her considerable creative skills and energy on her own home. But she has read enough to know that she's talking about at least one hundred yards of fabric, and frankly, she's afraid to start.

Dr. Bill really hates going home at night. Living alone again with the odds and ends of a ten-year marriage is so depressing that, to the astonishment of his friends, he has begun to pore over decorating magazines, searching for ideas to help him pull this chaotic new apartment together. He doesn't want to call in a professional interior designer. He doesn't plan to be here long enough to justify a serious investment. What he really needs are some simple and unifying ideas plus the basic technical input before he turns the whole thing over to a dressmaker recommended by the wife of a friend.

Nancy has moved into her first apartment. Sitting in the middle of her new living room is, in all probability, the ugliest table she has ever seen—a hand-me-down from her mother's attic. Nancy knows that a wonderful, all-concealing table skirt like the ones she's seen in magazines could turn this eyesore into the center of positive attention in her nearly empty new home. She'd also like to fill the place with big, soft pillows rather than a traditional sofa-and-chair arrangement. But Nancy can do little more than thread the sewing machine and sew a straight seam. To make matters worse, she works a long day, and the idea of complicated and time-consuming sewing is very unappealing. What can she manage with modest skills, a tight schedule, and an even tighter budget?

Pamela, Mary, Dr. Bill, and Nancy are all real people. They are among the hundreds who have contacted Lang/Robertson, Ltd. Interior Design for professional help. More significantly, they are people we were unable to work with directly, because they weren't willing or able to make a commitment to the very large number of dollars necessary to bring a professional design firm into a project. Each of them had decorating problems that could be solved by sewing. Each was reluctant to make the decisions or to try to go it all alone. But, we're pleased to report, each solved the problem successfully, either on his or her own or with a local upholsterer or dressmaker, and within the available budget. Pamela, following a copy of our working instructions, sewed a version of the lace curtains we've photographed on page 53. Mary talked with us one afternoon just to firm up her own ideas and then started off on her own. What she ended up with in her new guest room looks like nothing in this book. It does, however, look just as Mary wanted it to, and it's wonderful in her home. Dr. Bill turned our notes over to the dressmaker and had just finished putting the last pillow in his comfortable and attractive bachelor apartment when he married again. He'll smile and tell you his new wife admits it was love of the man—and his home—at first sight! And Nancy enjoyed the inexpensive and easy-to-sew solution we offered for her apartment so much that she has gone back to school to earn a degree in interior design and plans to make a new career of helping other singles to environmental happy endings.

The simple truth is, if you can sew a blouse, you can sew curtains. If you're undaunted by a dress pattern, you can make your own slipcovers. And even if your skill level won't get you too far beyond a straight seam, you can sew beautiful, practical, problem-solving items for your home. What's more, you can do it using fabrics available directly to you through local sources. None of the fabrics we feature in this book were unavailable to us as retail shoppers. They were sold through fabric shops, in the dress goods departments of larger stores, or in seconds or mill-ends shops. Some were designed specifically for home furnishings but marketed through retailers all over the country at very affordable prices. And some were picked up for pennies as remnants or at flea markets.

It's a common belief that dress goods are unsuitable for home furnishings. In some instances, of course, this is true. But it shouldn't surprise you to learn that the very same silk pongee that goes into dresses can, and in fact does, go up at the windows in rooms designed by top interior designers. Or that simple wool flannels make spectacular decorating fabrics. Or that washable woolens, cottons, and blends wash just as well sewn into slipcovers as sewn into pants.

To be sure, there are things to avoid. There are fabrics that won't wear well at all, and others that won't work in certain situations. If you're in doubt about a particular fabric, check the alphabetical Fabric Glossary, beginning on page 277, for suitability. There are times, however, when long-wearing isn't the final criterion. When you are doing all the labor and the goods are reasonably priced, perhaps the fact that even with careful use, gingham will wear out in a few years isn't such a problem. After all, when the fun is in the doing and the price is right, the excitement of a change in three or four years becomes something to look forward to and not something to dread.

We understand that not everyone who sews does so for reasons of economy. Some people sew for the same reasons others do needlepoint or knit or paint pictures. If for you the craft is more important than the savings, you might use this book as a way to keep all the fun for yourself without employing a professional designer. Or you may, like Dr. Bill, wish to use this book as a textbook for a local dress-maker or upholstery workroom and let that person or shop do the sewing for you. We've tried to write and organize in a way that will allow this book to function in a variety of situations and fill a variety of technical and design needs.

We've written the technical sections of the book as clearly and simply as possible, but we've begun with the assumption that whoever you are and for whatever reason you've chosen this book to be your decorating guide, you are reasonably familiar with the basic techniques of sewing or you have someone else on board who is. This is really no place to first lay your hand on the sewing machine. For this reason, you won't find the nitty-gritty sewing instructions in here. You will find, however, projects of varying degrees of difficulty ranging from simple, straight-seam sewing (such as the tie-on curtains found on page 115), to more complicated and time-consuming ones like slipcovers. Before beginning *any* project, read carefully through all the instructions and consider the time needed to complete it. This will, of course, depend greatly on your level of experience and expertise, but reading through will help ensure that you don't begin a difficult project the day before the boss comes for dinner.

"Every Room in the House" is a presentation of some real solutions in real rooms with sewing projects featured prominently in each of them. We've covered a variety of decorating situations, from foyers to nurseries, and added chapters that deal with sewing for outdoor spaces and vacation homes as well. It's important to note here that even though a particular project might appear in the chapter titled "Living Rooms," it could be perfect for your bedroom or family room. Our decisions about where to show a project and in which color and fabric were, of course, greatly influenced by the realities of what fabrics were available and suitable, in what colors, and, perhaps most important, what locations were available for photographing them. Since nearly every picture in this book is of a room that was created specifically for the book, the realities of time and location played a key role when deciding just what could be included. Choices had to be made and some ideas eliminated, either from the start or somewhere along the way. The projects you don't find here, however, should be less a disappointment than a challenge. The possibilities are as limitless as your imagination. In any case, you will find here enough basic techniques to spur you on to hundreds of other solutions you can visualize on your own.

The third part of the book is a very special technical section titled "Tools, Terms, and Techniques." This section acts as an introduction to the technical portion of the book. It includes a list of sewing equipment you will need to execute the projects in the most efficient way and an alphabetized list of sewing terms and techniques we use over and over again in the step-by-step instructions that follow. Specific terms and techniques referred to in project instructions are singled out by **boldface** type. Thus, the word **gather** will appear in the project instructions for a gathered dust ruffle, thereby referring you to the "Tools, Terms, and Techniques" section and the detailed directions for each of three methods of gathering. Experienced sewers may choose to proceed without checking back for terms and directions; less experienced sewers will be able to check the procedure quickly and/or answer to any technical questions they might have. In either case, reading through this section will help you to organize your tool kit and your procedural thinking before you actually begin to sew.

The fourth part of the book, "Project Instructions," is the textbook of actual sewing instructions, arranged in eleven sections by project type. Here you will find complete directions for every project in the book, listed by type (Pillows, Slipcovers, Kitchen Accessories, etc.). These instructions are as complete and detailed as was necessary to ensure the successful execution of the project. We've spent many professional years designing crafts and home furnishings patterns, and we are extremely sensitive to the frustrations caused by inaccurate or incomplete directions. We felt, therefore, that it was far more important to be thorough than to seem deceptively brief. Some of the instructions might, for this reason, look long and complicated, when, in fact, the length simply means that they are adequately explained rather than edited down, leading to confusion or, worse yet, omission. You can trust that we've given this sizable portion of the book our most serious and experienced attention.

Even though, in the final analysis, you must be your own expert, allowing your personal vision, needs, and style of living to influence your choices, we'd like you to consider Lang/Robertson, Ltd. your consulting interior design firm and this book the beginning of our client/designer relationship. *Decorating with Fabric* is our way of coming to visit you in your home and working with you on your individual decorating projects. Although we may never have the opportunity to meet you and share directly in that creative process, we'd like you to know before you begin that, page by page, project by project, we're in this with you, sharing our twenty years of pattern and design experience with you. We both hope that you will use this book over and over again through the years, that this is just the first of many decorating ventures we can help you to accomplish, and that the very special experience of sewing to decorate your home will continue to excite and reward you and your family for many years to come.

Before You
B·E·G·I·N

Color

Color is the magic in a beautiful room. More than any other element in design, color enhances our environment. Close your eyes and imagine a bedroom the color of a ripe peach. A child's bathroom in festive crayon brights. A delft blue and sparkling white kitchen. An earth-tone study. A plum living room. Each of these color images conveys a vivid message about the room and tells us a great deal about the kind of person who might live there.

Most of us are intensely aware of the power of color and the importance of suitable color choices. We take color tests in magazines, toy with paint chips for days on end, squint, choose, and then pray that the gorgeous coral on the two-inch chip won't give us a headache when it goes up on the walls. Color on a little piece of paper is, of course, one thing, and a coral living room is quite another. If there is one simple message designers should pass along at the outset, it's always to be careful about color. By this we don't mean it is necessary to live in a white and beige environment for the rest of your life, but that it's always best to take color chances in careful ways, in special places, and to tread a more conservative path when you can't afford to be wrong.

As part of our research for this book, we went back through our clipping files. There among the tearsheets was a room photographed nearly fifteen years ago for a national magazine. It was a bedroom with white rough-plastered walls, a white canvas bed, and white canvas upholstered pieces. But the floor was a master stroke of surprise. It was painted a brilliant red-orange. Now this room wasn't perfect for everybody, we understand, but it was nonetheless a very successfully decorated room and one that cleverly illustrated a creative use of color. The investment elements in the room—the wall treatment, the bed accessories, the upholstered furniture—were all white. But the floor—the accent piece —was a giant swath of glorious, dangerous color. By painting the floor, the owners found the easiest, cheapest way to try out what would have cost a fortune to undo in the rest of the room. Using this philosophy, you might choose to sew a dozen chintz sofa pillows in lipstick red, or a long table skirt in turquoise blue, and put them in a quietly colored room. Dramatic touches of extreme colors can be an effective face-lift for a conservative room, and like the painted floor, these things can be accomplished easily, quickly, and for a minimum of expense.

A quietly colored room with one bright shot of color is one way to handle color carefully but with flair. But what about rooms that are full of colors? In either case, the secret to the successful integration of color is in the balance. The white room with the red-orange floor had one additional color element—a number of natural wood accessories. Without them, the scheme would have been off-balance—too strongly bicolored. The key word here is *relief*. Every scheme needs relief

from its basic color palette. A room with what the handbooks might tell you is a technically good mix of color, warms to cools, might need a dab of a totally unexpected tone or concentration of color to make it special and exciting. Quite often, even to professionals, that little something extra isn't apparent until the room is completely finished.

Take a look at the photograph on page 36. The walls of this room were already painted a soft cream. We added the floral sateen with its gentle lemon ground color and rose, bluebell, and lavender flowers. Then, as you might expect, we picked up the blue from the print and repeated it on the pair of French side chairs. The sisal rug was chosen to add another textural element to the room and to carry the wall color down onto the expanse of dark wood flooring. The greens were repeated by the natural landscape outside the window. All seemed logical and balanced. But the day we came to photograph the room, we realized that something was missing. The warms and cools were neatly divided, the print colors were picked up here and there, but the room lay flat and unexciting in the test photo. We added the little needlepoint pillow with its navy blue ground, and that helped a bit. Then one of the photography crew carried a brilliant scarlet gloxinia in from the kitchen, and the room came alive. The offbeat color added a special, slightly out-of-sync touch that made the whole room work. In your room it might be real or silk flowers, a brightly colored bowl, a pillow, or a piece of lacquered furniture, but something with color whimsy should be there just to keep the scheme interesting.

The design process we used when we were styling this living room for photography is one we use often with clients. We always begin with a color feeling, a mood. Often, that color is already there—on the floor, on the walls, in a valuable piece of furniture or art. This room, for example, was already painted in a lovely, rich cream. How do we then decide what colors to bring into the room in the form of new fabrics and furnishings? First, we remove all the superfluous furniture and clutter and pare the room down to its essential pieces. We may then

move these pieces around a bit—shift the sofa away from the "sofa wall," for example, and float it out in the middle of the room just to get a good look at it and reconsider its position in the new scheme. Then we begin to carry cuttings and half-yard pieces of fabrics to which the client has responded during shopping trips. We place them over the pieces of furniture or tape them near the windows, exactly where they might go in the finished room. Everyone expresses an opinion as the fabric pieces go in, and often out again. We build the room together, color by color, fabric by fabric, using only the small pieces of fabric and without ever committing ourselves to yardage on a particular one until we're all sure. The room grows before our eyes until the basic color and print balance has been struck. The object is to keep each individual area in the room interesting while integrating it into the whole space by carefully orchestrating color and print to repeat around the room.

Of course, the process isn't simple. It takes a good eye and a splendid imagination. Perhaps the most difficult part of the job is knowing just when to stop. To be honest, knowing when to stop adding little touches of color and print or that last tabletop accessory item has caused us more trouble over the years than any other major design problem. It's always apparent when you've taken the one step too far, however. Something in the room says, "Whoops! Get that purple [red, blue, green] out of here! That print is too bright, or too large, or simply too much!"

We advise with color, as with nearly every element of design, that you take it slowly, one small step at a time. Wait awhile between major decisions. Get the wall and the ceiling and the trim colors just right and then live with them for a few days, or a few weeks, or a month, before going on. Let the new elements become a bit more familiar so that the next step is clearer and less of a gamble. Start with the surfaces—walls, ceilings, floors—then add the slipcover in that print you've always loved. Then try the half-yard cut of the fabric you're considering at the window and make sure. Buy a full length if you need to and look again. Save yourself from the pain of discovering that the curtains you labored over for days look just awful when they're hung up in the room. No one

needs a thirty-five-yard disaster. What you do want is the unique pleasure of watching your new room with its pleasing colors coming together in a bright, attractive, and comfortable place to live in and enjoy.

Color, as the best of the color tests will tell you, is a most personal experience. One man's peach is another man's pumpkin. We each see and sense and react to color in our own unique way. But no matter what color it is, one that pleases you will definitely enhance the quality of your life. Blue paint generally costs the same as yellow or white, and a print in the prettier color combination can be well worth the search. A thoughtfully colored environment can make all the difference in the world. There are millions of possibilities, and the ones that are perfect for you are out there waiting to catch your eye and change your life.

Color Tips

• Before beginning a decorating project, open your clothes closet. Chances are, the colors you enjoy wearing are the ones you'd like to live with, too.

• When selecting paint, buy a quart of a color (or colors) you think you would like. Paint a square of at least 12″ on each of the walls and take a good long look. Check the color at various times during the day and in sun and shade situations. If it's not perfect, pick another shade of the color and try again. It's worth the few extra dollars to eliminate unpleasant surprises. And remember, color reflects on itself in a room, so just one little swatch on one wall isn't enough to tell.

• The finish of the paint you select can be just as important as the color itself. You may be warned by your paint dealer that gloss paint tends to highlight every imperfection on the wall, but in some cases the advantages of gloss or semigloss walls far outweigh the disadvantages. Soft pastels, for example, tend to look dusty and dull in flat finishes and are livelier in a higher gloss. Flat darks are like velvet; they absorb light, show dust, and, for some people, make a room feel close and confining. Gloss darks, on the other hand, are like satin. They show up surface flaws and require considerable preparation, but the finished room will glow like a jewel. Both options can, and should, be balanced with the careful use of mat or lustrous fabrics and through the careful placement of paintings, fabric, screens, and the like to break up the painted surface of the walls and add textural interest.

• Even though the selection of wall color is important to the overall success of a room, try to keep in mind that the walls generally act as a background for the furnishings. Brighter paint colors or those with strong personalities can take away some of the need to furnish expensively. Designers know that all-neutral rooms demand the finest in surface finishes and furnishings to be truly successful. The more conservative the palette, the more visible the quality.

• When working with color chips at the paint store, it's always safer to select the color you think you want and then move up one or two chips lighter on the chart. Most paint colors are far more intense than they seem on paper, and when all the walls are covered, they can be overwhelming. Unless you're opting for a strong color, two steps lighter is a good rule.

• When planning room color, don't forget your ceiling. Ceiling colors don't have to be white or off-white. It is true that a dark ceiling will tend to descend into the room, and in a standard room height of 8′ or 8′6″, that can be a problem. But you can tint white base paint and make a ceiling special without lowering the boom. Soft apricot ceilings, pale rose pinks, and delicate blues and yellows all have a place. Just be sure you pick a color that looks nearly white on the chart, and that, just as you did for the walls, you paint a small section to check the intensity before going ahead with the whole job.

• Using contrasting colors for door and window frames and ceiling moldings can be a room-enhancing decision, but more often than not, it draws the eye to too many details at once and serves to break up the room rather than unify it. When in doubt, white or off-white trim is the best. Most rooms need definition at the ceiling line. We often suggest that a crown molding be added to a room that has none. This can be done inexpensively with a stock molding from a lumberyard. You'd be surprised what a difference a pretty crown molding can make in an ordinary room.

• There's an exciting color computer that is available in progressive paint stores. The operator simply feeds in a swatch of the paint, fabric, or photographed color and the computer automatically breaks down the pigment elements and formulates an exact match. In the case of tonals such as the mixture of yarns in a tweed, or a variegated yarn fabric like wool flannel, the computer will select a paint color that translates the mix—a complementary color that, on woodwork, for example, matches the mixture created in the eye by the different elements in the fabric or texture. Check in your area for a store that offers this service, or, if you are prepared to order your paint by mail, write to the source listed in the Source Listing to have the job done.

Rich darks or jewel tones can add sophistication, drama, and romance to a room. Here are two rooms done in deep colors, each with a different finished look. The tartan plaid room has a handsome, slightly masculine style. Darks are played against darks, creating a room that is particularly warm and inviting. The living/dining room on the left uses rich darks as well, but plays them against neutrals. The result is a room with strength and drama but with far less intensity than it would have had without the relief of the café au lait print ground, the pale pine floor, and the off-white walls and ceiling.

QUICK LIFTS
with Color

• Try brushing or sponging several coats of a warm-colored paint on the inside of your paper lampshades. Soft pink and apricot are especially effective and take years off the faces of the people who sit near them.

• Arrange a collection of pottery in a basically neutral room to lend color and interest. Cool, blue and white Canton will add elegance, glazed terracotta from Mexico will add warmth, and a collection of old majolica or Staffordshire will add personality.

• Consider painting the inside of your closets in bold, room-related colors. And while you're at it, do the same inside your kitchen cabinets.

• Paint one old piece of furniture an offbeat color and put it in a dark corner of a room to brighten up the whole space.

• Spray a group of inexpensive baskets in a cheerful color and use them for open shelf storage.

• Flowers used as the single bright color accent can dramatically change a basically monochromatic or neutral room. Blooming plants add color all through the house and they last longer than cut flowers.

• Area rugs can contribute color to a room. If you choose less expensive rather than investment rugs, you can afford to pick something you might not want to live with forever but that cheers you up right now. Rag rugs, for example, make a beautiful but gentle color contribution to nearly every scheme.

• Painting a floor an exciting color can be a stroke of genius. Have the floor sanded professionally before painting it, to ensure that the finished floor won't chip. If you tire of it in a few years, you can lightly sand and paint again.

• Food can act as a color accent in rooms where it is being stored, prepared, or served. For parties, food can create beautiful and festive color accents. Try arrangements of fruits and vegetables, alone or mixed with fresh flowers. After the party, you can eat the centerpieces.

• Painted canvas or plywood or fabric covered screens can add color and pattern to a room. The easiest way to create a screen is by upholstering fabric on stretchers purchased at an art supply store. Three or more of these panels can be hinged together and the resulting screen placed in a corner of a room to add zest and create additional hidden storage.

• Commercially available trimming can be applied along the edges of shelves to enhance the interior of kitchen, bedroom, bathroom, or linen closets. With a small investment in time and money you can make a charming color and pattern statement in what might otherwise be boring storage spaces.

• Simply by adding brightly colored potholders, tea towels, and other sewables to a monochromatic kitchen you can turn the whole room around.

• Buying spare sets of bathroom towels in varying colors allows for a quick change in a neutral or white bathroom every wash day.

Fabric

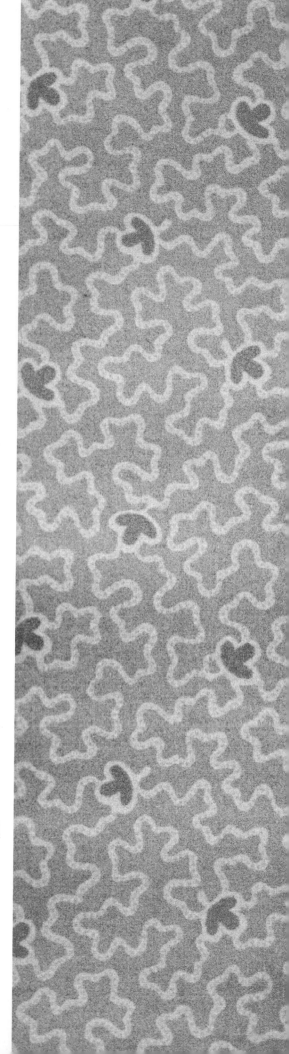

An army of fabrics is advancing toward us, loose ends blowing like banners. Over the hill comes a battalion of broadcloths, closely followed by companies of failles, batistes, and cotton lawns. Special-care tickets flapping, they march on, regiment after regiment. Suddenly, one bolt tumbles over and rolls, knocking down everything in its path. Swatches fly. Clippings flutter. In a swirling vortex of cloth, we surrender.

As professional designers who spend the better part of every working day handling fabrics and making fabric choices and recommendations to our clients, we can tell you that this bad dream is a recurrent nightmare. The biggest problem with fabrics is simply that there are too many of them. Making a commitment to the one or two or three perfect choices for the job at hand is no easy task. The options are endless. The problems are legendary. This one stretches. That one shrinks. This one pills. That one pulls. Silk rots in sunlight. Wool scratches. Linen wrinkles. Cotton fades. It's enough to drive you mad.

But since, in order to decorate, you must choose, we'd like to reassure you that there are some practical guidelines you can employ to make decision making a safer process. These guidelines fall into four basic categories: appeal, suitability, maintenance, and cost. Before you purchase a single yard of anything, we suggest that you read through and consider each of these areas carefully and well.

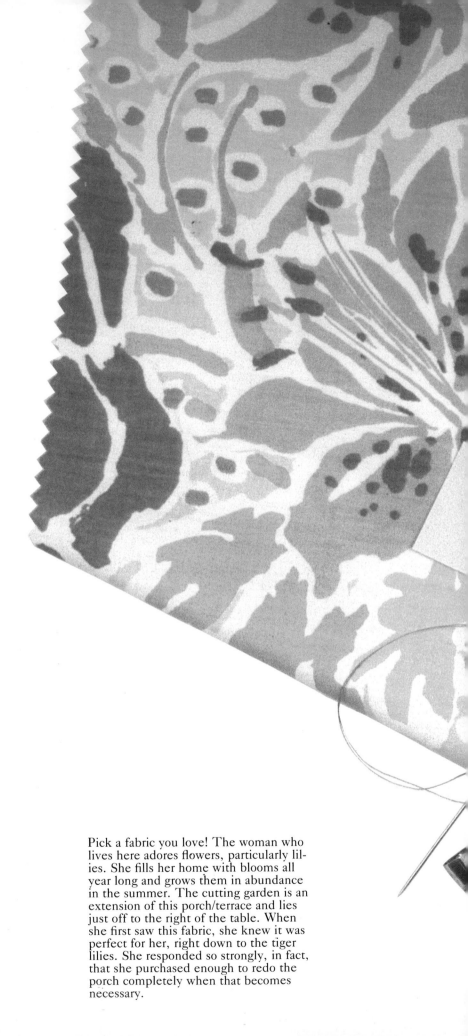

Appeal. To our way of thinking, the biggest consideration when selecting fabric for decorating projects is that you love it. Not like it, but *love* it. Never, never pick a fabric just because it's there. Ignore advice from friends or family urging you to go with a fabric because of availability. The green lily in the print you hated in the shop, you will hate in your living room—day after miserable day. Now this isn't to say that we don't all tire of fabrics after years of having them around, but disliking them from day one is another matter entirely. What you're considering, after all, is a lot of yardage, and a lot of money, and (please don't ever forget) a lot of your energy and time. So look around, and if you don't find something that causes your heart to flutter, look some more. If necessary, postpone your painter. First find the fabrics you love, then decorate around them.

Suitability. We do have to caution you that although we firmly believe in appeal as the first step, it does have inherent complications, especially in the area of dress goods for home furnishings. You might fall head over heels for a printed cotton batiste when what you really need is canvas. Or it might be a cloth with very little dimensional stability when stability is of prime importance. Occasionally these things can be worked out. You can have many fabrics quilted, for example, to increase their weight and dimensional stability, and then use them for such things as slipcovers or window treatments. But it is more prudent to check out the fabric you've selected for possible end uses (see Fabric Glossary, page 277) before making the commitment to hang it at five windows or slipcover the sofa and two chairs. If you can't have it for the sofa, perhaps you can use it for pillows or a table skirt. You can build a room around a fabric without using it everywhere in sight. Check before buying. Better safe than sorry in six months.

A few words of advice on the subject of fiber content. Fiber plays a crucial role in how a fabric performs on the job. When you're buying fabrics, the fabric content should be printed right on the bolt-end tag. If it's not there, ask. You should be aware of the fiber content and care recommendations of the fabric you're considering, and in some cases that information should influence your choice. You may notice that we refer frequently to "pure cotton" or "natural linen" in this book.

Pick a fabric you love! The woman who lives here adores flowers, particularly lilies. She fills her home with blooms all year long and grows them in abundance in the summer. The cutting garden is an extension of this porch/terrace and lies just off to the right of the table. When she first saw this fabric, she knew it was perfect for her, right down to the tiger lilies. She responded so strongly, in fact, that she purchased enough to redo the porch completely when that becomes necessary.

Even though there are advantages to man-made fibers and blends, we strongly believe in the correctness and suitability of natural fiber fabrics. You may have your own preferences. In any case, there are certain truths on the subject of fiber content we can briefly mention here that might influence your fabric choices. Yes, silk can rot—and will, if used at a window with direct sunlight. Yes, wool can scratch, and, in fact, should be immediately eliminated from your plans if someone in your family is allergic. Yes, linen wrinkles like mad at the windows or in slipcovers, and the dyes on printed linens used for seating pieces may rub off after a while, no matter how much they cost or how careful you are. And, yes, cottons can fade and chintz will, after consistent use, lose its waxy sheen. But we hasten to add, nothing in the world is as beautiful as lustrous silk curtains with the sunlight filtering gently through. Wools can be as soft and luxurious as cashmere and wear for fifteen years. And there is enormous, unaffected charm in wrinkled linen or a sun-softened floral chintz. Natural fabrics take dyes beautifully. They wear well without pilling, and they definitely age more gracefully than synthetics.

If you're not convinced about 100 percent natural fabrics, perhaps blended fabrics would suit you and your life-style better. Most upholstery weight wools used in the architectural specification end of the design business, for example, have a little nylon woven in for stability. Other man-made fibers are frequently added to natural fiber fabrics to control shrinkage or fading or sun rot. Even in the case of 100 percent man-made fabrics, the final success or failure will depend on performance, suitability, and aesthetic acceptability. If it wears like iron, promises to outlive your grandchildren and three generations of dogs on the sofa, releases stains from hot fudge and red wine, but it feels boardy, makes unappealing noises when disturbed, dyes up in colors that remind you of Kool-Aid, and has the undeniable touch of a plastic bag, forget it. No amount of perfect performance can replace the sheer sensual pleasure of a fabric that feels good, looks great, and makes you smile just to see it in your living room.

Finally, there is the issue of special surface treatments. Yes, Teflon®, Zepel®, and Scotchgard® finishes do repel stains, at least initially. But to those of you who have found a fabric you'd love to use on the sofa that comes with no such special finish, a word of hope. Our upholstery workroom has a theory about stain-repelling treatments. They have found over many years of working with fabrics and having pieces cleaned after normal use that the finishes rub off unevenly and that cleaning pieces upholstered with treated fabric is more difficult because of the broken film of stain repellent. As with a Teflon-treated pan with scratches, the magic is gone. It's definitely something to keep in mind.

If, however, the idea of treated fabrics allows you to sleep better at night, there is an alternative to treating them individually. A process in which a liquid sealant is sprayed directly on all fabric surfaces and all wall coverings is available nationally directly to the consumer. With their surfaces sealed in this way, fabrics release soil, thus preventing permanent stains in most cases. Spills can be quickly and safely removed with a cleaning kit provided at the time of the treatment. Educating the consumer about fabric maintenance and proper care and cleaning is all part of this service, and the psychological as well as pragmatic effects of the treatment are well worth the cost.

In the final analysis, the suitability of a particular fabric can surely make or break a successful decorating scheme. No one wants a home where you can't sit down or must draw the curtains against the sun. But, like most things, the rewards are sometimes worth the risks. If performance were all that mattered in interior design, we'd probably live in plastic capsules. You must weigh the choices. Analyze the advantages. Accept the liabilities. Then pick something beautiful and enjoy it to the fullest.

Maintenance. It's no secret that with fabrics, a big percentage of the commitment is to maintenance. It seems that in life, 10 percent is acquisition and 90 percent is maintaining the acquisition. Cotton organza priscilla curtains, for example, are among the prettiest things on earth, but how many of us would commit ourselves to the endless hours of starching and ironing? We sleep on no-iron sheets, dress in permanent press shirts, and encourage a wardrobe of jeans for

everyone under eighteen to avoid maintenance. Lang/Robertson once designed for a special display a full canopy bed, sewn from 120 yards of Swiss cotton organdy. The enormous number of yards was somewhat offset by the reasonable cost of the material. It took weeks to sew, of course, but the results were spectacular. The real bottom line, however, was the simple question: How many people could handle what would happen when it needed to be laundered in five or six months? Answer: not many. Take the matter of families with small children. An equally valid set of maintenance questions for them might be: How does it look with peanut butter? Will it match pizza and fried chicken, or will it need to be dry-cleaned every Monday morning? One client picked a sturdy multicolored tweed for a sofa that got a lot of family use, because it was the only one that she felt would match her family's afternoon snacks. One of life's great mysteries concerns rooms in magazines that look as if they're uninhabited. Who can live in a room filled with white satin upholstery? Obviously, somebody can and does.

Soil-release factors should influence everyone's fabric choices, but families with kids and pets and a hard-use life-style should probably consider them first. If, on the other hand, high maintenance doesn't cause you to pause for a moment, then barrel ahead with the pink silk slipcovers.

Cost. Everyone is sensitive to the spending of money. *Everyone.* Even affluent clients care about cost. In fact, in our private design practice we find that the more comfortable a client is, the more considered his expenditures. Not even the very wealthy are immune to the need for cautious handling of disposable income. In any case, getting the most for your money is an intelligent and admirable goal. There are several ways to ensure that your budget, whether large or small, will go as far as possible.

First, if cost is all-important, you will have to face up to that fact very early on and let it eliminate anything you can't afford before you decide you can't live without it. Don't take a second look at costly fabrics for big jobs. They are not an option.

Second, limit the amount of fabric you will need to the most important areas and eliminate the rest. Obviously, the sofa must be covered in something. The walls do not have to be. Neither, in some cases, do the side chairs. If you use chairs of chrome and wood rather than fabric-covered club or wing chairs, you may save a considerable amount of money. And windows can be beautifully treated with fabric, wood, or metal blinds rather than draperies. If you feel that fabric at the windows is a must for your room, try balloon or Roman shades rather than full panels and valances. It will save yardage and money.

Third, if you do fall in love with a costly fabric, limit its use to one or two very special, very small items, like sofa pillows or a little cushion for a chair. That way, you can spotlight one small piece rather than going into receivership by using it at four windows.

And, fourth, don't forget seconds shops or mill-end outlets when you're shopping for fabric. Just be careful to examine every yard you buy. A small imperfection or minor off-register in the printing can be forgotten in a room full of print, but a seriously off-grain printing can spell disaster. Always allow extra yardage when buying this way, both in anticipation of flaws you might have missed and in the realization that often these seconds or mill ends are the last yards of that fabric in existence and you can't casually come back for a bit more in a few weeks. The bedroom pictured on page 68 was sewn entirely from seconds. In a room lavished with fabric like this one, no one notices that the tulips are printed slightly off-register. What counted was the $2-per-yard ticket price.

In the end, flair and style can more than make up for the lack of boundless funds. Remember, you'll be saving hundreds of dollars in labor charges by sewing it yourself. That reality should make the cost of the fabric a lot easier to justify. Never, though, lose sight of just how valuable your time and energy are. Be realistic about what you can accomplish and just how much of your leisure a project will require. Make certain that the fabrics you finally select deserve your labor. Saving money on something wonderful is one thing—wasting hours of your free time on a compromise is another.

Where to Find Fabrics for Home Decorating Projects

Fabric shops. Look through the dress goods area for fabrics that can be adapted or used just as they are in home furnishings projects.

Home furnishings fabric shops. There may be shops in your area that specialize in upholstery and home furnishings fabrics. Some dress goods shops have in-store home furnishings boutiques that specialize in heavier weights.

Department stores. Check the piece goods departments of major department stores. In some of them, special home decorating boutiques may have been set up. These one-stop shopping centers can offer everything from fabric to wallpaper to paint—all precoordinated.

Paint and wallpaper stores. You can often order fabrics that go with wallpapers offered in the books at your local paint and paper dealer. Wallpaper books which include companion fabrics make the job of mixing patterns and prints much easier. Often store personnel can guide you in estimating yardage and making correct fabric choices.

Seconds and mill-end shops. This is a fabulous way to buy big yardage for less. It's best, however, to shop the outlets with an open mind. Let something wonderful catch your eye and then select a new carpet. And always check the goods carefully before buying. There is always a reason why they are there, after all. Small imperfections probably won't matter. Big ones might. Serious off-grain printing can jeopardize an entire decorating project. Also, always plan to buy a few extra yards. You might encounter flaws in the yardage you need, and the chances of finding that fabric at that store next week are slender at best. The basic rule for seconds and mill ends is *caveat emptor*—let the buyer beware!

Novelty stores. This might surprise you, but there are some tasteful fabrics to be found as precut pieces at stores that don't specialize in fabrics at all. Collections of home furnishings fabrics, put together by jobbers and sold as lots, often end up on the remnant tables at the five-and-dime. This is rarely a place to find enough of a particular print to redo a room completely, but as a source for incidental fabrics for pillows or an ottoman or the like, such a shop can be a treasure trove. Recently we found a number of five-yard cuts of a beautiful cotton sateen, known to be from a famous fabric designer, that normally sold for $24 per yard. At the novelty store, it was marked $5.95 for five yards. The four packages totaled twenty yards for less than $24—the cost of a single yard at its regular retail price. With careful management and seaming, the twenty yards were enough to do a slipcover for a sofa. Keep your eyes open for bargains like this.

Antique shops and flea markets. If your taste runs to softly aged fabrics, beautiful old chintzes, handworked linens, and the like, you should check these places for fabric. Actual yardage put away by someone long ago can be found from time to time. Drapery fabric in lengths of two and a half or three yards can be recycled. Old quilts make fabulous upholstery fabrics, and worn patches can be carefully replaced. Old fabrics have a warmth and friendliness that add patina to a new room.

Three windows with a view: three fabric solutions. Lace is a perfectly suitable choice for windows with a pretty view but where a little privacy is needed. Lace softens both the view and the light and is a delicate and decorative answer for rooms with a Victorian or elaborately detailed point of view. Lace can also add pattern without adding color. Lightweight woven gingham offers inexpensive and unaffected charm for country rooms. Because these priscillas are stationary on the rod, however, shades are necessary for privacy. Chintz is a very versatile fabric and can add color, print, and sheen to a traditional room. It's a perfect choice for shirred drapery styles where the attractive waxy finish can be shown to best advantage. These draperies draw for privacy.

Accessories can be sewn from nearly any fabric, but sometimes the pragmatics must be the first consideration. Because it gathers beautifully, a lightweight chintz was a logical choice for this ruffled tableskirt. The delicately printed fabric was too costly to be used for draperies and slipcovers, but the ten yards needed to make this extravagant-looking tableskirt made the fabric the star of the room. A very suitable choice for placemats, this jacquard fabric is totally reversible, allowing for double duties. Cotton broadcloth, used for the napkins, releases soil easily and makes sense for an item that requires constant laundering. Not one but two medium-weight, printed fabrics were combined to make these Turkish pillows and tie-on covers. This sturdy cotton was perfect because it is heavy enough to hold its shape, yet light enough to knot for the tie-ons.

Seating pieces have special requirements. These director's chairs, for example, require strong, tightly woven fabric to adequately support body weight. Canvas is a perfect choice, although corduroys or other lighter-weight cloths with added fabric backing will also work well. Try to use woven patterns such as this stripe for seating that gets heavy use; wovens don't show the wear as quickly as printed patterns do. This wing chair, on the other hand, gets more limited use. It was upholstered in a surprising and successful way—with an old quilt. Worn areas in the quilt were cut away, leaving enough good pieces to cut a cover for the chair. Our tree branch chair sits on a screened porch and is exposed to a great deal of dampness. A cotton blend with mildew-resistant qualities was the perfect, practical choice for this location.

CHOOSING
a Suitable Fabric

It's difficult to make a definitive list of fabrics that are unquestionably suitable for curtains, draperies, slipcovers, and accessory items because fabrics of the same name can vary greatly in weight, fiber content, and quality. We compiled lists, however, to help you in your search for the appropriate fabric type for your particular projects. For additional data, and to help in selecting fabrics for accessory items, read the introductory information at the beginning of each project category.

Don't forget, if you feel you *must* use a fabric that is not inherently suitable (for example, a lightweight classic gingham check for slipcovers), you can have it backed or quilted to give it the body it needs. Some of the most interesting projects are the result of breaking the rules with unexpected fabric choices.

Fabrics suitable for curtains

Batiste
Bedford Cord
Broadcloth
Calico
Cambric
Challis
Chambray
Chintz
Dimity
Dotted Swiss
Eyelet Embroidery
Fiberglass
Gingham
Habutai
Hopsacking
Lace
Lawn
Linen (handkerchief and lightweight)
Madras
Muslin
Nainsook
Ninon
Nun's Veiling
Organdy
Organza
Osnaburg
Oxford Cloth
Piqué
Percale
Percaline
Plissé
Polished Cotton
Pongee
Poplin (lightweight)
Sailcloth
Sateen (lightweight)
Seersucker
Terrycloth
Ticking
Toile de Jouy
Voile

Fabrics suitable for draperies

Antique Satin
Antique Taffeta
Barkcloth
Brocade
Chino
Chintz
Corduroy
Covert Cloth
Cretonne
Damask
Dupion
Drill
Faille
Flannel
Gabardine
Gingham
Homespun
Hopsacking
Jaspé
Khaki
Linen (medium-weight)
Moiré
Osnaburg
Peau de Soie
Piqué
Polished Cotton
Poplin
Popline
Sailcloth
Sateen
Satin
Shantung
Surah
Taffeta
Tartan
Thai Silk
Toile de Jouy
Tussah
Velvet
Velveteen

Fabrics suitable for upholstery

Antique Satin
Bagherra
Broadcloth (heavyweight)
Brocade
Brocatelle
Canvas
Chino
Chintz
Corduroy
Covert Cloth
Cretonne
Damask
Denim
Drill
Duvetyn
Faille
Felt
Flannel
Frieze
Gabardine
Haircloth
Harris Tweed
Homespun
Jaspé
Khaki
Leatherette
Linen (medium- to heavyweight)
Matelassé
Melton
Mohair
Moiré
Nacre Velvet
Piqué
Polished Cotton (medium- to heavyweight)
Poplin (medium- to heavyweight)
Popline
Ratiné
Rep
Sailcloth
Sateen (heavyweight)
Satin
Suede Cloth
Tartan
Ticking
Velour
Velvet
Velveteen
Vinyl
Whipcord

Fabrics suitable for slipcovers

Butcher Linen
Canvas
Chino
Chintz
Corduroy
Cretonne
Damask
Drill
Flannel
Gabardine
Jaspé
Khaki
Linen (medium-weight)
Piqué
Polished Cotton
Poplin
Popline
Sailcloth
Sateen (medium-weight)
Tartan
Terry Cloth
Ticking
Toile de Jouy

Decorative
Trims and Notions

Trimming is an enhancement in interior decoration. It can make the difference between ordinary and extraordinary for very little additional cost. It's true that in our private design practice the cost of the trims can equal, and, in some memorable cases, has actually exceeded the cost of the fabrics, but these trimmings are generally lavish, handmade, and are usually not available over-the-counter. Added to the already considerable cost of their production (mainly in Europe) is the reality of their being available exclusively to the professional trade. Even though very few of us will ever choose to make the commitment to use tassels at $600 or $700 a pair, all of us can utilize tasteful, machine-made, and readily available trimmings in our homes.

If you take a few minutes and look through the photographs in this book, you'll notice that there's hardly an item that doesn't feature a trimming of some sort. Fringe, ruffle, simple bias banding, cording—nearly every edge has a finishing detail. The reason for this is simple: we believe in trims. We find them useful and aesthetically pleasing. An uncomplicated application of bias tape can set a drapery panel off from the wall or highlight the shape of a piece of upholstered furniture in an appealing and exciting way. Whether subtle or dramatic, trims make the job look more professional, and, like the perfect hat or pair of shoes in a wardrobe, they can complement the room scheme and add a classy and personal finishing touch.

Left to right, first row: flat band trim; fringe with decorative header; shirred jumbo welt; wide crochet lace edging. Second row: mini ruffle as welt; decorative woven band; bias binding on gauze window panels; fabric borders; cable cord and hardware. Third row: braid and tassel of floss; eyelet and ribbon; accordian-pleated ruffle; fabric border, braid and tassel; beading with ribbon. Fourth row: bias binding with rick rack; applied fringe; hand-knotted yarn fringe; crochet edging; custom sawtooth edging.

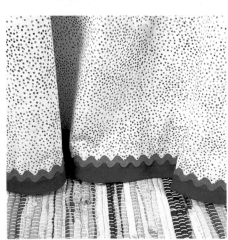

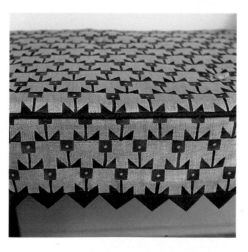

Trims are an excellent way to personalize decorative fabric choices. Hundreds of people might choose the same print in the same colorway during its lifetime in a collection of home furnishings fabrics. The way you trim that fabric is one critical factor in making it uniquely your own. In recent years, over-the-counter trimmings manufacturers and importers have spent considerable time and effort in improving their collections of trims, and some lovely fringes, braids, cordings, and bandings are now widely available. You may search through your local fabric shops and never find silk tassels in the style of Marie Antoinette, but the basic selection of volume trims offers many tasteful options.

Trims can be used just as they are, straight out of the package, for such direct applications as trimming the edges of shelves in kitchens, bedrooms, linen closets, and the like. They can, of course, be inserted into seams or applied to the fabric directly. You can combine two or more trims to create a totally new look. Twisting two colors of rick rack together, adding rick rack to a simple bias tape, or applying brush fringe or lace to the outside edge of a flat braid are just a few examples. Another customized trick is to double the application of trims to add to their luxuriousness and importance. The living room on page 34 combines braids, fringes, cordings, ruffles, and bias tapes to create a room that is rich with embellishment and detail. Trims can be used in traditional settings and ways and can add appropriate charm—ball fringe on kitchen curtains or eyelet ruffles in a little girl's bedroom (see the photograph on page 102, for example)—but the surprise of a machine-made crocheted lace on all the edges in our tea-toweling kitchen on page 58 turned the whole space into a more special and customized place in an unexpected way. Lace trimmings like this one add "age" and luxury wherever and whenever they're used, and in rooms with a country or old-world point of view, they can lend credibility as well.

In addition to the wide and varied selection of trimmings you can purchase by the yard, trims can be created to match specific fabrics and decorating needs. The simple process of cutting bias strips of fabric and applying them as flat tapes, or sewing them into bias welting to finish off seams and edges, can be an extremely effective trimming technique. Carried one step further, fabric tapes and cords can be created from a compatible fabric or fabrics and applied to accent, without actually repeating, the main fabric. (For this technique, see the bathroom on page 88.) Fabric, either matched or contrasting, can be cut, pleated, or shirred, and applied in a seam or on the surface as ruffling, either as bias or straight-grain. Borders or contrasting prints can be used effectively as hem treatments, as piping on cushions, or to outline decorative accessories (see the kitchen on page 62). Of course, all handwork used to trim fabric items falls into the category of trims you can create yourself. Appliqués, embroidered motifs, and contrasting blanket stitching used to finish edges are all very personal trimming touches you can use effectively. And if you choose, you can even create your own silk, cotton, or wool cords and tassels (such as the ones we've featured in the foyer on page 26) by plaiting embroidery floss or yarns for the cords, and wrapping and tying the same floss or yarns for the tassels. (Instructions on page 130.)

For purposes of clarity, we specifically refer in the Decorative Trims and Notions Glossary to all trimmings used in the construction of sewn items, or very basic, packaged trims, as *notions*.

These include shirring and shade tapes, crinoline, pleater tapes, cording and the like, as well as such items as rick rack, covered cordings, and bias tapes of varying widths. Some of these notions make excellent decorative trimmings. All of the scallop edged accessories shown in this book, for example, utilize simple, attractively colored bias tapes for the finished edges. (See the porch on page 106.) An inexpensive, commercially available bias tape in a polka dot print became the main design element in the baby's room, photographed on page 96, where it was used to finish off all edges, and effectively tied the whole room together with great style. And, perhaps the most dramatic decorator trimming touch—shirred jumbo welt (see page 27)—is, after all, created from lowly, cord-wrapped cotton filler and is available by the yard alongside the cordings in the notions area of any good fabric shop.

The secret to the creative use of trims is, then, to experiment with new combinations, think of ways you can turn fabrics and yarns into your own trimmings, and always to look on that bottom shelf! Often, the most exciting trimming possibility lies, dusty and long-forgotten, somewhere behind the lilac-colored ball fringe and the upholstery zippers, just waiting to be discovered and put to good decorative use.

Eight Tips for Better Trim Application

- When selecting trims, the most important consideration is compatibility. Trims and fabrics should be compatible in both weight (heavy trims won't work on delicate fabrics) and fiber content.

- Always check trims for colorfastness if you intend to machine wash, and, if the trim isn't marked "preshrunk," preshrink it before use.

- A water-soluble ink pen used to draw the exact placement lines makes trim application easier and more precise.

- If pins distort or pucker the trim, a glue stick may be useful for temporarily holding the trim as you sew.

- Do not pull the trim taut when applying, since this may cause the fabric to pucker when sewn.

- If at all possible, work from one long length of trim. If you must precut trim lengths, be sure to cut generously to allow for corners or take-up on the machine.

- Always allow extra trim for corners. Experiment first and then baste the trim at the corners before sewing.

- Sometimes the only way to apply a trim successfully is with white craft glue. Trims applied in this manner, however, cannot be laundered and will require dry cleaning.

Every Room in the H·O·U·S·E

Foyers

Whether you call them entryways, center halls, vestibules, or foyers, these passageways, like the synopsis of a story, should capture the spirit and announce the style of all that follows. At their best, foyers are a sneak preview of the whole house, and the most exciting and successful are those which transcend the expected and add a touch of drama and flair. In this chapter you'll find examples with very individual points of view. There's a rustic country entryway decorated with antique furniture and handmade accessories; a bright and cheerful Georgian stairhall with one sensational silk accent; a tailored and quietly colored traditional hallway; and an imposing Tudor foyer done with theatrical panache in high-contrast color. In every case, a dash of the dramatic, the addition of a handcrafted item or two, and a generous amount of personal style has imprinted the mark of the owner and raised these passageways to a new and very special status.

Americana Entry

Family and guests alike walked through this tiny, fieldstone-floored entryway en route to the living and family rooms. Since it was clearly too narrow for any major piece of furniture, the ingenious use of an old bench and a versatile Shaker pegboard met both practical and aesthetic requirements with ingenuity and charm. The sawtooth edging on the bench cushion is an authentic Early American quilt technique, done here in solid fabrics played against an old-fashioned potato-stamp printed cotton with great effect. The pegboard provides a handy solution for hanging up everything from mittens to herb bouquets to extra chairs from the dining room. The finished entryway is a delightfully pragmatic solution to space and traffic demands and a tasteful introduction to the country style of the home within.

In keeping with the handcrafted look of this entryway, *above*, this handsome, plaited trim, color-matched to the mini jacquard fabric, was created from strands of worsted woolen yarn that were braided, knotted, and then handstitched in place.

A rendition of a traditional potato-stamp print, *left*, turns this entryway into an appealing bit of Americana. When accented with contrast welting and trimmed, small patterns can have great impact in tight spaces.

A CHARMING
Georgian Stairhall

Even the tiniest of foyers can be memorable. The period architecture of this stairhall with its traditional carved wood and plaster moldings was combined with a contemporary, textured wallpaper and a surprising and unexpected silk dupion bench cushion. An extravagant fabric like this is best used where a little bit will go a long way. Here in this hall, with nothing to compete with its brilliant color and sheen, one and one-half yards looks like a million, and since few visitors will actually sit here, the fact that it is an extremely fragile upholstery fabric can be forgotten and its beauty enjoyed without worry.

The cushion for the shaped seat of the antique English bench, *above*, required an accurate template. Trace around the pattern with a felt-tip marker onto a foam slab of the desired thickness, and cut out the shape. (An electric knife gives the best and cleanest results.) You may then choose to wrap the foam piece with polyester fiberfill for added loft and softness. The charming, six-strand embroidery floss tassels, *top left*, were made of twelve different colors selected to correspond to the silk check.

A TAILORED
Traditional Hall

The owners of this home are gradually collecting fine American furniture and accessories, but they have not as yet found anything really special for their entrance hall. The answer was a carpenter-built, half-round plywood table, custom cut to fit neatly between the doors to the kitchen and dining room. The fabric is a classic camel wool flannel with a companion flannel in vanilla for the trim. The limited color range and the simple lines of the skirt are enhanced by one true dressmaker touch—a shirred jumbo welt trim that effectively sets the skirt off from the floor and softens it without making it fussy or demanding. When the ultimate antique piece replaces it one day, the table will move down the hallway to the wall just beside the front door.

The semicircular table skirt, *top*, was cut from a half circle of fabric with an additional eight inches along the diameter edge. This extra fabric was allowed to fall over the back edge of the table and was attached to the back piece by self-gripping tape fasteners.

Shirred jumbo welting, *above*, is an effective and beautiful trimming technique. When deciding upon the fullness of the shirring for your project, let the weight of the fabric be your guide. One good rule of thumb is that sheers can be shirred at a ratio of 2½:1 to 3:1; heavier fabrics at 2:1 to 2½:1.

Tudor Foyer

Tudor architecture, though stylish, is often so imposing that it can visually swallow up any attempt to decorate. This dramatic foyer, for example, overwhelmed most accessories and made all but the most assertive prints seem incidental. This solution, however, suited both the house and the owners, who felt that the high contrast between the dark woods and carpeting and the pale walls was appropriate to the dark and dramatic personality of their home. The fabric choice was a luxurious but affordable moiré. It was draped over an otherwise undistinguished table, and taking advantage of the grandeur of the hall and its lack of active traffic, the table skirt was cut long enough to spill out onto the floor. This pleated ruffle trim was heat-set by a professional pleater before it was applied. Brown was selected because by keeping the color range narrow, the skirted table adds a quiet and elegant finishing touch rather than competing with the architecture. Cut flowers in summer and blooming plants in winter lend seasonal color to the scheme.

Extra long table skirts that spill out, or "break," on the floor are dramatic and elegant additions to some rooms; simply add four inches to the diameter of the circle. The accordion-pleated ruffle, *above*, added a few inches more. Remember, however, that long skirts can be a nuisance in high-traffic areas.

This tableskirt, *opposite*, was completely lined to add to its luxuriousness and enhance the opulent fabric. Lining also helps the skirt to lie beautifully on the floor. Lining tableskirts in a fabric that offers a different style and point of view and then reversing the skirt for a seasonal change is an interesting option. When sewing a reversible skirt with a fabric ruffle trim like this one, remember to make certain that your choice of fabric for the ruffle is suitable on both sides.

Living Rooms

The living room is the main public space in our homes, a room where design choices are most visible and mistakes most apparent. It's the place for a grandstand play, for a major personal and financial commitment to fabrics and furnishings. This room, therefore, demands practiced skills. The projects featured in this chapter are among the more demanding in the book, requiring considered choices and considerable time. They include beautiful curtains and shades, carefully engineered and meticulously made slipcovers, and very special accessories. You'll find a wide variety of decorating styles, with examples of traditional, country, contemporary, and eclectic; from dramatic to romantic to a fabulous first apartment assembled from foam shapes you can glue together and slipcover for instant furniture. Decorating your living room is a serious commitment. This chapter was designed to help you avoid costly and disheartening mistakes and to inspire you in the creation of a truly memorable finished room.

Contemporary Style

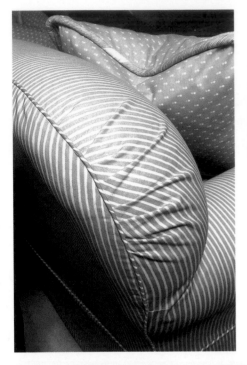

The family who lives here numbers three active children, two comfort-conscious parents, and a miniature Sheltie who joins in on everything. These over-sized, cozy seating pieces added a perfect contemporary touch to the Tudor living room. The problem was that they were upholstered in off-white cotton. Slipcovers provided a practical solution to the maintenance problem, but something more than practicality was added with the slipcovers. The charm of the mixed stripes and plaid gave the room personality, and the whole family loves the result. Stripes can add zest without making too many visual demands, and when contrasting stripes outline the seating shapes in this way, the furniture takes on a new, crisply tailored silhouette. The window panels in sheer gauze allow the room to remain open and airy while softening the quality of the light by day and providing something more than a black hole in the wall by night. The newly decorated room is the favorite gathering place for the family, including the dog, because even though it's very pretty, it's clearly not hands-off.

When slipcovering upholstered pieces with soft, rounded outlines, *top left*, fabric can be eased around the curves by softly gathering it, adding interest to the slipcover while solving the technical problem. By outlining the seating pieces in welting made from the blue and cream stripes, the clean and uncluttered look of the room was reinforced, and the size and shape of the rather bulky furniture was more clearly defined. Be careful with this kind of detail, however; it demands fastidious sewing.

When working with a diagonal plaid, *top right*, it's very important that you carefully lay out the fabric over the cushions before cutting to ensure that the plaid will achieve the best possible placement and will match along the seams.

Comfortable cotton stripes and a companion plaid add a relaxed touch to this living room, and using the same bias trim motif on the window panels and on the sofa pillows adds to the coherence of the overall design. Keep in mind that sewing something this complicated and time-consuming requires considered fab-

ric choices: Medium-weight fabric like the cottons we used here allow you to sew through the four layers of cloth necessary in slipcover construction without too much difficulty. Heavyweight fabrics are not just more demanding; they can actually be impossible to sew. In order to ensure the alignment of the edges to the

bias binding on the sheer gauze window panels, we applied the bias to the back edge first, finishing the trim with top-stitching along the front edge.

Color and Romance

A pleated ruche hem, *right*, is one of the prettiest ways to finish the bottom edge of a tableskirt.

The pillow appliqué, *below* and at *right*, was created by cutting flowers and leaves from the overall fabric and placing them on a solid muslin ground. To guarantee a clean outline when you are appliquéing, leave a margin the desired width of the satin stitch. This allows you to outline without ever changing the color of your thread and to keep the central motif clear and unbroken.

The design concept of this living room was, quite obviously, elaboration. The ornamental and patterned style of the fabrics and furnishings, all played against the drama of the richly colored walls, lends a romantic, Victorian air to the room, even though there's not a single piece of real Victoriana in evidence. In truth, this room was designed to be deliberately busy in order to disguise the rather undistinguished heritage of the furniture. It's a theatrical set with one element and pattern playing off against another, carefully planned so that the eye never rests on one particular thing. Look for example at the extraordinary number of trims and decorative fabric finishes used here. Loop fringe trims the drapery, braids outline the chair, cloths are finished with self-fabric pleated hems, and laces and appliqués abound. It's a veritable reference work of ornamentation! The addition of several authentic antique collectibles—the Staffordshire ceramic dogs, the majolica pottery, and the 18th-century English tea caddies—add a touch of legitimacy and class.

Slipcovers, no matter how carefully fitted, will soften the outline of a piece. In the case of this off-white wing chair cover, *left*, the addition of a simple line of burgundy welting kept the chair from becoming clumsy and tied it into the color scheme of the room. When combining darks with lights in this manner, it's vital to pretest the fabrics and trims for colorfastness.

AN UPDATE ON
Provincial

This lovely little house came filled with provincial French details. The owners had added more. Armoires filled corners. Period French chairs populated the main rooms. Our aim here was to downplay provincial and to create a less contrived, more relaxed mixture of international styles. The sofa, an elderly velvet piece, was slipcovered in a glorious English garden print, chosen both for the way the pale lemon ground relates to the cream walls and for its light-handed freshness. The ruffled corner pillows disguise the dated style of the sofa arms while emphasizing the window and the view beyond. The fabric shades are a stationary installation—they neither raise nor lower but are there simply to frame the view. The period French chairs remain, but the addition of the extraordinary ruffled welt is a dressmaker touch that gives them new life and interest. Traditional French gingham checks were used here just to pull the whole room back to its origins.

In this small, dark room, *opposite*, lightness was all-important. The airy, floral sofa with a pale background and the balloon window shade float in the room, allowing the outside view to remain an important visual element. The stationary fabric shade required less fabric than one that will fully raise and lower; too much fabric results in a bulky shade that looks overdone. The ruffled pillows are a lovely addition to rooms with a romantic point of view and, when sewn with a hemmer foot and a ruffling attachment, are far easier to make than they appear.

A traditional French open arm chair was given a new seat cushion and a delightfully shaped and buttoned backrest, *above*. Narrow self-fabric cords secure the back pillow by tying through the caning. The truly special dressmaker touch is the insertion of a tiny ruffle of bias-cut gingham, where welting might be more expected. Working with a ruffle as narrow as this one takes some getting used to, but the technique is easy to master, and the finished effect is worth the extra effort.

PERSIAN
Prints

This exceptional paneled living room/library was full of cast-off furniture. The dated and awkward styling of the upholstered pieces spoiled the architectural beauty of the room. The antidote was a slightly exotic set of slipcovers, sewn from a group of paisley coordinates. Using these fabrics, however, called for very careful planning. Yard cuts of each of the print possibilities were placed on the furniture and scrutinized before the final fabric choices were made. In the end, the printed border of one cloth was cut off and sewn onto a second, allover print to achieve the proper mixture of prints and to set the slipcovered pieces off from the dark carpeting. Part of the fallaway was used for the window seat cushion and the floor pillow.

The second problem was to keep the room exciting without letting the patterns take over. This was accomplished by selecting a print with the same dark brown background as the carpet and wood walls. Definitely out of the ordinary, the unusual scheme never betrays the unexceptional furniture it so dramatically conceals.

By pulling the corners of a loosely fitted throw into soft gathers and securing them with self-fabric ties, *top*, a relaxed and easy slipcover was created. This technique also succeeds in disguising the narrow, dated arms of the sofa. Even though this slipcover has the look of a casual throw, its construction makes it secure and practical.

What was once a stiff, boxlike sofa, *above*, has been transformed into a plush, stylish one by replacing an old foam slab seat and back cushions with dense feather pillows. Three thirty-inch squares compress neatly to fit the seat, while five smaller squares across the back allow for individual placement and slight overlapping.

Turkish corner pillows, always have a slightly exotic look and translate beautifully into paisleys like these. Due to the gathered corners, they will appear slightly smaller than their actual dimensions, so you may want to make them an inch or two larger than you would a knife-edge pillow. Also remember that an applied border, like the one on the floor pillows, must be placed far enough from the edge that the full motif remains visible on top of the finished pillow.

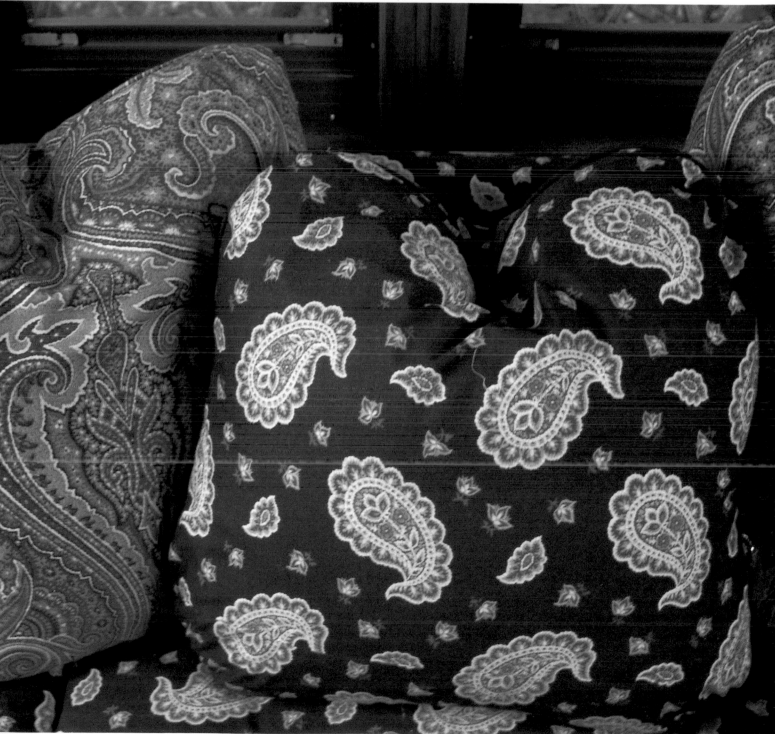

A KEEPING ROOM
in Traditional Patterns

Large-scale prints like this one often work best when they are repeated at least once in a room. For this reason, enough fabric was purchased for both a new slipcover on the existing sofa and for upholstering a new wing chair. Perfect placement of a bold, colorful print is very important to guarantee a successful slipcovering or upholstery job.

Although more time-consuming than ring tape, the hand-sewn rings on this Roman shade, *right*, give a more attractive look and are the choice of professional workrooms. Metal rings are sturdier than plastic and won't break under heavy use.

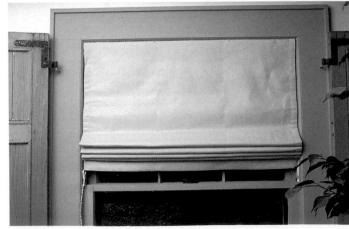

This room, an addition to a too-small house, had to serve many needs for a growing family. The idea of a colonial keeping room appealed greatly, from the standpoint of both style and function. At one end, a shuttered pass-through from the kitchen allows food to come directly to a large family dining table. At the other end, a comfortable and inviting living area serves family and guests. Even though the style is authentic colonial, some practical compromise entered into the decorating decisions. The random pine floor, for example, was cut from old beams, but a bit of pigment stain was added to lighten the color and thereby disguise dust. A traditional braided rug nods to its colonial past while obscuring clutter. The end result is a happy and serviceable combination of the old and the practical. But it's the brilliantly colored tree-of-life print and its smaller companion prints that keep the whole room focused and attractive, even under continual hard use by this young family.

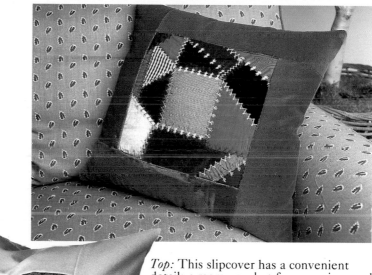

Top: This slipcover has a convenient detail: a roomy pocket for magazines and newspapers. Another interesting detail here is the combination of two trims, rick rack and bias binding, to make a unique trim finish.

These pillows effectively turn a small bit of old, beautiful patchwork into an appropriate size by the addition of four fabric strips joined in the style of log cabin quilting around the center piece. Each pillow was backed with the same fabric as the front strips. To protect fragile fabrics in this or other such projects, use a fine netting placed over the face of the delicate fabric before seaming.

A STYLISH AFFORDABLE
First Apartment

*T*his bright and cheerful multipurpose room is full of real furniture to sew. It's a simple and inexpensive solution to the first apartment, a vacation home, a dorm room, the spare room, or the kids' room. The secret to the furniture is basic foam shapes, available directly from foam stores or by mail order from catalogs. All the sizes are standard; the pieces are assembled by stacking or arranging the foam to the right heights and configurations. After the foam elements are glued together, they're slipcovered, first in muslin, then in a decorative fabric. The resulting furniture is lightweight, portable, and—perhaps most important to our point of view here—inexpensive. A big part of the success of this room is the choice of a striped linen and cotton canvas. The use of boldly colored stripes (which, when mitered, become the design element in the room) gives the room such a young and spirited design lift that the rather simple furnishings look important and stylish.

The sofa in the room, *opposite*, was built from three standard lounge pads stacked and glued together. Two foam wedges were glued at each end. Covering the foam shape first with muslin, then with fabric slipcovers, allows you to remove the covers for dry cleaning or for a seasonal change. The quilted pad can be rolled up into a sofa bolster or seat pad and rolled out to become an exercise mat. It was created from two lengths of individually channel-quilted fabric. Director's chairs can make clever and affordable dining chairs. The addition of an extra seat cushion raises the height of the chair to allow comfortable dining use.

Artfully joined by fabric hinges, the ottoman sections, *top left*, open out to become lounge pads that can be propped up, stretched out, and used for just lounging around.

Roman shades, *above*, are the simplest and best way to treat awkward or unevenly sized windows. They require very little yardage and give you the option of partially shaded windows in sunny rooms like this one. Always make sure that the rings, here purchased as Roman shade tape, are properly aligned across the shade, or it will never raise or lower properly.

Graphic squares were created on the front panel of the sofa and floor pillows, *top right* and *opposite*, by mitering the striped fabrics. When estimating yardage for mitered pillows, allow at least one-third more fabric than you would need for a plain pillow front and back, and be sure to cut all the pieces in the same place on the stripe pattern, with the stripes going in the same direction.

Dining Rooms

No longer a special-occasion room used on Sundays, holidays, and for parties, but off-limits at other times, the dining room has become an important and often multipurpose part of the house. This chapter covers a wide range of dining room styles—from a converted service porch, newly decorated for breakfasting, to an extravagant formal room. In between are a brightly colored family dining room that occasionally doubles as a work/play space for young children, and a charming provincial room with the ease and style of a country inn. We've also included a party view of one room with a table set up for a kid's birthday bash, and a Christmas Eve supper table with spectacular holiday flair. Each one has a decorating twist or two, and each offers a bounty of tabletop projects and ideas.

BRIGHT AND

Contemporary

These attractive unlined side panel curtains, *right*, incorporate the bias band motif as an inside edge trim detail. Notice that the band was cut to repeat visually the width of the fabric-covered curtain pole. The casings were purposely cut large to add an easy, contemporary flair to the window treatment. The pole itself is a plastic tube, covered with a bias-cut tube of the curtain fabric.

To make this mitered tableskirt, *opposite* and *below*, without piecing, use fabric fifty-four to sixty inches wide, and allow one and one-half times the normal amount of fabric to accommodate the extra required by the bias cut. The bias banding was made from the fall-away from the cut-out circle plus a bit of additional fabric.

How do you best decorate the dining room when you've got little kids, little space, and less money? This bright, cheerful, virtually kid-proof room was furnished from a catalog and sewn in rough-and-tumble cotton and linen canvas with jazzy awning stripes. The choice of yellow and white keeps the room light and sunny and adds considerably to the feeling of spaciousness. Everything was kept supersimple. The Cheska chairs and sisal rug are classics and their laid-back style is undemanding. In fact, these same chairs can do double duty in the living room for extra guest seating. As for the fabric accessories, everything was preshrunk so it gets pitched into the washing machine as necessary. The finished room is so easily maintained that the kids are welcome to use the unskirted table as a work/play area during the afternoon, so there's never a moment—or an inch of space—wasted. This dining room has the same strong and appealing contemporary style as the living room photographed on page 42 and, like that room, would fit well into the active life-style and limited budgets of young singles and growing families.

Sunny yellow and white stripes are engineered to make a bright and pleasant dining room. To add to the comfort and multi-use capacity, a collection of matching pillows was sewn for the window seat, with two cut on the straight grain and two cut on the bias. In order to stabilize the bias pillow pieces, a lightweight fusible interfacing was applied to the wrong sides of the pillow fronts and backs. This trick guarantees that the pillow covers won't stretch out of shape after repeated launderings.

Splendor

This formal dining room comes with a few surprises. Even though the look is expensive, the reality is not. Only the floor was a serious investment, painted by an artist to look just like marble and then sealed in practical polyurethane. The furniture was handed down and none too wonderful, so an ingenious system was devised to keep most of it out of view. The table was simply skirted out in beautiful, natural linen. The awkward chairs were slipcovered in a way that can be easily adapted for any wood dining chair. One reason why so much fabric works in this room is the notable absence of window curtains. With the sleek metal blinds, the table skirt and chair slipcovers are a soft relief. Even the unsightly chandelier cord has a soft fabric casing. Everything was well planned to hide what wasn't pretty with something that was. And since the overall color scheme is monochromatic, the real splash and drama come from the foods that are brought to the table, the flowers, and the colorful addition of family and guests who dine here.

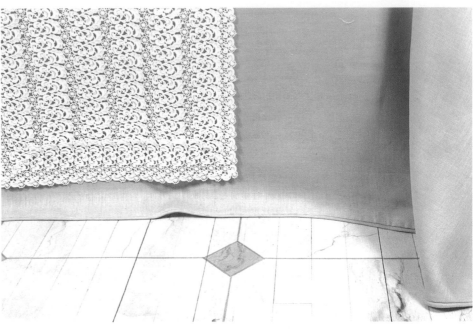

Notice the carefully mitered finish on the lace table runner, *above.* These seams were sewn by hand to guarantee a perfect match and to allow for the overlapping of the lace, rather than have bulky seaming. You may choose to use a wide, close machine zigzag stich to accomplish this match.

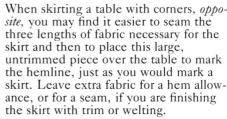

When skirting a table with corners, *opposite,* you may find it easier to seam the three lengths of fabric necessary for the skirt and then to place this large, untrimmed piece over the table to mark the hemline, just as you would mark a skirt. Leave extra fabric for a hem allowance, or for a seam, if you are finishing the skirt with trim or welting.

In order to make the fabric in these chair slipcovers more substantial and help keep it from wrinkling, a thin layer of fiberfill was added as an interfacing between the linen face fabric and the sateen lining. The use of a brush fringe in place of the more expected bias welting added a nostalgic touch to the room.

IN THE STYLE OF
a Country Inn

This tiny dining alcove is situated just to one side of the living room pictured on page 36 and combines, as does that room, some of the best elements of American and French country style. By isolating the gingham check (featured in the living room on a pair of open arm side chairs) and adding a contrast binding in red and cream as the trim detail, the dining room echoes the living room without being boring or repetitious. The overall feeling here is one of friendliness and comfort. The Windsor chairs were somewhat uncomfortable for long dinners, thus the addition of the shaped seat cushions. The window treatment, identical in style to that in the adjoining living room, is translated here into the gingham scheme, and, because the fabric shades are short and stationary, they not only fit well into a rather awkward bay window without looking gimmicky or contrived, but they allow the sunlight and the beautiful garden to become an active part of the room.

The simple, nearly foolproof decorating scheme, *top left*, keeps a small space interesting without making it too busy. Notice how the addition of sulphur yellow Quimper dinner plates gives the whole room the color relief it needs.

When using a clearly geometric pattern like this one, let the width of the check be a cutting and trimming guide. The bias band around these napkins and tablecloth, *top right*, was sized to correspond to the width of the check.

Antique furniture is a visual joy but a problem to fit. Since no two Windsor chairs are identical, it is necessary to cut a separate template for each chair seat when making cushions, *above*. You may find it helpful to code each cover permanently by numbering it on iron-on tape, which you can then apply to the inside of the cushion cover.

Birthday Table

E van and three special friends will celebrate at a table created just for his birthday. The ceiling is a cloud of helium-filled balloons and on the table, balloons again! Balloon placemats are sewn in brightly colored chintz, as are balloon party bags, one for each child with the names inked on just to keep things straight. Sewing something special for a party is an art unto itself. Sewing techniques should be kept relatively simple and the fabrics chosen with limited use in mind. You may choose to pass along the clever balloon birthday party cloth and accessories to the next child in line, but the obvious goal of these projects is immediate effect rather than technical brilliance or durability.

The multicolor hem treatment on this party skirt, *top*, was created as a simple adaptation of the more complicated version seen on the reading chair slipcover, page 41. In this application, the hem is constructed from wide bias tape with jumbo rick rack applied on top.

The top layer of these charming balloon placemats, *above*, was backed with polyester batting. Then we topstitched around the balloon shape, one-quarter inch in from the outside edge, just to make sure that after laundering the placemat would retain its nice, round shape.

Breakfast Room

Once an unused service porch tucked between the old butler's pantry and the dining room, this tiny space was perfectly situated to become a sunny breakfast room. Since it was clearly visible from the very formal dining room, something extra special was required to keep it from looking like an afterthought. The choice was to use relaxed, country prints in an elaborate way and to finish the scheme with an abundance of elegant cotton lace. The walls were upholstered in one of a charming collection of French country prints, then borders were created by cutting strips from a companion stripe. Finally, other prints from the group of coordinates were added for the slipseats and tableskirt. The lace curtains gave just enough privacy and made a sensible and consistent choice for the pantry cabinets as well. Now the pantry and the breakfast room make a delightful twosome, and since the kids generally opt for the kitchen counter, this little corner of the house has become the favorite spot for Dad and Mom to spend a few minutes together over coffee and the morning paper.

If you have any concern about cutting into a loosely woven fabric like lace, you may want to stabilize it first by sewing narrow twill tape to the inside of the cut line. This way you can split the fabric without risking stretching and fraying.

When constructing curtain panels that are attached at top and bottom, it is easier to install the bottom rods last, after the panels have been made and installed on the top rod. This ensures that the finished curtains will be perfectly taut. After laundering, rehang sheer curtains like these while they are still slightly damp. They will fit the rods more easily and will dry without wrinkles.

GREYSCALE

BIN TRAVELER FORM

Cut By _Michael A Huerta_ Qty _12_ Date _8-5_

Scanned By_____ Qty_____Date_____

Scanned Batch IDs

_____   _____   _____

Notes / Exception

_____

_____

_____

_____

_____

The walls of this breakfast room were upholstered over polyester batting. The staples along the unfinished corner edges were covered with flat self-fabric bands made from bias strips which were cut, folded, and secured with a strip of fusible web, then applied to the walls with a hot glue gun. The border was cut from the companion stripe fabric and ironed on under the crown molding with a hot iron and fusible web cut to width. The Cluny lace used for the window curtains is a forty-eight-inch cotton galloon. Because it is finished with a decorative edging on both sides, it was possible to use a mitered finish across the bottom, thereby beautifully continuing the scallop motif around the entire curtain panel.

A CHRISTMAS EVE
Supper

Straight out of a Dickens novel, this extravagant and romantic Christmas Eve supper setting holds the promise of good food, good drink, and good times. The table is a celebration of traditional taffetas, which were gathered, bustled up, and gloriously overdone in honor of this event. Part of the excitement is the surprise of a table in an unexpected location, creating a dining room where there was none a moment before—on a terrace, on a lawn, in a hallway, in the library, in the bedroom. The significant point here is that no matter where and no matter what the style, the gesture is a sign of a new attitude toward dining: the moveable feast, created from a collection of varied, portable tables to gussy up and turn out for parties and special evenings like this one. No rules, no regulations—only your fancy and preference and the spirit of the event. This one is our suggestion for Christmas Eve. Dream up your own fancy dress evening, designed just for you and one or more special friends to enjoy and remember fondly long after the last toast has been made.

A draped, long tableskirt, *top*, that spills out over the floor is festive for this kind of special event. If you run short on time, you might choose simply to cut the skirt long and tuck it under for the evening rather than hem it.

Our festive Christmas wreath, *above*, was created from three bias-cut plaid taffetas, stuffed, and plaited into a circle. The bow was also made from taffeta fabric.

The gathered-up overskirt, *opposite*, was created by single-cord shirring tape sewn around the edge of the skirt, which was drawn up to an attractive puffiness. The overall length of the top skirt is five inches shorter than the actual drop to the floor. The festoons were formed by gathering up the overskirt, attaching it in fabric bands, and adding the bows (actually two bows, crossed and sewn together with a self-covered button).

Kitchens

For most of us, the kitchen is the heart of the home. Our families gather here, many of our waking hours are spent here, and, inevitably, most of our day-to-day family memories center around this active, purposeful room. As more kitchens become entertainment and social centers as well as family nurturing spaces, the need to make them attractive as well as practical increases. The truth is, a kitchen can easily be both functional and pretty. This chapter deals with a variety of kitchen styles, each given a personal touch with a group of sewn accessories. You'll find some of the traditional items like appliance covers, potholders, aprons, placemats, napkins, and the like done in some fresh and untraditional ways. There's a kitchen with a touch of authentic Provence; another group of accessories straight from the heritage of American handicraft; and a bright and cheery kitchen chock full of accessories sewn from tea toweling by the yard and all trimmed in crocheted lace. This chapter and the pretty ideas here could be just as important to the heart of your home as the pots and pans.

TEA TOWELING

and Crochet

This remodeled kitchen with its white walls, cabinets, and appliances needed a generous dash of color and pattern to finish off its new look. The classic choice of colors and the tattersall pattern might not surprise you, but the choice of fabric might. All the dressmade accessories in this room were sewn from readily available linen and cotton tea toweling purchased by the yard from a local fabric shop. Since tea toweling is only available in very narrow widths, all of the items were designed to utilize the cloth in the most attractive and economical way and to make the most of the woven selvage. Then all the edges were trimmed in cotton crocheted lace with a homemade look. Unfortunately, when laundered, tea toweling does require light starch and ironing, but in a room that looks like this one, that occasional bit of extra effort seems well worth the result.

This roll basket insert, *above*, was sewn from three equal circles of trimmed fabric, which, when snapped together, create a charming and functional accessory that fits a variety of baskets. Tea toweling is ideal for this project because the design is the same on both sides of the fabric and, therefore, each of the pockets will look the same, whether seen from the right or wrong side.

Decorative potholders, *top*, can add a colorful accent to your kitchen. These are not heatproof or fire resistant, however, and should be used carefully for handling hot cooking utensils. The idea here is to use them as you might use a picture or a wall plaque—to enhance the room with an additional decorative touch.

Our tea toweling valance, *above*, was engineered to take advantage of the bolder stripes woven in near the selvage edge. The addition of a line of crocheted trim further emphasizes the decorative border and adds a handcrafted touch.

When selecting special fabrics for a kitchen, *opposite*, remember that washability is a primary concern. Many fabrics are not guaranteed against shrinkage and can change size dramatically when laundered. What's more, the uniformity of the shrinkage is unpredictable, and the dimensions of the woven pattern can alter. Always launder these fabrics before cutting so that there will be no surprises.

Patchwork

What could be more American than a patchwork quilt? Few crafts are more appealing than the intricate patching of mixed and matched fabrics to create patterns like the log cabin, the flower basket, or the Texas star. Here is a special group of kitchen accessories sewn in traditional quilt styles. The secret is in the arrangement of the prints and the assortment of the colors. Start with two that work well together and add little snips of additional prints or colorways to the group, keeping them or removing them as your eye dictates. Be sure of the final arrangement before buying yardage. A good tip is that it's always easier to stay within specifically designed and coordinated groups of fabrics from one manufacturer. Some fabric companies specialize in large ranges of color-coordinated miniprints like these, and since they've done most of the planning for you, your job will be made easier.

Polyester batting plus the top and bottom fabrics give these decorative potholders, *above*, a bulky edge. Extrawide double-fold bias tape can accommodate the loftiness of all three layers. Perhaps the single most important factor in successfully executing these projects is accuracy. Each piece must be sewn on the exact seamline to guarantee that the

pieces will assemble perfectly into the finished patch designs.

Quilting through two layers of fabric with a layer of polyester batting sandwiched between, as in these appliance covers, top, is made far easier by using a walking foot on your machine.

When binding outward corners as on this tablecloth, *right*, be sure to allow enough extra bias binding at the corners so that it will lie perfectly flat. Pin or baste the binding in place and check the corners before you begin to sew.

à la Provence

For all who have longed for a true French country kitchen, these are the prints and this is the style. Take one sleek, ceramic-tiled kitchen with a natural wood or terra-cotta floor. Add an assortment of authentic Provençal fabrics in traditional French colorings. Mix carefully, one print, one color at a time, and voilà! The real beauty of these natural cotton prints is their strength of color and the intricacy of their patterns. When combined and played one against the other, they can give a neutral room a color and print lift. The border print was used around the placemats and as the boxing strip on the stool cushions to give the miniprints definition and to provide the traditional bordered style in the room. Even though the sewing involved some demanding techniques such as quilting and mitering, the finished kitchen shows that the time and effort were well spent.

The group of kitchen accessories, *top* and *opposite*, was designed around a purchased, printed border and a coordinating fabric. The width of the border determined the construction of each piece, so the patterns for these accessories will need adjusting if you choose a border wider or narrower than this one. For instance, the border fabric determined the height of the boxing on the stool cushions.

If you choose to use shirred rather than flat curtains in glass-front cabinets, *above*, it's necessary to measure carefully the amount of space available between the glass and the edge of the shelves to determine whether or not it will accommodate gathers.

On an item as small as a placemat, *above right*, it may be impossible to make a perfect match at all four mitered corners. Instead, center a motif on the two long sides, letting the corners fall where they may, then do the same on the two shorter sides. This way the corners will present a consistent appearance.

Using Bristol board as a stiffening material is the traditional way to construct this little roll basket, *above*. You may, however, choose to substitute plastic mesh needlepoint canvas which would let you hand-wash the basket when necessary.

CHRISTMAS PRINTS
and Appliqués

It's Christmas morning and the troops are gathered for a festive breakfast buffet. You've set the buffet table with holiday dishes and some special Christmas accessories sewn just for the occasion. The old folding chairs are brought out, but this year you've dressed them up for the holiday with cheery, Christmas red quilted slipcovers. Even the centerpiece has a handcrafted touch. Freesia is arranged in a container made from candy canes you've glued over an empty jar. Handicraft is a wonderful, personal way to say, "Merry Christmas!"

Most people enjoy dressing up their homes for the holidays. Both sewn accessories and fabric trimmings can be used to accomplish this personal and festive effect. Here, yards and yards of inexpensive florist's ribbon were used to decorate a wreath, while two pattern pieces, prequilted fabric, and purchased welt transform battered folding chairs into stylish holiday seating.

Even though these buffet roll-ups and table runner, *top* and *above*, are clearly designed for holiday use, they involve skills and a time commitment that make repeated use, Christmas after Christmas, both sensible and desirable. It's wise, then, to make sure that all the fabrics used in these projects be carefully preshrunk and completely washable.

The buffet roll-up holds the flatware and napkin for each guest in a tidy and manageable package. When unrolled, it becomes a handy placemat or lap covering.

Bedrooms

Is there anyone among us who hasn't dreamed of having a splendid bedroom, a personal retreat filled with all the little comforts and lavished with a favorite color or print? No matter what your idea of style and decoration, the bedroom is definitely a decorating priority and a room for which most of us are eager and willing to sew. This chapter features five special rooms, each with a highly individual design point of view. They cover a wide range of sewing projects—from spectacular canopy beds and upholstered walls to simple, more tailored country looks; from mixed and matched tartans in masculine colorings to a curtained bed constructed from four-by-fours and draped with graceful scallop edged panels. Nearly one-third of our lives is spent sleeping. This chapter, then, is devoted to sleeping in beauty.

A cardboard stiffened flap was slipped between the mattress and box spring to secure the caddy, *right*, to the bed. The cardboard is removed before laundering the caddy.

When combining upholstered walls and free-hanging items such as curtains in one room, *below*, there's really no way to match the print down the entire length of both. This problem is caused by the stretching of the fabric during upholstering. Cover the walls first and then, holding a length of the curtain fabric up against the wall, determine the best visual placement for the match. It's usually best to line up the print at the top of the curtain or valance, or at eye-level along the wall.

Chintz

These stationary chintz side panels with a casing top, *below left*, are difficult to control on the rod. They tend to creep and the fullness becomes unevenly distributed. There are two ways to solve this problem. If the casing is small, you can roll a rubber band onto the rod, pushing it until it meets the inside edge of the panel. If, however, the casing is larger, pin a ribbon to the inside edge and pull the ribbon back to the outside edge or the return, and pin it again. The ribbon will hold the panel in place.

It's the little personal touches that made the accessories in this room truly special. The daisies on this neckroll, *below*, were purchased by the yard and cut apart—only the leaves and stems were chain stitched.

If you love English garden florals and dramatic style, this glorious chintz and piqué bedroom should be just your cup of tea. When designing around a strong and visually demanding print like this one, it's sometimes best to lavish it on all the main fabricated pieces, letting that one print become the decorating theme, rather than trying to mix in others. In this room, even the stenciled flowers on the floor have been copied directly from the main fabric motif. The relief from the floral was provided by the extensive use of white—white paint as the ceiling and trim color, white antique linens on the bed and tabletop, and white piqué for the lining of the canopy, the curtains, and the dust ruffle. By this careful balance of dark and light, print and plain, the room remains crisp and fresh rather than becoming visually overwhelming.

A brass bed, *left*, is a beautiful piece of furniture, but it can be extremely uncomfortable for reading or breakfasting in bed. This ruffled, chintz headrest was made from a piece of foam cut to length and wrapped with polyester batting for additional softness. It ties to the headboard in three places along the length.

SCOTTISH
Plaids

This bedroom, as Scottish as a kilt, was sewn from literally hundreds of yards of practical, washable wool and polyester plaids. The design direction here is very strong and obviously not for everyone. But the details and the design thinking can be easily translated into other, less specific decorating situations. The consistent use of bias ruffles to soften the edges of the bed hangings and the window curtains illustrates one way of creating a room that suits both a masculine and a feminine design requirement. The effective use of a simple bias banding reiterates the ruffle as a trim motif and efficiently finishes off all raw edges, including the staple lines on the upholstered walls. The successful mixture of plaids and solids throughout the room provides a good lesson in balance and proportion that could be applied to hundreds of other print and solid mixtures. This wonderful room of warm and inviting color, filled with the scent of pine potpourri, and lit by the glow of the fire, is eminently successful just as it is. It's a room to warm you to the tips of your toes.

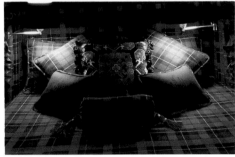

This collection of pillows, *above*, was based on the very same shapes used for the white piqué pillows shown on page 69. The dramatically different look obtained here eloquently illustrates the power of color and fabric choice. Note the attractive tartan tassels, cut from an authentic Scottish bagpipe tie, at either end of the neckroll.

Plaids are tough! Be sure you feel technically proficient and confident before attempting to upholster a room in a plaid fabric. Work slowly with at least two plumb bobs and a level. The first wall will be the hardest, but things should get a little easier as you proceed. Never try to upholster a room with a printed plaid fabric—they're rarely printed straight enough. With wovens, you can tug to adjust and pull the plaid back on-grain.

Being able to custom fit accessories to any bed, even an antique, *opposite*, is just one of the advantages of sewing your own. Here the dust ruffle was cut extra long to accommodate the unusual height of the bed, built up intentionally to give the bed an old-fashioned look. A good way to accommodate a full canopy bed visually in a modestly sized room is to cover the walls and sew the canopy from the same fabric. If this isn't possible, match the color of the painted or papered wall to the ground color of the fabric. Try to keep the floor color a compatible tone, too. In this way, you'll integrate the bed into the room to make it appear less bulky.

A canopy bed can have the cozy feeling of a room within a room. To save on yardage, the backdrop was cut just long enough to end below the headboard. Short backdrops can be shirred onto brass rods and secured to the wall, or simply left to fall freely behind the bed.

Notice the careful placement of the scallops on the bed valance. To ensure that the scallops would fall at exactly the same place at each of the two end posts, a scallop was placed at the exact center point. Then the valance was hung from the center out, working first to the right and then to the left.

Bouquets

The dressing table skirt, *below*, was designed to open on a pair of wooden swing-arms that are hidden beneath, thus allowing access to the drawers. The skirt was gathered on two-string shirring tape and attached to the table with self-gripping fastener tape. The green single-fold bias tape, used for subtle contrast on the duvet cover, makes a decorative trim down the inside edges and across the bottom of the skirt.

Recently, we've seen a great deal of a stylistic trend called "American Country," which uses primitive furniture and accessories and handwoven gingham or small-scale prints to create authentic rustic rooms. The style is warm and inviting and has great appeal. The room photographed here, however, offers country with a plus—a stylistic departure that retains that down-home charm but adds a dash of old-world elegance. The use of beautiful, scallop edged detailing on the canopy bed hangings and at the windows adds romance to a room that still happily incorporates such authentic Americana as the old milk paint chest, jug lamp, hand-embroidered linen shams, rag rugs, and rough willow baskets. The canopy frame may look old, but it was constructed from new four-by-fours, distressed and stained to repeat the color of the random-plank pine floor. The finished room balances all of these elements subtly and effectively.

This fabric valance, *below*, was attached to the frame by stapling it over one-inch-wide strips of cardboard to ensure a straight top edge. For cleaning, the valance is pulled down, cleaned, and then restapled to the frame over fresh strips of cardboard.

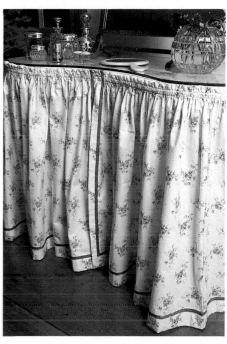

Florals

This softly and romanti-
cally colored bedroom
was designed around a four-
poster bed, some inherited
mahogany side tables and
accessories, and a fine primitive portrait. The pleasant
surprise is some untradi-
tional pastels played against
the dark woods of the period
and reproduction furniture.
A finely rendered chinoiserie
print like this one blends
well with period furniture.
The addition of the geometric
pattern of the wallpaper and
the little squiggle print of the
contrast fabric keeps the
scheme alive and interesting,
and ties the space together in
a quiet, understated way.
All in all, it's a conservative
but charming solution that
pleases without ever boring
the traditionalists who live
here.

When you're using a print with a strong
personality, *above*, consider using a contrast print of a smaller scale as a bind-off
fabric—one that relates to the wall color-
ing as well as to the main print. Here,
we used the little squiggle print to bind
off the dust ruffle and the ruffled shams
and to trim the duvet cover.

A reversible duvet cover, *left*, allows you
to change the look of the room just by
flipping the duvet. This one opens and
closes with self-gripping fastener tape.

Balloon shades and shutters, *opposite*,
weren't just the prettiest solution for this
room; they were the only solution. That
awkward corner and the adjacent closet
door to the right of the bed made curtains of any kind an impossibility. The
balloon shades were designed to lower to
just below the top of the shutter.

TAILORED
Silks

Handwoven fabrics are nearly impossible to match exactly at the seams, but the slight irregularity of these fabrics is part of their charm. Simply match the pattern in crucial areas and let the rest fall randomly. The handwoven silk tattersall used on the straight grain for the dust ruffle had seams hidden in the corner pleats to alleviate this problem. It was also lined for added stability. By quilting some of the natural silk fabric used in this room, it was possible to sew the bedspread and the curtain valances without any interfacing or lining. Quilting adds dimension and personality to the fabric and cuts down on the sewing steps, even though it does add to the cost.

When creating your own upholstered headboard, nailheads should be arranged in a pattern that is related to the plaid or print. Let your choice of fabric help you to make the decision. You may, however, find a height of twenty-four to twenty-six inches above the mattress is the best and most workable design. You might try a higher headboard for a more dramatic effect. Be careful, though, about the practicality of a lower one.

These lined draperies, *top*, have a pleated heading. Pinch pleats like these fall more evenly and gracefully than do panels that are simply gathered on a rod. They can also be installed on traverse rods, allowing them to be opened and closed easily. When you are using bias strips of plaid or printed fabrics, first fold a piece on the bias, letting the pattern caused by the fold determine the finished width of the trimming.

The very special heading on this dressing table skirt, *above*, was made by taking tiny tucks in the fabric. The silk fabric on the dressing table top was stabilized with iron-on interfacing to keep it flat and smooth under the glass and prevent the edges from fraying.

If ruffles or mixed prints aren't your style, plaids give you astigmatism, and florals make you sneeze, perhaps the solution is a crisply tailored room like this one. Built around a bicolor scheme, this room has an airy and peaceful atmosphere. The main design theme here is texture played against texture—slubbed, handwoven silk tattersall and sleek silk broadcloth; quilted and unquilted fabrics; a wooly Greek flokati rug on a highly polished floor; woven rush and pine Scottish cottage chairs set against ceramic tiles; and so on. The subtheme is the use of applied bias trim on nearly every fabric item, which establishes a decorative pattern on its own that's repeated over and over again around the room. Everything here is pared down, simple, and understandable, but the use of these two decorative themes keeps the room interesting. Take a good, long look. The more you study the quiet details, the better it gets.

Bathrooms

The usual decorating rule for the bathroom is that the finished room be uncluttered and easily maintained. But for those of us who would choose a more distinctive and decorative approach to the bath, we offer several solutions that manage to be both practical and interesting. The rooms we feature here run the gamut from a tiny maid's bath in an older home, which was given new life with yards of hand-dyed batiks, to a contemporary bath complete with the requisite whirlpool and a few tailored accessories. In between are armloads of ideas. We've even photographed four ways to treat the same window in a pristine, all-white bathroom that forever dispels the notion that white baths are boring. For everyone who has ever despaired of finding the perfect shower curtain, or a pair of bathroom curtains with unaffected and unplasticized charm, or yes, even a tasteful toilet seat cover, here is a chapter full of wonderful ways to transform your bathroom in your own style, in colors and fabrics you love.

WHITE

on White

Nothing is as clean and fresh as pure white, and white cotton towels, just washed and smelling of sunshine, could be the ultimate bathroom luxury. This white-on-white bathroom was created around white terry toweling with just that sybaritic thought in mind. Toweling by the yard was sewn into the double shower curtain and valance, the window curtains, and a group of accessories. Quilted toweling created a bath mat and toilet seat cover. The purchased towels were all monogrammed, again in white, and yards of white crocheted lace were lavished on everything. It's a room that is every bit as comforting as it is beautiful. Terry makes a wonderful, soft fabric addition to the room and its highly textured surface plays attractively against the glistening ceramic tiles. A decorating touch to note here is the use of pine to create a vanity cabinet, and the use of the pine shutters at the window. This adds not only relief from the bright white color palette, but also the warmth and patina of wood, stained to look as though it had been there forever.

The seams of all of these terry accessories were designed so that there would be no raw edges left to ravel during use and laundering. After the raw edge on the shower curtain valance, *top*, was enclosed in a hem, the lace was stitched to the back side.

One of the advantages of sewing this bath mat, *above*, from terry yardage rather than simply trimming a purchased mat was that the size of the mat could be adjusted to allow for the perfect fit of the mitered trim.

Decorated towels, *above*, are easy to sew and can make a dramatic difference in the look of a room. It is, however, of utmost importance to remember to preshrink both the towels and the trimmings so that they will not pucker during normal washing.

To be sure that the shape you cut will fit perfectly around your toilet seat lid, make a template by slipping a piece of kraft paper under the seat and tracing around the outside edge. Add two and one-quarter inches all around the template except at the back edge, where only one inch is added. Remember to include enough drawstring to allow you to release the gathers again for laundering.

All-cotton terry toweling, teamed with all-cotton lace trim makes serviceable and attractive bathroom accessories. Both the toweling and the lace were carefully prewashed in hot water before cutting and sewing to keep shrinkage to a minimum. Occasional bleaching keeps everything in pristine condition.

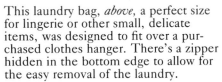

This laundry bag, *above*, a perfect size for lingerie or other small, delicate items, was designed to fit over a purchased clothes hanger. There's a zipper hidden in the bottom edge to allow for the easy removal of the laundry.

A bath salts bag, *top right*, may not be the first bathroom accessory you think of, but it adds more than just good looks to the room. Use it for storing scented salts or fill it with herbals or potpourri.

Although this bath mitt, *right*, looks as if it is secured at the wrist with a cable cord, the bow is actually tacked on. The mitt opens to allow the hand to slip in or out easily by means of an elastic hidden in the casing.

*Here are four fresh views
of the same window:*

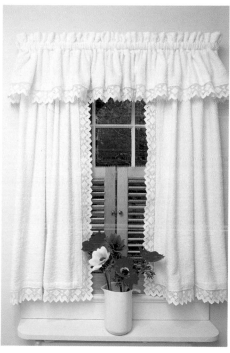

1. Sewing the rings on this Roman shade by hand, rather than using ring tape, makes it possible to align the placement with the crochet pattern perfectly and eliminated the rows of machine stitching. Since there were only two dozen or so rings, the job wasn't formidable, and the result is far more pleasing.

2. A lovely hand-crocheted valance made these simple cotton cord side panels more special. To tie the panels visually to the valance, a delicate crochet trim was added down the inside edges. Both this bit of old crochet and the larger piece used in the Roman shade were found for a few dollars at a flea market and recycled into handsome decorating accessories.

3. Few things can compare with the beauty of pure cotton organdy priscilla curtains. These were further embellished by the addition of a delicate trim at every edge. Since this fabric takes hours to wash, starch, and iron, you may choose to sew these curtains in an easy-care fabric instead.

4. Cotton terry toweling, iced with yards of white lace, makes the perfect bathroom curtain—attractive, unaffected, and easily maintained.

TAILORED

Tattersalls

No frills, please. Just good sense and simple style." The couple who lives here had just renovated this bathroom, complete with a whirlpool tub. They wanted to keep the clean, architectural style but did agree that something extra was needed to keep the room interesting and less ascetic. These fabric accessories added just enough softness. The Roman shade is easily raised and lowered for privacy. The little bench is an inexpensive piece, skirted and cushioned for both style and comfort. The owners love the handy extra towel holder, even though it was included more for aesthetic than practical reasons. And the final touch of the bright coral and jade towels brought the soft beige and apricot bathroom to life. In the final analysis, there is little more here than the bare essentials, but the little comforts these accessories brought with them please the psyche and the eye.

The Roman shade, *opposite*, is big and heavy, and raising and lowering it for privacy can be a cumbersome task. To make the job a little easier, the cord was knotted at the place where it would best hook onto a metal cleat when raised. Then the cleat was installed upside down so the knot can be easily hooked over without checking the height or twisting the cords around the hardware.

The fabric for this towel holder, *above*, was first stiffened with heavyweight, iron-on interfacing and then edged with bias tape to add sturdiness. It's perfect for use in a guest bath where it will not get constant, heavy use. Here it becomes an attractive decorative accessory, adding color and print to a bare wall.

RUFFLES

and Lace

This bath, with its fixtures and tiles dating back to the late 1920s, was basically white and totally boring. Fanciful feminine color and style were added by painting the ceiling a pretty, cotton candy pink and sewing a collection of floral fabric accessories. These accessories were sewn from the same group of coordinated cotton chintzes that were used in the child's bedroom, photographed on page 102, and these delicately romantic prints, covered with bouquets of miniature carnations, add a girlish glamour to the bath. Borders were created from the striped cloth and were applied to finish the edges of the sink skirt and shower curtain, as well as being used as a detail on several of the towels. The collection of bath, face, and hand towels is the true star of the room. The addition of eyelet trims, monograms, and appliquéd bouquets and individual flowers cut from the remnants makes ordinary white terry towels hand-crafted works of art.

The shower curtain, *above*, ties back to only one side since the radiator interfered at the other end. To continue the fabric pattern across the width of the room, the valance was added. The surprise is that the liner was carefully cut and pieced from two large, machine washable and dryable vinyl lace tablecloths.

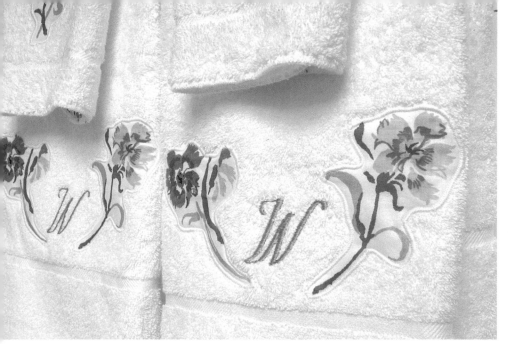

The personalized bath linens, *left*, were decorated with large and small motifs cut directly from the allover printed fabric and appliquéd in place. The monograms were professionally done after the appliqué work was finished.

Sink skirts can provide an additional fabric touch as well as hiding extra storage space in baths without ample closets. There are two ways to mount a sink skirt: one is on the underside of the sink apron; the other, shown *below*, is on the outside, around the edge of the sink bowl. The outside mount is made by attaching self-gripping fastener tape to the skirt and to the sink edge. Attach the fuzzy side of the tape to the skirt as the loops tend to fill up with lint in the wash.

In this bath the decision to glue fabric to the walls and ceiling was made because of the awkward angles created by the garretted ceiling. A heavy duty vinyl fabric paste made the job easier, but it was necessary for one person to hold the fabric in place while another smoothed the ceiling.

Batiks

This tiny bathroom lay unused and nearly forgotten in the back hall of an older home. The fixtures were in good working order, and since there was very little money to invest in a major renovation, a clever face-lift was devised with inexpensive cotton batik fabrics. The walls were covered with fabric, pasted on right over the original dingy paint, and layers of trim were cut and sewn from the batiks and applied with white glue at all the edges. A shower curtain, sink skirt, panel print area rug, and skirt for the old vanity were sewn, again from the same collection of fabrics in an effort to unify all the elements and to give the room charm without making it look smaller. Finally, a sisal rug was cut and its edges sealed with latex to keep them from raveling. The total job cost less than the price of a new bathtub.

Since this bathtub has no showerhead, the shower curtain, *left*, is a purely decorative addition and requires no plastic liner. Notice the repetition of the border on the curtain and its use as the actual casing across the top edge.

Batik or other panel prints are a natural for small area rugs. This panel, *below*, was backed with batting and an attractive companion print, and the motif was quilted following the border design.

In an undermounted sink skirt installation, *right*, the loop side of the self-gripping fastener tape is glued to the underside of the sink apron and the skirt is applied from underneath where it will stay fresher and cleaner and require less laundering.

Above: These trims—a flat ribbon and a single welt—were designed to repeat the mixture of prints in the room. The welting was sewn and applied first. Then the ribbon trim was cut in bias strips folded into thirds and glued on the wall to the inside of the welt. White glue was used to apply all of the trim.

Children's Rooms

The truth is, most of us do very little about decorating children's rooms. After all, they're usually buried under a camouflage of toys and assorted hand-me-down treasures. Who ever looks at the wallpaper? In our work experience, however, we've learned that children *do* look and that, from a very young age, most of them appreciate. What we've chosen to photograph for this chapter may represent too much concentrated effort for your idea of real childspace, but you can certainly edit from this collection of ideas to give the kids a new room geared to your—and their—idea of what's just right for your budget and life-style. We begin at the very beginning—with nurseries, replete with beautiful and practical baby accessories. Then there's a learning quilt for a toddler to love, a playroom built from cushions, a bath, and a young boy's bedroom, all done in primary brights. Finally, we've included two little girls' rooms chock full of florals and eyelets, pink and pretty as a picture. This chapter was designed for the children born, perhaps not with the proverbial silver spoon, but to parents who care enough to take the time to make the kids' rooms into special places.

This room was designed around eyelet, also called *broderie anglaise,* which is available as a trim as well as yard goods in a variety of styles and widths. You can mix eyelet styles and widths in one space if you shop carefully for fabrics and trims that have compatible motifs and ground colors.

BABY

Sleeping

An unused room, tiny and awkward, was transformed into a new home for the baby. Everything was painted white. A lovely antique crib was tucked neatly into the existing alcove, and a crown, constructed of wood and hung with beautiful eyelet panels, was suspended overhead. The same fabric was sewn into the dust ruffle, and compatible eyelet and band trims were applied to the quilt and an assortment of bed and chair pillows. The mixture of white trims and fabrics, just touched with blue, gives the room the delicacy of a Victorian christening dress without seeming monochromatic. But the practical beauty of this room is that it has remained basically a white room with a blue carpet and will require little if any change when the baby begins to grow and his (or her) needs change. All things considered, this room is far more than a nursery. It's a sensible and practical answer to a temporary space for the child who will, all too soon, grow up and out of it.

The most beautiful and effective way to utilize this bordered eyelet, *left*, was to miter the corners so that the border continues across the hem. The panels were cut long to add elegance and to display the mitered finish.

A baby pillow, made from eyelet yardage and trimmed with ruffled eyelet beading, is mixed with an antique lace pillow in the crib, *below*. The pillow will be removed when the baby is sleeping.

A half-round wooden frame supports the eyelet side panels, backdrop, and valance on the crown canopy, *above*. The backdrop was sewn with a top casing and is gathered on a brass rod. French taffeta ribbon tied into a luxurious double bow finishes the canopy with a touch of color.

PIQUÉ AND
Polka Dots

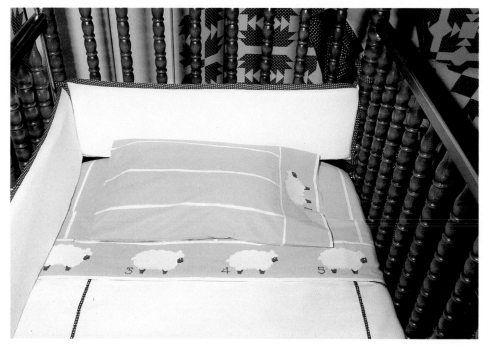

Little Keith was born into a family of avid quilt collectors whose only spare room was papered in a bold navy and white American quilt pattern. But when Keith came home, the Jenny Lind crib was moved right in and baby accessories were sewn in compatible white cotton and polyester piqué, trimmed with navy and white polka dot bias tape. Within this limited color scheme, the wallpaper provides just enough drama and, in fact, is a handsome background for the white accessories. The scallop edged detail on the window shades is repeated on the crib spread, and the use of the polka dot bias tape, chosen to match the polka dots in the wallpaper pattern, ties all the elements and accessories together. Notice the welcome addition of a comfortable old rocking chair, the perfect accessory for Mom and Dad on late-night visits to the nursery.

For a change of color and style on the crib, *top*, these commercially available sheets were customized to fit, and then the charming sheep appliqués were added. A fitted crib sheet was used as a pattern to size the bottom sheet, and a bias tape casing with elastic was added to the new corners.

The bed linens, *above*, were sewn from the same cotton and polyester piqué used throughout the room. They are easily laundered and require little or no ironing. Notice the simple but interesting details here that work well in a room designed for a small boy.

The alphabet on the dust ruffle, *opposite*, was designed from a type face which had a classic, versatile, and visually effective style. It's an alphabet you might return to again and again to personalize any one of a number of other sewing projects. Prepackaged bias binding of a compatible navy and white polka dot was used on the window shade, crib spread, baby pillow, and bumper guard.

PIQUÉ AND POLKA DOTS

The same navy and white polka dot yardage was cut and sewn into the appliquéd alphabet and seat cushions, *right*, and then used to bind off the dust ruffle and window valances.

A changing table cover, *above*, was cut from a template to be the same size as the tabletop. The cover was constructed from two layers of fabric with several layers of polyester batting sandwiched between.

Fabric-covered window shades, *right*, can give the maximum in light control and privacy for a minimum investment.

They can be rolled up and down easily, which is especially convenient for a room where the baby naps. When making your own fabric-covered window shades, avoid textured fabrics because they don't bond as easily or as well as smooth fabric surfaces.

A LEARNING

Quilt

A-B-C—*zipper me! What a wonderful learning toy—a cozy and comforting toddler's quilt, constructed of thirty squares, each with a letter to learn or a skill to master. There's a shoelace to lace, snaps to snap, a zipper to zip, and ribbons to tie. Although this is clearly not a project you can sew overnight, this quilt could well be the ultimate baby gift.*

Each of the four corners of this quilt features a learning skill square. The child can lace up a turtle shell, zip an apple, tie a floral bouquet, and snap the wheels on a little train. If you prefer, you can use this quilt as a beautiful wall hanging in a baby's room, rather than as a nightly cover. The pieced top, batting, and quilt back are box-quilted together using clear monofilament thread, which enables you to do all of the stitching without changing thread colors. It's really the only way with so many colors coming together. This is a project for someone with good skills and patience.

Playspace

Once an unused garret on the third floor, this cheerful playroom was designed with a minimum of furniture for maximum versatility. The cabinets were custom-built to house games and toys, and a board was installed along the left-hand wall to create an empty storage space for stacking the foam lounge pads, three deep. The extra-giant pillows add to the casual comfort of the room and can be stacked or tossed about as the kids wish. Simple metal window blinds repeat the colorful design, as does the carpeting, a commercial grade that cuts and pieces easily. Notice how all the intense colors were kept at floor level or slightly above, with white, glossy wallpaper and white cabinets selected to add height and light to the otherwise confined space. It works so well that these kids always bring their friends home to their place to play.

Standard-size foam lounge pads were covered with bright cottons and stacked to make this seating space. The pads can be removed from the storage bin and laid out to create a wall-to-wall sleep-over or lounging area.

Pillow-form sizes can vary, and a form that is sold as a 30″ × 30″ might actually measure 28″ × 28″. The type of filling in the form will make a difference in the size of the cover as well. Always be sure to measure pillow forms carefully before cutting fabric for the covers.

Bathtime

Right down the hall from the playspace at left is this bath, designed just for kids. Small and awkward, with another garret ceiling to consider, it was a perfect place for an amusing and eye-catching wallpaper. This scribble-print paper, run up the walls and over the ceiling, pulls the little room together. Because every other element in the room is simple (plain white fixtures and solid green vinyl flooring), it sets the stage for a group of wonderful accessory towels. These cotton terry towels were appliquéd with glossy cotton chintz. Personalized towels not only make any bathroom more special, but make wonderful gifts, and children gleefully respond to the whole idea of "my balloon towel" and "your cars."

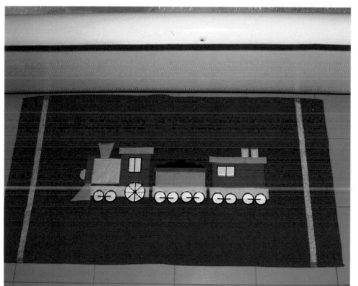

Chintz was used for these appliqués because it comes in a wide range of beautiful colors and, being so closely woven, it frays less readily than other fabrics. Use a glue stick to hold the individual appliqué shapes in place on the toweling while you zigzag them on the machine. You'll find this the easiest way when working with a multitude of little, individual pieces.

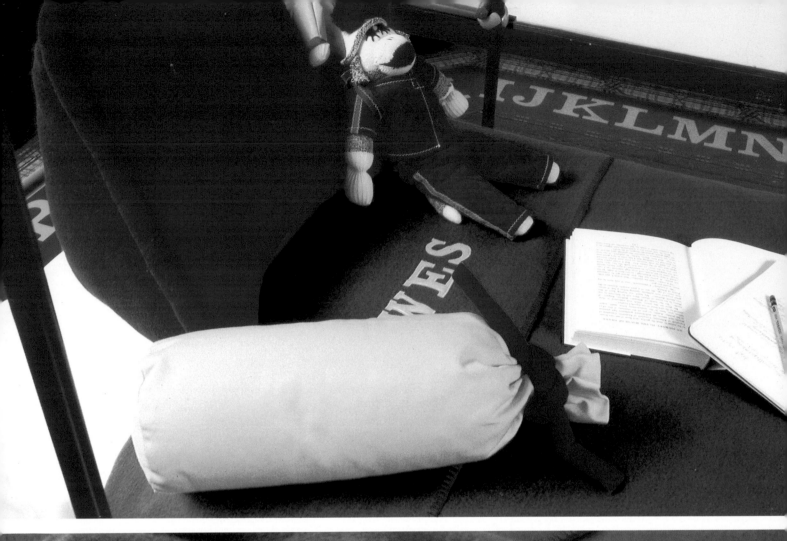

Retreat

The young fellow who lives here loves to draw, read comics in bed, and have his friends stay overnight. He also loves the color red. Primary colors have played an important role in most of the kids' rooms we've designed. Children, even at an early age, seem to respond to fire-engine red, school-bus yellow, banner blue, and the like. Dark greens mix so well with these bright colors that we often incorporate them to tone down a primary room. This room had no real bed wall, so, using plastic-covered metal tubing, a bunk bed was constructed like a jungle gym in the middle of the room. Since the bed is open, the room remains bright and airy, and because it's fun, the young man thinks it's terrific. Sure, he may not really appreciate his blanket-stitched and appliquéd blankets on a day-to-day basis, but they give his mother a lift every time she makes the bed. If it's any indication of a successful kid's room, this guy has friends standing in line for a chance to sleep over.

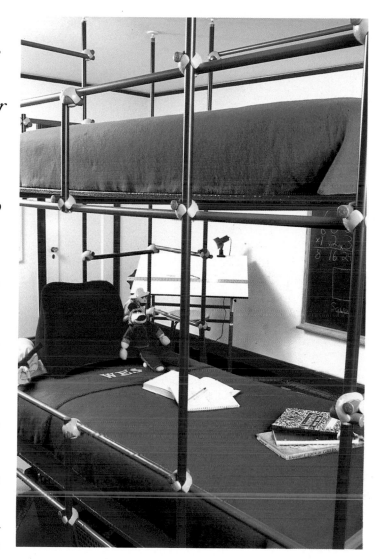

Jumbo welting trims the reading pillow and is repeated for the cord tie on the sack neckroll, *opposite top*. It's an uncluttered but visually effective trim for rough and tumble rooms like this one, and it's masculine enough to appeal to little boys.

Blankets, *opposite bottom*, can be easily decorated to make them more appealing and personal. As with all added trims and finishing details, be sure that your choice of trim fibers or fabric corresponds with the blanket in washability.

Every fabric in the room, *above*, can be washed and rewashed. The blankets are acrylic, the canvas is cotton and polyester, and the reading/TV pillow is tough, soft, stretch terry. Easy-care stretch terry makes sense in kids' spaces, and it's a perfect fabric choice for an oddly shaped item like this pillow where a nonstretch fabric could look lumpy and wrinkled.

WHITNEY'S
Fairy Tale

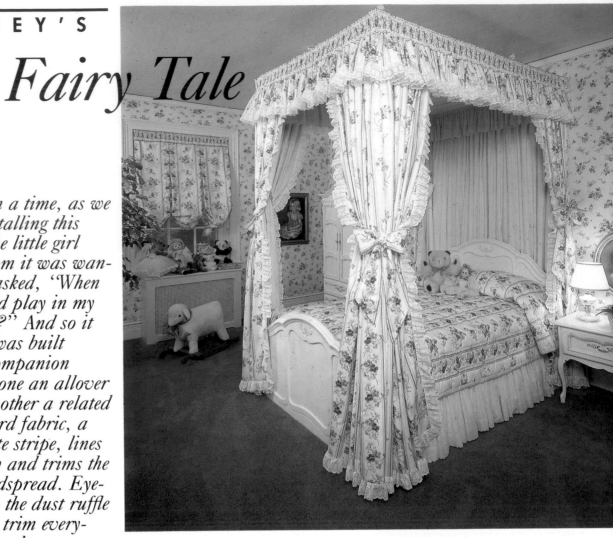

Once upon a time, as we were installing this canopy bed, the little girl whose new room it was wandered in and asked, "When can I come and play in my princess room?" And so it is. The room was built around two companion print fabrics: one an allover floral and the other a related stripe. The third fabric, a pink-and-white stripe, lines the bed canopy and trims the edges of the bedspread. Eyelets, sewn into the dust ruffle and used as a trim everywhere else, give the room a delightful charm. As is always the case, the little touches make a big difference. Look at the sheets, for example. Tiny, washable pink satin ribbons were woven through the eyelet trim, and Whitney's name was chain stitched on the top sheet and the pillowcases. This is a very special bedroom, designed for a child who, we hope, will live here happily ever after.

Canopy beds can work, even for young children. The important safeguard is to be sure that they are securely suspended from the ceiling. It's always safer to have a carpenter build and install the frame for a bed such as this one, whether you choose to hang the frame from fabric-covered chains, as we did here, or to install it flush up against the ceiling. The girlish tiebacks with their oversized bows attach to the existing bedpost by means of a casing sewn in the tie which slips down snugly over the post. This attachment also serves to keep the end panels in place in a room with a great deal of activity.

Purchased sheets with a wide eyelet trim were embellished with one-eighth-inch satin ribbons, *right*. The ribbons were interwoven through the eyelet and then secured with little bows.

KARIN'S

Own Room

Karin's mother and father had looked long and hard for an apartment with enough extra space to give Karin a room of her own. When a suitable apartment was finally located, they discovered that because of the additional rent, the overall decorating budget had to be kept to the barest minimum. But Karin's mother was willing and able to sew, and so an acceptable compromise was worked out. Nothing about the actual room was changed. The walls were left white and the floor remained in its uncarpeted condition. Most of the budget went immediately for the few pieces of pretty white wicker furniture, the rag rug, and the large ficus tree that effectively filled an empty corner. Then Karin's mother went to work. Eyelet flounce and inexpensive cotton and polyester seersucker and broadcloth were purchased for all the fabric accessories. The most impressive decorating element in the room became Karin's mother's handiwork, including the repetition of the charming rosebud appliqué used throughout. Karin loves her room. She doesn't mind that she hasn't got much of a view from her window, because the room is full of pretty things her mother sewed just for her. And the real beauty of it all is that, should her parents find another apartment someday, everything here can be neatly packed up and moved.

If economy is of primary importance in your decorating plans, a room like this one could be easily sewn from twin-size sheets, the best yardage bargain anywhere. Any one of a number of delicate sheet patterns might have worked as well as the seersucker and broadcloth used here.

Vacation Homes and Outdoor Living

Congratulations! You've just signed the papers on a little hideaway cabin by a lake or a passive solar house in the heart of ski country. And now that you've made the commitment and thoroughly depleted your bank account, what can you do to decorate the place? Sheets or fabric seconds will quickly and inexpensively spruce up the cabin, and by using simple sewing techniques, they can be finished in time for the first warm weekend. What warms the body and soul in the Vermont mountains? Use snuggly trappers' blankets to make slipcovers that cover inexpensive foam furniture, and keep an extra blanket or two for use in front of the wood stove on snowy nights. If your idea of rest and relaxation centers around a two-week rental at the shore, try our beach package for a personalized carry-along. Even a simple picnic at a local park can become an event with the picnic gear on page 100, designed to turn fried chicken into a glamorous gourmet experience. Finally, if you choose to stay at home and the notion of an outdoor living room full of brightly flowered fabric is appealing, try turning the scallop edged technique, featured in the bedroom on page 72, into romantic porch accessories. Nearly every idea in this book could be adapted, through careful choice of fabric and trim, for open air or partially enclosed spaces. Let your imagination be your guide and spend a few hours sewing up something designed to make the outdoors or your vacation hideaway much more special.

Living Room

This lovely Victorian porch and terrace had all the basics—the simple, clean lines of the white frame house wall, the cool gray fieldstone floor, a collection of fine old wicker furniture, and a colorful garden beyond. What it lacked was personality. A few large-scale floral prints were considered here. Half-yard samples were draped across the seating pieces and scrutinized on sunny afternoons, hazy mornings, and even by candlelight after dark. This is the print that worked. It pleased the owners and kept its color in any light. Color tends to soften in natural light, so here, unlike in many other decorating situations, stronger is better. Even the choice of a very bright green bias tape for the scallop edged detailing was predicated on its visibility from a distance in bright sunlight. The careful addition of the softer pink/red dotted fabric to relieve the strength and brightness of the floral brought the whole area into balance. This is the favorite gathering place for family and friends all season long.

The pillows, *above*, illustrate the flange-type construction, created by stitching the shape of the pillow form into the cover. Flanges can be straight, or shaped into scallops, or other decorative patterns. Flanges of two to four inches work best; if they are cut wider they won't stand up, and their beauty will be lost.

Bright green bias binding was used throughout this space, *left*, as an integrating design element. Mastering the technique of applying narrow bias binding to fabric edges requires a good eye and a steady hand. One application technique—appropriately called "stitch in the ditch"—allows you to do the entire job by machine without the machine stitches showing on the right side.

In order to avoid seaming, the tablecloth, *below*, was designed so that it could be cut from a square the width of the fabric. Since decorator fabrics generally come in greater widths than dress fabrics, they offer an advantage in situations like this.

Gear

This cheerful beach package began with a trip to a local umbrella shop where custom beach umbrellas are available by special order. We had the choice of bringing our own canvas or selecting from the variety offered. Enough extra was purchased to sew these handy accessories. The beach blanket was a nice find at a bed linens store. It's a pure cotton thermal blanket that works well in a twin size. We applied a decorative grosgrain ribbon to tie it to the yellow, gray, and white color scheme. The completed beach pack solves travel and comfort needs for a trip to the shore, or makes a fabulous going-away gift for a friend. This beach gear provides a practical and handsome way to get away from it all in great style.

When putting together a group of items like this, be sure to find all the color-coordinated elements before buying any of them. It's frustrating to discover that webbing, for example, isn't made in the color you've decided to use. The quilted beach mat, *opposite*, was designed with its own webbing strap to secure it in a tight roll and allow it to be easily packed away into the duffel. Turning corners on any fabric, especially heavyweights like the canvas used for this tote, can pose problems. To form a sharp corner, sew two diagonal stitches across the corner rather than pivoting sharply and forming a right angle.

The hardware and grommets for this duffel, *top*, were purchased, not at a fabric shop, but at a marine supply store.

This ensured that they would resist salt water damage and be virtually rustproof.

When fusing appliqués to thick fabrics like this terry towel, *center*, it's helpful to place a piece of aluminum foil, shiny side up, over cardboard and to use this as a base under the towel.

Picnic

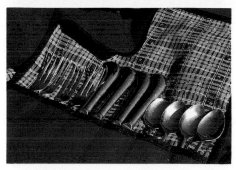

One of the many plea-sures of sewing is that you can design and make eye-catching and very per-sonal accessories like this col-lection of picnic gear. This stylish assortment, sewn for autumn in washable wool flannel and a cotton and polyester plaid, represents just a few of a whole list of items you'll never see in a catalog or in someone else's station wagon. Protect your wine in a wine bottle case. Carry along your flatware in a utensil wrapper and keep your glasses safe from chips in a case of their own. There is a customized picnic basket liner and, of course, a basic set of napkins and a flannel tablecloth, complete with a monogram. Far more than a delicious luncheon spread, this picnic is a real feast for the eyes.

In order to make a liner, *top*, that will fit your own basket, take a large piece of muslin or other scrap, and, using our diagram on page 275 as a guide, adjust the muslin pattern to fit. The actual liner is constructed of two layers so it can be totally reversible. If your basket needs more than ties, an elastic in a casing around the top edge will work well. If your basket has a very unusual shape, you may need to make separate pattern pieces for the sides and bottom.

The wine bottle sack, *above*, is fully lined, not to keep the wine cool, since fabric will not perform that function, but to make the sack sturdier and to protect the bottle from bumps.

When using printed plaids, such as the one that lines the cutlery and wine glass holders, *center left* and *bottom left*, it is always necessary to cut the pieces according to the lines of the plaid, even if they do not accurately follow the grain lines of the fabric. The rule is that the plaid must always look straight—even if it isn't.

To eliminate any seams, the square picnic cloth, *opposite*, was made from one width of the wool fabric. The monogram was professionally done after the cloth was bound.

A SKI HOUSE
in the Mountains

This passive solar ski house was furnished as quickly and inexpensively as possible with some pretty nylon upholstered furniture. A set of wool blanket slip-covers solved the problem with sensational style. Classic Hudson's Bay or trappers' blankets, purchased from a catalog, were cut out and sewn together with great attention to the placement of the stripes. The resulting covers are both stylish and practical. They can be removed and sent out to the dry cleaners at the end of the season, and since these blankets are remarkably soft to the touch, no one finds them uncomfortable or scratchy when they're in use. Add on an extra twin-sized blanket or two to use as a throw for cold nights in front of the fire. Wouldn't this be a wonderful idea for a winter version of your family room, too?

The lush fringe, *right*, was made from worsted knitting yarn. Since these blankets are rather densely woven, small holes, first marked at equal intervals along the edge, were punched through with the tips of a scissor to allow a crochet hook and five 12″ strands of yarn to pass through more easily.

Four 66″ by 90″ wool blankets were cut and sewn into slipcovers for the armless sofa and two chairs, *below*. To figure out the most economical sizes of blankets and the number you will need, you must know the greatest distance required to cover one piece. For each individual cover, measure the total distance from the floor at the front, across the seat, up and over the back, and down to the floor at the back. Add an allowance for tucking under the ends.

An indispensable, but down-and-out, studio couch was rejuvenated with a simple and serviceable throw sewn from a queen-size sheet. Three of the four edges were bound with a bias strip of plain white sheeting. The rag pillows were made from prefinished rag yardage plus muslin for the backs. The windows were treated in the same style as the studio couch, but here the colors were reversed, and the ties are, in real country fashion, just hooked over nails to pull the curtains back.

Cabin by a Lake

*H*aving stretched finan-
cially to purchase this
lovely lakefront property, the
family who summers here
was resigned to living in the
existing ramshackle cabin
until they could afford to
replace the whole structure.
However, creative planning
and some sewing quickly
turned ticky-tacky into rustic
charm. Twig seating pieces
found in a local secondhand
shop were made more com-
fortable with the addition of
large sacklike cushions filled
with a combination of feathers and chopped foam, and
then slipcovered in a botanical print cotton purchased as
seconds at a dollar a yard.
Careful attention was paid
to the color of the ceiling and
walls of the long, narrow
porch. Unlike the bright
white interior of the cabin,
dark brown, the color of tree
bark, was chosen. It effectively causes the walls to fall
away and the eye to be
aware only of the green and
blue of woods and water
beyond.

The seat cushions on the twig furniture, *above* and *opposite*, were designed as large sacks, made first in down-proof ticking and then covered in this botanical print cotton. They were stuffed with feathers recycled from the cushion of an old sofa which was found at a flea market. The backrests were traced from a template which was drawn to duplicate the curves. Five layers of polyester batting were cut and stacked together to fill out the shapes. Since the backrests were made without zippers, the polyester batting allows them to be laundered without removing the interior stuffing. These simple, tie-on curtains were sewn quickly and easily from fabric seconds and then tied on to branches harvested from fallen trees in the woods. The ties were planned at 9″ intervals to allow for gentle folds.

A HIDEAWAY
CABIN BY A LAKE

In the bedroom, sheets were turned into bed hangings and inexpensive cotton lace dressed the windows. The kitchen was freshened up with blue and white gingham, and a sheeting cover became a practical, washable throw for the ancient studio couch. Rag rugs sewn from yardage and some rag pillows were added along with a bountiful collection of old linens found in thrift shops and garage sales. The little cabin is such a comfortable place to be now, and the family loves it so much, there's some doubt they'll ever bring themselves to tear it down.

When sewing with sheets as in this bedroom, *top*, try to size your project to correspond to the most economical sheet sizes. Twins cost far less than larger sizes. The easily removable pillow covers are made from a piece of sheeting long enough to wrap around once and then tuck back under so that none of the pillowcase hidden beneath is visible. Only the bottom corners of this blanket cover, *near right*, were fitted. The addition of the ties here and on the sham repeats the design theme in the room and anchors the cover on the bed.

The old ladderback chairs on this dining porch, *center right*, were painted white and dressed up with new back and seat cushions. To push out the corners and cutouts on an item like a shaped cushion, the best tool is a Chinese chopstick. It allows you to push firmly and completely without punching a hole in the corner, as so often happens with sharper tools.

Placemats made from dishcloths, *near right*, are sturdy and washable, as well as an interesting conversation piece. Prewash both the cloths and the trim before sewing. Pick up a few extra dishcloths for napkins.

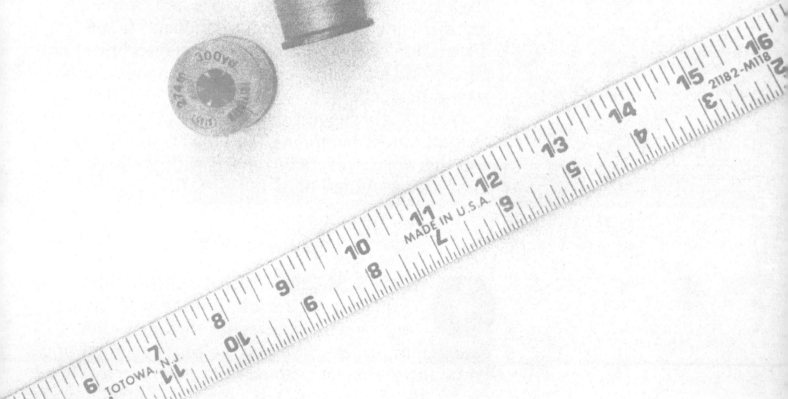

Tools, Terms, and T·E·C·H·N·I·Q·U·E·S

Tools

This section introduces the technical portion of the book. In it you will find two separate areas of information: a comprehensive list of sewing and sewing-related equipment that you might find helpful in the execution of book projects, and an alphabetized list of sewing terms and techniques we use over and over again in the step-by-step instructions. These terms and techniques are indicated by **boldface** type throughout the instructions. If you are an experienced sewer, you may not need to refer to this section for a further definition of a term or to review a technique. If, on the other hand, you are less experienced, or you are interested in trying a method with which you are unfamiliar, "Tools, Terms, and Techniques" will act as a technical reference guide and clarify any questions about the best way to proceed.

We strongly suggest that you glance through this chapter before beginning the projects in this book and that you familiarize yourself with the kind of information offered here.

Obviously, the most basic sewing tool is the sewing machine itself, but there are many other sewing accessories that are either essential or can be extremely helpful in completing a home sewing project. Some of them you may already own. Others may seem less crucial additions to your tool kit, but might spell the difference between an acceptable job and one that looks professional and first-rate.

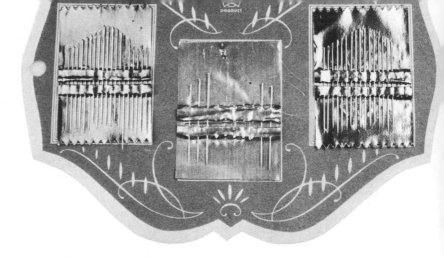

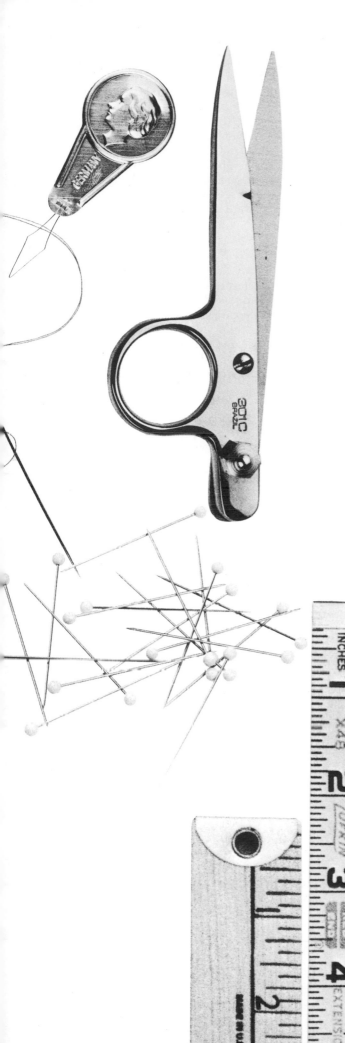

Sewing Machine Attachments

Zipper foot: designed for inserting zippers and welting. It should be adjustable to the right or the left side of the needle.

Hemmer foot: allows for the turning and stitching of a narrow hem in one operation. ⅛″ and ¼″ sizes are the most useful.

Ruffler: makes a gathered or pleated ruffle. The fullness is controlled by a special screw and by varying the stitch length.

Quilting foot: a guide for spacing the stitching lines by means of an adjustable bar.

Blind stitch foot: used for sewing hems by machine. Stitches do not show on the right side of the project.

Even-feed foot (plaid foot or walking foot): helps to feed layers of fabric evenly through the machine. It is especially useful for sewing seams where designs are matched, for quilting, and for topstitching through several thicknesses of fabric.

Seam guide: device for controlling seam width; attaches to the machine bed with screws or a magnet and is adjusted for the distance desired from the needle. (A substitute could be a strip of tape placed on the machine bed parallel to the line of stitching.)

Measuring Devices

Tape measure (60″): a flexible synthetic or fiberglass measure that won't tear or stretch.

Metal tape measure (8′ to 12′): a longer measure used for measuring large areas such as windows, beds, etc.

Yardstick (meter stick): a wood or metal measure.

Transparent ruler (12″ to 18″): a flat see-through measure used for checking grainlines, marking lines, and measuring for small projects.

Small ruler or seam gauge (6″): a small metal or plastic ruler with a sliding indicator used for measuring seam allowances, pleats, etc. See-through plastic ones are the most useful.

T-square (carpenter's square): made of clear plastic or metal; used for straightening grainlines, locating opposite grains, squaring off edges, and similar applications.

Marking Devices

Tailor's chalk: chalk or wax wedges. Also comes in pencil form but the points break easily.

Water soluble ink pen: a marking pen, the ink of which is removed easily with cold water.

Tracing paper and wheel: a form of carbon paper and wheel for transferring the carbon to fabric. It also comes in a water soluble form.

Leftover soap wedges: will do in a pinch on washable fabrics.

Needles

Hand needles: sharps—a medium-length all-purpose needle—the most versatile for a variety of fabrics.

Machine needles: Sizes 11 (75) and 14 (90) are used most often. Size 9 (65) is used for only the finest sheer fabrics, 16 (100) and 18 (110) for very heavy ones.

Upholstery needles: A heavy duty curved needle. Optional but can be handy for many projects.

Scissors (Shears)

Dressmaker shears (7" to 9"): bent-handle shears used for cutting fabric. They allow the fabric to lie flat while being cut and are also easier on hands.

Embroidery scissors (sewing) (4" to 5"): a small round-handled scissor used for clipping, trimming, and other small jobs.

Pinking shears: bent-handle shears with a zigzag blade used to finish seams and raw edges.

Thread clips: a scissor with short blades and spring mechanism convenient for cutting threads and seams.

Pins

Stainless steel dressmaker pins: best because they don't rust or leave pin marks in fabric, and they can be picked up with a strong magnet!

T-pins: longer and sturdier than dressmaker pins. Useful with heavier fabrics and for pinning fabric to a padded surface.

Quilter's pins: extra long, but finer than T-pins. A luxury but very useful.

Safety pins: for threading elastic and cording through casings.

Miscellaneous Accessories

Cutting board: a fold-up cardboard mat, marked off in 1" squares. If you are planning a cutting table, 36" is a good height.

Seam ripper: a tool with a sharp, curved edge for opening seams and a point for picking out threads. Use with care!

Loop turner: a long wirelike tool with a hook at the end for grasping fabric and turning it right side out. Use for tubing, ties, etc.

Bodkin: a tweezerlike object with gripper teeth used to draw elastic and cording though casings. A safety pin can also be used for this purpose.

Tools from the hardware store: small screwdriver; tweezers for picking out threads, helping to thread needles, extracting pins while you sew, removing lint from machines, etc.; small needle-nosed pliers for removing caught threads from the machine, holding fabric where it's hard to grasp with fingers, etc.; magnet for picking up pins.

Pressing Tools

Steam iron: those with burst of steam and/or spray features are especially handy.

Ironing board: must be sturdy and well padded.

Press cloth: a piece of unbleached muslin or white sheeting. It protects fabrics from scorch and iron shine.

Plastic spray bottle: to hold water for extra moisture.

White vinegar: for helping to remove stubborn crease lines.

Point presser: a wooden tool useful for pressing corners, points, or other awkward areas. It usually comes as part of a pounding block.

Glues

Craft or white glue: best of the decorator variety. It is tackier, faster-drying, and less likely to bleed through. Great for attaching trims to nonwashable items.

Glue stick: excellent for positioning trims and appliqués before stitching. Available in office supply stores.

Spray adhesive (aerosol): for fabrics or foam. Available in hardware or art supply stores.

Terms and Techniques

Here we offer brief but comprehensive explanations of terms we will use frequently in the step-by-step instructions, as well as special sewing techniques you will need to understand before completing many of the home sewing projects. The terms and techniques listed alphabetically here are referenced to this chapter by **boldface** type in the instructions.

Even if you are very experienced, it makes good sense to read through this material before beginning. You may discover some new ways to execute projects and learn a few tricks that will speed up your sewing time.

Ruffles

A strip of fabric cut and sewn to create full, luxurious look. Plan ruffles wide and full enough to give the desired finished width. Be sure to add seam and hem.

Strips for ruffles are usually cut on the straight of the fabric. If, however, your fabric has a design (plaid, check, etc.) that would be more decorative on the bias, plan to cut them as described under this chapter.

After the strip is cut, seam along the length of the fabric.

Railroading

Tufting

A means of joining fabric and pulling together stitches tightly to hold the layers as regular stability and decorative detail. Tufting can be ways.

Selvage

Preshrink

To treat fabric before cutting, to allow shrinkage to occur before fabric is cut.

Repeat

Transfer

To copy a design.

Template

Quilting

A means of holding two layers of fabric together in a decorative fashion.

Slip-Baste

Used to hold fabric design in place while you stitch. Pin the fabric on the edge along the seam line. Lap the creased edge over the other material. Insert the needle through the crease on the top layer and through the lower section, making the stitches about 1/4" apart. Stitch along the basting.

Zippers

Side zipper.

Centered zipper.

1. Close the zipper seam with machine basting stitches. Press seam open.

2. Open the zipper and position it face down on the extended seam allowance (a single layer of fabric).

Welting

Appliqué

To apply one fabric to another as a decorative feature. There are four basic appliqué techniques:

Method A:
1. With the two layers pinned together, cut out the shapes to be appliquéd from both fabric and fusible web.
2. Lay the shapes out on the background fabric and fuse them in place with a damp press cloth placed over the appliqué.
3. Appliqué with a satin zigzag stitch.

Method B:
1. Trace the shapes to be appliquéd onto the wrong side of the fabric. *Do not* cut them out.
2. Place a piece of fusible web on the wrong side of the fabric, larger than the shape, but not larger than the piece of fabric. Use a piece of heat resistant glass (e.g., the bottom of a clean glass baking dish) on the ironing board, and, placing the web onto the glass, fuse with a dry iron. Let it cool. The fabric with the fusible web adhered to it peels off the glass.
3. Cut out the shape. Lay out on a background fabric and fuse it in place.
4. Appliqué with a satin zigzag stitch.

Method C:
1. Cut out the shapes to be appliquéd. Then cut a shape slightly larger than the appliqué from lightweight plastic food wrap, or dry cleaner's bags.
2. Place the plastic between the background fabric and the appliqué. Cover this with a brown paper bag (dime store weight) and press with as hot an iron as the fabric permits. The excess plastic will stick to the brown bag. Do not use this method for permanent fusing.
3. Appliqué with a satin zigzag stitch.

Method D:
1. A glue stick also provides good temporary adhesion for appliqués. Apply the glue to the wrong side of the cut-out appliqué and position it on the background fabric.
2. Appliqué with a satin zigzag stitch.

For ease of stitching and the best finished appearance, use a stabilizer between the fabric and the sewing machine bed. The stabilizer can be tissue paper, pattern tracing paper, or tracing fabric. If paper is used, tear it away after stitching is completed. Tracing fabric may be left in place, as it will not be seen on the back of the finished piece.

Bias Strips

Pieces of fabric cut on the true bias (see **grain** in this chapter for explanation of "bias").

Yardage Chart

Amount of Fabric	Approximate Running Yards of 1⅝"-wide bias strips		
	36" fabric	48" fabric	54" fabric
¼ yd.	4½	5½	7
½ yd.	10	13	14
¾ yd.	16	20	22
1 yd.	22	26	29½

Use this chart as a general guide for other widths also, e.g., the amount of 3"-wide strips is about half the yield for 1⅝".

Making Separate Bias Strips

This method is primarily used for projects where you need only a small number of strips, or where strips must follow a certain design line on the fabric.

Fold the fabric diagonally so that the lengthwise grain aligns with the crosswise grain. Press, then cut off the triangle along this fold. Measure and mark lines parallel to the cut edge, spacing them the desired bias width until you have as much as you need. Mark ¼" seam allowances along the lengthwise grain. See Diagram A.

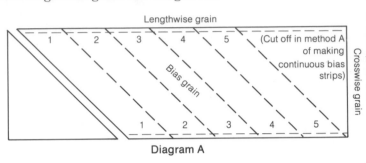

Diagram A

Trim the strips if necessary so that the ends are on the straight grain.

With right sides together, align two strips at right angles, matching seam lines. See Diagram B. Stitch and press the seams open. Trim off the extending points.

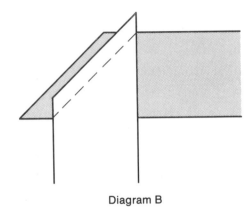

Diagram B

Making a Continuous Bias Strip

Method A: This method may be quicker than making separate bias strips, but it does not yield quite as much yardage since you do not use the triangles at each end.
1. Cut off a triangle and mark the fabric as described in Making Separate Bias Strips. Cut off the triangle at the other end of the fabric length. (See Diagram A.)
2. On the wrong side, number the strips, marking the same number at each end of the strip. With right sides together, form a tube by pinning the lengthside edges together. Align the seams and markings so that one strip extends beyond the edge on each side. Stitch the edges along the seamline. Press the seam open.
3. Cut in a spiral along the marked lines starting between strips 1 and 2.

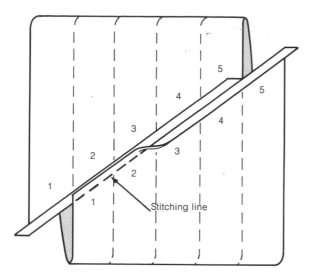

Method B:

1. Cut a square of fabric, making certain the **grain**lines are perfect.

2. On the wrong side of the fabric, mark a diagonal line along the bias from one corner to the opposite corner. Measure and mark lines parallel to the center line, spacing them the desired bias width. Mark ¼" seamlines along both the lengthwise and crosswise edges.

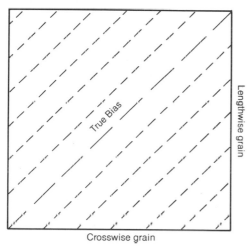

3. Cut the square in half along its center line, making two triangles. With right sides together, match the marked bias lines along the seamline (*not* along the cut edge) of the lengthwise grain. Stitch and press the seam open.

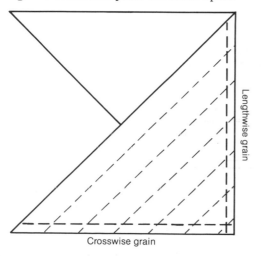

4. With right sides still together, sew the crosswise grain edges, forming a tube. Align the markings so that one bias strip width extends beyond the edge on each side. Match the marked bias lines along the seamline (*not* along the cut edge).

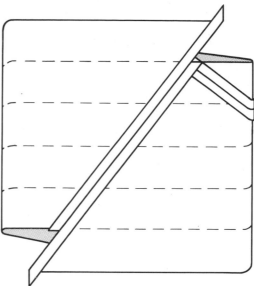

5. Starting at one end, cut in a spiral on the marked lines until the tube is all cut.

Binding

A method of finishing an edge without a hem. You can use commercial bias or decorative tape, or you can make your own (see **bias strips** immediately preceding).

Binding an Edge

Method A: "Stitch-in-the-Ditch" application
1. Open out one fold of binding, and pin the crease line to the seamline of the fabric, right sides together. Stitch along the crease line.
2. Leave the fabric seam allowance untrimmed or trim it to just less than the finished width so that it will fill up the binding for a slightly puffed, firmer appearance.
3. Bring the binding around to the wrong side, encasing the raw edge. Pin the binding in place so that the other folded edge covers the previous stitching by at least ⅛".
4. From the right side of the fabric, "stitch-in-the-ditch" (the groove created where the binding joins the fabric), being sure to catch the binding on the wrong side.

Method B: Hand-finished application (the method of choice when the edge has batting between fabric layers)
Follow Steps 1 to 3 of Method A. Then pin the binding in place so that the other folded edge just covers the previous stitching. **Stitch** in place by hand.

Method C: Topstitch application
Follow Steps 1 to 3 of Method A, but start the application of the binding with the right side of the binding to the wrong side of the fabric. Bring the binding over to the right side and topstitch it in place along the folded edge.

Binding Outward Corners

1. Open out one fold of the binding strip. Pin the crease line of binding to the seamline of the fabric. Stitch along the crease line, stopping at the intersecting seamline. Backstitch.

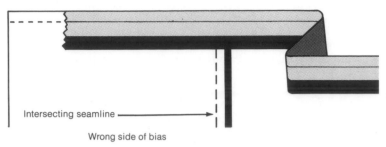

Intersecting seamline

Wrong side of bias

Right side of bias

2. Fold the binding on the diagonal to make it turn the corner. Measure from the center fold line of the binding to a point that is twice the distance of the finished width of the binding. Mark this point with a pin.

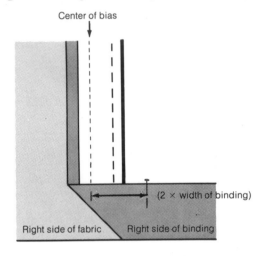

Center of bias

(2 × width of binding)

Right side of fabric   Right side of binding

3. Fold the binding straight back from the pin. Align the binding at the second edge and pin it. Stitch it along the diagonal crease. Repeat at all corners.

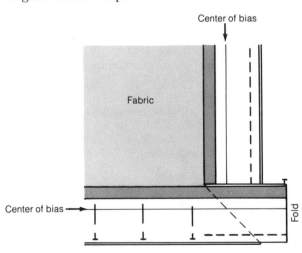

Center of bias

Fabric

Center of bias

Fold

4. Turn the binding over the raw edge to the other side of the fabric, folding a **miter** in the binding at the corners on both sides. To distribute the bulk, fold the binding on the back in the opposite direction from that on the front.
5. Position and stitch the binding in place by hand or machine as described earlier under Binding an Edge.

Binding Inward Corners

1. Reinforce the corner with small stitches close to the seamline for 1″ on either side of the corner. Clip into the corner.
2. Spread the slashed corner and pin the opened-out edge of the binding to the fabric so that the crease line of the binding aligns with the fabric seamline. Stitch to the fabric along the seamline.

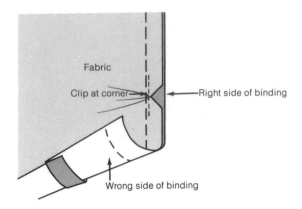

Fabric

Clip at corner

Right side of binding

Wrong side of binding

3. Fold the binding to form a **miter** on the right side and pull it through the clip to the other side of the fabric. Fold the binding down over the seam allowance to form another miter on the wrong side. Position and stitch the binding in place by hand or machine as described in Binding an Edge.

Joining the Ends

To seam the ends, start the binding application 2″ from the beginning point, allowing an extra 1½″ of binding. Stop the binding application 2″ from the other side of the beginning point, also allowing an extra 1½″ of binding.

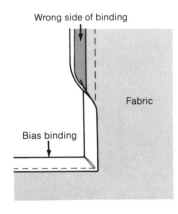

Wrong side of binding

Fabric

Bias binding

Adjust the length to fit the fabric, trim the ends on a diagonal, allowing a seam allowance, and stitch. Press the seams open and continue stitching the binding to the fabric piece.

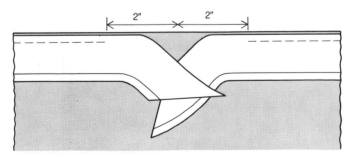

2″   2″

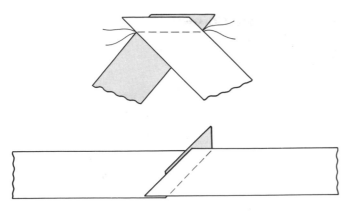

To lap the ends, turn the beginning end under ½″ on the straight or diagonal. Pin and sew in place. When you come to that end again, overlap the binding ¾″ and finish stitching.

Finishing an End

Apply the first edge of the binding to the fabric, extending the binding ¾″ beyond the fabric edge. Trim the seam allowance at the corner on a diagonal.

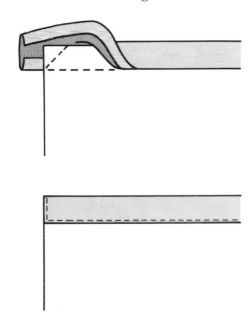

Fold the extending end of the binding back over the edge, then fold the binding down over the seam allowance and finish stitching, pivoting to sew across the open end.

Casing

A tunnel formed with fabric so that a curtain rod, drawstring, or elastic can be threaded through it.

Diagonal Basting

A series of parallel stitches used for holding layers of fabric and/or batting together. Take short stitches through the fabric at a right angle to the edge, spacing them evenly. The stitches on the top will be diagonal and those on the underside horizontal.

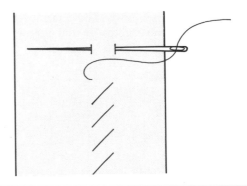

Drop

The distance from the top of a piece of furniture to the floor, rug, or other desired lower position.

Enlarging Patterns and Diagrams

A method of converting small patterns to the actual size.

Draw on a piece of paper a large grid of squares that equal the indicated grid size (usually 1″) or buy 1″ grid paper at an office supply or art store. Copy the pattern, one square at a time, onto the large grid.

Gather (Gathering)

The process of pulling up a given length of fabric to measure a smaller distance across, thereby creating soft, even pleats. The fullness of the gathers is determined by the use of the fabric, but is usually 1½ to 3 times the distance to be spanned, with double being the average.

Method A:
1. Using a long, loose machine stitch, make two parallel rows of gathering stitches. Place the first row alongside the seamline in the seam allowance and the second ¼″ closer to the raw edge. To avoid thread breakage, use extra-strength thread in the bobbin and a loose upper tension.
2. Anchor the threads at one end of the stitch line.
3. Pull gently on the bobbin threads until the correct length is reached. Anchor the threads. Adjust the gathers by sliding the fabric along the threads.

Method B:
1. With a long, wide zigzag stitch, sew over a strong, thin string ⅛″ above a seamline. Be sure that you do not stitch the string.
2. Secure one end of the string. Pull up the other end and adjust the gathers evenly.
3. Stitch the gathers in place. Remove the string.

Method C: Use a ruffler or gathering foot attachment which automatically gathers with each stitch the sewing machine makes.

Grain

The direction in which the threads composing the fabric run.

Crosswise. The direction of the fabric that runs perpendicular to the selvage or finished edge.

Lengthwise. The direction of the fabric that runs parallel to the selvage or finished edge.

Bias. The direction of the fabric formed by marking a line at a 45° angle to the lengthwise and crosswise grains. This is often referred to as "true bias."

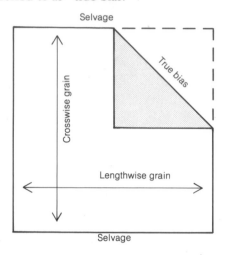

Mitering

Joining two corner edges at an angle to create a neat finish. (The mitering of an outward or inward corner is discussed in this chapter under **binding.**)

Mitering Hems

Press under the hem allowances on the lengthwise and crosswise edges. Open out the edges. Fold the corner up on a diagonal so that the pressed lines match.

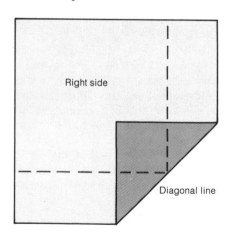

Press in the corner fold, then open it out. Fold the fabric diagonally, right sides together and raw edges even. Stitch along the diagonally pressed line.

Trim to a ¼″ seam allowance tapering into the corners. Press the seam open. Turn the mitered corner right side out and press.

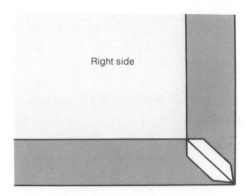

Mitering an Indented Trim

Stitch the trim to the right side of the fabric at the outer edge, stopping where it intersects the next seamline.

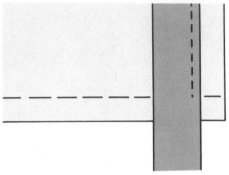

Fold the trim straight back on itself so that the fold is even with the intersecting seamline and pin.

Fold the trim across to create a right angle (a diagonal fold) at the corner and press. Lift up the trim and stitch it across the diagonal fold line. Trim away the excess fabric to reduce bulk.

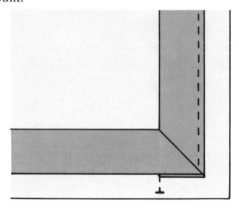

Fold the trim back and continue stitching at the outer edge. Repeat for all of the corners.

Stitch along the inner edge of the trim.

Mitering an Outside Border Trim

Take two lengths of the decorative border (be sure they are equal in width) and overlap them generously at right angles. Pin to a corner of the fabric. Adjust the borders as needed to match the design.

Diagonally fold one end of one border strip under at a 45° angle and press. **Slip-baste** the two pieces together.

On the wrong side, stitch along line of slip-basting. Trim the seams and overcast the edges as you feel appropriate.

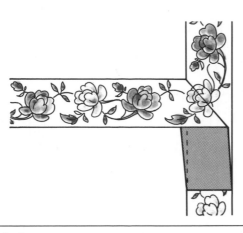

baste around the edges. Experiment with a sample "sandwich" of fabrics and batting to determine the best sewing machine tension, pressure, and stitch length. Usually, you need a looser tension and pressure and a longer stitch than you usually use.

Stitch straight lines, starting at the center and working toward the edges. To quilt fabric motifs, lower or cover the feed dog, remove the presser foot, and stitch around the designs as desired. Be sure the presser bar is down.

To accommodate bulk of fabric to the right of the needle, roll the fabrics tightly as you would a bedroll. To reduce bulk in seam areas, trim away the batting in the seam allowances.

Preshrink

To treat fabric before cutting, thus allowing any shrinkage to occur before fabric is cut.

Since washing tends to destroy some of the fabric finish and causes the fabric to lose its fresh, crisp appearance, we suggest taking fabrics to a dry cleaner who can steam-shrink them without these losses. If, however, you wish to do it yourself, put the fabric into the dryer at medium heat with two or three wet towels. Steam and heat will shrink the fabric.

Where washing is appropriate, put the fabric in a large tub of water. Soak it until it is thoroughly wet. Squeeze, do not wring, out the water or hang up until dripping stops. Put it in the dryer at the appropriate setting or air dry in a protected area.

Trimmings and zippers can be preshrunk by dipping them in warm water. Let them drip dry.

Quilting

A means of holding two layers of fabric and one of batting together in a decorative fashion.

Materials and Tools Needed

Fabric: face fabric; backing fabric. Allow about 10 percent extra fabric in length and width for drawing up that takes place when fabric is quilted.

Batting: polyester (recommended) or cotton.

Sewing Machine Attachments: quilting foot with guide bar that measures the distance between stitching lines, or an even-feed foot, which prevents fabrics from shifting.

Quilt Patterns

Trace onto the right side of the face fabric before you begin with chalk, water soluble ink pen, or thread:

Diamond shapes: quilt diagonally across the fabric.

Large squares: stitch lines along lengthwise and crosswise **grains** at equal intervals.

Lengthwise lines or channels: stitch parallel lines equidistant from each other.

Around a motif in the fabric: follow a stripe, plaid, floral, or other design motif.

Assembling and Sewing

Working on a large surface, spread the batting smoothly over the top of the wrong side of the backing fabric. Cover with the face fabric, right side up. Smooth all three layers from the center out. Pin with T-pins or quilter's pins.

Use a **diagonal baste** in contrast thread to secure the layers along the lengthwise grain, 6″ to 12″ apart, to keep the fabrics from slipping. Start at the center and work out, then

Railroading

To align patterns along the width of the fabric (horizontally) instead of along the length of the fabric (vertically). This method is usually used to eliminate or reduce seams or to follow a specific design line.

Repeat

One complete pattern on a print or plaid fabric. To determine an amount of repeat, measure the distance from one point in the design to the next identical point.

To figure how much extra yardage to allow for a pattern repeat, divide the cut length of the drapery panel, cushion, etc., by the size of the repeat. If the resulting number is a fraction, round off to the next highest number. (Example: each drapery panel is cut 98″ long. The repeat is 23″. $98 \div 23 = 4\%_{23}$ [round off to 5]. Buy five repeats per panel: $5 \times 23″ = 115″$ or 3¼ yards.)

To be safe, order an additional ½ yard of large repeat fabrics because you don't know where on the repeat the vendor will make the first cut.

Ruffles

A strip of fabric cut and sewn to create fullness.

Plan ruffles wide and full enough to give your project a luxurious look. Be sure to add seam and hem allowances to the desired finished width.

Strips for ruffles are usually cut on the straight **grain** of the fabric. If, however, your fabric has a design (stripe, plaid, check, etc.) that would be more decorative cut on the bias, plan to cut them as described under **bias strips** in this chapter.

After the strips are cut, seam them on the short ends. Make an **enclosed seam** on those that will be seen.

Single layer ruffles have the raw edges finished with a narrow hem, **binding,** or other decorative trim. To the desired finished width of the ruffle, add ½″ for a seam allowance and ⅜″ for each narrow hem. (A machine hemmer is great for this!)

A self-faced ruffle is a single piece of fabric folded back on itself. Double the desired finished width. Add 1″ for two ½″ seam allowances. Ruffles with a heading and double ruffles should have the seam fall on the back side at the point where the ruffles will be gathered.

There are basically three styles of ruffles:

Plain Ruffle   A ruffle with one finished, free edge and the other edge gathered in a seam or enclosed with a facing or hem allowance.

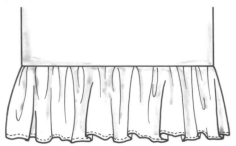

1. Make a narrow hem or otherwise finish off one edge. **Gather** the other edge to the desired size and distribute the fullness evenly.
2. Pin the ruffle strip, right sides together, to the raw edge of the fabric. Stitch the ruffle in place.
    When applying ruffle to squared corners, allow extra fullness in the corners.

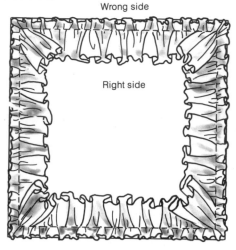

Wrong side

Right side

3. Join the second fabric layer or facing to the one with a ruffle attached (usually the top piece), right sides together. The ruffle is now attached between the two layers. It is best to stitch with the top piece up so that you can follow the previous stitching line.

Ruffle with a Heading   A ruffle with two finished, free edges that is gathered so that the top edge is narrower than the lower one. It is sewn to the right side of the fabric along the gathering line.

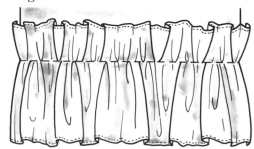

1. Make a narrow hem or otherwise finish off both edges.
2. **Gather** the ruffle strip the desired distance down from the top edge. Distribute the fullness evenly.
3. Place the wrong side of the ruffle to the right side of the fabric, with the gathering line on the ruffle just up from the stitching line on the fabric. Allow extra fullness in the corners. Stitch the ruffle in place on the gathering line.

Double Ruffle   A ruffle with two finished, free edges that is gathered halfway between the two edges. It is sewn in the same way as the ruffle with a heading.

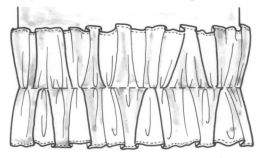

1. Make a narrow hem or otherwise finish off both edges.
2. **Gather** the ruffle strip through its center. Distribute the fullness evenly.
3. Follow Step 3 above.

Seams

Plain   Involves placing the fabric with the raw edges together, usually with right sides together. Stitch ½″ from the edge, or as otherwise specified in the directions. Press the seams open. The edges can be overcast or pinked, if desired.

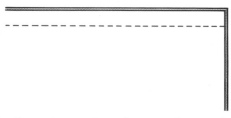

Enclosed   Is used to enclose the raw edges so the wrong side has no raw edges showing.

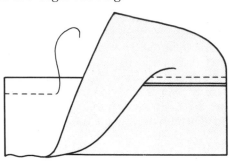

• *French:*   Place two pieces of fabric with wrong sides together. Stitch a ¼″ to ½″ seam, based on how easily your fabric frays. Press the seam to one side. Trim the seam allowance to ⅛″, and fold the fabric so that the right sides are together. Make a seam to enclose the raw edges.

• *Mock French:*   Place two pieces of fabric right sides together. Sew a ½″ seam (do not press it open).

Method A:
    Trim one side of the seam allowance to a scant ¼″. On the other side, turn under ⅛″. Fold the larger seam over the narrower one and stitch close to the folded edge on the seam allowance, not over the seamline.

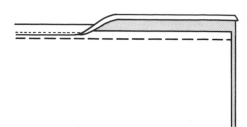

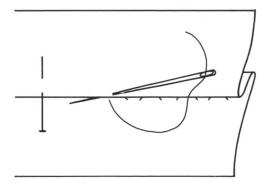

Method B:

Turn in ¼″ on the raw edges of the seam allowance to meet the seam and sew the folded edges together.

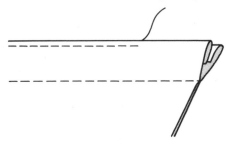

• *Flat-Felled:* A strong seam that looks the same on both sides of the fabric. Place two pieces of fabric wrong sides together. Sew a ½″ seam. Press the seam allowances to one side. Trim one side of the seam allowance to ⅛″ to ¼″. Turn in ⅛″ on the raw edge of the other seam allowance and fold over the trimmed edge. Pin it flat to the fabric. Sew close to the fold by machine or **slip stitch** by hand.

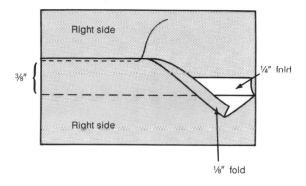

Selvage

The finished edge that runs along both sides of the length of fabric to prevent raveling. If the selvage is part of a seam allowance, it may be necessary to trim it off or at least clip it every few inches to reduce the chances of puckering.

Slip-Baste

Used to hold fabric design in place while you stitch. Turn in the fabric on the edge along the seamline. Crease it and pin. Lap the creased edge over the other section, matching the design along the lower layer's proposed seamline. Pin. Insert the needle through the crease on the top layer, then through the lower section, making the stitches on each layer about ¼″ long. Open out the seam allowance and stitch along the basting.

Stitches

Blanket Stitch A handstitch worked on the right side of the fabric from the left to right. Insert the needle at right angles through the fabric and bring it out to the edge of the fabric. Make a loop by keeping the thread under the needle.

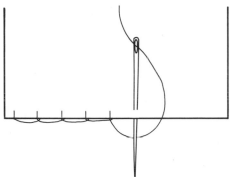

Blind Stitch By hand, see **slip stitch**.

By machine, use a blind stitch hem attachment for the sewing machine. Check your machine manual or insert pins about ⅛″ from the inner hem fold. Turn back the hem along the pins so the hem edge extends ⅛″ beyond the fold. Using the attachment (or a long, wide zigzag stitch) sew along the fold, catching a thread on the wrong side of the fabric with the extended stitch. Pull the hem down and press well.

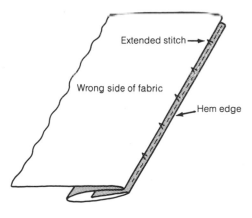

Chain Stitch A continuous series of looped stitches that form a chain. Thread needle with embroidery floss. Fasten thread and start the stitch from the wrong side of the fabric. Bring needle up to the right side. For each stitch, hold the thread down in a loop with your thumb. Pass the needle down exactly where the thread came up. Bring the needle up again a small distance along the line at the top of the loop held down by your thumb. Draw the thread through, forming a loop with the thread coming out within its base. Repeat for each stitch.

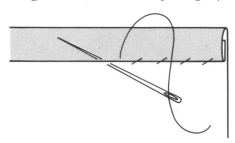

Hemming Stitch A handstitch worked on the wrong side of the fabric from right to left. Insert the needle into the fabric, catching a single thread, and bring the needle up through the edge of the hem. Do not pull tightly.

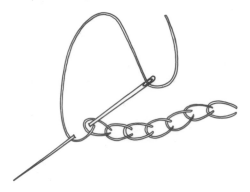

Overcasting Stitch A handstitch worked from left to right, bringing the needle through at an acute angle and taking the thread over the edge.

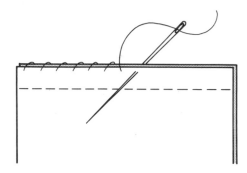

Slip Stitch (also called Blind Stitch) A handstitch used to join folded edges together invisibly. Pick up the thread from one fold and slide the needle through the fold for ¼". Then put the needle into the other fold the same way and carefully draw up the thread. Do not pull it tightly. The stitches should be about ¼" apart.

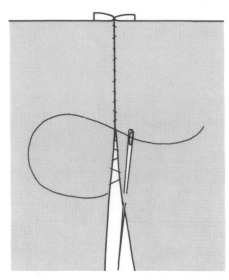

Staystitch A machine stitch of regular length used to keep fabric from stretching or ripping, and to serve as a guideline for clipping corners and curves. Staystitching should be done in the direction of the grain and should fall in the seam allowance ⅛" away from the seamline.

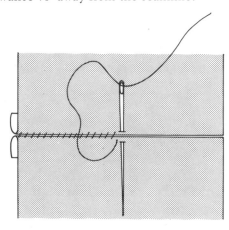

Whipstitch A fast, strong handstitch often used for closing openings on pillows, casings, etc. Insert needle at a right angle close to the edge, picking up only a few threads with each stitch.

Tassel

A decorative element made with yarn or embroidery floss. The following instructions use yarn. To use embroidery floss, plan three to four times as many strands.
1. Purchase 4-ply yarn in the desired number of colors (approximately 6 oz. per tassel). Cut a piece of cardboard 6" to 8" wide and 12" long. Adjust the length of the cardboard for longer or shorter tassels.
2. Wrap the yarn around the cardboard lengthwise with the two cut ends at the bottom edge. Slip a 6" piece of strong thread under the yarn at the top of the cardboard and tie ends of thread securely to draw yarn strands together. If you plan to attach the tassel to a pillow, use a longer piece of thread to bind the tassel top; the excess can be threaded into the fabric to secure the tassel.

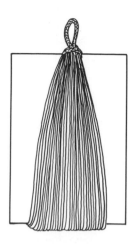

3. With twelve strands (each 10 to 12 inches long) of yarn, make a braid 6″ long. Knot the ends together to form a circle. Slip the circle under the yarn at the top of the cardboard. Make a loop by pulling one side of the circle over the yarn and through the opposite side of circle.

4. Cut the yarn at the bottom of the cardboard.

5. Wrap one strand of yarn around all the strands about a third of the way down from the loop to make a tassel head. Leave an end as you begin wrapping. Tie this to the other end when you are finished.

6. Shake out the tassel to free the strands. Trim the bottom ends evenly. If tassel is attached to a long braid, eliminate the braided ring at top. Divide the strands of long braid in half and slip under the yarn. Tie securely.

Template

A pattern which reflects the exact size and shape of a particular object.

To make a template, trace around the object onto newspaper or brown paper to make an exact representation of the outlines. In order to draw templates for more complex shapes, you may have to lay the paper over the object, clipping and folding to get a shape as close to that of the object as possible. Cut out the approximate shape and then lay it over the object and make any necessary changes. In either instance, after the exact size and shape have been determined, add the needed seam allowances before tracing onto fabric.

Transfer

To copy a design or shape onto fabric. First, copy the design onto paper, **enlarging** it if necessary, and put onto fabric in one of the following ways:

• Using colored tracing paper and a special tracing wheel, trace the lines of the design with the wheel, applying just enough pressure to make faint lines. Be sure to use the type of paper that makes removable markings.

• Use a special "transfer pencil," available at most craft and fabric stores. These make an impression that can actually be ironed onto fabric.

• If appropriate, as in an appliqué design, cut out the paper pattern and trace around it with a pencil or tailor's chalk, right side of pattern to wrong side of fabric.

Tufting

A means of joining fabric and padding together by drawing stitches tightly through the layers at regular intervals to add stability and decorative detail. Tufting can be done in two ways.

Method A:

Use a long needle threaded with a double strand of strong thread, pearl cotton, or yarn. Sew through all the layers twice and cut the thread at the needle. Tie the ends tightly in a double knot so that it forces the fabric to dimple on both sides. Clip the ends no shorter than ¾″.

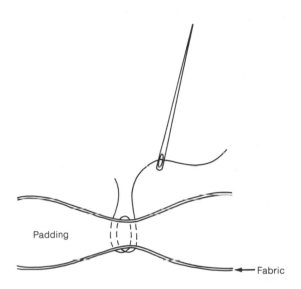

Method B:

Using a long needle threaded with a double strand of strong thread, secure one end of the thread to one button shank. Pull the needle to the other side and cut the thread at the needle. Put one of the two threads through the shank of the second button, which should be positioned opposite the first one. Pull the threads tightly so that the buttons make the fabric dimple on both sides. Tie the threads securely and clip.

Welting (also called cording or piping)

Fabric-wrapped cord used to define or finish seams, to give seams added strength, and to add a decorative touch.

Materials Needed to Make Welting

Cord: cotton or polyester cord comes in diameters ranging from ⅛″ to 1″ and can be purchased at fabric and upholstery shops. Buy enough for all the seams in which you plan to insert welting, plus extra for finishing the ends.

Bias strips: yardage, cutting, and assembling instructions are in this chapter under **bias strips.** To determine the width of the bias strips needed to go around the cord, wrap a piece of fabric (or paper) around the cord. Pin it, encasing the cord snugly. Measure ½″ (¾″ on very fat cord) from the pin. Cut along this line. Unpin and lay it out flat. Use this piece as a width guide.

Zipper foot: for the sewing machine.

Assembling the Welting

1. Wrap the bias strip, right side out, around the cord with the raw edges even.

2. Using a zipper foot positioned to the right of the needle, stitch next to the cord, but not crowding it. Let the cord extend beyond the bias strip at both ends.

Sewing the Welting to the Fabric

1. Position the welting on the right side of one piece of fabric (usually the one on top), raw edges together. The stitching line should be in the seam allowance just inside the seamline. Start the welting midpoint on a long edge, not a zipper edge, and not at a corner.

2. Using the zipper foot, sew the welting in place along the stitching line, starting and stopping 2″ in from the ends.

3. Pin the fabric with the welting on top of the second piece of fabric, right sides together.

4. Stitch the layers together, using the welt stitching line as a guide, with a zipper foot tight against the cord so that the welt stitching line is inside the seam allowance. Stitching will now be on the seamline and stitching lines should *not* show on the right side of the project.

Be sure to stitch across the welt, crowding with the zipper foot in any opening areas.

Turning Corners and Curves

For a very square corner, make a slash close to the stitching line in the welting seam allowance at the corner point.

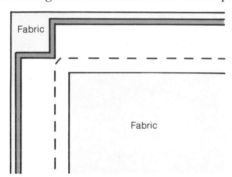

For a slightly curved corner, make clips in the welting seam allowance 1½″ on either side of the corner point.

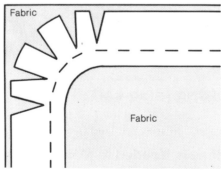

On the other curved areas, make clips at intervals as needed to make the welting lie flat.

Joining the Ends

Method A: Butting the Ends

1. Sew the welting around the fabric piece to within 2″ of the beginning of the welt. Cut the end of the welting so that it will overlap the beginning by 2″.

2. Rip out the stitches at the beginning of the welting for about 2″ and at the end for 4″ to expose the cording. Make a diagonal cut on the beginning section of the bias strip. Mark a ¼″ seam.

3. Lay the end of the bias strip over the beginning and fold it back along the marked seamline of the beginning side. Cut, leaving a ¼″ seam allowance. Stitch the ends of the bias strips, right sides together. Press the seam open.

4. Cut the cord so that the two ends butt together and finish stitching the welting in place.

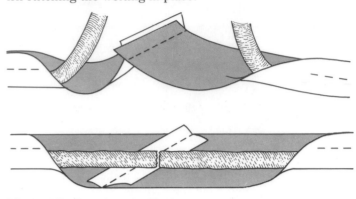

Method B: Crossing the End

1. Sew the welting around the fabric piece to within 1″ of the beginning of the welt. Leave the needle in the fabric. Cut the end of the welting so that it will overlap the beginning by 1½″.

2. Pull out ¾″ of the cord from each end of the welting and cut it off.

3. Extend both ends of the welt into the seam allowance, crossing the empty casings, and finish stitching the welt in place.

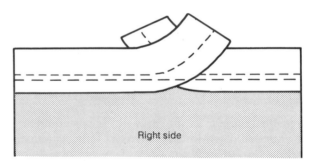

Zippers

Slide fasteners for seams that need to be opened and closed.

Centered Zipper

1. Close the zipper seam with a machine basting stitch. Press the seam open.

2. Open the zipper and position it face down on the extended seam allowance (a single layer of seam allowance with no fabric underneath) so that the teeth rest against the seamline.

Machine baste the length of the zipper along the woven guideline on the zipper tape.

3. Close the zipper and spread the fabric flat, with the zipper still face down. Baste the other side in place in the same manner.

4. Turn the fabric right side up with the zipper underneath. Starting at the top of the zipper, stitch down one side, across the bottom, and up the other side, ¼″ from the basted zipper seam. Stitch across the other end if necessary. Remove the basting stitches.

Lapped Zipper in a Plain Seam

1. Follow the first two steps under Centered Zipper, above. Close the zipper and turn it face up. Fold and smooth the fabric so that it rests against the zipper teeth.

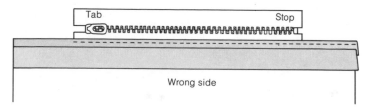

Tab

Stop

Wrong side

2. Sew along the narrow fold of the seam allowance between the zipper seam and the zipper teeth.

3. Spread the fabric flat, turning the zipper face down. Pin and baste the unstitched zipper tape to the other seam allowance through all thicknesses.

4. Turn the fabric right side up. Stitch across the bottom of the zipper and up the basted side ⅜″ to ½″ from the zipper seam. Stitch across the top edge if necessary. Remove the basting stitches.

Lapped Zipper in a Welted Seam

1. Press under the seam allowance along the seamline in the zipper opening on the unwelted side.

2. With the welted piece on the bottom and the right sides together, pull back the seam allowance on the top piece to expose the welted seam allowance. Open the zipper. Lay it face down over the extended seam allowance with the zipper teeth on top of the welt. Stitch close to the teeth on the zipper tape.

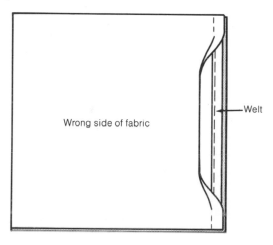

Wrong side of fabric

Welt

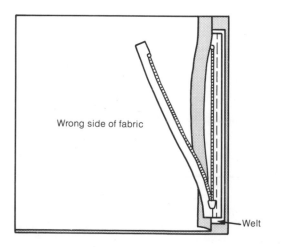

Wrong side of fabric

Welt

3. Open the pieces, positioning them so that the right sides are up. Close the zipper and lay the pressed-under edge of the unwelted side over the teeth so that it rests against the welt. Baste it in place.

4. Stitch as for Lapped Zipper in a Plain Seam, above.

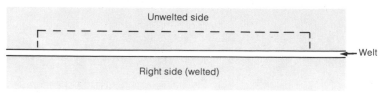

Unwelted side

Welt

Right side (welted)

Project
I·N·S·T·R·U·C·T·I·O·N·S

Now that you've carefully thought through your color and fabric choices and researched styles and solutions in the first two sections of this book, you are ready to begin the actual sewing. If you are doing the work yourself, there are several guidelines you will need to follow to ensure success. At the beginning of each set of individual project instructions you'll find a sketch of the item with size information where pertinent, page references for the room or rooms which feature the project, and any special information. Estimates for yardage for each project are based on the sizes we've featured. You may wish to individualize your project and make it in a different size; our dimensions are merely a point of reference. You may, therefore, need to establish your own yardage requirements based on the guidelines provided. When estimating yardage, the goal is to keep your calculations moderate, that is, neither extravagant nor miserly.

It is imperative that you read through all the steps of a project before beginning so that there will be no surprises at any point. Keep the overall project in mind during each step so that you will know what you're working toward. Never lose sight of the finished project and how it should look and function. At first glance some of these instructions may appear to be rather complicated. We ask you to keep in mind that when you are actually working, holding the fabric and using the machine, the instructions will make sense. It's often harder to describe a step than to do it. These directions were compiled while actual work was in progress, and they incorporate numerous shortcuts or warnings developed over the many years we have been designing patterns and working out decorative treatments for clients.

Before beginning a project, it's wise to check back in the section where that project is photographed and to read the photo caption describing the picture. We've tried to include many helpful sewing tips in these captions, which you will want to keep in mind as you begin the project. The color pictures, aside from suggesting a suitable and attractive color and fabric choice, will also help you to visualize the finished project as you work.

Even if you are leaving the actual sewing to a dressmaker, friend, or local workroom or upholstery shop, you will want to go over these points with this person or persons rather than simply indicating the instructions. The more familiar you are with the overall contents of this book, the more you will enjoy the process of realizing your design projects, and the more professional and successful your finished projects will be.

Pillows

Very little need be said about the versatility and decorative potential of pillows. For a minimum of expense and effort, they supply color, pattern, and personality. Even more, they can lend newness to a room. Although pillows come in many diverse sizes and shapes, there are basically two pillow constructions: knife-edge and box-edge. The knife-edge pillow is thicker in the center and tapers off to the outer edges. It requires only one seam. The best looking knife-edge pillows are square or oblong. Circular knife-edge pillows tend to pucker at the edges unless they have ruffles added. The box-edge pillow is of an equal thickness throughout and requires two major seams.

Two variations on the knife-edge construction are also described here: the flanged pillow, with flanges or flaps; and the Turkish corner pillow, a knife-edge with the look of a box-edge pillow. These basic types can be made with the addition of decorative trims, or can be embellished with a self-welt, ruffles, or other fabric finishes.

Pillows can, of course, be made from a great variety of fabric types. It is wise to consider, however, just how the pillow will be used and to let that application guide you in selecting fabrics that are decorative (for light use) or that are easily laundered or dry-cleaned (for heavy use).

Forms

Ready-made pillow forms are widely available in standard shapes and sizes. They may be made of polyester fibers or foam; or fabric cases filled with shredded foam, polyester fibers, down, or feathers. Be sure to choose a filler that suits the requirements of the job. Firmer, shredded foam or polyester fiber fillers, for example, require little attention and are best if economy is a crucial concern. Down or feather forms, on the other hand, are more costly, require "fluffing up" after use, and can pose a problem if someone who uses the room has allergies. In our experience, however, the soft and deluxe appearance of down or feather pillows is so superior to any substitute that, in all cases except those where they cause sneezing or rashes, they're the best choice.

It's important to measure a pillow form before purchasing it. The actual measurements often vary from those printed on the package or tag. A pillow form slightly larger than the finished size of the pillow cover will give the pillow a smoother, more professional look. You might choose to make a size adjustment by wrapping the form with batting to increase its fullness and make the pillow cover fit more snugly.

If you choose to make a nonstandard size or shape, you'll need to make your own form. Construct a pillow from a strong, firm fabric, like muslin or ticking, sewn to the desired measurements, and fill it with one of the fillings listed above.

Box-edge forms are occasionally difficult to find. You can make your own by covering a cut piece of foam with batting or by using a square knife-edge pillow form larger than the desired finished square box-edge pillow. To determine the size knife-edge form you'll need, add the depth of your box-edge cover to its width. For example, an 18″ square box-edge pillow with a 2″ depth could be filled with a 20″ knife-edge form. For instructions on making box-edge pillows, refer to Box Cushion with Welt, page 190.

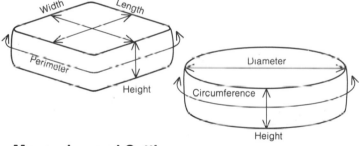

Measuring and Cutting

In order to decide on the style and size of pillow for your particular decorating need, you'll have to consider its end use, and the width and pattern of the fabric you've chosen. For example, a bed or modestly scaled sofa pillow is usually between 14″ and 22″; a floor pillow is between 27″ and 30″; and dramatically oversized corner pillows for a large-scale sofa are between 24″ and 30″. If you can't cut two sections of the pillow side by side across the width of the fabric you've selected because the fabric is too narrow or the repeat makes this impossible, you will have to purchase considerably more fabric. If cost is a primary concern, you may decide to make a smaller pillow rather than purchase more fabric.

To determine the basic measurements of the pillow pieces, measure the length and width across the center of the form. For a circular form, measure the diameter. You

will need to buy enough fabric for both the front and the back pieces.

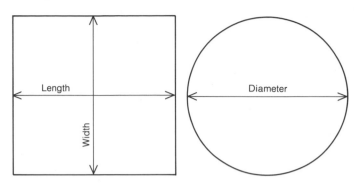

Pillows are usually cut on the lengthwise and crosswise **grain.** When using plaids or stripes, however, you might want to create a diagonal pattern by cutting the pillow on the bias. It takes more fabric to use the bias (usually 1½ times as much), but often the visual effect is well worth the extra cost. For instructions on cutting bias pillows, refer to the section on specific pillows using bias on page 140.

You'll also need extra yardage if you want to add a self-welt, ruffles, or the like. Instructions for figuring the extra amounts for these trim details are given either with the specific pillows that feature them on the following pages or in the "Tools, Terms, and Techniques" chapter under the appropriate heading.

Closures for Pillows

The two most frequently used pillow closures are hand **stitching** and **zippers.**

If your pillow is to be primarily decorative, or is constructed of a lightweight fabric, stitching the opening closed by hand is generally best. For pillows that are to be reversible (that is, useable on either side), or those styles not suited to zippers (such as those with heavy, double ruffles added into seams), closing by hand is usually the better choice as well.

Pillows that will be used a lot are better closed with zippers. For the best appearance, insert the zipper after any in-seam trims (like welting or ruffles) have been added and before stitching the pillow sections together. If the trim is too heavy to allow you easily to insert a zipper in the seam, you can create a seam across the back of the pillow, as illustrated. Remember to allow an extra 1½″ for the zipper seam when cutting the pillow back. It's a good idea to make this seam low on the pillow back side. In this way it will be nearly invisible and may even allow you to reverse the pillow, back to front, without the zipper showing at all.

A round knife-edge pillow is usually constructed with the zipper across the center back, as illustrated.

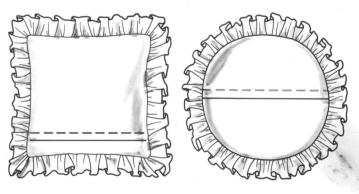

Constructing a Basic Knife-Edge Pillow

1. To avoid exaggerated points at the corners (as sometimes happens when pillows are perfectly square) and to help the cover fit the form more precisely, mark points ½" in from each corner along the raw edges. Measure along each side and mark a second set of points at one-quarter of the length edge. Connect this point to the ½" mark on the adjoining edge. Trim the pillow fabric along these lines.

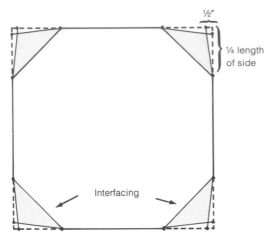

2. To keep the corners sharp, especially in lighter weight fabrics, fuse a triangle of interfacing to each corner of both the front and back pieces.

3. Apply any trim, welting, or ruffle that is to be sewn into the seam. For exact application, see the specific pillow instructions that follow, or refer to the "Tools, Terms, and Techniques" chapter.

4. Insert the **zipper** if you have chosen this method of closure. Open the zipper.

5. Stitch the pillow pieces together with a ½" seam allowance. If you are planning a closure stitched by hand, pin the front to the back, right sides together. On the side of the pillow cover to be left open for turning (usually the bottom edge), begin and end the machine stitching 1½" in from the corners. For a zipper closure, sew the pillow pieces together as above, beginning and ending at the zipper.

6. Clip the corners and press the seams. Turn the pillow cover right side out. Press the edges. Insert the pillow form and close.

Pillows with Ruffles

Ruffles are generally used only on knife-edge pillows and can be cut on either the straight **grain** or the bias. The bias cut is more effective with plaids, checks, and stripes, but remember that it requires more fabric.

Ruffles can be a single thickness, finished with a hemmed edge, or a double thickness, finished with a self-faced hem. Single thickness ruffles are more frequently used for pillows which clearly have a right and a wrong side. Double ruffles look best in soft fabrics and are more successful for pillows that are reversible.

Ruffles tend to be bulky, making zippers difficult to install in an edge seam. With ruffled pillows, it's easier to plan either a closure **stitched** by hand, or to insert the **zipper** in a seam created in the back of the pillow, as described on page 137.

Different methods of making ruffles are discussed in detail in the "Tools, Terms, and Techniques" chapter.

Pillow with Top-Applied Ruffle

Pillow shown here and on page 115 is 24" square plus ruffle.

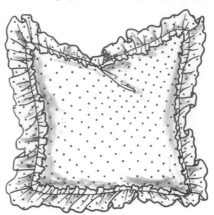

Fabric: Enough for the pillow front and back, plus 1¼ yards for ruffle. If bias ruffle is preferred, add an extra ½ yard.
Notions: Zipper (optional).
Pillow form.

1. Follow the preceding instructions for cutting and sewing a basic knife-edge pillow. If you are using a **zipper** closure, insert it in the pillow back.
2. Cut **ruffle** strips 7" wide and make a narrow hem along both edges. A hemmer foot is useful for this.
3. Gather the ruffle strip, ¾" in from one edge.
4. Apply the ruffle to the front side of the finished pillow cover, placing the gathering line ¼" in from the edge of the pillow. Sew on the gathering line through all thicknesses. Make an **enclosed seam** where the ruffle ends meet.

Pillow with Welt and Ruffle

Pillow shown here and on page 36 is 22" square plus ruffle.

Fabric: Enough for the pillow front and back, plus an extra 1¼ yards for the ruffle and a self-fabric welt. If bias ruffles are preferred, add an additional ½ yard.
Notions: 6/32" cording in an amount equal to the perimeter of the pillow plus 4"; zipper (optional).
Pillow form.

1. Follow the preceding instructions for basic knife-edge pillow.
2. Prepare the **welting.** Apply to the right side of the front piece.

3. Cut **ruffle** strips 4⅞″ wide and make a narrow machine hem on one long edge. Seam short ends with an **enclosed seam.**

4. Gather the cut edge of the ruffle strip ½″ from the edge.

5. Sew the ruffle to the right side of the front piece over the welting, aligning the stitch line for the welting with the gathering line for the ruffle.

6. Insert the **zipper,** if desired, in the back piece.

7. Stitch the pieces together. On the side of the pillow to be left open for turning, begin and end the machine stitching 1½″ in from the corners.

Pillow with Contrasting Jumbo Welt
Pillow shown here and on page 30 is 22″ square.

Fabric: Enough for pillow front and back; contrasting welt fabric—½ yard.

Notions: ½″ cording in an amount equal to the perimeter of the pillow plus 4″; zipper (optional, but not recommended). **Pillow form.**

1. Make the **welting** and sew it to the front pillow section.

2. Construct a basic knife-edge pillow according to the preceding instructions.

Note: A **zipper** is not recommended for pillows with jumbo welting because the installation is difficult. If you decide to insert a zipper, place it in the back piece, not in the seam. You will have to adjust the size of the back section accordingly.

Pillow with Applied Trim
Pillow shown here and on page 34 is 20″ square.

Fabric: Enough for pillow front and back, allowing for the centering of any motif or pattern.

Trims and Notions: Amount equal to the perimeter of the pillow plus 4″; zipper (optional).

Pillow form.

1. Construct a basic knife-edge pillow, following the preceding instructions. If **zipper** closure is chosen, insert the zipper in the back piece.

2. After the pillow is made, sew trim to the outside edge of the pillow front as close to the seamed edge as possible. If closure is **stitched** by hand, first stitch the trim to the front side of the pillow along the open seamline. Insert the form and close pillow by hand.

Boudoir Pillows with Applied Trim
Pillows shown here and on pages 92 and 93 are 12″ × 16″.

Pillow A

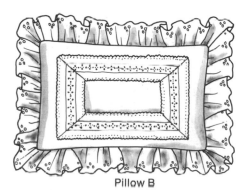

Pillow B

Fabric: ¼ yard for each pillow.

Trims and Notions: Pillow A—1¼ yards trim, approximately 2″ wide; 1¼ yards of ⅜″ ribbon; pillow B—1½ yards band trim, approximately 2″ wide; 4 yards unruffled eyelet trim, or 1¾ yards commercially pre-ruffled trim (these tend to be less full than preferable); zipper (optional).

Pillow forms.

Pillow A

1. Cut 2 pieces from fabric, each 13″ × 17″.

2. Weave ribbon through eyelet trim. Apply to one rectangular piece, centering trim over a drawn line 2⅜″ in from seamline. **Miter** corners of trim.

3. Finish according to the preceding knife-edge pillow instructions.

Pillow B

1. Cut two pieces from fabric, each 13″ × 17″.

2. Apply trim to front pillow piece as above.

3. Gather and sew eyelet **ruffle** to pillow front.

4. Finish according to the preceding knife-edge pillow instructions.

Pillow with Braided Yarn Trim

Pillow shown here and on page 40 is 10" × 19".

Fabric: Enough for pillow front and back.
Trims and Notions: Knitting worsted (4-ply yarn) in three colors, approximately 15 yards of each color; zipper (optional).
Pillow form.

1. Make a basic knife-edge pillow, following the preceding instructions.
2. Cut each color yarn into five equal strands 3 yards long. Join and secure the five strands of each color at one end. Braid the three colors together.
3. **Stitch** the braided strand by hand around the pillow along the seamline. When the ends meet, tie a knot and tuck the ends under. Stitch the ends firmly in place.

Bias Cut Pillow

Pillow shown here and on page 47 is 22" square.

Fabric: Allow 1½ times the normal fabric allowance for the pillow front and back to accommodate cutting on the bias (i.e., if ½ yard is needed for a straight grain cut, ¾ yard would be needed for a bias cut); lightweight nonwoven fusible interfacing for pillow front and back.
Notions: Zipper (optional).
Pillow form.

1. Cut squares for pillow front and back on the diagonal. Fuse interfacing to wrong side. (Interfacing may have to be pieced for large pillows.)

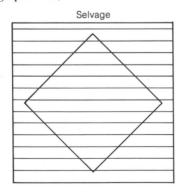

Selvage

2. Construct as basic knife-edge pillow according to preceding instructions.

Mitered Pillow

Pillows shown here and on page 42 are 24" and 30" square.

Fabric: Allow approximately one-third more fabric than needed for a plain pillow front and back this size.
Notions: Zipper (optional).
Pillow form.

1. Make a pattern on a piece of paper by drawing a square the desired finished size of the pillow, plus a ½" seam allowance on each side. Cut one square of fabric for the pillow back, and then fold paper pattern in quarters on the diagonal. Open out to square again and add a ½" seam allowance to the diagonals on one of the triangles. Cut out. This is the pattern piece for the four front sections.

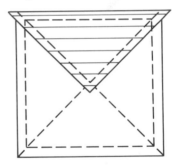

2. Cut triangles from fabric, matching the fabric stripes along the diagonal seamlines on all four pieces. Sew together to create a square, carefully matching the stripes.
3. Construct pillow, following the preceding instructions for a basic knife-edge pillow.

Appliquéd Pillow

Pillow shown here and on page 35 is 20" square.

Fabric: Enough for pillow front and back; printed fabric for cutting motifs.

Trims and Notions: Welting in an amount equal to the perimeter of the pillow plus 4″; zipper (optional).
Pillow form.

1. Cut the pillow front and back. **Appliqué** the motifs. (On the pillow pictured, a background fabric was chosen with a color similar to that of the printed fabric from which the motifs were cut. As the shapes were cut, a margin of ⅛″ of background fabric was left on the motif. A ⅛″ zigzag stitch was used to appliqué the motif to the pillow. This was so that the thread did not have to change color as the motif color changed, and we were not obliged to follow any pattern lines exactly.)
2. Sew the **welting** to the appliquéd side of the pillow cover.
3. Finish the pillow, following the preceding instructions for the basic knife-edge pillow.

Patch Pillow

Pillow shown here and on page 41 is 22″, with an 11″ patchwork square.

Fabric: Decorative square of fabric for center; enough for pillow back and border strips on pillow front.
Notions: Zipper (optional).
Pillow form.

1. Cut the border strips. (For our 22″ pillow, we used 5½″ wide strips.) The strips for the border should equal the desired finished width plus 1″ for seam allowances. The length of each strip should be the finished length of the center square plus the finished width of the strip plus 1″ for seam allowances.
2. Sew the first border strip to one side of the center square, aligning the border strip and the square at one end. With right sides together, stitch only between seamlines on the center square.

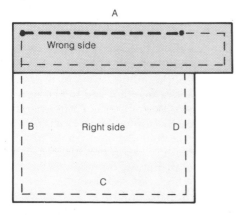

3. Press the seam open. Sew a second border strip to side B, aligning the strip with the square on one end and the end of the border strip on the other. Press seam open.

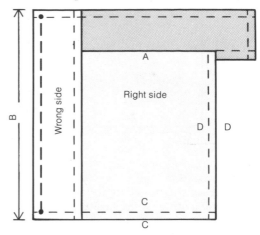

4. Repeat for sides C and D. Side D requires an extra seam at the end where border D meets border A.
5. Construct a basic knife-edge pillow as per preceding instructions.

Rag Pillows

Pillows shown here and on page 114 are 22″ square and 12″ × 16″.

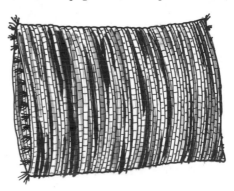

Fabric: Prefinished rag piece for front (handwoven fabric, placemats, etc.); fabric for pillow back equal to the size of the front piece, plus ½″ seam allowances.
Pillow form.

1. Press under seam allowances on the pillow back.
2. **Stitch** the back to the front on three sides by hand. Insert pillow form. Close the fourth side with hand stitches.

Constructing a Basic Turkish Corner Pillow

1. Cut pillow front and back the size of the form you are covering plus ½″ all around for seam allowances. Remember that Turkish corner pillows are "mock" box-edge pillows, and, when finished, will appear smaller than the same size form done with a knife-edge. Therefore, if you want the finished pillow to appear to be 18″ with a 2″ depth, use a 20″ form. For an 18″ pillow with a 4″ depth, use a 22″ form, and so on.
2. On the wrong side, mark each corner at an angle, as illustrated. Distance A should be approximately 3″ for a small pillow, 4″ for a large one.

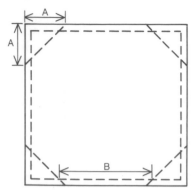

3. Insert the **zipper,** if desired, in distance B, as illustrated. If a zipper is not used, leave B open.

4. Sew pillow sections, right sides together.

5. Run **gathering** stitches along the marked corner lines. Zigzagging over a string is the best method.

Wrong side

6. Pull the string or threads to form tight gathers. Sew several times across each gathered corner, just inside the string or gathering stitches. Remove the string.

7. Press the seams open.

8. Turn the pillow right side out. Press again and insert the form. **Stitch** by hand to close if a zipper was not inserted.

Turkish Corner Pillow with Welt

Pillow shown here and on page 39 is 30" square.

Fabric: Enough for pillow front and back plus an extra ½ yard for the welt.

Notions: ⁶⁄₃₂" cording in an amount equal to perimeter of pillow plus 4"; zipper (optional).

Pillow form.

Method A: (Traditional but exacting)

1. Follow the preceding instructions for a basic Turkish corner pillow, marking and **gathering** corners of front and back pieces separately (gather eight corners).

2. Stitch **welting** to pillow front following the line of gathering stitches at the corners.

3. Insert **zipper,** if desired. You will find it easier to complete the pillow if you continue the zipper seam with standard stitches around the gathered corners.

Method B: (Quicker and easier)

1. Make a knife-edge pillow, following the basic instructions in this chapter, applying **welting** and inserting a **zipper,** if desired. The welt can stop approximately 1½" short of each corner. Be sure that the zipper is short enough not to extend into what will be the gathered corners.

2. Mark the corners and gather up through all thicknesses, following the preceding instructions for a Turkish corner pillow, Steps 2 and 5 to 8.

Turkish Corner Pillow with Border and Braid

Pillow shown here and on page 38 is 30" square.

Fabric: Enough main fabric for pillow front and back; border print—amount equal to the perimeter of the pillow plus extra for mitering and matching at corners (double this amount if the border will appear on both sides of the pillow).

Trims and Notions: Braid or trim in an amount equal to the perimeter of the pillow plus 4". (*Note:* The braid featured on this pillow was made by braiding three strands of a commercially available ½" braided trim to make a more impressive trim. To do this, buy 4 times the perimeter of the pillow, cut the trim into thirds, and braid. Interweave the braid where the ends meet.) Zipper is optional.

Pillow form.

1. Cut front and back pieces.

2. Cut four border strips (eight if the bottom will be treated with a border as well), each the finished depth of the border plus ½" on each side for seam allowances. The length of each border strip should be the outside finished length desired plus ½" at each end for **mitering.** If the border has a print to be matched at the corners, plan before cutting. Also keep in mind that the pillow will have a boxed look and that the border will, as a result, need to be inset more toward the center of the pillow.

3. With the right sides together and the corners and raw edges matching, sew two of the four strips together. Fold down the corner on the top strip to determine the diagonal line. Be sure that the folded corner comes to ½" below the long edge of the border strip to provide a seam allowance. Pin, check the alignment and direction of the miter, and mark the stitching line. Sew, stopping ½" before the inside raw edge. Repeat for all corners.

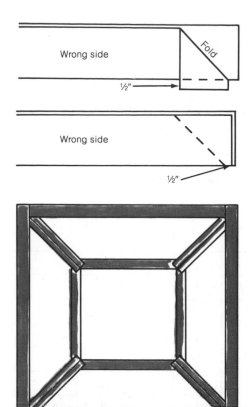

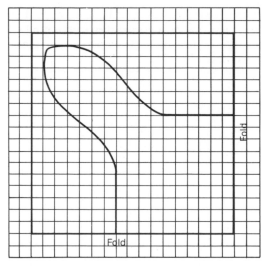

Scale: 1 square = 1″

4. Trim the corners, press the seams open, and press under the seam allowances on the inside and outside edges.

5. Center the border on the pillow front. Stitch the border in place close to the inside and outside edges.

6. Construct the pillow according to the preceding directions for basic Turkish corner pillows.

7. After the pillow is complete, **stitch** the braid or other trim by hand along the seamline. If the braid is suitable, use any remnants to make **tassels.**

Tie-ons for Turkish Corner Pillows

Tie-ons shown here and on page 39 cover a 24″ square pillow.

Fabric: Enough to cut two squares, each twice the dimensions of the pillow it will cover. (For example, a 12″ x 12″ pillow requires 2 squares, 24″ x 24″)

Notions: Single-fold bias tape in an amount equal to twice the perimeter of one square plus 1 yard.

1. Enlarge pattern to the desired size and cut two fabric thicknesses.

2. Bind raw edges with bias tape.

3. Place the tie-ons on the front and back of the pillow, with the ties falling in the center of each pillow side. Double knot and adjust fullness.

Constructing a Basic Flanged Pillow

1. The flange is cut with the front and back pieces of the pillow cover. Flanges are usually 2″ to 4″ wide and are created by stitching the shape of the pillow form into the cover, as illustrated below in Step 6. Keeping this in mind, cut the pillow front and back pieces with flange extension plus ½″ all around for seam allowances. *Note:* If you are planning a **zipper** closure, cut the back piece 1½″ longer.

If you are planning a sham back (a pillow back with two-piece construction with an overlap for the insertion of pillow), cut the back piece 6″ to 7″ longer. If you want a reversible pillow, leave one edge open during construction, insert the pillow form, and then finish stitching. Since this technique isn't easy, we recommend either a zipper or the sham back construction as described here.

2. For a zipper closure, cut the back piece into two separate pieces, dividing it into one-third and two-thirds sections as illustrated. Sew the two pieces back together with a ¾″ seam and insert the **zipper.** The zipper must be inserted inside the lines of topstitching that will form the flange.

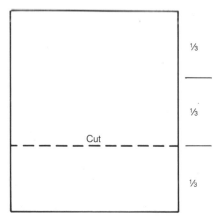

3. For a sham back, cut the back piece into two separate pieces, dividing it into one-third and two-thirds sections as above. Make a narrow hem on each of the two cut edges. Lay the two back pieces over the front piece with the hemmed edges overlapping and the raw edges aligned as illustrated. Pin or baste together the overlapping edges of the back piece. Treat the back section as one piece for the rest of the procedure.

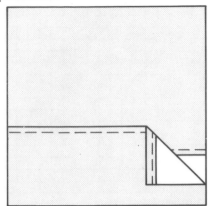

4. If you've inserted a zipper, open it. Align the front and back, right sides together, and sew around the outside edge with a ½″ seam.

5. Clip corners and press seams open. Turn the cover right side out through the sham or zipper opening, or the unsewn edge and press again.

6. Trace or draw the shape of the pillow form with chalk or water soluble ink pen onto the back side of the pillow cover. Topstitch along these lines. If you have chosen to stitch the flange with the pillow form in place, do this according to the illustration.

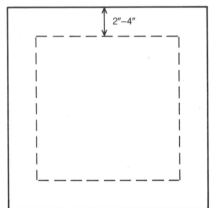

2″–4″

Topstitch to size of form or around form

Scallop Edged Pillows

Pillows shown here and on page 106 are 16″ and 22″ square with 2″ to 2½″ flanges.

Fabric: Enough for pillow front and back including flange.
Trims and Notions: Single-fold bias tape in an amount equal to perimeter of the pillow plus ¾ yard; zipper (optional, but recommended).
Pillow form.

1. Enlarge pattern to desired pillow size. (This will be much easier if you fold the paper into quarters and enlarge one-fourth of the diagram. Cut all quarters at one time for a full pattern.)

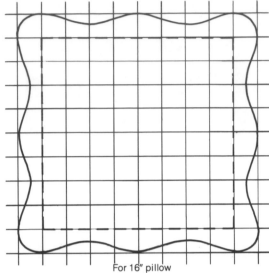

For 16″ pillow

2. Follow Steps 1 to 3 of the preceding basic instructions for constructing flanged pillows.

3. Cut out the pillow front and back, shaping the border edges into the scallop design as shown in pattern diagram. Pin the front and back together to hold them securely in place.

4. Bind the unfinished edges with bias tape.

5. Trace or draw the shape of the pillow form with chalk or water soluble ink pen onto the back side of the pillow cover. Topstitch along these lines.

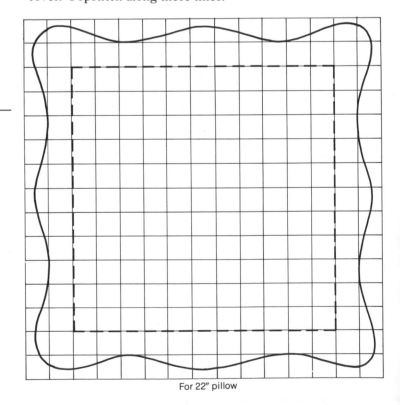

For 22″ pillow

Tabletop Accessories

Creative table settings and accessories are a delightful way to brighten up your home. A simple round table gracefully skirted to the floor can add drama and color to a spiritless room or hallway. Attractive placemats, napkins, and table runners can make any meal more special, and the addition of a few unusual items like fabric napkin rings, bun warmers, and tea cozies can make table settings memorable for family and guests.

Even if your busy schedule does not allow you the luxury of sewing table accessories from scratch, you can personalize purchased accessories by the addition of trims or appliqués, and by sewing or embellishing a collection of tablecloths, skirts, and accessories, you also add the magic of seasonal change to your home and personal style to your entertaining.

Tableskirts and Cloths

The skirted table is one of the least expensive and most effective solutions to a myriad of decorating problems. It also provides an ideal display surface, and by bringing color or pattern into a room, it eliminates the need for costly upholstered or wood pieces. There are, of course, as many different looks for a skirted table as there are fabrics available, and the choice of any one of a number of decorative hem finishes only increases the style possibilities.

Although most of the table covers in this book are floor length, any of them could be sewn in shorter versions. To measure for a table cover, figure the diameter of the top and add twice the desired **drop,** plus hem allowances. Then use the appropriate charts in this chapter to determine yardage. Normal cloths and overskirts have a 10″ to 12″ drop. For a more formal look, consider a 16″ to 24″ drop. Floor-length tableskirts are generally more permanent accessories than simple cloths and, as such, should have overskirts or cloths added for mealtime to avoid constant laundering.

Basic Round Tableskirt or Cloth

Tableskirt is photographed on page 54.

Fabric: Measure the diameter of the tabletop and add twice the distance from the tabletop to the floor, or twice the **drop** desired. For example, a 36″ tabletop diameter with a 30″ drop to the floor would measure 36″ + 30″ + 30″ = 96″. This measurement is the finished diameter of the cloth. Add a hem allowance to this measurement for the cut size.

Fabric is usually not wide enough to make the cloth, so it is necessary to join 2 or 3 lengths of fabric or panels to create the necessary width. The number of panels you will need to make the cloth depends on the width of your fabric. Use the following chart to make this determination:

Fabric Width	Diameter of Tableskirt	Lengths Needed	Hem Allowance
36″	up to 69″	2	2″
	69″–105″	3	3″
44″–45″	up to 85″–87″	2	2″
	88″–131″	3	3″
48″–50″	up to 93″–97″	2	2″
	over 93″–97″	3	3″
54″–60″	up to 53″–59″	1	1″
	up to 105″–113″	2	2″
	over 105″–113″	3	3″

Measuring for Hem Treatment:
Calculate the distance around outside of the circle (the circumference) by measuring the diameter of the circle and multiplying by 3.14.

To determine the yardage needed, multiply the number of inches in each length (including the hem allowance) by the number of lengths. Divide this total by 36″. For example: 96″ cloth, fabric 45″ wide, 3 lengths needed. 96″ + 3 ″ = 99″ × 3 = 297″ ÷ 36″ = 8¼ yards. You should always add a few inches as a safety measure.

To determine fabric yardage for a semicircular table, measure the height and add half the tabletop diameter plus 8″. If this measurement is the same as or less than the width of the fabric purchased, the tableskirt can be made without piecing. The yardage needed is equal to twice the table height plus the table diameter. If narrower fabric is used, additional yardage is required for piecing.

If you are using a print fabric, you have to allow extra yardage for matching the pattern **repeat.** Add an amount equal to the repeat for each length of fabric needed except the first length.

Many special hem treatments, such as welts, ruffles, fringes, are discussed later in this chapter. For these, you will have to figure the circumference (the distance around the circle edge) of the tableskirt or cloth. To do so, multiply the diameter of the skirt in inches by 3.14.

1. Construct a square slightly larger than the cut size of the tableskirt or cloth by cutting the fabric into the number of lengths needed and matching any designs as necessary. Use one panel of fabric for the center panel of the cloth. (Tableskirts and cloths are never seamed down the center unless the cloth has a special design.) Pin the side panels to each side of the center panel. Sew the panel's right sides together, with ½″ seams. Press seams open.
2. Fold the cloth in half, matching the edges and seams. Fold again into quarters. Pin together to prevent slipping.
3. Determine half the diameter of the cloth (48″ on a skirt cut 96″, for example). Using a measuring tape or string tied to a pencil as a compass, measure out that distance on the fabric to draw a quarter circle. Cut through all four layers along the marked line.
4. Finish the basic tableskirt with a narrow ½″ hem.

Tableskirt with Welt

Tableskirt is photographed on page 53.

Fabric: Refer to chart for Basic Round Tableskirt or Cloth and add ¾ yard to cut bias for the welting.
Notions: ½" cording in an amount equal to the circumference of the tableskirt plus 4".

1. Follow the instructions for the Basic Round Tableskirt or Cloth, cutting the skirt the finished dimension with no hem allowance.
2. From the remaining fabric, cut **bias strips** 3" wide. Join the strips to create one piece of the length you need.
3. Make **welting** from the bias strips and cording. Sew the welting to the bottom of the skirt right sides together, with a ½" seam allowance. Trim seam allowance to ¼" and overcast, if desired.
4. Press the seam allowance toward the skirt.

Semicircular Tableskirt with Shirred Welt

Tableskirt photographed on page 27 is for semicircular table, 36" diameter, 32" high.

Fabric: *Main fabric*—3 yards 54" or wider or 5 yards for 44" to 45" (for table photographed); *contrast fabric for welting*—2 yards 54" or wider or 3 yards 44" to 45".

Notions: ²²/₃₂" cording—5 yards; 2" to 3" self-gripping fastener tape (optional); batting (optional).

1. To determine the pattern for your table, follow the preceding measuring directions for the Basic Round Tableskirt or Cloth. Divide the pattern for a whole cloth in half and

add 8" to the diameter edge. The cord suggested here (²²/₃₂") adds about 1" to the length of the tableskirt, so provide for this amount plus seam allowances in your planning.

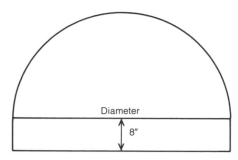

2. Cut the cloth. If fabric is 54" to 60" wide with no specific direction to the weave or pattern, cut with the diameter of the skirt along the selvage. If fabric is narrower or has a specific design, piece as for a Basic Round Tableskirt or Cloth.
3. Cut contrast fabric into **bias strips** 4" wide and seam to a length of 2½ times the circumference of the semicircular skirt. (For the skirt photographed, we used 12½ yards.)
4. Make the **welting** by sewing the bias over the cording. To shirr, sew for 1 yard, stop, and then gather up the amount. Continue in this manner until all the fabric is shirred over the cord.
5. Sew the welting to the right side of the skirt. You may need to stop sewing periodically and adjust the welting, as it tends to pucker up as you sew. At the ends, trim only the cording to the skirt edge. Tuck in the ends of the fabric and sew closed.
6. If the skirt was not cut with the diameter along the selvage, make a narrow hem there.
7. Lay the skirt over the table with the 8" **drop** over the back edge. Bring the extra fabric around to the back of the table and create a **miter** fold at each corner. Self-gripping fastener tape may be sewn here to hold the corners in place.
8. If the skirt has too sharp a line when it drops over the table edge, cut a piece of batting the size of the tabletop plus a 3" drop.

Tableskirt with Bias and Rick Rack

Tableskirt is photographed on page 69.

Fabric: Refer to chart under Basic Round Tableskirt or Cloth in this chapter.
Notions: 1" wide bias tape in an amount equal to the cir-

cumference of the skirt, plus 12″ for piecing; medium or jumbo rick rack in an amount equal to the circumference of the skirt plus 4″.

1. Construct the tableskirt as in Steps 1 to 3 of the preceding instructions for a Basic Round Tableskirt or Cloth.

2. Bind the bottom edge of the skirt with bias tape. Sew right side of the bias to wrong side of the skirt along the fold line, ½″ up from the cut edge of the skirt.

3. Fold the bias tape along the seamline, bringing it to the right side of the skirt. 1″ of the bias tape will be on the right side of the skirt. Pin the bias in place and topstitch close to the upper folded edge, easing as necessary.

4. Apply the rick rack over the top edge of the bias tape.

Lined Tableskirt with Accordion-Pleated Hem

Tableskirt is photographed on page 29.

Fabric: *Face fabric*—refer to the chart in this chapter for a Basic Round Tableskirt or Cloth. For a tableskirt that spreads out, or "breaks," onto the floor, add 4″ to the skirt diameter; *pleated hem*—fabric enough to cut strips on the straight grain 6″ wide by three times the skirt circumference. If you want this lined tableskirt to be fully reversible, choose a hem fabric without an obvious right or wrong side; *lining fabric*—amount equal to face fabric.

1. Cut and sew the fabric strips for accordion pleating. Make a narrow hem on one long edge. You will have to locate a professional pleater to have the strip finished with heat-set pleats (see Source Listing).

2. Construct a tableskirt following Steps 1 to 3 of the preceding instructions for a Basic Round Tableskirt or Cloth. When sewing the lining fabric, leave a 12″ opening in one seam for turning.

3. With right sides together, sew the accordion-pleated hem around the circumference of the tableskirt (not the lining) with a ⅜″ seam. Make an **enclosed seam** where the ends join.

4. Pin the lining to the face fabric, right sides together. Sew around the tableskirt circumference with a ½″ seam.

5. Turn the skirt through the opening in the lining seam and press. **Slip stitch** to close the opening.

Tableskirt with Pleated Ruche Hem

Tableskirt is photographed on page 35 and page 68.

Fabric: Refer to chart under Basic Round Tableskirt or Cloth in this chapter, subtracting 6″ from the total finished diameter of the skirt. You will need four additional yards for the hem treatment on a cloth up to 96″. For a considerably larger or smaller cloth, adjust yardage accordingly.

1. Cut and sew the cloth according to instructions for the Basic Round Tableskirt or Cloth, Steps 1 to 3.

2. From remaining fabric, cut **bias strips** 5″ wide. Join together to make a strip 3 times the circumference of the cloth. Press this bias strip in half lengthwise, wrong sides together. Machine baste ¼″ in from the raw edge. Pleat the bias strip, making pleats 1″ deep with a 3″ return between each fold.

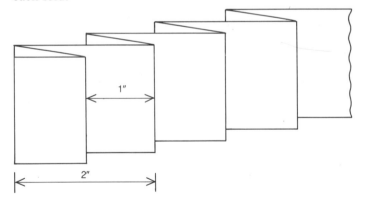

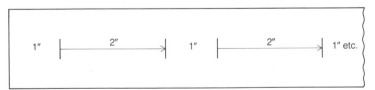

Pin pleats, baste, press, and stitch over previous basting line.

3. Sew the pleated strip to the bottom edge of the tableskirt with right sides together, using a ½″ seam allowance. Where the ends of the pleated strip meet, interfold pleats so that the raw edges fall into the folds.

Tableskirt with Top-Applied Ruffle

Tableskirt is photographed on page 14.

Fabric: Refer to the chart for a Basic Round Tableskirt or Cloth in this chapter, subtracting 21″ from the desired diameter of the skirt (before hemming). In addition, for the ruffle, you will need fabric to cut strips 13″ wide by 2½ times the circumference of the skirt.

1. Make a tableskirt following the preceding instructions for a Basic Round Tableskirt or Cloth, but adjust the diameter of the skirt to 21″ less than the desired diameter (before hemming).

2. From the remaining fabric, cut strips for the ruffle, each 13″ deep. Sew the strips together to make a circle. The finished strip should be 2½ times the circumference of the skirt.

3. Make narrow hems on both edges of the ruffle strip. (A hemmer foot is helpful.)

4. **Gather** 1″ down from the top edge and fit the ruffle to the circumference of the tableskirt hem.

5. Pin the ruffle to the right side of the skirt so that the gathering line of the ruffle is about ¼″ above the edge of the skirt. Sew through the gathering stitches.

Basic Tableskirt with Festooned Overskirt

Tableskirt is photographed on page 55.

Fabric: *Underskirt and bows*—refer to the chart for Basic Round Tableskirt or Cloth in this chapter, adding 7″ to the skirt diameter for the "break" onto the floor; *overskirt*—refer to chart for Basic Round Tableskirt or Cloth, cutting the skirt 5″ shorter than the actual length to the floor.

Notions: Five 1½″ button forms to cover with fabric; single cord shirring tape in an amount equal to the circumference of the skirt plus 4″; five self-gripping fastener tape spots.

1. Make an underskirt following the preceding instructions for a Basic Round Tableskirt or Cloth.

2. From underskirt fabric, make bows by cutting 10 **bias strips,** each 9″ wide by 22″ long.

3. Fold the bias strips lengthwise, wrong sides together, and stitch. Press so that the seam falls down the center of each strip.

4. Fold each end to the center, overlapping slightly, and stitch by hand. **Gather** the center of each strip to create a bow.

5. Attach two strips at right angles. Stitch by hand to secure the pieces. Finish with a covered button, sewing it into the center of the bow.

6. To make the overskirt, follow Steps 1 to 3 of the instructions for a Basic Round Tableskirt or Cloth.

7. Apply single shirring tape all around the bottom edge of the overskirt, folding the fabric over the tape as you sew to enclose the tape in a hem.

8. Lay the overskirt on the table. Divide it into five equal segments. Measure down from the edge of the table 4″ on each of the five segments and mark the position with a pin or chalk.

9. From the same overskirt fabric, cut five rectangles, each 2″ × 3″. Sew, turn, and press to make the tabs, 3″ in length and ½″ wide. Using one tab as a test length, gather the overskirt from the bottom edge to the pin or chalk mark to create a festoon.

10. Sew one end of each of the five tabs onto the wrong side of the overskirt at the pin or chalk mark.

11. Attach self-gripping fastener tape "spots" with looped side on one end of each tab, and the fuzzy side on the right side of the cloth at each of the positions marked in Step 9. Tabs and self-gripping fastener tape will allow you to gather up the overskirt at the five points to form festoons. (If you are doing this skirt for a party or for short-lived holiday use, you can simply attach the tabs to the skirt with large safety pins. This will eventually cause damage to the fabric, however, and is not recommended for long-term use.)

12. Using the cord encased in the shirring tape, gently gather the overskirt to pull it in evenly around the table. This shirring will keep the "poufs" turned under. (*Do not cut the string.* Conceal the string in the folds of the fabric. When you are ready to launder, dry clean, or store the overskirt, release the shirring tape to allow the skirt to lie perfectly flat.)

13. Once the skirt has been evenly shirred all around, bring the tabs up over the skirt from beneath, adjust the folds, and fasten the tabs to the self-gripping fastener tape on the overskirt.

14. Stitch by hand or pin the bows to each of the five attachment points. The bows should conceal the tabs and complete skirt.

Mitered Round Tableskirt with Bias Hem

Tableskirt is photographed on page 47.

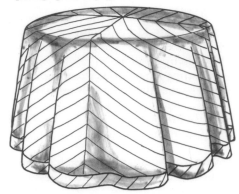

Fabric: 1½ times the amount of fabric indicated in the chart for a Basic Round Tableskirt or Cloth in this chapter. We suggest you choose fabric 54″ to 60″ wide; if you use narrower fabric, add two extra yards.

1. To make a pattern for the quarter circle needed to construct this cloth, determine half the diameter of the cloth and measure that distance on a large square of paper using a measuring tape or string tied to a pencil.

2. Cut four quarters from the fabric as illustrated. A stripe should be centered at the point of each quarter circle. (If you're using fabric narrower than 54″, the shaded section of the circle should be cut from the fall-away or from the extra fabric.)

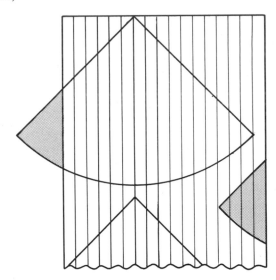

3. Sew two quarters together, matching the stripes along the seams. Repeat for the other two quarters. Then sew the two halves together, carefully matching the centers and stripes.

4. To allow for the hem treatment, trim the circle to the tableskirt diameter minus 2″.

5. Cut 3 ″ **bias strips** from the fall-away and the remaining fabric. Join them to make a strip equal in length to the circumference of the tableskirt plus 16″.

6. Press the bias strip in half lengthwise, wrong sides together, and machine baste ¼″ from the raw edge.

7. With right sides together, sew the bias strip to the bottom edge of the tableskirt, easing the bias onto the skirt (i.e., put more bias strip onto the circle than the circumfer-

ence of the circle actually measures). Make a bias seam where the ends meet.

8. Trim the seam allowance to ¼″ and overcast the raw edges. Press the seam allowance toward the skirt.

Round Tablecloth with Scalloped Edge

Tablecloth is photographed on page 107.

Fabric: Refer to chart for a Basic Round Tableskirt or Cloth in this chapter.

Notions: Single-fold bias tape in an amount equal to 1⅓ times the circumference of the cloth.

1. Follow Steps 1 to 3 under preceding instructions for a Basic Round Tableskirt or Cloth.

2. **Enlarge** diagram pattern, following the scale indicated. The diagram represents one-quarter of the total circle, but you need to cut out the full circle for your pattern. To do this, draw one quadrant at a time, either on brown wrapping paper or directly on the fabric, flipping the quarter pattern piece and matching the edges as you go. Cut the hem edge of the tableskirt according to this pattern.

3. **Bind** the raw edges with bias tape.

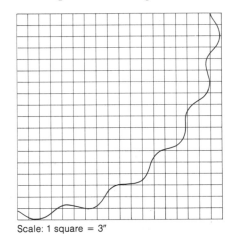

Scale: 1 square = 3″

Constructing a Basic Square Tablecloth

Measure the width of the tabletop and add twice the desired **drop.** This total is both the width and the length of the cloth. Add the needed hem allowance to determine the cut size of the unfinished cloth.

Use the chart and yardage information for a Basic Round Tableskirt or Cloth in this chapter, to determine the yardage needed.

1. Construct a square slightly larger than the cut size of the tableskirt or cloth by cutting the fabric into the number of lengths needed and matching any designs as necessary. Use one panel of fabric for the center panel of the cloth. (Tableskirts and cloths are never seamed down the center unless the cloth has a special design.) Pin the side panels to each side of the center panel. Sew the panel, right sides together, with ½″ seams. Press seams open.

2. Finish the basic tableskirt with a narrow ½″ hem.

Square Tablecloth with Bias Fabric Trim

Tablecloth is photographed on page 50.

Fabric: *Main fabric*—a square of fabric in the necessary width (if the desired square is larger than the width of the fabric you are using, use the chart for a Basic Round Tableskirt or Cloth in this chapter, to determine yardage); *contrast trim fabric*—amount to make a bias strip 3″ wide by the perimeter of the tablecloth plus 10″. (¾ to 1 yard is usually sufficient.)

1. Cut a square in the desired size from main fabric. If piecing is necessary because of the width of the fabric, consult the instructions for Constructing a Basic Square Tablecloth.

2. Cut 3″ wide **bias strips** from contrast trim fabric. Piece them to make a strip equal to the perimeter of the cloth plus 10″ to allow for matching and **mitering** corners.

3. Apply the bias strip to the cloth following the instructions for Binding Outward Corners in "Tools, Terms, and Techniques." When the bias strip is folded to turn the corner, allow the folded edge to extend approximately ¼″ beyond the top raw edge. This accommodates the wider width of bias used on this cloth.

Square Tablecloth with Binding and Patchwork Corners

Tablecloth is photographed on page 61.

Fabric: A square of fabric in desired width for tablecloth (if the desired square is larger than the width of the fabric you are using, refer to the chart under Basic Round Tableskirt or Cloth in this chapter, to determine yardage); *patchwork motifs*—¼ yard tablecloth fabric and ½ yard contrast fabric.

Notions: 1″ wide bias tape in an amount equal to the perimeter of the cloth plus 10″.

1. Cut a square the desired size from fabric. If piecing is necessary because of the width of the fabric, consult the instructions for Constructing a Basic Square Tablecloth.

2. Bind the edges with wide bias tape, following instructions for Binding Outward Corners in "Tools, Terms, and Techniques." When the bias is folded to turn the corner, allow the folded edge to extend approximately ¼″ beyond the top raw edge. This accommodates the greater width of bias used on this cloth.

3. For each one of four patchwork blocks, cut a square of the main tablecloth fabric, four squares of contrast fabric, eight triangles of main fabric, and eight triangles of contrast fabric. See pattern, page 151.

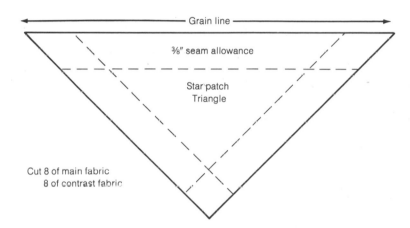

Grain line

⅜″ seam allowance

Star patch Triangle

Cut 8 of main fabric
8 of contrast fabric

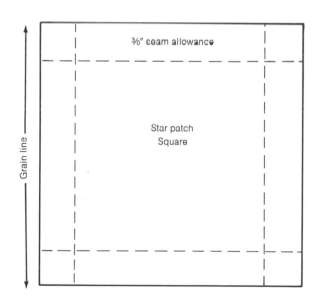

⅜″ seam allowance

Grain line

Star patch Square

Cut 1 of main fabric
4 of contrast fabric

4. To make patchwork blocks, begin by joining a triangle of each fabric along one short edge to form eight larger triangles, using a ⅜″ seam.

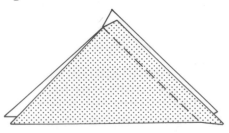

5. Next, make four squares from the pieced triangles by stitching the long edges together. Be sure colors alternate and intersecting seams match.

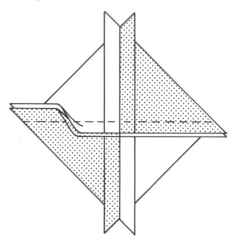

6. For the center row of patchwork, join two pieced squares to the main tablecloth fabric square at sides. Be sure colors alternate; check before stitching.

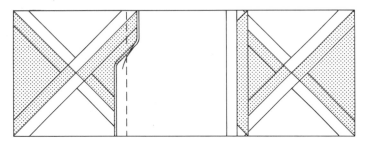

7. For each top and bottom row of patchwork, join two squares of contrast fabric to each pieced square at sides. Check that colors alternate before stitching.

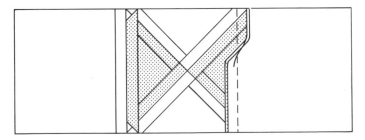

8. To complete the block, stitch the three rows together. Intersecting seams should match.

9. To make squares larger for tablecloth, cut two border strips 1¾″ by 6¾″ (including ⅜″ seam allowance) from contrast fabric and stitch to opposite sides of the patchwork block, right sides together, using ⅜″ seams. Press seams open.

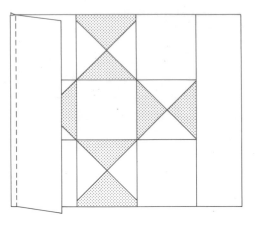

10. Cut two border strips 1¾″ by 8¾″ (including ⅜″ seam allowance) from contrast fabric and stitch them to the other two sides of the patchwork block. Press seams open.

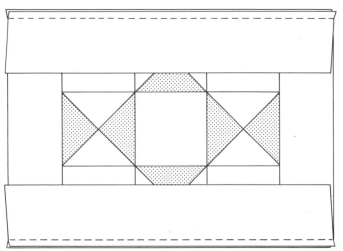

11. Press under ⅜″ on all outer edges of block.

12. Pin the patchwork squares to the corners of the tablecloth, placing them 2″ in from the edge of the binding. Stitch them in place close to the pressed edge.

Constructing a Basic Rectangular Tableskirt or Cloth

Measure the length, width, and height of the table as illustrated. The finished cloth will be:

Width + 2 times Height = width of the cloth
Length + 2 times Height = length of the cloth

Using the chart and yardage information under the instructions for a Basic Round Tableskirt or Cloth, determine the yardage needed.

Make the rectangular tableskirt by following Steps 1 and 2 under instructions for Constructing a Basic Square Tablecloth, page 150.

Rectangular Tableskirt with Self-Welt
Tableskirt is photographed on page 49.

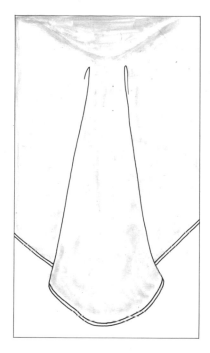

Fabric: Refer to Constructing a Basic Rectangular Tableskirt or Cloth, immediately preceding. Add an extra ¾ yard for welting.
Notions: ⁵⁄₃₂″ cording—amount equal to the perimeter of the tableskirt plus 4″.

1. Follow Step 1 under instructions for a Basic Round Tableskirt or Cloth in this chapter.
2. Round off the four corners as illustrated:

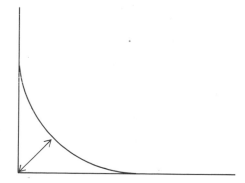

3. Prepare the **welting** and stitch to the bottom edge of the tableskirt, right sides together. Trim the seam allowance to ¼″, **overcast** the edges, and press toward the tableskirt.

Table Runners

Runners are a versatile tabletop accessory that can overlay a tablecloth or tableskirt or be used alone to accent the natural beauty of your table. A runner requires less fabric than a cloth or skirt and can be used for purely decorative purposes or as a long placemat.

Most runners are at least 12″ wide. They can, of course, be cut to any length you desire, as you will see in the projects that follow.

Tea Toweling Runner with Lace Trim
Runner photographed on page 58 is 72″ × 12″.

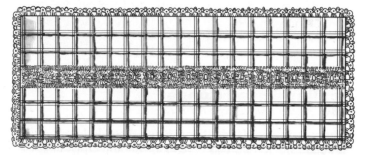

Fabric: Tea toweling the length desired plus 4″ to 6″ to allow for shrinkage.
Notions: Lace edging in an amount equal to the perimeter of the runner plus 4″; lace band trim for center of runner in an amount equal to the length of the runner plus 4″.

1. **Preshrink** tea toweling.
2. If you are making a runner narrower than tea toweling width, cut and seam the runner lengthwise with a **flat-felled seam** through the center, in order to narrow the toweling to the desired width. Sew lace trim over the seam.
3. Trim the toweling to the desired length, adding a hem allowance on both ends. Hem short ends of runner and sew lace edge trim on all four sides.

Lace Runner
Runner is photographed on page 48.

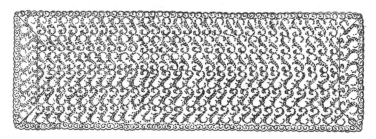

Fabric: To determine the amount of lace panel to purchase, add the desired length of the runner and the width of the lace panel, plus 8″ to 10″ for mitering.

1. Cut the lace panel the desired length. Split the remaining piece in half through the center of the panel, as illustrated.
2. Pin one half panel across one end of the runner so that cut edge of runner extends ½″ or more. To ensure that

both corners end at the same point of the design, center a lace motif across the width.

3. Turn under the raw edge of the half panel at a pleasing point in the pattern, **mitering** at the corners.

4. Stitch the mitered piece in place using a wide, close zig-zag stitch, or sew by hand, overlapping lace.

5. Trim away any excess fabric on the wrong side.

6. Repeat Steps 2 to 5 for other end.

Scallop Edged Runner
Runner photographed on page 107 is 72" × 13".

Fabric: 2 yards of fabric that can be **railroaded.**

Notions: Single-fold bias tape in an amount equal to 1⅓ times the perimeter of the runner.

1. Enlarge the diagram pattern, following the scale indicated. To lengthen or shorten the table runner, add or subtract length at the fold line on the diagram pattern. Cut the edges of the runner according to this pattern.

2. Bind the raw edges with bias tape.

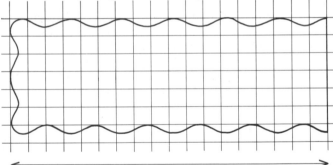

Lengthwise grain of fabric (crosswise grain if fabric width is greater than runner length)

Scale: 1 square = 2"

Table Runner with Christmas Appliqué
Runner photographed on page 65 is 44" × 14".

Fabric: *Face fabric*—½ yard of fabric 44" wide, or wider if length of runner is to be no longer than width of fabric, or an amount equal to desired length of **railroaded** fabric; *lining fabric*—same amount as face fabric; *remnants*—10" × 14" green for leaves and 8" × 4" red for berries.

Notions: Extrawide double-fold bias tape in an amount equal to the perimeter of the runner plus 4"; polyester batting—a piece slightly larger than the runner size.

1. Enlarge the runner diagram to make a pattern. Adjust the pattern at the fold line to create the desired length and cut out runner fabric and lining.

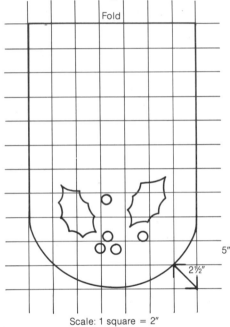

Fold

5"

2½"

Scale: 1 square = 2"

2. Cut the leaves and berries from remnant fabrics. **Appliqué** in place at each end of the runner.

3. Align the two layers of fabric, wrong sides together, with the batting in between. Pin and baste layers together along the raw edges.

4. Bind the raw edges with bias tape.

Scale: 1 square = ¼"

Cut 10 Berries   Cut 4 Leaves (2 reversed)

Placemats

Like runners, placemats can be used either alone on the tabletop or over a cloth. The size of placemats can vary but most fall into the range of 12" to 14" deep by 16" to 18" wide. The placemats in this section cover a broad variety, from simple to more complicated styles.

Bordered Placemat

Placemats photographed on page 63 are 12" × 18".

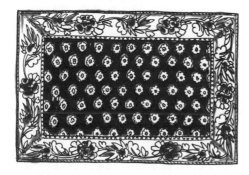

Fabric per placemat: 13" × 19" piece for top; 13" × 19" piece for back; 2 yards of border fabric (we have used a border 2½" wide).

Notions per placemat: Polyester batting—13" × 19."

1. Quilt the top fabric with batting and backing fabric. If you have a walking foot for your machine, use it in this step.

2. Arrange the border strip around the quilted piece, allowing a ½" seam allowance on the outside edge of the placemat. **Miter** the corners of the border strip.

3. Turn under and pin the raw inside edge of the border. Stitch close to this fold.

4. Stitch around the placemat close to the outside edge but not at the edge. Trim only the quilted fabric to ⅛" less than the finished size of the placemat.

5. Turn the border strip to the back side of the placemat along the outside line of the border design. Turn under the raw edge and pin. Stitch from the right side on the previous stitching line, catching the hem on the back side.

6. Slip stitch or topstitch the mitered corners in place.

Churn Dash Design Patchwork Placemats

Placemats are photographed on page 61.

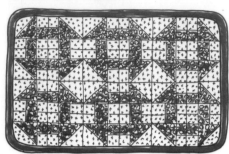

Fabric per placemat: ½ yard main fabric (A)—44″ to 45″ wide; ¼ yard contrast fabric (B)—44″ to 45″ wide; ⅝ yard backing fabric (C)—44″ to 45″ wide.

Notions per placemat: 2 yards extrawide double-fold bias tape; polyester batting—13″ × 19″.

1. For each one of the six churn dash patchwork blocks, cut four triangles of Fabric A, four triangles of Fabric B, four bars of Fabric A, four bars of Fabric B, and one square of Fabric A.

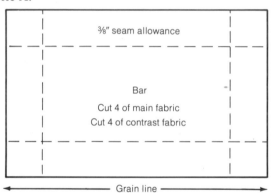

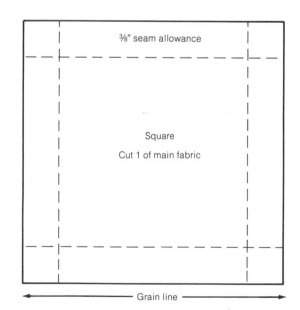

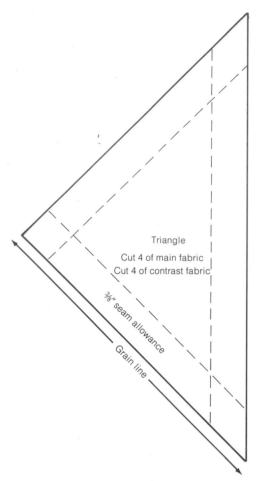

2. Piece the triangles by stitching each Fabric A triangle to a Fabric B triangle along the long edge, forming a square (use ⅜″ seams). You should have four pieced squares.

3. Piece the bars by stitching each Fabric A bar to a bar of Fabric B along the long edge, forming a square. You should have four pieced squares.

4. For the center row of patchwork, join two bar-pieced squares to the unpieced square of Fabric A. Be sure colors alternate; check before stitching.

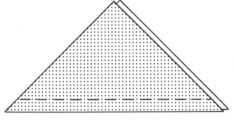

5. For each top and bottom row, join two triangular-pieced squares to one bar-pieced square at the sides. (The seam on the bar-pieced square should be horizontal.) Check the color placement before stitching.

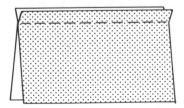

6. To complete the block, stitch the three rows together. Be sure intersecting seams match.

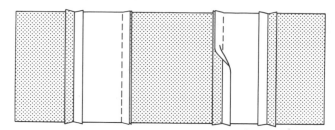

7. To construct the front of the placemat, join two patchwork blocks, right sides together, with ⅜″ seams. Repeat with the other blocks, creating three rectangles, then stitch the three rectangles together.

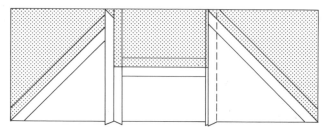

8. Lay the placemat top over the back piece, wrong sides together, with the batting in between and pin. Baste layers together along raw edges.
9. Round off the corners of the patchwork and trim the back and the batting until they are even with the front.
10. Bind raw edges with bias tape.

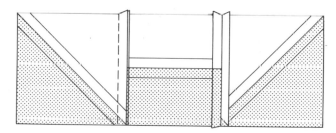

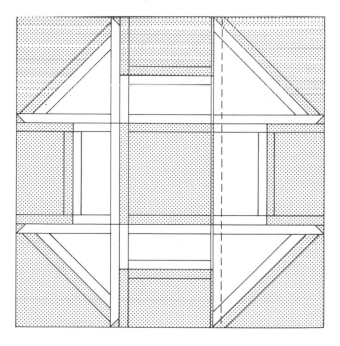

Balloon Placemats
Placemats are photographed on page 51.

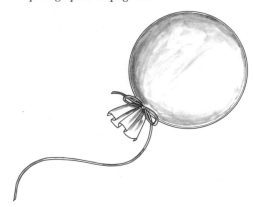

Fabric per placemat: ½ yard.
Notions per placemat: 1½ yards spaghetti cording or ribbon; polyester batting—16″ x 16″.

1. Enlarge diagram for balloon and base. Cut out the fabric shapes as directed.

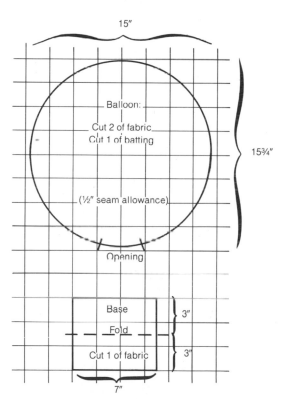

Scale: 1 square = 2″

15″

Balloon:
Cut 2 of fabric
Cut 1 of batting

15¾″

(½″ seam allowance)

Opening

Base   3″
Fold
Cut 1 of fabric   3″

7″

2. Using a ½″ seam allowance, stitch balloon pieces, right sides together, with batting pinned to one side. Leave an opening as indicated to allow for turning and inserting base.
3. Trim away the batting to the stitching line. Trim the fabric to ¼″. Clip all around, turn, and press.
4. To make the balloon base, fold cut fabric on the fold line, right sides together. Sew ½″ seams on the short sides. Trim the seam allowances to ¼″, turn, and press.
5. Gather along the open edge of the base to fit the opening in the balloon. Insert the base ½″ into the opening. **Slip stitch** the edges of the balloon to the base on both sides.

6. Topstitch around the balloon ¼″ from the edge.
7. Tie with spaghetti cording, leaving one end long.

Dishcloth Placemat with Lace Trim
Placemats are photographed on page 116.

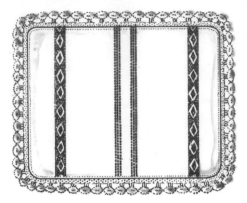

Fabric per placemat: Purchased dishcloth.
Notions per placemat: Narrow crochet lace trim in an amount equal to the perimeter of the dishcloth plus 4″.

Preshrink dishcloth. Sew the crochet trim around the outside edge of the dishcloth.

Napkins

Napkins are easy-to-make accessory items and the varieties are almost endless. The size can range from a small cocktail napkin to a large dinner size, 22″ × 22″. It's more economical to let the width of the fabric you've chosen determine the finished napkin size. Some fabric widths can accommodate three napkins across, and make the most sense when the cost per yard is high or the budget is low. Napkins can be finished simply with a double hem, or they can be embellished with any one of a number of trims.

Basic Square Napkin
Napkin is photographed on page 63.

Fabric: Squares of fabric the desired size plus hem allowance.

To hem napkin squares, turn ¼″ to the wrong side. Turn up again and stitch in place. If you have a hemmer foot attachment for your sewing machine, you can use it for this step.

Basic Square Napkin with Lace Trim
Napkin is photographed on page 44.

Fabric: Squares of fabric the desired size plus hem allowances, or purchased napkins.
Notions: ¾″ to 2½″ wide lace trim in an amount equal to one side of the square plus 2″ per napkin.

1. Make a Basic Square Napkin following the instructions above.
2. Sew lace trim to one side of napkin so that the lace extends over the napkin edge by ¼″. Turn lace under at each end of the napkin and stitch in place.

Tea Towel Napkin with Crochet Lace Trim
Napkin is photographed on page 58.

Fabric: Tea toweling—use the width of the toweling as a guide for the napkin size and allow an extra 3″ in length to allow for shrinkage and hems.
Notions: Crochet lace trim in an amount equal to the perimeter of the napkin plus 3″.

1. **Preshrink** tea toweling.
2. Make a Basic Square Napkin, following the preceding instructions.
3. Sew the crochet lace trim around the outside edge. Based on the trim chosen, sew to the right or the wrong side of the napkin, stitching over the previous hemstitching line if possible.

Square Napkin with Wide Bias Trim
Napkin is photographed on page 50.

Fabric: *Main fabric*—squares of fabric the desired size; *contrast fabric*—enough to make a bias strip 3″ wide by the perimeter of the napkin plus 3″. (1 yard of 44″ to 45″ fabric should be enough for four napkins up to 24″ square.)

1. Cut 3″ wide **bias strips** from contrast fabric. Piece them together, following the pattern of the fabric, if necessary to make a strip equal to the perimeter of the napkin plus 3″.
2. Using a ½″ seam allowance, apply the bias strip to the napkin, following the directions for Binding Outward Corners, page 138. When the bias is folded to turn the corner, allow the folded edge to extend ¼″ beyond the top raw edge; this accommodates the wider width of bias used on this napkin.

Miscellaneous Tabletop Accessories

Roll baskets, bun warmers, tea cozies, and napkin rings are just some of the special extras you can sew for your table. We've included a selection of the more conventional items and some of the less expected, like cheerful balloon gift sacks for a child's party and a fabric wreath to coordinate with your holiday table. These items can make attractive gifts as well as add charm to your own home, and because they are sewn from small amounts of fabric, they're a delightful and economical way to utilize those leftover bits and pieces from major sewing projects.

Napkin Rings of Bias-Covered Welting
Napkin rings are photographed on page 47.

Fabric: ½ yard for four napkin rings.
Notions: ½″ cording—2 yards for four napkin rings.

1. Cut a **bias strip** approximately 20″ long × 2¾″ wide.
2. Make a tube by sewing the strip lengthwise with a ½″ seam. Trim to ¼″ and turn.
3. To thread the cording through the tube, wrap a fabric scrap tightly around one end of the cord, as illustrated, so that it is smaller than the cording. Turn the end of the fabric down next to the cord and pin it with a large safety pin. Use safety pin to feed cord through the tubing, but when moving tubing down the cord, grab the end of the cord, not the safety pin, to keep pin in place.

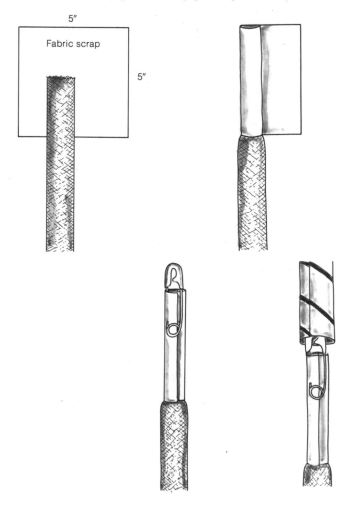

4. Close one end of the tube. Trim the other end to ½″ beyond the cording. Turn in ½″ of fabric and close up the end.
5. Tie the tube into a pretzel knot and insert the napkin.

Roll Basket Insert

Roll basket insert photographed on page 58 will fit 10" to 12" basket.

Fabric: 1½ yards tea toweling, or 1 yard 44" to 45" fabric.
Notions: 4 yards crochet lace trim; 2 snaps.

1. **Preshrink** tea toweling.
2. **Enlarge** pattern diagram.

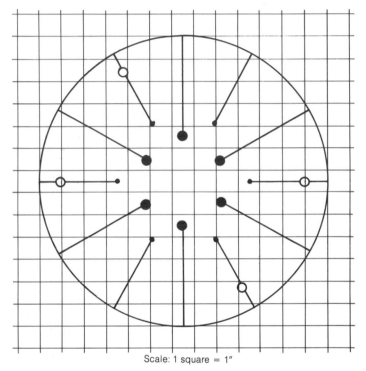

Scale: 1 square = 1"

3. Cut out three circles, centering each on the fabric design, if appropriate. Mark one circle with all the lines; mark another circle with long lines only and snap marks "x" and "o." Mark third circle with short lines only.
4. Make a ½" hem around the outside edge on each circle. Apply the lace trim to each circle.
5. Sew the snaps to the right side of the circle so marked; the ballside of the snap attaches at "o" and the socket side at "x."
6. Pin the wrong side of the circle with the long lines to the right side of the circle with all the lines, matching the long lines. Stitch through the long lines only, ending at the large dots.
7. Pin the right side of the circle with the short lines to the wrong side of the circle with all the lines, matching the short lines. (The circle with all lines is in the middle of the other two.) Stitch through the short lines only, ending at the small dots.
8. Snap the opposite sides together and place in the basket.

Roll Basket

Roll basket is photographed on page 62.

Fabric: Two fabric remnants, 12" × 14" of inside fabric; 12" × 24" of outside fabric. (More fabric will be needed if the ties are cut on the bias.)
Stiffening Support: Heavy cardboard, or plastic needlepoint canvas—8" × 14".

1. **Enlarge** diagram to make pattern piece.
2. Cut one pattern piece from each fabric. Cut eight strips, 1" × 10" from the fabric to be used on the outside. (If the fabric is a stripe or plaid design, you may wish to cut on the bias.)
3. Make ties by folding each strip in half lengthwise and then sewing along the length with a ¼" seam. Trim, turn, and press.
4. Place the ties on the right side of one piece of the fabric, at the square marks (see pattern) just inside the interior stitching lines on three sides, leaving them off the "open" end.
5. With the right sides together, sew the two main sections with ½" seams, leaving one end open. Trim the seam allowances to ¼"; clip the curves; turn; press. Topstitch close to the edge around the seamed area only.

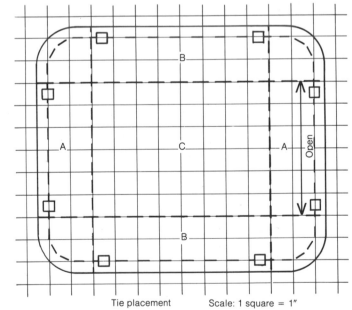

Tie placement   Scale: 1 square = 1"

6. Cut out the stiffening support pieces as follows: two pieces 5⅞" × 1⅞" (A); two pieces 7⅞" × 1⅞" (B); one piece 5⅞" × 7⅞" (C).
7. Mark one side of the basket with stitching lines, using a water soluble ink pen.
8. Insert one piece of stiffener A at the end opposite the opening. Stitch along the marking lines to enclose that piece.

9. Insert and sew stiffeners B and C in the same manner.
10. Insert the second stiffener A. Pin the two remaining ties in place. Turn under ½″ seam allowance and **slip stitch** the opening, catching the ties in the stitching. Topstitch close to the edge.
11. Finish off the raw ends of the ties with machine zigzagging.

Tea Cozy

Tea cozy is photographed on page 58.

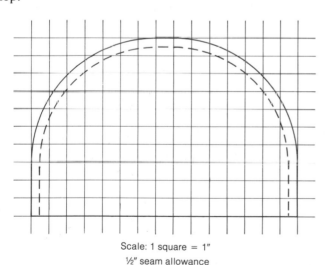

Fabric: 1 yard tea toweling, or ⅓ yard 44″ to 45″ fabric; ⅓ yard muslin.
Notions: 1 yard crochet lace trim; polyester batting—two pieces, each 11″ × 16″.

1. **Preshrink** tea toweling.
2. **Enlarge** diagram to make pattern piece.
3. Cut two rectangles, 11″ × 16″, from both the tea toweling and the muslin. Sandwich batting between fabric and muslin. **Quilt** them together (we followed the plaid lines). If you have a walking foot for your machine, use it in this step.

Scale: 1 square = 1″
½″ seam allowance

4. Cut out the tea cozy pattern from both quilted pieces, lining up the bottom of the tea cozy pattern with the stripe along the selvage of the toweling and centering the pattern on the design. *Do not cut off the* **selvage.** The material between the stripe and the edge of the toweling is your seam allowance. (Don't forget to include a ½″ seam allowance on the pattern if you are using cut yardage.)
5. Make a loop for the top from the extra fabric, cut either on the bias or the straight **grain** of the fabric. Baste the loop at the center top of the tea cozy.

6. Sew the lace to one quilted piece along the seam allowance of the curved edge only.
7. Using a ½″ seam, sew the quilted pieces, right sides together, along the curved edge only. Trim the seam allowances to ¼″ and **overcast.** Turn the tea cozy right side out.
8. Press the seam allowance along the bottom edge to the inside. Hand- or machine-**stitch** the hem in place.

Balloon Gift Sack

Gift sack is photographed on page 51.

Fabric per sack: One piece 10″ × 14″.
Notions per sack: ¾ yard spaghetti cording or ribbon; fusible web—¾″ × 12″; fabric marking pen.

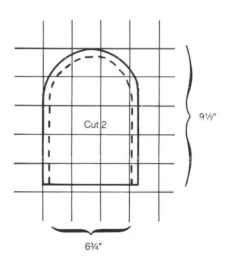

Cut 2

9½″

6¾″

Scale: 1 square = 2″
½″ seam allowance

1. **Enlarge** pattern for the sack and cut out as directed.
2. With right sides together, sew the two sack sections, leaving the bottom edges open. Trim the seam allowance to ¼″, clip the curve, turn, and press.
3. On the open edge, turn fabric under ¾″ toward the inside of the sack. Fuse the hem to the sack with fusible web.

Tabletop Accessories/161

4. Cut the folded edge with pinking shears.

5. Write a name on the sack with a fabric marking pen. Fill the sack with a gift or party favors and tie with spaghetti cording.

Buffet Roll-up

Buffet roll-up is photographed on page 65.

Fabric per roll-up: 22″ × 20″ piece for inside (A); 21″ × 16″ piece for outside (B); *remnants*—4″ × 12″ piece of green for leaves and 2″ × 4″ piece of red for berries.

Notions per roll-up: 3¼ yards double-fold bias tape; *fusible web*—2″ × 3″; *polyester batting*—4″ × 6″.

1. From Fabric A, cut a band 22″ wide × 4″ deep. Fold the band in half lengthwise, right sides together. Sew with a ½″ seam along the long edge. Trim the seam allowance to ¼″; press open. Turn right side out and press so that the seam falls in the center, not at an edge.

2. From both Fabrics A and B, cut out rectangles 20½″ wide × 15½″ deep. Round the corners slightly.

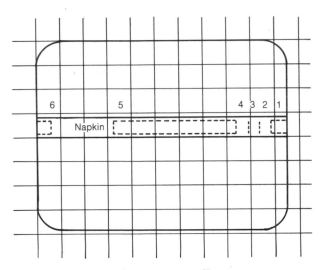

Scale: 1 square = 2″

3. Pin the seamed side of the band (Step 1) to the right side of the rectangle of Fabric A only, using the diagram as your placement guide. Starting at the right-hand edge, mark and pin the utensil slots. The first stitching line should be 1½″ from the raw edge; the other three utensil slot stitching lines should be 1¼″ apart. It is necessary to ease a little extra band across the 1¼″ distance on the rectangle to allow room for the utensils and, on the other side, for the napkin. From the fourth to the fifth stitching lines, the band is applied flat and the total distance covered is 9½″. The sixth and last stitching line is 1½″ from the left-hand edge.

4. After sewing all the vertical lines, stitch down the horizontal lines at each end and in the middle.

5. To make the ties, trace around the leaf pattern on the right side of half of the green fabric remnant and mark the veining. Trace a second leaf shape, keeping within the same half of the remnant piece. Place the traced half of the green fabric remnant over the other half, wrong sides together, and slip a piece of batting between the two layers. Pin or baste the two pieces together. Then stitch along the traced center lines with a narrow zigzag satin stitch; stitch the outside of the leaf shapes with a medium zigzag stitch. The outside stitching must be as close together as possible. Cut out the leaves as close to the outer stitching as possible without cutting the stitches. (If batting is visible, simply touch up with permanent green marker.)

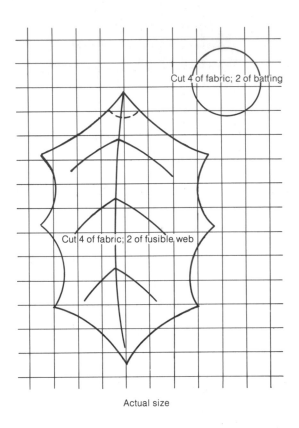

Cut 4 of fabric; 2 of batting

Cut 4 of fabric; 2 of fusible web

Actual size

Trace four berry shapes from the red fabric. Instead of batting, however, place pieces of fusible web between the layers and fuse. Cut out the berries on the traced lines *without* sewing them.

Cut a strip of bias tape 40″ long. Stitch the long edges together and sew a leaf at each end to make the tie.

Baste or fuse a berry to each side of both leaves where they join the tie. Stitch around the outer edge of the berries with a medium width, satin zigzag stitch.

6. On the right side of Fabric B, sew the center of the tie to the mark as shown on the diagram.

7. To make the roll-up, place Fabrics A and B wrong sides together. Baste together along the raw edges and **bind** with bias tape.

8. To roll up, turn in the top and bottom edges and roll, starting at the end with the utensils, and tie.

Plaid Wreath and Bow

Wreath is photographed on page 54.

Fabric: ¾ yard *each* of three different fabrics for wreath; ⅞ yard of 44″ to 45″ fabric for bow.

Notions: Bone ring for hanging; polyester fiberfill, 24 oz.

1. From each wreath fabric, fold the yardage for the greatest length on the bias. Cut along the bias fold. Using the larger piece, cut two strips one at a time so the first piece can be matched, if necessary, to the second where they will be seamed. Each strip should measure 7½″ wide by about 54″ long.

2. Seam the matching fabrics to make one long strip.

3. Fold each strip in half lengthwise with right sides together. Leaving a ½″ seam allowance, stitch the long edge. Trim and press the seam open.

4. Turn right side out. You now have three tubes.

5. Baste one end of each tube closed about 3″ from the end. Stuff with fiberfill to about 3″ from the other end.

6. Baste the wreath tubes together at one end. Braid the tubes, shaping the wreath as you braid.

7. To join the ends of the tubes, tuck one end of each tube into its corresponding end, turning under the raw edges. **Slip stitch** them together securely.

8. Sew the bone ring on the back of the wreath on the edge opposite the area where the tubes are joined.

9. To make the bow, cut two fabric pieces, each 14″ × 30″. Stitch the short ends of the pieces together to make a strip 14″ × 60″.

10. Fold the strip in half lengthwise with right sides together. Stitch the long edge with a ½″ seam allowance, leaving an opening in the center for turning. Press the seam open.

11. Bring the seam to the center of the bow, cut the ends in a "W" shape, and stitch them with a ½″ seam. Clip the corners and turn. Press with the seam at the center of the bow. Close the opening with **blind stitches.**

12. Tie the bow and attach it to the wreath in the area where the tubes are joined.

Window Treatments

It may surprise you to learn that window treatments are among the easiest of home decorating projects to make. All that is required is time, patience, and basic sewing skills. Since, however, most window dressings require considerable amounts of fabric as well as a substantial investment in trims, notions, and window hardware, it is best to plan carefully.

Success depends largely on accurate measurement and appropriate choices of fabric and style. After you have determined the treatment style you prefer, select and install the hardware in the window *before* taking the final measurements. It is also a good idea to read the instructions thoroughly before you shop, so that you understand the project and can make any changes you feel may be appropriate to your own specific design. When approached in this manner, window treatments can be quite simple to execute.

In this chapter, we offer a variety of projects. They fall into three basic categories: decorative shades, curtains, and draperies.

For many people, the traditional window shade is a green or white heavy paper or plastic sheet pulled down over the window to control light and ensure privacy. The fabric window shades that follow, however, are a far cry from practical, but unaesthetic, paper or plastic shades. While still allowing for privacy and light control, they add style to the room and, in the case of Roman and balloon shades, lend dimension and softness to the window. They can be used alone or in combination with curtains or draperies, with shutters, or with valances.

In this chapter we describe three different types of shades: the roller shade, the Roman shade, and the balloon shade. The roller shade is the simplest and is usually tailored. The Roman shade is similar in appearance to the roller shade when it is lowered, but in the raised position it falls into neat, horizontal folds. Balloon shades fall into swags and poufs in the raised position, and they give a softer look to the room.

Curtains and draperies are the most commonly used of all window treatments. They can be made in many attractive, diverse styles. Curtains are also among the simplest window treatments to sew. They attach by hooks, rings, or fabric tabs to a rod at the window, or they may have a fabric casing through which a rod is inserted. They are usually stationary, but could be closed manually. Short curtains have a more casual appearance. Full-length curtains lend an air of sophistication and luxury to the window.

Draperies tend to be heavier and more formal in appearance than curtains. They are usually lined and most often have pinch-pleated headings that are hung on rods by hooks or rings. Some draperies traverse the window. Others are simply stationary panels at each side of the window opening.

We have used valances as the sole window treatment, as well as combining them with roller shades (pages 73 and 94), and with a variety of curtains and drapery panels throughout the book.

This chapter includes a section with basic information pertaining to all curtains or draperies, whether they are to be lined, unlined, shirred, or pinch-pleated. That information is followed by individual projects. Note that, except in special instances, we have not specified the type or size of curtain rod to be used, as this consideration depends largely on your window. If there is an existing rod in your window —go ahead and use it; most standard rods will be accommodated by the casings we allow.

Roller Shades

Roller shades are both visually and technically the simplest in design of all the window shade varieties. They require the least sewing, the least fabric, and the least amount of work. Although they can be purchased ready-made and trimmed to fit your decorating scheme, we describe here how they can be made by the simple process of laminating a decorative fabric to shade cloth backing. If you have access to a shop which provides a laminating service, you might choose to have your fabric professionally laminated or vinylized. This option ensures the most professional looking shade.

Fabric roller shades can be made in several ways. The simplest is to purchase a prepackaged kit containing all the materials you will need (except for the decorative fabric). You can also purchase iron-on shade backing which is sold by the yard. Both the kits and the shade backing are sold in fabric, decorator, and window shops. If special shade backing is not available, heavy duty iron-on interfacing or fusible web with lining fabric can be used. When fusing roller shades, it is important to work on a large surface. A shade that hangs over the edge of a table or ironing board can be easily stretched or distorted. If you are not using a kit, you will need the necessary hardware including the roller, brackets, slat, and pull.

Roller shades are mounted at the window in one of two ways: conventional roll or reverse roll. With a conventional roll, the shade comes down from the back of the roller and fits closer to the window. This means that the wrong side of the shade will show on the roll unless a cornice or valance conceals it. With a reverse roll shade, the shade comes from the front of the roller and the fabric or face side always shows. For this installation, you will need reverse roll brackets. With either of these rolls, the shade can be installed inside the window frame to expose attractive woodwork, on the window frame, or on the wall for total coverage of the window area. For an inside mount, install the brackets 1½" to 2" from the top of the window, depending on the thickness of the rolled-up shade. On an outside mount, place the brackets at least 1½" to 2" beyond the window opening on each side.

When making roller shades, it is best to select closely woven, light- to medium-weight fabrics with a smooth surface. Avoid fabrics which are difficult to fuse, such as sheer, nubby, stretchy, or heavy fabrics. Try to make the shades from one width of fabric since seams tend to interfere with the smooth operation of the finished shade. If you do have to seam the fabric, center a full-width panel and add half of the additional fabric on either side. Adding a valance to a simple roller shade can make a very special window treatment. Although we have only photographed the scallop hemmed roller shade with two different valance styles, any of the valances in the chapter could be combined with any straight or decoratively hemmed shade.

The seam allowances are bonded to the face fabric with fusible web. If you have to piece the backing material, try to do so horizontally rather than vertically and piece by overlapping rather than seaming.

Hems on roller shades can be shaped, trimmed, or perfectly plain. Shaped hems follow a design or scallop pattern. These edges can be finished with a trim or they can be faced with fabric. The pocket for the wooden slat is planned about 4½" to 5" above the bottom edge of the shade. For a shade with a straight hem, make the slat pocket at the very bottom of the shade, by folding under the lower edge 1¾" and stitching 1½" from the fold.

Roller Shade with Scalloped Hem
Shades are photographed on page 73 and page 94.

Fabric: Yardage 3″ wider than the finished width and 12″ to 14″ longer than the finished length of the shade.

Notions: Iron-on shade backing, slightly larger than the shade fabric; double-fold bias tape—⅓ yard more than the width of the shade.

Tools and Hardware: Shade roller and brackets (heavy duty roller is best); one wooden slat for the bottom; staples or flat-headed tacks; one shade pull; T-square; glue or fray retardant (optional).

1. Accurately measure the window using a metal tape measure between the points where the outside edge of the brackets will fall. (If you will be making shades for two or more windows, be sure to measure *each* one.) Cut the roller to the size needed.

2. Working on a large flat surface, unroll the backing, paper side up, and peel off the paper liner. Note any special instructions that came with the shade backing.

3. Place the fabric, right side up, on top of the backing. Remove any loose threads that may be sandwiched between the decorator fabric and backing. Use a dry iron at the appropriate fabric setting (unless the manufacturer's backing directions say otherwise) and fuse the fabric and backing from the center out toward the edges. Let the shade cool completely. (We suggest that you try a sample before doing the entire shade.)

4. Lay the roller across the back of the shade. The finished width of the shade is equal to the visible wood part of the roller. Trim the side edges of the shade to this measurement using *sharp* scissors. Using a T-square, square off both ends of the shade so all corners are perfect right angles. If you want to guard against fraying edges, apply white glue with a cotton swab along the back edges, keeping the front of the shade clean, *or* apply to the edges the commercially available liquid that retards fraying.

5. Enlarge the scallop design and use it to cut the bottom edge of the shade. **Bind** the cut bottom edge with double-fold bias tape by gluing or sewing.

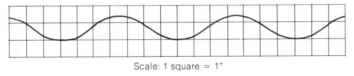

Scale: 1 square = 1″

6. To make the slat pocket, measure at least 4¼″ from the bottom edge of the shade. Fold the shade along this line, wrong sides together. Stitch across the shade 1¼″ from the fold line. Insert the slat.

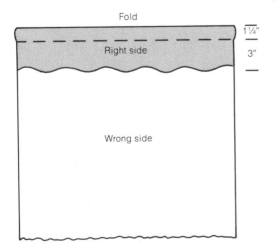

Fold

1¼″

Right side

3″

Wrong side

7. Place the roller over or under the shade according to the desired "roll." Be sure the top edge of the shade is aligned with the printed guideline on the roller. If the roller has no guideline, draw a straight line from one end to the other. Tape the shade to the roller to hold it in place temporarily, then attach the shade to the roller with staples or flat-headed tacks.

Scallop Edged Valance for Roller Shade
Valance is photographed on page 73.

Fabric: ½ yard fabric (1 yard if the rod plus the returns is longer than the width of the fabric); 1 yard lining.

Notions: Single-fold bias tape—½ yard more than the width of the valance.

Hardware: Standard adjustable rod.

1. Mount the rod on the window as desired. Measure the rod plus the returns.

2. Cut the fabric 15″ deep by the length of the rod plus the returns plus 1″.

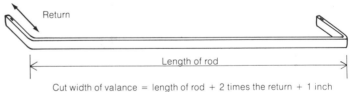

Return

Length of rod

Cut width of valance = length of rod + 2 times the return + 1 inch

Piece the fabric if necessary along each side of a center piece.

3. Enlarge the scallop design from the shade hem and trace it onto the decorator fabric, starting at the center of the valance and working to each end.

4. Fold the lining in half (½ yard by the width of the fabric). Place the decorator fabric piece on the top with the lowest point of the scallop about 1″ above the folded edge. Pin the fabrics together.

5. Trim the sides of the lining to match the top fabric. At the sides, press ½″ on both the fabric and lining to the wrong side. Topstitch the folded edges together. **Bind** the scalloped edge with bias tape.

6. Measure up from the bottom of the scallop to a distance of 13¾″ and trim off the top edge of the valance.
7. Press under 3¼″ to the wrong side of the valance. Sew across the valance 1¼″ from the folded edge to make the heading. Turn under ½″ on the raw edge. Pin this in place and stitch it close to the folded edge to make a casing.
8. Slip the finished valance over the installed rod.

Shaped Valance for Roller Shade

Valance is photographed on page 94.

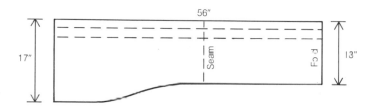

Fabric: 1½ yds of 44″ to 45″ fabric for a window up to 50″ wide. (See Curtains and Draperies basics, page 173, planning the valance unlined with a rod-pocket heading.)
Notions: Extrawide double-fold bias tape in an amount equal to the length of the valance.
Hardware: Standard adjustable rod.

1. Cut and seam together the valance panels as needed to allow 2½ times fullness. Fold in half and shape the bottom edge using the diagram below as a guide.

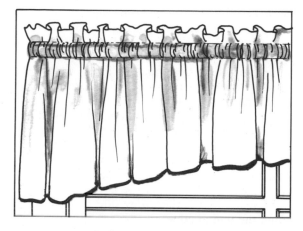

2. Finish the side edges and make the top rod-pocket heading (page 174).
3. **Bind** the bottom edge with extrawide double-fold bias tape.
4. Slip the finished valance over the installed rod.

Roman Shades

While Roman shades are similar to roller shades and have the same tailored look, they present a more elegant appearance. The Roman shade hangs smoothly when down, but when it is in the raised position, the fabric falls in graceful, horizontal folds.

The Roman shade, like the roller shade, is an economical window treatment. It requires only enough fabric to fill in the window area plus side, top, and bottom hems. Firmly woven fabrics of medium to heavy weights are the best choices. Lightweight fabrics must be lined to work well. Loose or open weave fabrics can be used as well, but they require extra care and time to construct.

The accordion effect of Roman shades is created by rings and cords attached on the back side of a shade. Rings can be sewn on individually or they can be attached by using Roman shade tape which has rings already sewn on at even intervals.

Roman shade tape or rows of rings should be placed at each side of the shade, with additional rows spaced 8″ to 12″ across the width of the shade. You may find it helpful to align the tape or rings with the window mullions. If you are installing individual rings, place a ring at the top and bottom of each row, with other rings spaced 5″ to 6″ apart. In any case, it is important for the rings, cords, and screw eyes to be perfectly aligned.

Lightweight traverse cord, Roman shade cord, or other nonstretch fine cord is rigged through the rings to raise and lower the shade. To estimate the cord yardage for each shade, add the length of a row of rings or tape, plus the width of the window, plus at least 3′ (which will hang down the side of the window), and multiply the result by the number of ring or tape rows across the shade. An awning cleat is attached to one side of the window to wind the cords on when the shade is raised. To make it easier to raise the shade to the desired height, the awning cleat can be installed upside down, and the cord knotted so that it hooks over the bottom of the cleat. (The cord can be knotted to accommodate more than one raised shade position.)

Unlined Roman Shade with Roman Shade Tape

Shades are photographed on page 42.

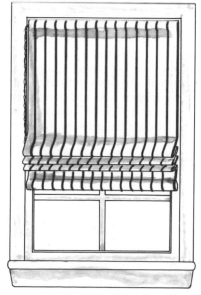

Fabric: Finished width of the shade plus 2″ by the finished length of the shade plus 11″.

Notions: Roman shade tape in the length of the fabric for each row, plus ½ yard to allow for cutting waste; cord for rigging shade (see above); self-gripping fastener tape or snap tape equal to the width of the mounting board, or staples, or flat-headed tacks.

Hardware: 1″ × 2″ board that is ¼″ narrower than finished width of the shade; screw eyes large enough to accommodate all the cords—one for each row of tape; small awning cleat and screws; two angle irons and screws; ⅜″ diameter brass or solid metal rod 1″ shorter than the finished width of the shade.

1. Cut the mounting board to ¼″ less than the width of the shade. The board can be covered with a lining fabric or painted before mounting, if desired.

For an inside mount, the board will be screwed directly into the top of the window frame or secured with angle irons into the sides of the frame.

For an outside mount, angle irons will be used to secure the board above the window either on the frame or the wall above it.

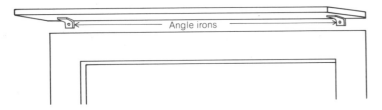

Angle irons

2. Cut the fabric 2″ wider than the finished width of the shade and 11″ longer than the finished length. If the fabric widths need to be joined, plan the seams to fall in front of a row of rings (tape). The shade must be a perfect rectangle, i.e., square corners and parallel sides. Use a T-square if necessary.

3. Turn under a 1″ hem on each side edge to the wrong side of the fabric. Baste in place.

4. Press up a 4″ bottom hem. Stitch across the shade 1½″ from the hem fold to make a rod pocket. Fold up another 4″ and press (4″ double hem). Do *not* stitch yet.

5. Measure up from the bottom and mark the finished length of the shade with pins along the top edge.

6. Pin the Roman shade tapes to the wrong side of the shade. Plan a tape at each side with the other tapes spaced evenly between them at 8″ to 12″ intervals. Start at the lower hem edge, placing the edge of the tape over the raw edge of the side hem ½″ from the outside edge, with the bottom ring at the top of the hem. Make sure the rows of tape are perfectly parallel to the sides of shade. Leave 1½″ of tape below the bottom ring.

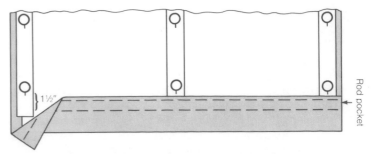

Rod pocket

Apply the shade tape up to the top edge of the shade. Remove any rings between the top raw edge and 3″ below the line marked for the finished top edge.

7. Sew the tapes to the shade using a zipper foot. Tapes tend to stretch and pucker. Test and adjust your stitch tension as needed.

8. Pin up the double hem, tucking in the ends of the tapes, and, keeping the rings free, stitch across the shade ¼″ down from the top fold.

9. Insert the rod through the rod pocket. **Slip stitch** the open edges at the sides, encasing the rod.

10. Prepare top of shade for mounting to board. *For a self-gripping fastener tape or a snap-tape mounting,* press a fold along the finished top edge line, wrong sides of the shade together. Sew the fuzzy side of the fastener tape (or socket side of the snap tape) to the wrong side of the shade ⅛″ down from the folded edge.

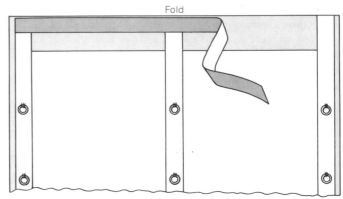

Fold

Trim away any extra shade fabric. The other side of the tape is fastened to the front edge of the mounting board with glue, staples, or tacks.

For staple attachment, trim the top edge of the shade to 1½″ beyond the line for the top finished edge and overcast the raw edge. Align the top front edge of the board with the finished top edge marks on the shade so that the shade extends 1¾″ over the top of the mounting board. Staple the fabric onto the top of the board.

11. Position the screw eyes in the bottom of the board above each row of rings.

12. Cut the cords to rig the shade. Each one will be a different length, but they must go up through a row of rings, across the top of the window through all the screw eyes they pass, and at least halfway down the opposite side of the window. Tie one end of each cord to the bottom ring.

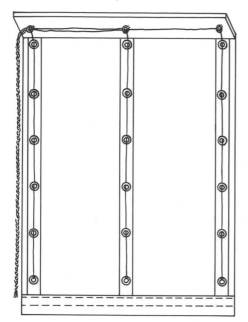

13. Mount the board with attached shade in the window. Lower the shade and adjust the strings so they draw up evenly. Knot the cords and trim off the excess. The cords can be braided together while the shade is in the down position.

14. Attach the awning cleat to the side of the window.

Lined Roman Shade with Individual Rings

Shades are photographed on page 40 and page 84.

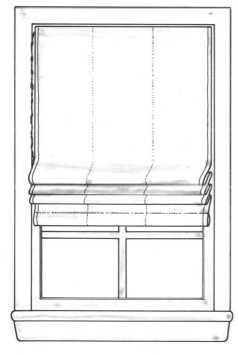

Fabric: *Face fabric*—an amount equal to the finished width of the shade plus 2", by the finished length of the shade plus 11"; *lining fabric*—same amount as the face fabric.

Notions: ½" diameter brass or plastic rings; cord for rigging shade (see page 167); self-gripping fastener tape or snap tape equal to the width of the mounting board, or staples, or flat-headed tacks; clear nylon thread (optional).

Hardware: 1" × 2" board —¼" narrower than the finished width of the shade; screw eyes large enough to accommodate all the cords. Use one for each row of tape; 1 small awning cleat and screws; 2 angle irons and screws; ⅜" diameter brass or solid metal rod ½" shorter than the finished width of the shade.

1. Follow Steps 1 and 2 under Unlined Roman Shade with Roman Shade Tape, page 167.

2. Cut the lining fabric the same length as the face fabric, and 1" narrower than the face fabric. If the lining must be seamed to achieve the correct width, plan the seam to fall in line with a seam in the face fabric or where a row of rings will be sewn.

3. On the face fabric press up (do *not* sew) a 4" double hem.

4. On the lining fabric, press up a 4" hem. Stitch across the hem 1½" from the hem fold, making a rod pocket. Backstitch well at the ends. Fold another 4" and press to make a 4" double hem.

5. With right sides together, place the lining so that the bottom of its hem is ¼" above the hem edge of the face fabric. Match the side edges, pin, and sew together with ¾" seams.

6. Lay out the shade with the lining side up. Make a small slit, ½" to ¾" wide, at one end of the rod pocket, cutting through the top layer of lining *only*. The rod will be inserted here later.

7. Turn the shade right side out and press. The lining is narrower than the face fabric, so ½" of face fabric will extend to the lining side of the shade.

8. From the lining side, stitch the bottom hems in place 3¾" up from the bottom edge of the face fabric.

9. On the right side of the shade, measure up from the hem edge and mark the finished length of the shade at the top edge of the shade with pins. Fold the top down to the lining side along the row of pins and press in place. Measure 1¾" from this line toward the raw edge at the top of the shade, and trim off the excess fabric and lining. Overcast the raw edges together.

10. On the lining side of the shade, mark the placement of the rings with a water soluble ink pen, keeping the rows even and parallel. Mark the vertical lines first. At the outside edges, the lines should be 1" in from the edge. The rows in between should be evenly spaced, 8" to 12" apart. Use a yardstick to draw these lines. (If desired, you can sew the lining and fabric together by machine along these vertical lines, using a straight seam with the bobbin thread matching the face fabric and the top thread matching the lining.)

11. Mark spots for the rings along the vertical lines. The first ring at the bottom is just above the rod pocket. The last one at the top should be down more than half the distance between the rings. The rings between them should be 5" to 6" apart. (If deeper folds are desired, however, or if the fabric is quite heavy, the rings can be up to 8" apart.) All the rings *must* align perfectly across the shade.

12. Sew the rings to the shade at the marked spots, by hand, using a double strand of clear nylon thread or a color that matches the face fabric. If you did not sew through the vertical lines, be sure to catch a tiny amount of the face fabric as you sew. If you did sew vertical lines, be sure to catch the lining only and use thread which matches the lining.

You can also sew the rings to the shade by machine, using a zigzag button stitch (lower the feed) and covering the ring with 8 to 10 stitches. (You can move from one ring spot to the next without cutting the threads.)

13. Turn out the bottom hems to expose the rod pocket. Insert a rod through the slit. **Whipstitch** the slit closed and turn the hem down again.

14. To mount the shade, follow Steps 10 through 14 under Unlined Roman Shade with Roman Shade Tape, page 167.

Crochet Lace Roman Shade
Shade is photographed on page 83.

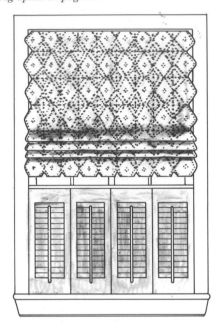

Fabric: Hand-crocheted lace the width of the window by the length of the window plus 1½".

Notions and Hardware: See Lined Roman Shade with Individual Rings.

1. Sew the rings to the back of the lace according to the preceding instructions for Lined Roman Shades with Individual Rings, Steps 10 through 12. If you want the bottom edge of the lace to show, start the first row of rings up from the bottom more than half the distance you plan to space the rings vertically. For example, if the rings are to be 6" apart, the first row of rings must be more than 3" up from the bottom. The amount more than 3" is the amount of lace you want to show.

2. Cover the rod with a fabric that matches the lace color and tack the rod to the bottom row of rings.

3. For mounting the shade, follow Steps 10 through 14 under Unlined Roman Shade with Roman Shade Tape, page 167.

Balloon Shades

The balloon shade is closely related to the Roman shade. It is constructed on the same principles, but it uses more fabric so that when it is in the raised position, the balloon shade billows into soft poufs of fabric along the bottom edge. (Refer to Roman Shades introduction, page 167.)

Headings on balloon shades can be gathered or pleated according to your design preference. With a gathered heading, the shade has a puffed look even in the lowered position. The gathered-heading technique uses less fabric width than the pleated method and is somewhat easier to make. The pleated version falls into inverted box pleats and is flat in appearance in the lowered position.

Balloon shades can be made in most light- to medium-weight fabrics, but it is a general rule that the softer the fabric, the more graceful and softer the poufs.

Balloon shades can also be made in a shorter version to be used as valances over roller shades, curtains, draperies, or shutters.

Balloon Shade with Gathered Heading
Shade is photographed on page 75.

Fabric: *Face fabric*—an amount equal to a generous 1½ times the width of the window (2 times for very soft, light-weight fabric) by the length of the window plus 11" to 32", depending upon the "poufiness" desired; *lining*—the same amount as the face fabric (this shade can be made unlined).

Notions: Roman shade tape in the length of the fabric for each row, plus ½ yard to allow for cutting waste; four-string shirring tape in an amount equal to the width of the window shade plus 2"; cord for rigging shade; self-gripping fastener tape or snap tape—the width of the mounting board, or staples, or flat-headed tacks; Roman shade tape or ½" brass or plastic rings.

Hardware: 1" × 2" board ¼" narrower than the finished width of the shade; screw eyes large enough to accommodate all the cords (use one for each row of tape); small awning cleat and screws; 2 angle irons and screws; ⅜" diameter brass or solid metal rod 1" shorter than the finished width of the shade.

1. Prepare the mounting board as in Step 1 of Unlined Roman Shade with Roman Shade Tape, page 167.

2. Cut the face fabric to desired width and length. If the shade is to be hung on an outside mount, add 3½" to the width so that the shade, when installed, will come around the sides of the board. The amount you add to the length will determine how much pouf you have at the bottom, especially when the shade is in the lowered position.

3. Cut the lining the same length as the face fabric, and ½" narrower than the face fabric.

4. Join the fabric widths, if necessary, planning the seams so they will fall in front of a row of rings.

5. With right sides together, pin the lower edge of the lining 2″ above the lower edge of the face fabric. Match the side edges and sew them with a ½″ seam.

6. Turn the shade right side out. Press so that ¼″ of face fabric extends to lining side of the shade.

7. Press up 2″ for a hem along the bottom edge of the face fabric. Turn under 1″ of the hem (to make a 1″ double hem) and stitch in place. This hem is also the casing for the weight rod.

8. Trim off the top of the shade so that the face fabric and the lining are even and the corners are perfectly square.

9. Press under 1″ at the top to the lining side. Sew the shirring tape across the top, starting the tape ¼″ down from the top folded edge. Stitch at the top and bottom of the tape and on each side of the cords (eight rows of stitching).

10. With tailor's chalk or other removable marking, draw vertical lines on the lining for center of tapes or rings. The side lines should be 1″ from the edge. The lines in between should be evenly spaced. The spacing is determined by the number of poufs desired, with 18″ being the maximum distance. Along the vertical row place one ring at the top of the hem and one just below the shirring tape. The rings in between should be spaced 6″ to 10″ apart. The larger the space, the bigger the poufs. The shades in the photograph have rings spaced 6″ apart. Sew on the rings or tape, following instructions under Unlined Roman Shade with Roman Shade Tape, page 167, Steps 6 and 7, *or* Lined Roman Shade with Individual Rings, page 169, Steps 10 through 12.

11. To gather the top edge of the shade; tie the shirring tape cords together at one end. Draw up the fabric by pulling the cords at the other end until the shade is the width of the window (plus 3½″ for an outside mount). Adjust the gathers evenly.

12. To make a flap which will be stapled to the mounting board, cut a piece of fabric (face fabric or lining) 4″ wide by the length of the mounting board plus ½″. Fold it in half lengthwise and sew along the long edge with a ¼″ seam. Turn and press. Turn in ¼″ at each edge and stitch. Sew this strip to the wrong side of the top of the shade, stitching along the top stitching line on the shirring tape. (Instead of using a strip, you can mount the shade to the front edge of the mounting board with self-gripping fastener tape. Sew the fuzzy side of the tape to the top edge of the shade, starting ¼″ down from the top. Glue and/or staple the loop side of the tape to the front edge of the mounting board.)

13. Make a tube of fabric long enough to cover the metal rod, plus allowance to extend ⅜″ beyond each end of rod for "tabs." Insert covered rod into hem casing at bottom of shade. Tack the rod cover "tabs" to the hem casing at each end and the rod cover to the hem casing at each row of rings. Adjust the gathers on the rod.

14. Rig the shade with cords and mount in the window as instructed in Unlined Roman Shade with Roman Shade Tape, page 167, Steps 10 through 16.

Balloon Shade with Pleated Heading
Shade is photographed on page 36 and page 102.

Fabric: *Face fabric*—see below for estimating yardage; *lining fabric*—an amount 1″ longer and 1″ wider than the finished, flat size of the shade.

Notions and Hardware: The same as for Lined Roman Shade with Individual Rings, page 169. Roman shade tape can be used as well; special instructions will be noted at the end of the instruction section.

Planning the Shade
1. Measure the window for the finished width of the shade. Remember that this balloon shade is flat when it is lowered.
2. Divide the above measurement by the number of balloon panels desired to determine the width of each panel. The panels can be any width (8″ to 12″ is suggested). Adjust the number of panels to obtain the desired panel widths, if necessary. Consider the position of seams when deciding the width of each panel.
3. Determine the width of the box pleats, 9″ to 12″ depending on the fullness desired. Multiply the number of balloon panels by the width of the box pleats; e.g., 3 panels × 10″ = 30″.
4. Add the above measurement to the width of the finished shade plus 4″. If the panel needs to be pieced, add 1″ for each seam (½″ seam allowance). (Seams in a balloon shade must fall within a pleat, either on a back fold or at the center of the pleat. Plan the purchase of fabric accordingly.)
5. The length needed per shade is equal to the distance from the top of the window to its bottom plus 11″ to 32″. The longer the shade, the more "poufiness" when the shade is in the lowered position.
6. The amount of Roman shade tape or the number of rings needed will be basically the same as for Roman shades. Plan one tape or row of rings per pleat. The number of pleats equals one more than the number of balloon panels because there are half-box pleats at each side; i.e., three balloon panels have four rows of rings.

Constructing the Shade
1. Prepare the mounting board as in Step 1 of the Unlined Roman Shade with Roman Shade Tape, page 167.
2. Cut the fabric according to the measurements established above. Join the fabric widths, if necessary, planning the seams within a pleat. If the fabric has a specific design (stripe, plaid, etc.) as in the photograph, page 36, plan the pleats so that the design falls in the appropriate places.

3. Following the diagram below, mark off the location of the pleats, fold lines and the center of the pleat on a strip of paper 6″ wide by the width of the shade piece. Allow 2″ extra at each side edge.

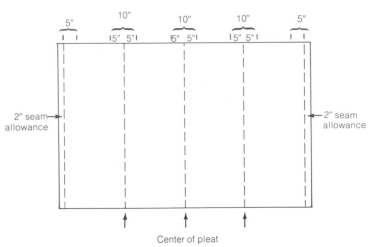

Center of pleat

4. Transfer these markings to the wrong side of the shade fabric. Form the pleats, stitching them together 1½″ up from the bottom and 4″ down from the top. Baste the rest of each pleat in place.

5. Cut the lining fabric ½″ narrower than the face fabric *after* the pleats are formed.

6. With right sides together, match the bottom and side edges of the lining and the face fabric, and pin. Sew with a ½″ seam. Turn the shade right side out, and press so that ¼″ of face fabric extends to back.

7. Using a T-square, trim off the top of the shade so the face fabric and lining are even and the corners are perfectly square. Overcast the raw edges together.

8. On the lining side of the shade, mark the location of the center of the pleats with removable marking, making a vertical line at each side 2¼″ in from the edge. Mark the ring positions on the vertical lines, placing a ring ½″ up from the bottom edge, and one ring no less than 5″ down from the top edge. The rings in between should be spaced 6″ to 10″ apart. (In the photograph the rings are spaced 7″ apart.)

9. Sew the rings at the marked spots through the lining fabric, catching the face fabric at the center back of each pleat. For detailed instructions, see Lined Roman Shade with Individual Rings, page 169, Steps 10 through 12. *Note:* If you are using Roman shade tape, you have to buy and cut your lining the same size as the face fabric. Sew them together. Turn right side out. Mark your pleat locations on the lining as determined in Step 4 above. Sew the shade tapes to the vertical line designating the center of the pleat, except at the side edges where the center of the tape should be 2¼″ in from the side edge. Plan the first ring 1″ up from the bottom edge. The last ring should be no less than 5″ down from the top edge. Form the pleats as in Step 5 above. Complete Step 8. Cover the rod. Attach and mount the same as described in Steps 12 and 13 above.

10. At the bottom edge of the shade, turn under 1½″ at each side edge. Tack in place along the bottom edge of the shade and 1″ up each side.

11. Cover the brass or metal rod with a piece of lining fabric. Sew the rod by hand to the bottom edge of the shade at each of the rings.

12. Rig the shade with cords and mount it in the window as instructed in Unlined Roman Shade with Roman Shade Tape, Steps 10 through 14, page 167. When stapling the shade to the mounting board, bring the shade 1½″ around the ends of the board.
Note: If you choose to make an unlined balloon shade, make ½″ double hems at each side edge and a 1″ double hem at the bottom edge. The rings should start at the top of the bottom hem. Otherwise, construction is the same as for the lined version.

Shirred Heading for Balloon Shade
Shirred heading is photographed on page 102.

Fabric: *Border or stripe fabric*—the width desired plus 3″, by a length equal to 2½ times the width of the window.
Notions: Buckram or heavyweight interfacing in an amount equal to the width of the window; self-gripping fastener tape in an amount equal to the width of the window; 3- or 4-string shirring tape in an amount equal to 2½ times the width of the window.

1. Cut the border strip the desired width (we recommend 5″) plus 1½″ seam allowances on both sides. If the fabric will not give that large an allowance because of the design, plan to face the border print. The length of the strip should be 2½ times the width of the window.

2. Press under 1½″ on the long edges of the border design and ½″ at each short end.

3. Sew shirring tape (3- or 4-string, depending on the width of the strip) to the wrong side of the border design, centering the tape on the strip. Sew the tape on the top and bottom edges and on both sides of the strings (six to eight rows of stitching).

4. Tie the cords at one end and pull them up from the other end until the strip is the width of the window. Tie the cords at the other end and arrange the gathers evenly.

5. Trim the buckram or interfacing to ½″ less than the size of the smocked strip. Sew it to the back of the strip, stitching over the top and bottom rows of the previous stitching.

6. Sew the fuzzy side of the self-gripping fastener tape to the top edge of the border strip. Sew the loop side across the balloon shade at a point where the shade covers the front edge of the mounting board.

Balloon Shade Valance

Balloon valances are photographed on page 50.

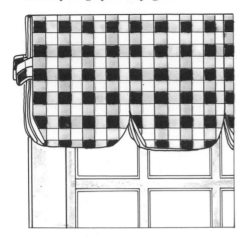

Balloon shade valances can be constructed following the instructions for either the gathered (page 170) or box-pleated (page 171) balloon shades. The valance width remains the same as for a shade; however, since the valance is not lowered, shorten the length to the exact window measurement. For a very tall window, the valance shade can be cut shorter than the length of the window. If you want a decorative trim at the bottom edge of the shade, make or purchase trim as desired and insert it in the seam at the bottom edge of the shade.

After the valance is constructed, raise to the desired position and tie the cords under the valance so they do not show. Tuck the cord ends in, but do not cut them off because the shade must be lowered for cleaning.

Different looks can be achieved by the arrangement of the poufs at the bottom of the shade. In our photographs, they are tucked in to create a more tailored look.

Curtains and Draperies

The first step in making curtains and draperies is measuring the window. This will be the basis for designing the units and determining the necessary yardage.

There are three lengths usually used for curtains and draperies: from floor to ceiling (or bottom of crown molding); from the top of the window molding (facing) to the floor; or from the top of the window molding to the sill or to the bottom of the apron (facing).

If the window has no molding, allow 4″ to 5″ above the window opening. Curtains or draperies should fall about ½″ above the floor or carpet for the best appearance.

Select a location for the rod placement and install it. To determine the width of the curtain, measure the length of the rod, including the returns (the distance from the corner of the drapery rod to the bracket on the wall) and the overlap (the distance at the center of a two-panel treatment where one panel overlaps the other, usually adding about 3″ on each panel). When planning for shirred curtains of heavyweight fabrics, allow 2 times the rod length; for medium-weight fabrics, allow 2½ times the rod length; and for lightweight fabrics, 3 times the rod length. In addition,

you will need 2¼ times the rod length for pleated headings plus 2″ per side for the side hems (1½″ plus a ½″ turn-under).

To determine the finished length of each panel, measure from the bottom of the rod for a shirred treatment, or from ½″ above the traverse rod for pinch pleats, to the desired point for the lower edge. Allowing for the hem, add 8″ to 10″ for floor length panels, or 4″ to 6″ for sill/apron length panels.

To these measurements, you must also add for the casing and/or heading. A simple casing for rod-pocket curtains requires 2 times the depth of the casing plus a ½″ turn-under. A casing with a heading requires 2 times the depth of the casing (allowing for ease), plus 2 times the heading desired, plus a ½″ turn-under. For standard rods, allow 1¼″ to 1½″ for the casing. For large decorative rods, measure the circumference of the rod, add ½″ for lightweight fabric, ¾″ for medium-weight, and 1″ for heavyweight fabric. Divide this number in half for the casing size. For more information on sewing rod-pocket headings, see page 174.

For pleater tape heading or self-pleated heading on lined curtains/draperies, add ⅝″. For a self-pleated heading on unlined curtains/draperies, add 6″ with a 3″ stiffener or 8″ with a 4″ stiffener.

Add 1″ to the final per-panel length to allow for raveling and squaring the ends.

Allowance must also be made for any pattern **repeat** on material with a design. (See page 127 in "Tools, Terms, and Techniques," for calculating the repeat allowance.)

Lining fabric can be purchased in the same yardage as the curtain fabric.

Valances require much the same construction techniques as curtains and draperies. Most valances require ½ yard of fabric or less per panel but, unless the valance is perfectly flat, more than one panel will be needed to achieve the necessary width. The average valance is about 10″ in finished depth, but depth can vary from 6″ to 18″. Be guided by the height of your ceiling and the size of your windows.

Check for fabric shrinkage and preshrink, if needed, before cutting the panels. Working on a large, flat surface, measure and mark one panel at a time. If you are working with a solid color fabric or a design without an obvious direction, mark the top or the bottom of the panels as you cut. Printed fabrics follow the lines of the pattern design, not the grain of the fabric.

Unlined Curtains and Draperies

1. Cut the fabric according to the previous instructions.
2. Sew the curtain panels right sides together, with ½″ seams. Sew from the bottom to the top, and trim or clip the selvages to reduce puckering. Since curtains will not be lined, you should use **enclosed seams.**
3. To hem the bottom edge, turn up half the amount allowed for a bottom hem. Turn up an equal amount again to create a double hem and press. Insert weights, if desired, placing one at each seam and one 3″ from each outside edge. Tack them to the hem allowance. Chain weights rest in the hem fold. Tack them occasionally to keep in place. Sew the hem by hand with a **blind stitch,** or by machine with a line of stitching close to the upper fold line.
4. To make the side hems, press under 2″. Press under ½″ on the raw edge and stitch it in place as is done on the bottom hem. **Miter** the side hem where it meets the bottom hem at the corners.

5. Finish the top edge for the rod pocket or pleated headings according to separate directions which follow.

Lined Curtains and Draperies

1. Cut the face fabric according to the measurements desired.

2. Cut the lining fabric the same length as the face fabric, but plan the total lining width to be 6″ narrower than the total face fabric. For single width panels, 54″ decorative fabric is compatible with 48″ lining fabric.

3. Sew the curtain panels right sides together, with ½″ seams.

4. Make bottom hems on the face fabric as described in Step 3 of Unlined Curtains and Draperies, above. On the lining, make a 2″ double hem and sew it in place by machine.

5. Position the fabric and the lining with right sides together. Place the lining so that its lower edge is 1″ above that of the face fabric. Match the side edges. Stitch the sides with ½″ seams.

6. For a rod pocket or pleater tape heading *only*, press the seams open and turn the lining and curtain right side out. (Self-pleated headings use a different method, so stop with Step 5 and go to the directions for Self-Pleated Headings which follow.

7. Center the lining over the face fabric and press. 1½″ of the face fabric should show on either side of the lining.

8. At the bottom corners turn under the side hems of the curtain below the lining. **Miter** the corners and **slip stitch** in place.

9. Finish the top edge for a rod pocket or pleated heading according to the following instructions.

Rod-Pocket Heading for Curtains and Draperies

This heading can be used with a standard adjustable curtain rod or a fat, round pole, as well as with a tension rod, sash rod, or a ⅜″ brass or solid metal rod.

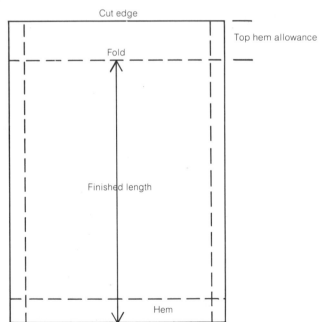

1. With the wrong (or lining) side up, measure and mark the finished length of the panel. Trim away *only* the lining to this line. Measure and mark the top hem allowance on the face fabric. Fold the top hem allowance down onto the wrong side of the panel, and press.

2. Turn under ½″ on the raw edge of the top hem allowance. Pin it in place. Stitch the heading line, if called for, and then stitch the hem in place.

3. Insert a rod through the pocket.

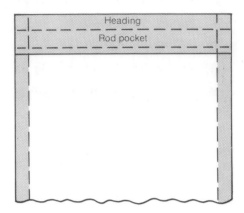

Pleated Heading for Curtains and Draperies

This heading can be used with a traverse-style rod for drawing the panels, or a standard adjustable curtain rod for stationary panels. The pleated heading can also be used with a decorative wooden pole and rings. Although this heading style is more complicated than the rod-pocket casing, the panels do hang more beautifully.

1. Cut pleater tape to go across the full width of each panel. (For short curtains, use 3″ width; for long styles, use 4″ width.)

2. Trim the upper edge of the fabric (and lining if used) so the panel is the finished length plus ⅝″ to accommodate seams; turn back.

3. Center the pleater tape at the top of the panel with the right side of the tape (the side with the openings for hooks) to the right side of the face fabric. Align the top edges. Pocket openings on the tape should be on the bottom. The distance from the side edge of the panel to the pocket that will start the first pleat should be the length of the return on the rod (the distance from the front of the rod to the wall).

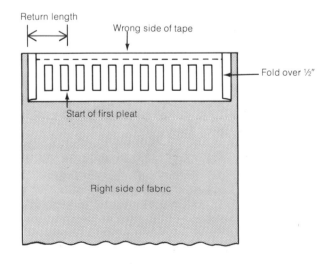

4. Fold ½″ on each end of the tape to the wrong side of the tape and pin. Stitch the tape to the panel across the top edge, ¼″ from the edge. The tape usually has a colored thread line to guide you.

5. Fold the tape over to the wrong, or lining, side of the curtain, with ¼" of fabric showing above the tape. Press.
6. Pin the lower edge of the tape to the panel and stitch ¼" from the edge of the tape.
7. Insert a 4-prong hook into four pockets, working it in first ½" into each pocket and then pushing it in all the way. Adjust the front of the pleats. Lock the hook in place. Insert an end pin in the last pocket at each end. Leave one or two pockets between the pleats as needed to create the correct width.

Self-Pleated Heading for Unlined Curtains and Draperies

1. Cut crinoline or buckram (stiffener) to go across the full width of each panel plus 1½". (Use 3" stiffener for short curtains and 4" for longer styles.)
2. Measure and mark the finished length of the panel on the wrong side.
3. Fold under 1" on each end of the stiffener and center on the panel, wrong sides together, with the folded ends ¼" from each side of the panel. Align the lower edge of the stiffener with a line marking the finished length of the panel. Pin in place.
4. Press the top hem allowance above the stiffener down over the stiffener. Remove the pins from the stiffener and pin through the top layer, stiffener, and bottom layer of fabric.

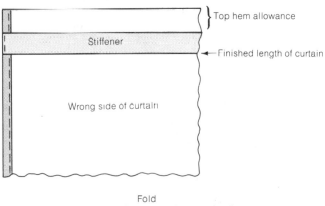

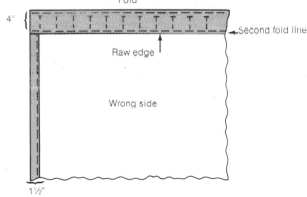

5. Stitch through these layers ¼" from the fold and ¼" from the raw edge.
6. Fold down a "hem" again on the second fold line (a line marking the finished length of the panel). You now have a double-folded hem with the stiffener enclosed. Pin it in place.
7. Close the sides of the top hem by **slip stitching** the edges together.

8. Plan and sew the pleats and set the folds following the directions below.

Self-Pleated Heading for Lined Curtains and Draperies

1. Cut the stiffener ½" narrower than curtain panel.
2. With the wrong sides still out, and lining centered on the face fabric, press the seams toward the lining. Stitch across the top edge with a ½" seam.
3. Center one edge of the stiffener across the panel on the seam allowance and stitch it in place.

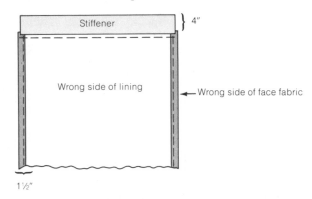

4. Turn the curtain right side out through the hem edge (like a pillowcase) and press. The stiffener will lie between the lining and the face fabric.
5. **Miter** the hems at the lower corners and **slip stitch** in place.
6. Plan and sew the pleats and set the folds following the instructions which follow.

Planning the Pleats

1. Determine how much fabric will be used for the pleats in each panel:
Take the total width of the panel: _____ "
Subtract the finished width of the panel:
(rod length + returns + overlap) − _____ "
Equals the total inches for pleats _____ "

2. Determine the number of pleats per panel:
Divide the total inches for pleats by a number between 4 and 5. This number will be the amount of fabric in inches in each pleat. The result is the number of pleats to make. An uneven number of pleats looks best, so adjust between 4 and 5, until the result is an uneven number of pleats.
3. Using pins, mark the side returns and the overlap at the front edge. Where there is neither overlap nor return, leave 2" at each end. Mark the first pleat next to the return, the second pleat next to the overlap.

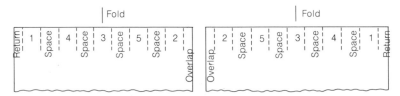

4. Fold the panel in half so that the pins next to the overlap and return meet. The fold is the center of pleat #3 or the middle pleat.
5. Determine the fourth pleat by bringing together pleats #1 and #3, the fifth pleat by bringing together pleats #2 and #3, and so on.

6. On the wrong side of the heading, bring together the pins at each side of the pleat (the fold is the center of the pleat). Pin each pleat on the right side and remeasure the panel width to be sure it is correct. Make any necessary adjustment.

Sewing the Pleats

1. Sew each pleat along the pin line, stitching from the top edge to ½″ below the lower edge of the stiffener. Secure the ends by backstitching.

2. To create pinch pleats, fold the pleat into three equal parts.

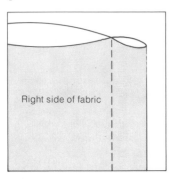 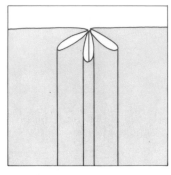

Right side of fabric

3. At the lower edge of the pleat, either hand-tack the pleats together using a sturdy needle and thimble, or machine-stitch across each pleat. If machine stitching is used, start ¼″ from the folds of the pleat. If you have trouble getting through all these thicknesses, try a small amount of silicone lubricant on the fabric and needle. Test a small sample first. Pleats can also be tacked using a zigzag stitch with the feed dog in the lowered position.

4. Finger-press the folds of the pleat rather than using an iron.

5. Insert pin-in drapery hooks in the back of each pleat and at each end of the panel. The pin should catch the stiffener but not the face fabric.

6. Hang the curtain from the rod.

Setting the Curtain and Drapery Folds

Push the panels open to the sides of the window. Starting below each pleat, arrange the folds evenly, pulling the pleat folds forward and pushing back the folds in between. Tie the panel loosely with soft cord or fabric scraps about every 12″ to 18″. Leave the curtains tied for three days.

Tie-on Curtains

Curtains are photographed on page 115 and page 116.

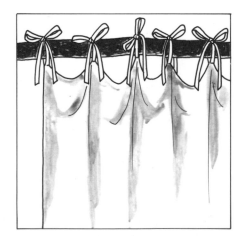

Fabric: See page 173 for yardage estimate, plus ½ yard for ties.

Hardware: A tree branch the desired length for the rod; molly bolts (optional).

1. Hang the tree branch from the ceiling (use molly bolts, if necessary).

2. Cut the panels the desired length, allowing for 1¼″ hems all around.

3. Sew the hems on all sides.

4. To make ties, cut strips, each 30″ long by 2½″ wide (we used six on each 40″ panel width). Sew the long edges of each strip with a ½″ seam. Trim, turn, and press. Close the ends. Fold the ties in half and sew at the fold to the top edge of the panels, approximately 8″ apart. Place a tie at each end and space the others evenly in between. Tie the curtains to the branch.

Curtains with Contrast Trim and Tiebacks

Curtains are photographed on page 114.

Fabric: See page 173 for yardage estimate, eliminating side and bottom hems and planning double fullness.

Hardware: 1 yard of contrast fabric for trim and tiebacks; curtain rod (see Rod Pockets, page 174, for options); cup hook.

1. Follow the measuring and cutting instructions for unlined curtains with rod-pocket heading, starting on page 174, eliminating the side and bottom hems.

2. Cut **bias strips** from contrast fabric 4″ wide by the distance around the sides and bottom of the curtain.

3. **Bind** the side and bottom edges of the curtain with bias strips. Sew them to the curtain with a ½″ seam. The trim should be 1½″ wide when finished.

4. Make a rod pocket.

5. From remaining contrast fabric, make a tieback that will be 1½″ wide when finished. Length is determined by your window but allow enough extra to make a knot and have 6″ to 7″ tails.

6. Install curtains on the rod and decide the location for the tieback knot. Place the cup hook there to catch a section of the knot and hold the tieback in place.

Priscilla Curtains
Curtains are photographed on page 83.

Fabric: See page 173 for yardage estimate, plus 1½ to 2½ yards for the ruffles, depending on the length and width of the curtains.
Trims and Notions: Narrow lace edge trim in an amount equal to the distance around the ruffles; 4 plastic rings; 2 cup hooks.
Hardware: Standard adjustable rod.

1. Cut the curtain panels ¾" shorter than the desired finished measurement. Seam the panels, if necessary, with an **enclosed seam.** Make ½" hems on the sides and bottom of all the panels.
2. To make the top-applied ruffles, which go on the front, bottom, and top edges of the curtain and on the tiebacks, cut 6" wide strips, on the straight grain or bias, from the remaining fabric. Make the ruffles with a heading according to the instructions in "Tools, Terms, and Techniques," page 127, planning a ¾" wide heading and 2½ times fullness. Make a narrow hem at the ends of the ruffles. Apply the ruffles to the front edge and across the bottom. (Later, the ruffles will be sewn to the top edge also.) Remember that the ruffle along the top edge has to go across the ruffle at the front edge, so allow at least 4" to accommodate the front edge ruffle width. Apply the lace trim to the bottom edge of the ruffles if desired.
3. At the top edge of the panel, turn down 2¾" to the wrong side, including the ruffle at the front edge. Stitch across the panel ¾" from the top fold line. Turn under ⅜" on the raw edge and stitch in place to create a **casing.** Take out the gathers on the front edge ruffle in the casing area and trim off the excess fabric.
4. Sew the ruffle to the top edge, placing the gathering line of the ruffle along the bottom row of stitching for the casing.
5. To make the tiebacks, cut two fabric strips 21" × 2½" and sew each in half lengthwise. (Finished band should measure 21" × 1¼".) Tiebacks can be longer or shorter if desired. Apply a ruffle piece to this strip along the seamed edge, so that the gathering line is ⅛" above the bottom edge of the strip. Sew a plastic ring to each end.
6. Install curtain on rod and attach tieback rings on cup hooks.

Curtains with "Tunnel" Casing
Curtains are photographed on page 46.

Fabric: See page 173 for yardage, plus estimate, plus ¾ yard per pair for bias trim and rod cover.
Hardware: Plastic plumbing pipe 1½" in interior diameter —the length of the rod desired; two elbow joints; 3" square bend screw hooks; two plastic screw anchors or molly bolts (optional).

1. To install the rod, put the elbow joints and the rod together and position them on the wall as desired. Mark the wall at the top center point on the elbow joints.

Drill a hole for the screw hook ⅜" below these marks. Insert the screw hooks in the holes. For additional support, use plastic screw anchors or molly bolts. Be sure the screw hooks are firmly installed.
Measure the distance that the screw hooks protrude from the wall, approximately 1½". Drill a hole in the top of the elbow the same distance from its wall end. Be sure the hole is large enough to accommodate the screw hook. Hang the rod over the screw hooks.
2. Cut two panels, each the desired length and width, allowing 10" for the bottom hem and casing.
3. Cut **bias strips** 5" wide and join them to make two strips, each the length of the curtain panel. If you are using a striped fabric, seam strips so that the stripes are evenly spaced.
4. Make 1" hems on the side back edge of both panels. Trim away the selvage. Make a 3" double bottom hem at the bottom of each panel.
5. **Bind** the front edges of the panels with the 5" wide bias strips, making sure the stripes go in the same direction on both panels. Sew the right side of the bias to the wrong side of the panel with a ½" seam. Trim the seam to ¼". Press the seam toward the bias.
Bring the bias to the front of the panel, and turn under a ½" seam allowance. At the bottom edge, fold up 1" of bias to the inside before bringing the bias around to the front of the panel. Stitch close to the folded edge.
6. To make a **casing,** turn down 4" at the top edge. Turn under ½" on the raw edge and stitch the casing in place.
7. Cover the center section of the rod with a bias strip going in the same direction as the bias trim on the drapery panels. The fabric can be glued or taped to the rod under the drapery panels.

Tea Toweling Valance

Valances are photographed on pages 58 and 59.

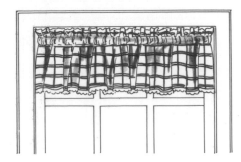

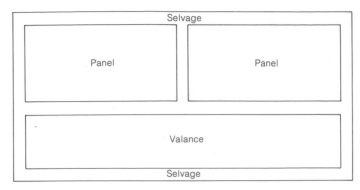

Fabric: Tea toweling yardage in amount equal to 2 to 2½ times the width of the window opening plus rod return.
Trims and Notions: 2″-wide bias tape *if* the valance is to be deeper than the tea toweling width; crochet-lace edge trim in an amount equal to the length of the valance.
Hardware: Curtain rod.

1. Preshrink tea toweling fabric.
2. Hem the toweling along the short edges.
3. Press under one long edge so that the design stripe is at the bottom edge. Sew the lace trim along the fold.
4. To make rod pocket, turn 3″ on the top edge to the wrong side. Turn under raw edge ½″ and stitch in place. Sew 1″ from folded edge to create the heading.

Panels with Attached Valance and Trim

Curtains are photographed on page 33.

Fabric: Twice the height of the window or the width of the window (whichever is greater) plus ½″; contrast fabric—¾ yard for bias trim.
Hardware: ⅜″ diameter brass rod—½″ less than the inside dimensions of the window and hardware.

1. Following the diagram layout, cut the panels the desired finished length by the desired finished width plus ½″. Cut the valance 12½″ to 13″ deep by the desired finished width plus 1″.

2. Cut **bias strips** 2¾″ wide by the total length of the sides and bottoms of the panels and the bottom of the valance, plus 6″. Cut bias strips 3½″ wide by the length of the valance plus 1″ for the top edge of the valance.
3. Make a ¼″ double hem at one side of each panel, along the sides of the valance and the top of the panels.
4. **Bind** the edges of the panels and the bottom of the valance with the narrower bias strip using a ¾″ seam. **Miter** the corners at the bottom of the panels. Press the seam allowance toward the bias. The finished binding should be ¾″ wide.
5. Apply the wider bias strip to the top edge of the valance in the same manner using a 1″ seam for a 1″ finished bias.
6. Before sewing the second side of bias in place, pin the panels behind the valance at each side. The top of the panels should extend ½″ above the seamline that joins top bias to valance. Stitch the panels to the valance along the previous stitching line on the bias. Finish application of bias and insert a rod through the bias strip.

Curtains with Rod-Pocket Valance

Curtains are photographed on page 81.

Fabric: See page 173 for yardage estimate for curtain panels and a valance 9″ to 10″ deep.
Trim: 1½″- to 2″-wide crochet lace trim in an amount equal to twice the length of the curtain plus twice the width, with 6″ to 8″ added for mitering the corners, plus the length of the valance.
Hardware: Standard adjustable double rod.

1. Make a valance 9″ to 10″ deep following the instructions for sewing unlined curtains on page 173, and finishing the top with a rod-pocket heading described on page 174. The side and bottom hems should be 1″ to 1¼″ wide, and the heading should be 1½″ deep.

2. Apply the lace trim to the front and bottom edges of the curtain panels, **mitering** the lace at the bottom corners. Apply the lace also to the bottom edge of the valance.

3. Install the valance on the outside rod, and the curtain panels on the inside of the double rod.

Curtains and Valance with Appliquéd Border

Curtains are photographed on page 103.

Fabric: See page 173 for yardage estimates. No bottom allowance is needed, and 4″ can be subtracted from the length per panel. Do the same for the valance; contrast fabric for bands—1¼ yards per single window; fabrics for appliqué (bud—5½″ × 17″, petals and leaves—11½″ × 26″).

Hardware: Double adjustable rod.

1. Make the curtains following the instructions for sewing unlined curtains, page 173, and finishing the top with a rod pocket heading, page 174, eliminating the bottom hem. Trim the curtain panel at the bottom edge to 4″ less than the desired finished length. Repeat for the valance, planning the finished valance depth at 11½″.

2. Cut the contrast bands, 10″ wide by the width of the panels and the width of the valance plus ½″ seam allowance at each short end. Press the bands in half lengthwise with wrong sides together, turning in ½″ at each end. On the top long edge, press under ½″. On the other long edge, press under ⅜″ (facing side).

3. Cut out rosebud appliqués, page 263, spacing them evenly across the bands.

4. **Appliqué** the design to the top half of the bands, making sure that the motif will be upright when the band is stitched to the bottom edge of the curtain. Do not catch the facing side.

5. Pin the band to the bottom of the curtain panels and the valance, allowing ½″ of the curtain as a seam allowance. Stitch from the top side, close to the folded edge, catching the facing as you sew. Stitch across the ends of the bands.

Curtains with Antique Lace Valance

Curtains are photographed on page 83.

Fabric: See page 173 for yardage estimate on curtain panels; lace piece wide and long enough for the valance.

Trims and Notions: Bias tape wide enough to make or complete a rod casing (if lace is not deep enough for self-casing); ½″- to ¾″-wide lace edge trim in an amount equal to twice the length of the curtain plus twice the width plus several inches.

Hardware: Standard adjustable double rod.

1. Make the curtains following the instructions for sewing unlined curtains, page 173, and finishing the top with a rod-pocket heading, page 174.

2. To make the valance rod pocket, turn enough lace to the wrong side to accommodate the rod **casing** and a heading, if desired, and stitch. If necessary, sew the bias tape across the wrong side of the valance to create the rod pocket.

3. Hang valance on the outside rod and curtain panels on the inside of the double rod.

Curtains with Ruffles and Valance

Curtains are photographed on page 70.

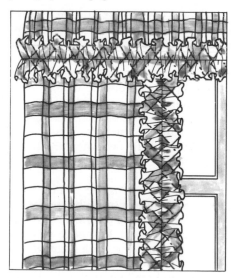

Fabric: See page 173, on planning unlined curtains, and valance with shirring tape top, for yardage estimates, adding 2 to 2½ yards for ruffles for each pair of curtains and valance.

Notions: 4-string shirring tape in an amount equal to width of valance.

Hardware: 1″ × 6″ mounting board wider than the window frame; 2 or more angle irons and screws; curtain rod.

1. Cut the curtain panel lengths. Trim away the inside front corners to form a curved shape that measures 4½″ from point of corner to curve.

2. Make a narrow machine hem on the sides and bottom of each panel.

3. To make rod pocket, turn 3″ on the top edge to the wrong side, turn under raw edge ½″ and stitch in place. Sew 1″ from folded edge to create a heading.

4. To make **ruffles,** cut and join enough 6½″ wide **bias strips** to finish the bottom and inside panel edges of the curtains and the bottom edge of the valance. Make a narrow hem on both long edges.

5. Gather the bias strips through the center. You may ruffle by hand as you sew, or zigzag over a string which is pulled up. If you use the string method, sew about two yards, stop and pull up the ruffles; continue sewing two yards and pulling up the ruffles to the end of the fabric.

6. Sew the ruffles to the inside front edge and across bottom of panels, starting at the bottom of the rod pocket.

7. To prepare the mounting board, cut a board the length of the curtain rod plus 2″–3″ for hardware and fabric bulk. The board can be covered with a lining fabric or painted before mounting, if desired. Use angle irons to secure the board above the window.

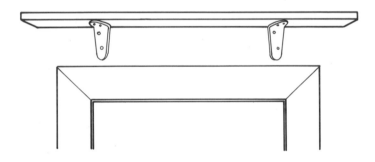

8. For the valance, cut 16″ deep panels and seam as needed. At the side edges, make 1¼″ double hems. Make a narrow machine hem at bottom of valance, and press under ½″ along the upper edge.

9. Sew the shirring tape on the wrong side of the valance, starting the tape ⅛″ down from the folded edge. Sew at both top and bottom and on each side of all strings (eight rows).

10. Sew the bias ruffles to the bottom edge of the valance with the center of the ruffle on or near the hem. Pull up the strings until valance is the length of the mounting board plus returns.

11. To make a flap for stapling the valance to the mounting board, cut a piece of fabric 4″ wide by the length of the board plus ½″, plus twice the return. Fold the piece in half lengthwise and sew along the long edge with a ¼″ seam. Turn and press. Turn in ¼″ at each edge and stitch. Sew this strip to the wrong side of the top of the valance, stitching along the top stitching line on the shirring tape.

12. Install curtains on rod and valance on mounting board.

Curtains with Shirred Valance
Curtains are photographed on page 34.

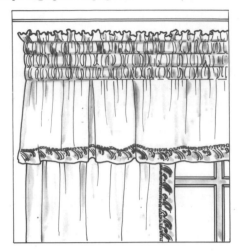

Fabric: See page 173, on planning unlined curtains with a pleated heading. Valance has shirred heading in these instructions.

Trims and Notions: Drapery hooks; 4-string shirring tape in an amount equal to the length of the valance; pleater tape or stiffening in an amount equal to the width of the curtain panels; 1″ fringe-style or band trim in an amount equal to twice the length of the curtain plus the length of the valance.

Hardware: Standard adjustable rod or traverse rod; 1″ × 4″ board wider than the window frame; 2 angle irons and screws.

1. Make curtain panels, following the instructions for sewing unlined curtains, page 173, and finishing the top with a pleated heading on page 174.

2. Apply the trim onto the front edge of the curtains, so that the trim starts 1¼″ in from the edge. If the curtains are to be washed, **preshrink** the trim. (Some trims tend to make curtain edges pucker when they are sewn on by machine. If you have this problem, consider gluing trim on with a thin coat of special fabric glue, *or* sewing on the trim by hand.)

3. Prepare the mounting board and install it, following the directions, preceding, for an outside mount.

4. For the valance, cut 17½″-deep panels and seam as needed. Make 1¼″ double hems at the side edges.

5. Press up 1½″ on the bottom edge. Press up 1½″ again, making a 1½″ double hem, and stitch in place. If the trim will cover the stitching, you can sew the hem by machine.

6. Turn under the top edge ½″ and apply 4-string shirring tape ⅛″ down from folded edge. Stitch the top and bottom edges and on both sides of the cord (eight rows).

7. Apply the trim to the bottom edge of the valance so that the trim starts 1¼″ up from the edge.

8. Pull the strings until valance is the length of the mounting board.

9. To make a flap for stapling the valance to the mounting board, cut a piece of fabric (face or lining) 4″ wide by the length of the board plus ½″, plus twice the return. Fold the piece in half lengthwise and sew along the long edge with a ¼″ seam. Turn and press. Turn in ¼″ at each edge and stitch. Sew this strip to the wrong side of the top of the valance, sewing along the topstitching line on the shirring tape.

10. Install curtain panels on rod and valance on mounting board.

Draperies with Tailored Valance and Contrast Trim
Draperies are photographed on page 76.

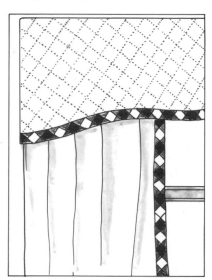

Fabric: See page 174, on planning lined draperies with pleated heading. Prequilted fabric for valances in an amount equal to the length of the mounting board plus the two returns plus 6″ for side hems (Since the fabric will be railroaded, this yardage makes two valances.); lining in the same amount as the face fabric; ¾ yard contrast fabric for trim (1 yard for more than two pairs).
Notions: Pleater tape or stiffener in an amount equal to the width of the panels.
Hardware: Standard adjustable or traverse rod; 1″ × 4″ mounting board wider than window frame; 2 angle irons and screws; cardboard—1″-wide strips; flat-headed tacks.

1. Follow the instructions for sewing lined draperies and finishing the top with a pinch-pleated heading on page 174. Do not finish the front edges of the draperies when constructing the panels. Face fabric and lining should meet at the front raw edge.
2. Cut **bias strips** from contrast fabric and **bind** the front raw edges. 3 yards of 3″ bias is needed per panel for a 96″ length.
3. Prepare the mounting board and install it as described on page 180.
4. **Enlarge pattern** for the shape of the bottom of the valance, adjusting it for your mounting board size. The valance goes across the front and around the sides of the board.

Scale: 1 square = 4″

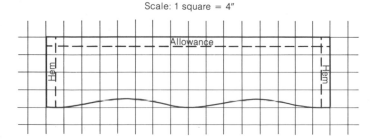

5. To make the valance, **railroad** the fabric, thus eliminating the need for seams. Cut the valance the correct length by 16″ deep. Transfer the shaped design to the bottom edge of the fabric and cut out.
6. Turn under 2″ at each end of the valance. Turn under ¼″ on the raw edge and **slip stitch** the hem in place.
7. **Bind** the bottom edge of the valance as you did the drapery panels in Step 2.
8. **Overcast** the raw edges on the top edge of the valance. Press 2″ to the wrong side along the top edge.
9. Install the valance on the mounting board as described in Canopy Bed with Scallop Edged Panels, page 222, Steps 21 and 22.

Draperies with Shirred Valance and Undercurtains
Draperies and undercurtains are photographed on page 68.

Fabric: See page 174, on planning lined draperies with rod-pocket heading. The shirred valance is 15″ deep. Lining in the same amount as face fabric; undercurtains—see page 173, for unlined curtains with pleated heading.
Trims and Notions: 4-string shirring tape in an amount equal to the width of the valance; pleater tape or stiffener for undercurtains in an amount equal to the width of the panels; 22 flower motifs; green 6-strand embroidery floss; ¾″ wide lace-edge trim in an amount equal to length and width of both undercurtain panels.
Hardware: Standard adjustable rod with deep return to accommodate undercurtain; ceiling-mounted traverse rod for undercurtains; 1″ × 6″ mounting board, wider than window frame; 2 angle irons and screws.

1. Follow the instructions for sewing lined draperies and finishing the top with a rod-pocket heading, page 174.
2. Prepare and install the mounting board as described on page 180.
3. To make the valance, cut the panels of fabric and lining 16″ deep (or the desired finished depth plus 1″). Seam the panels as necessary.
4. Sew the face fabric strip and the lining strip, right sides together, along the side and bottom edges with a ½″ seam.

5. Turn right side out, and press. Baste the raw edges together at the top ½″ from the edge.

6. For instructions on finishing the top edge and mounting, follow Steps 6, 8, and 9 of Curtains with Shirred Valance, page 180.

7. Make the undercurtains, following the instructions for sewing unlined curtains, page 173, and finishing the top with a pleated heading on page 174.

8. Sew the lace trim to the front and bottom edges of each panel. The straight edge of the trim should be on the wrong side of the curtain. Ease in the fullness at the corner. Stitch close to the edge of the curtain.

9. Apply the flower motifs, and, using three strands of embroidery floss, **chain stitch** the stems and leaves, following diagram on page 227. Place a triple bouquet at each bottom front corner with a double flower on either side. A single flower is next on the bottom and front edges. A double is last on the curtain front edge.

10. Install undercurtains on traverse rod.

Lace Curtains

Lace fabrics are available in many widths and a variety of edge treatments. You may find a narrow 12″ flounce width with one decorative edge, which is ideal for dust ruffles, valances for canopies and windows, and narrow window panels. Greater widths range from 22″ to 50″, some with one decorative edge and others with a galloon finish. Wider galloons can be split for use where only one edge need be ornate. All-over lace patterns with straight edges can be sewn together easily to create greater widths, and can have decorative lace edging applied for a more finished look. When estimating yardage for lace curtains, always allow extra for matching panels, as well as for options in cutting panels along decorative galloon edge. Finding the perfect lace fabric may require extra shopping time, but it is crucial to plan your projects around your choice of lace for the best results.

Lace Curtains for Cabinet Door
Curtains are photographed on page 52.

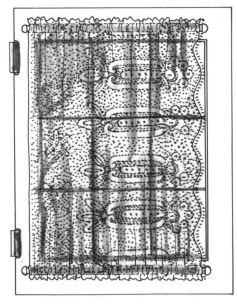

Fabric: 12″-wide lace panels with decorative border on one side in the length of the cabinet door (not the window opening).
Hardware: Sash rods or brass rods, ⅜″ in diameter, and mounting hardware—two rods per door.

1. Mount the rods on the cabinet door about 1″ in from the top and bottom edges. You may need to adjust this 1″ distance if your casing is larger or smaller than 1″ or if the lace has a lot of "give" (stretch).
2. Cut each panel the height of the cabinet door.
3. Make a **casing** at the top and bottom of the panel large enough to accommodate the rod. A 1″ casing is a good size, but be sure that it will not show in the window. Adjust the length so that the finished curtain will be taut when installed on the rods.
4. Install the curtain on the rods.

Lace French Door Curtains
Curtains are photographed on page 53.

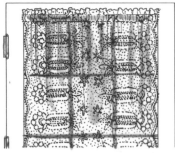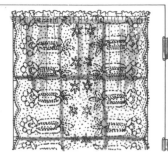

Fabric: 25″-wide lace panel with decorative border on both sides in the length desired plus 5″ for casings per panel.
Hardware: Sash rods or brass rods, ⅜″ diameter, and mounting hardware—two rods per door.

1. Install rod at the top of the glass only.
2. Cut each panel the desired finished length plus 5″ for rod pockets.
3. Turn 2½″ on the top and bottom edges to the wrong side. Turn under raw edges ¼″ and stitch in place.
4. Stitch 1″ from folded edges to create a 1¼″-wide casing.
5. Place curtain onto top rod. Put second rod in bottom casing and pull curtain taut to determine exact placement of bottom rod.

Lace Window Curtains
Curtains are photographed on page 53.

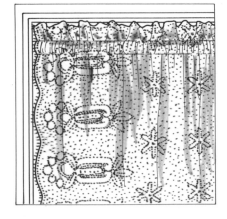

Fabric: 45″-wide lace panels with decorative border on both edges—for each pair, allow twice the length of the window plus 60″ for casing and mitering across the bottom.
Hardware: Curtain rod.

1. Cut each panel the length of the window plus 3″ for rod pocket.
2. Cut the remaining fabric (55″ to 60″) in half lengthwise.

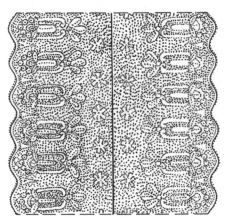

3. Turn under top edge of half panel at a pleasing point in the pattern and pin across the bottom of the window panel, matching the corners to create a smooth curve. (See Step 2 of Lace Table Runner, page 154.)
4. Miter the corners and stitch in place, using a wide, close zigzag stitch.
5. Stitch by hand or machine zigzag the bottom panel to the window panel across the bottom along the fold. Trim away the excess fabric on the wrong side.
6. Turn 3″ on the top edge to the wrong side. Turn under the raw edge ½″ and stitch in place. Sew 1″ from the folded edge to create a **casing** at the top.
8. Repeat this procedure for the other panel, using the other half of the split panel for the bottom strip.
9. Install curtain on rod.

Lace Curtains with Valance
Curtains are photographed on page 116.

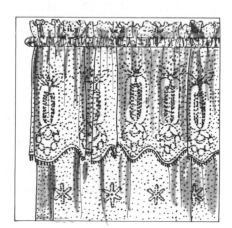

This treatment is suitable for short windows only, where the window opening to be covered is 37″ or less in height.
Fabric: 45″-wide lace panels with decorative border on both edges—allow 2½ times the width of the window.
Hardware: Curtain rod.

1. Make narrow hems at each cut end of the lace panel. The panel will be **railroaded** with borders at the top and bottom of the curtain.
2. Fold down one border edge to the right side so that the panel is now the desired finished length.
3. Stitch across the curtain ¾″ from the top fold. Stitch again 1″ down from that line to create the **casing.**

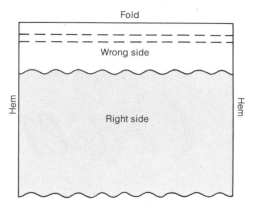

4. Install curtain on rod.

Seating: Cushions and Covers

This chapter offers technical information for making cushions and covers for chairs, benches, and stools. In addition to the more traditional items—boxed cushions with welting, flat cushions, director's chair covers, covered foam pieces, and versatile covers for dining room and folding chairs—we have provided some new ones, including a sofa made from foam lounge pads. For many projects, you will be covering an existing cushion form, or purchasing a readily available foam shape, but in some cases it will be necessary to create your own form.

If you choose foam (which is sturdier and will give maximum height) for your cushion, you can find it in many fabric and craft stores, as well as through large mail-order catalogs. Many stores even offer a foam-cutting service for a nominal charge. If you are doing your own cutting, we suggest using an electric knife to make the job easier. Simply draw your template shape on the foam and follow the lines with the knife blade. To create a knife edge with foam, apply rubber cement around the thickness edge and pinch together. If you find it necessary to glue layers together to achieve the desired thickness, use spray adhesive that is suitable for foam.

Polyester batting can also be used for seating projects in many ways. It can be wrapped and stitched by hand around the base form to soften the shape of purchased cushions and pads. Layers of polyester batting can be used to achieve the desired filling height for relatively flat cushions and back rests. You can even create a "crown," or a rise in the center of the cushion, on a seat by adding layers of batting. Loose polyester fiberfill or shredded foam encased in muslin liners can give a fuller cushion shape, and of course, feathers or down can be used in ticking liners for a truly luxurious look in seat and back cushions.

There may even be times when a readily available pillow shape, particularly those filled with feathers or down, can be used as a form for chair seat and back cushions.

You may find it helpful in locating foam, adhesives, batting, and other essential supplies to look under "Upholsterer's Supplies" in your telephone book Yellow Pages for sources of special materials and notions. Although their major business is wholesale, most sources will sell on a retail basis.

Be sure to check the suitability of any fabric for this group of projects in the "Fabric" chapter, page 16.

Knife-Edge Stool Cushion
Cushion is photographed on page 58.

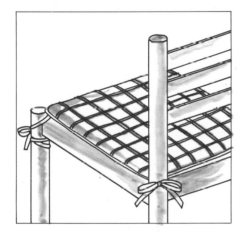

Fabric: 2 yards tea toweling (if cushion is to be smaller than width of toweling) or ¾ yard fabric; ½ yard to ⅝ yard muslin for liner (optional).
Notions: ⁶⁄₃₂" cording in an amount equal to the perimeter of the cushion plus 3"; five pieces of polyester batting the size of the cushion; zipper (optional).

1. **Preshrink** fabric.
2. Make a **template** of the seat. Add a ½" seam allowance to the pattern. Cut two pattern pieces from the toweling, centering the pattern on the plaid.
3. Cut five layers of batting ⅛" smaller than the size of the template. Do *not* add a seam allowance. Secure loosely together with a **diagonal basting** stitch.
4. If a liner is desired so that the cover can easily be removed for laundering, cut two pattern pieces from the muslin and sew right sides together, leaving an opening to insert batting. Trim the seams. Turn, press, insert the batting and close the opening.
5. Cut 1½"-wide **bias strips** from the toweling and make **welting.**
6. Sew the welting to the right side of one toweling cush-

ion piece. If the template has a cutout at the back corners for the chair back, stop and restart the welting at those points.

7. If you use a zipper, sew the cushion top to the cushion bottom at the back edge only. Insert the **zipper.**
8. To make ties, cut bias strips 9" × 1½". Fold the strips in half lengthwise, and sew them along the long edge and across one end with a ¼" seam. Trim, turn, and press. If the stool has a back, you will need four ties per cushion. If the stool has no back, you will need eight ties per cushion.
9. Pin and baste the ties to the cushion top at the back corners, or on all four corners if the stool has no back.
10. Finish sewing the cushion top to the bottom along the remaining three edges. Be sure to leave the zipper open for turning and inserting the liner pillow or batting if no lining is used.

Boxed Stool Cushion
Cushion is photographed on page 63.

Fabric: Two pieces of main fabric the dimensions of the seat plus 2" on all sides (i.e., a 15" square needs a 17" square of fabric), plus ¼ yard for ties; border fabric equal in length to the perimeter of the finished cushion plus 1", plus extra for centering the border on the cushion (i.e., a 15" square seat requires a minimum of 61" of border fabric); backing fabric for quilting.
Notions: Polyester batting—enough to quilt two seat pieces and to wrap around the foam form.
Cushion form.

1. **Quilt** the top and bottom cushion pieces, but not the border fabric.
2. Cut the quilted pieces according to your measurements, adding a ½" seam allowance to each.
3. Seam the border fabric to create a circle equal to the perimeter of the cushion. To make the border symmetrical on the cushion, center the border motif on the front of the quilted cushion piece and plan the border seam to fall at the center back. Pin and stitch with a ½" seam.
4. Make the cushion ties by cutting eight fabric strips 1½" × 16". Fold the strips lengthwise and sew along the long edge with ¼" seams. Turn and press.
5. Pin a tie to each corner on the right side of the remaining quilted cushion piece about ½" inside the point where the corner will be finished.
6. Pin and sew this cushion piece to the free edge of the border, leaving an opening between the ties on one side to

insert the pillow form. Turn right side out and press.

7. Wrap all sides of the cushion form with batting. **Whip-stitch** as needed to hold the batting in place on the foam. Insert into the cover. **Slip stitch** the opening closed.

8. Determine the finished length of the ties after wrapping around stool legs. Finish off the ties by turning in ends or simply tying knots at each end.

Stool Slipcover and Cushion
Stool is photographed on page 84.

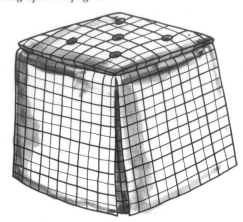

Fabric: 2¾ yards 54″ fabric.
Notions: Five ¾″ buttons to cover; self-gripping fastener tape or four "spots" (optional); polyester fiberfill for cushion. For the stool base, we used a readily available vinyl Parsons table/stool with a 16″ square top.

1. Cut three panels of fabric, each 19″ long × 54″ wide. Seam the panels together and cut away the excess to create a strip 19″ deep × 113″ long.

2. Start at one end of the strip to make pleats. Allow ½″ for the seam at either end and make the pleats 3″ deep. There will be a total of eight pleats, forming the four boxed corners. Allow 16″ between pleats.

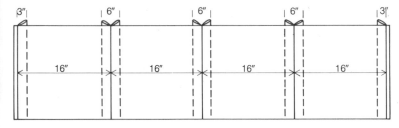

3. Join the short ends of the strip to create a tube.

4. From the remaining fabric, cut a 17″ square. Sew the skirt to the square, with ½″ seam allowance and centering the pleats at each corner.

5. Along the bottom edge of the skirt turn under ½″ and then turn under 2″ to create a hem. Sew it in place and press the pleats.

6. For the cushion, cut two 18″ squares. Stitch, right sides together, with a ½″ seam allowance, leaving an opening along one side for stuffing.

7. Turn and press. Stuff lightly but firmly with fiberfill, and **slip stitch** the opening closed.

8. Make covered buttons and sew them to the cushion through all thicknesses for a **tufted** effect.

9. The cushion can be secured to the stool cover by hand tacking or by sewing spots of self-gripping fastener tape at the corners of the cushion and stool cover.

Oval Bench Cushion with Tassels
Cushion is photographed on page 26.

Fabric: 1½ yards for cushion measuring approximately 18″ × 36″ × 2″ (as shown), or amount needed to cut two cushion shapes and 3″ boxing strips; ½ yard for welting.
Trims and Notions: ⁶⁄₃₂″ cording in a length twice the perimeter of the cushion plus 6″; 2″-thick foam form cut to size of cushion; batting to wrap around form; 12 skeins of 6-strand embroidery floss in different colors for tassels.

1. Make a **template** of your bench seat. Add a ½″ seam allowance all around.

2. Cut two template shapes from the fabric. Cut a 3″-wide boxing strip the distance around the cushion plus 2″. (You will probably have to cut two boxing strips and then match and piece them. Try to arrange the strips so that the piecing and finishing seams are both toward the back of the cushion.)

3. Place the cushion top and bottom pieces together and make small marking clips around the edges in the seam allowance. Use them to align the two pieces as you join them to the boxing strip.

4. Make **welting** and apply it to the top and bottom cushion pieces.

5. Sew boxing to top pieces. Seam the boxing ends together where they meet. Sew the bottom piece to the other side of the boxing, aligning the clip marks. Leave an opening in the back to insert the foam form.

6. Using the template you made (exact measurement without the seam allowances), cut the foam. To make a softer cushion, wrap the foam piece with batting. Baste the batting in place to hold it securely against the foam.

7. Insert the foam into the case and **slip stitch** the opening closed.

8. To make the tie-on cords, cut twelve pieces of 6-strand embroidery floss, each 36″ long. (We used one of each color.) Lay the strands together and knot them 6″ in from one end. Braid the strands and tie another knot, leaving 6″ unbraided.

For each tassel, cut 144 pieces of 6-strand embroidery floss, each 8″ long. (We used twelve pieces of each of the twelve different colors.) Lay out all strands together. Divide each cord end into two equal sections and tie securely around the center of the tassel pieces.

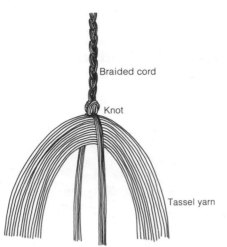

Braided cord

Knot

Tassel yarn

Fold the tassel lengths in half over the knot, and wrap three 6-strand pieces of floss securely around the tassel about ¾" down from top and knot ends. Thread the floss ends onto a large-eyed needle and "weave" ends in the tassel. Give the tassel ends a "haircut" to even their length. (Our tassels were 3" long after trimming.)

9. Sew the ties and tassels onto the cushion at a point where they can be tied around a spindle or leg.

Bench Cushion with Sawtooth Border
Cushion is photographed on page 24.

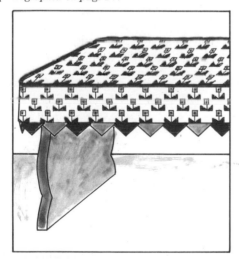

Fabric: 2½ yards main fabric (for a bench measuring approximately 60" × 13" adjust if necessary); ½ yard contrast fabric A; ¼ yard contrast fabric B.
Notions: ½" buttons to cover (we used 11); 3½ yards of ⁶⁄₃₂" cording; five 60" × 13" pieces of polyester batting (adjust if necessary).

1. Measure or make a **template** of the top of the bench

and add ¾" to all the sides. Cut the fabric for the top and bottom from this pattern, piecing fabric, if necessary, with a panel at the center and additional fabric at either side.

2. To make the overhang strip, cut enough strips 4½" wide from the main fabric to go around the entire bench twice plus 2". Piece this as needed to make two equal strips, avoiding a seam at the center front. Seam the strips at the back edge. Mark with pins or a small clip at the points for the corners of the bench.

3. From the two contrast fabrics, cut 3" squares, about thirty of each color. Press each square in half on the diagonal, creating a triangle. Press it in half again on the dotted line to create a smaller triangle.

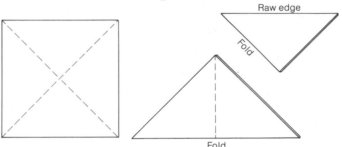

Raw edge

Fold

Fold

4. Along the right side of the bottom edge of one overhang strip, arrange the triangles along the strip, raw edges together. Slip one triangle inside the next at the folded open side of the triangles, alternating the colors.

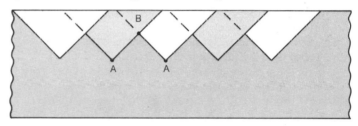

The distance from point A to point B in the illustration is about 1". (We planned the triangles to go across the front and both sides of the bench only; if all four sides of bench will show, continue triangles along back of cushion.)

5. With a ½" seam allowance, join the ends of each of the two strips. With the right sides together and triangles sandwiched in between, sew the two strips with a ½" seam along the bottom edge. Press seams open. Turn right sides out. Press well along the sawtooth edge.

6. From contrast fabric A, cut **bias strips** 1½" wide and make **welting** to go around the perimeter of the bench.

7. Sew the welting around the top fabric piece with a ½" seam.

8. Pin and sew the overhang strip, right sides together, to the top piece. Fold the overhang strip to the center of the cushion top and pin to keep it out of the way so you can sew the bottom piece to the top, right sides together. Leave a large opening at the back edge of the cushion. Turn through the opening and press.

9. Place five layers of batting together, join them loosely with **diagonal basting** about 1" from the edge. Trim the batting layers to slightly less than the bench top measurements.

10. Slip the batting layers into the cover through the opening and smooth in place.

11. To create a **tufted** effect, cover buttons and sew them on the cushion.

Knife-Edge Chair Cushion

Cushions are photographed on page 25.

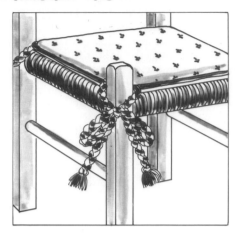

Fabric: ¾ yard for each seat 18″ square or less; ⅜ yard for welting.

Trims and Notions: ⁹⁄₃₂″ cording in an amount equal to the perimeter of the seat plus 2″; four or five pieces of polyester batting the size of the chair seat; yarn in three colors, about 14 yards of each color, for four ties, or 4 yards of decorative cording trim.

1. Make a **template** of the chair seat. Trim the corners to accommodate the vertical rungs, if necessary. Add ⅝″ all around the template. This is your pattern. (½″ is allowed for the seam allowances.)

2. Cut two pieces of fabric using the pattern.

3. Make **welting** from self or contrast fabric.

4. Sew the welting all around the right side of one chair seat piece, starting at the center of the back edge.

5. Sew the welted fabric piece to the other matching piece, right sides together, leaving most of the back edge open for turning.

6. Trim the corners and turn the cover right side out and press.

7. Layer four or five pieces of batting and sew them together loosely about 1″ from the edge with **diagonal basting.** Trim the batting layers to ⅛″ less than the original template before adding ⅝″.

8. Slip the batting into the cover. Smooth and close the opening with a **slip stitch.**

9. To make yarn ties (one for each corner), cut three strands of each color yarn 40″ long, a total of nine strands, for each tie. Knot all the strands together and braid, using one color for each of the three sections. Knot and trim the ends.

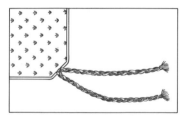

10. Fold either the yarn ties or purchased decorative cording (with ends knotted) in half and tack the center at the corners of the cushion. Bring the ties around each side leg post to the underside of the chair. Cross over and bring the ties around to the front; tie into a bow. If the ties are too long, move the knot and trim ends.

Shaped Chair Cushion

Cushions are photographed on page 50.

Fabric: ½ yard for each cushion; ⅜ yard contrast fabric for welting (½ yard to ¾ yard for several chairs); ½ yard to ⅝ yard of muslin for liner (optional).

Notions: ⁹⁄₃₂″ cording in an amount equal to the perimeter of the chair plus 3″; five pieces of polyester batting the size of the seat; zipper (optional).

1. Follow the procedure for Knife-Edge Stool Cushion, page 185, using the instructions below for the ties.

2. From the seat fabric, cut three strips on the bias or straight **grain,** as desired, 1″ wide × 17″ long. Sew the strips lengthwise with ¼″ seam allowances. Turn and finish the ends.

3. Fold the ties in half and sew the center point to the seat cushion at the center back and at the corners, to align with the chair spokes.

Ruffled Chair Cushion with Crochet Square

Cushions are photographed on page 94.

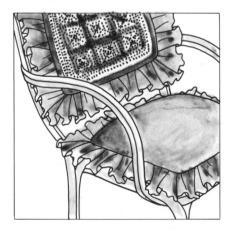

Same as for Pillow with Welt and Ruffle, page 138. In the photographed chair, a 12″ pillow form was used. Attach by hand a square of crocheted lace to the center of the pillow for the back. Both cushions should have ties to hold them to the chair. Make and attach the ties like the ones in Shaped Chair Cushion, above. The cushions in the photograph have self-faced **ruffles,** 3¼″ wide.

Ruffled Cushion and Headrest

Cushion and headrest are photographed on page 116.

Fabric: As needed for top and bottom seat pieces, plus 1¾ yards for bias ruffle and self-fabric welting, plus ⅜ yard for headrest; muslin for liners (optional).

Notions: ⁶⁄₃₂″ cording in an amount equal to the perimeter of seat cushion and backrest plus 6″; polyester fiberfill for headrest; two zippers (optional).

Pillow Form.

1. Follow the basic instructions for Knife-Edge Pillow on page 138. Use or make a pillow form 1″ larger than your chair seat dimensions. Make muslin liner for headrest. Cut top and bottom seat pieces and front and back headrest pieces from fabric.

2. Make enough **welting** to go around seat cushion and headrest plus 6″. Apply to the right side of the top seat piece and the front headrest piece.

3. For the seat, cut **ruffle** strips 9″ wide so that the finished self-faced ruffle will be 4″ wide (see page 127). The ruffles will begin and end at the back corners, 1″ from the corners to accommodate the ties. After determining the necessary lengths to make back and side/front ruffles, fold the strips lengthwise, right sides together, and seam the ends. Turn, press, and **gather** ruffles.

4. Sew the finished ruffles to the right side of the top seat piece, over the welt, aligning the stitch lines for the welt with the gathering line for the ruffle.

5. To make the ties (four for each cushion and four for each headrest), cut eight strips of fabric 3″ wide by 17″ long. Fold lengthwise, right sides together, and stitch on the long edges and across one end with ½″ seams. Turn and press.

6. Fold the raw-edged ends in thirds and pin on either side of the back corners (see illustration), and to either side of the top corners on the headrest. The ties should come in about ¾″ from the corners.

7. Insert **zippers,** if desired, in the bottom seat piece and the back headrest piece.

8. Pin and stitch the seat bottom to the top and the headrest front to the back. Either open zipper or leave openings for turning. Remember to pin the ruffles and ties carefully out of the way before sewing.

9. Trim seams, turn, and press. Insert pillow forms and either zip or **slip stitch** openings closed.

Turkish Corner Cushion and Backrest

Cushion and backrest are photographed on page 114.

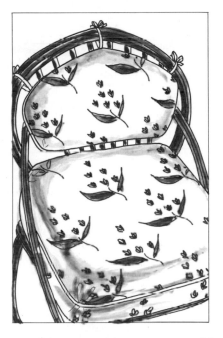

Fabric: As needed for top and bottom seat cushion pieces and front and back headrest pieces, plus ½ yard for welting and ties.

Notions: ⁶⁄₃₂″ cording in an amount equal to perimeter of seat cushion and headrest plus 7″; five pieces of polyester batting the size of the template for headrest.

Pillow Form.

1. For seat, follow instructions for Turkish Corner Pillow with Welt, page 142. If chair seat is not a standard size, you will need to make your own form (page 137).

2. To make headrest, draw **template** from the chair back using the chair's design lines as your guide. Add ½″ all around for seam allowances.

3. Cut two pieces from fabric using template as a pattern.

4. Make **welting** and sew it to right side of one fabric piece.

5. Make ties (see page 188), 1″ wide and long enough to go around chair frame and tie in a bow. Baste them to the right side of the welted piece at positions where they will attach to the chair frame.

6. Cut five layers of batting the size of the chair back template without the seam allowance. Secure the pieces together with **diagonal basting** 1″ in from the edge. Trim the edges of the batting so that they are even.

7. Sew the welted piece to the matching one, leaving an opening for inserting the form. Trim, turn, and press.

8. Insert the batting and smooth in place. **Slip stitch** the opening closed.

Box Cushion with Welt

Cushion is photographed on page 107.

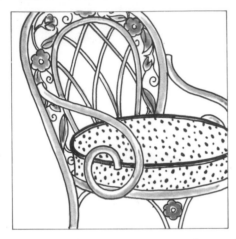

Fabric: As needed for the top and bottom pieces plus boxing, and ½ yard of self or contrast fabric for the welt.
Notions: 6/32″ cording—twice the perimeter of the cushion plus 8″; zipper (optional).
Pillow Form (or foam piece and batting to make form, as discussed on page 137).

1. Measure diameter of form and add 1″ to measurement for seam allowances. Cut two circles from fabric following this measurement.

2. Cut **bias strips** and make **welting** in an amount equal to twice the perimeter of the cushion plus 8″. Sew the welting to right side of cushion top and bottom.

3. Cut boxing strips. Measure height of form and add 1″ for seam allowances. If you are using a zipper, allow one-quarter of the overall boxing strip length for the zipper section. The boxing strip in the zipper section should be cut an additional 1½″ wider to accommodate the zipper seam.

4. Cut zipper section in half lengthwise. Sew back together with a ½″ basting seam. Insert the **zipper.**

5. Seam the zipper section to one end of the boxing strip. Press the seam away from the zipper. Determine finished length of boxing and seam at the other end of the zipper. Trim away any excess fabric.

6. **Staystitch** both edges of the boxing strip and clip frequently to make the fabric smooth and flat.

7. Open zipper, pin, and sew the boxing strip to the top and bottom pieces, right sides together, with ½″ seams.

8. Trim seam allowances, turn, and press. Insert cushion form.

Box Cushion and Flat Backrest with Ruffle Welting

Cushion and backrest are photographed on page 36.

Fabric: 3¾ yards (amount may vary with the size of the chair).
Notions: Five ½″ buttons to cover; four pieces of polyester batting the size of the backrest pattern.
Pillow Form (or foam piece and batting to make form, as discussed on page 137).

1. Make a **template** for the seat and chair back. Add ½″ all around for seam allowances. Add an additional ³⁄₁₆″ all around to the chair back pattern only for take-up from the batting. Cut two seats, one boxing piece (the distance around the seat pattern), and two chair backs. You may have to piece the boxing strip for the chair seat.

2. To make a ruffle welt, cut 2″-wide **bias strips** from the remaining fabric. Piece them together to make about 18 yards. Press the bias strip in half lengthwise to make it 1″ wide. Baste ½″ from the folded edge to hold the fabric together. **Gather** the bias strip along the basting line to 6 yards (a ruffler is helpful here). If you use the "zigzag over cord" method, sew the ruffles in place and remove the cord.

3. Sew approximately 2½ yards of ruffle to the right side of each chair seat piece as you would an ordinary **welting** so that about ¼″ of the ruffle will show when the seat is finished.

4. Sew the boxing piece to each of the chair seat pieces, right sides together. Match the center of the boxing to the center of the chair seat, leaving a large enough opening at the back to insert the cushion.

5. Clip the corners and curves and trim the seam allowances to ¼″. Turn and press. Insert the cushion and sew up the opening. Be sure to sew the full seam allowance in the opening area, so that the exposed ruffle there will be at the correct width.

6. Apply approximately 1 yard of ruffling to the right side of the top curved edge only of one seat back piece. Turn in the raw edges at the ends and taper the ruffle to nothing at the bottom corners.

7. Sew the seat back pieces, right sides together, leaving an opening along the top edge. Trim the seam allowances to ¼″. Clip the curves and corners. Turn and press.

8. Cut four batting pieces the size of the chair back template without any seam allowances. Secure the four pieces together with **diagonal basting.** Trim away an additional ⅛".

9. Insert the batting into the chair back. **Slip stitch** the opening closed.

10. Cover the buttons to match the area where they will be sewn. Sew buttons in place to create a **tufted** effect.

11. From the remaining fabric, cut five bias strips for ties, 17" × 1". Fold in half lengthwise, right sides together, and sew with a ¼" seam. Turn and finish the ends of each bias strip. Fold ties in half and tack to the back of the chair back cushion behind the buttons, so that they can be tied through the caning of the chair back. If the back cushion is used on a chair back with no caning, attach the ties to the back cushion at the back edge under the welt and tie to the frame.

Director's Chair Cover with Cushion

Director's chairs with cushions are photographed on page 42. Directions are given for a chair with a seat measuring 15½" × 19" and a back measuring 7" × 21½".

Fabric: ¾ yard, plus ⅝ yard for optional cushion (add ¼ yard for each cover if fabric is not reversible).
Notions: Five ¾" buttons to cover for cushion; polyester fiberfill for cushion.

1. Cut two pieces of fabric, one 17" × 21½" for the seat, and the other 8½" × 29" for the back. If fabric is not reversible, cut two backs and baste them wrong sides together. Trim away any excess fabric on "lining" piece to the finished size of the back. The hems will come over the raw edges.

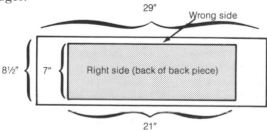

2. For the seat, make ¼" double hems on the front and back edges. Turn under 1¼" at each side end. Finish off the raw ends by zigzagging over edges. Make a **casing** for rods by stitching a line ½" from each fold.

3. For the back, make ¼" double hems on the top and bot-

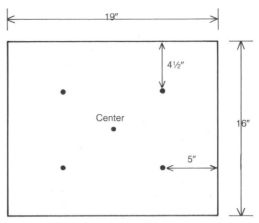

tom edges. Fold under 3¼" on each side edge and turn under ½" along the raw edge. Stitch close to this folded edge and again ¼" away to reinforce.

4. To make the cushion, cut two rectangles 17¼" × 20¼". Sew the rectangles, right sides together, with ½" seams, leaving an opening for the stuffing. Press the seams open. Clip the corners. Turn right side out and press. Stuff with fiberfill. **Slip stitch** the opening closed.

5. Cover the buttons and sew them on the front of the cushion as illustrated to create a **tufted** effect.

Lounge Cushion Cover with Welt

Cushions are photographed on page 98.

Fabric: Amount needed to cut cushion top, bottom, and boxing strip plus ½ yard for the welt.
Notions: ⁶⁄₃₂" cording in an amount equal to twice the perimeter of cushion plus 6" to 8"; foam lounge pad form; polyester batting for wrapping foam (optional); zipper—if upholstery zipper long enough to go across back of cushion and wrap around back corners is not available, purchase two zippers to equal necessary length.

1. Measure length and width of foam cushion and add 1" to each dimension to accommodate ½" seam allowances. Cut top and bottom pieces following these measurements.

2. Cut boxing strip (**railroad** fabric to eliminate seams) 1" wider than the thickness of the foam and long enough to go around two ends and the front of cushion. To make boxing for back of cushion where zipper will be applied, add an additional 1½" to the width of the strip to accommodate the zipper seam. (The zipper boxing section should extend beyond back corners so that the cover can be easily slipped over foam.)

3. Cut the zipper section of the boxing strip in half lengthwise. Sew the two sections back together with a ¾" basting seam. Insert the **zipper.**

4. Sew the zipper section to one end of the boxing strip. Press the seam away from the zipper. Determine length of finished boxing strip and seam at other end of zipper section. Cut off any excess fabric and press seam away from zipper.

5. Cut **bias strips** and make **welting** to go around top and bottom of the cushion. Sew the welting to right side of cushion top and bottom.

6. Center zipper across back of cushion and pin the completed boxing strip, right sides together, to the top piece. Stitch to within ½″ of the first corner. Leaving the needle in the fabric, raise the presser foot and make ⅜″ clips in the boxing strip to make turning the corner easier. *Do not remove needle from fabric or it will shift.* Continue sewing and clipping at the corners, pivoting fabric on the needle as necessary around the cushion.

7. Mark the unsewn side of the boxing strip with the corner locations. Pin and stitch the bottom piece to the unsewn side of the strip (remember to open zipper), matching the marks on the strip to the corners of the bottom piece.

8. Trim the corners, turn the cover, and insert form.

Ottoman/Lounge Pad

Ottoman is photographed on page 42.

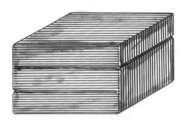

Fabric: 4 yards 44″ to 45″ fabric.

Notions: Three foam pieces 22″ square by 4″ deep.

1. Using layout as your guide, cut two hinges, 22⅞″ × 2½″ each; six boxing strips, 44″ × 5″ each; and six cushions, each 23″ square.

Selvage		
Hinge—cut 2		
Boxing strip—cut 2		
Boxing strip—cut 2		
Boxing strip—cut 2		
Cushion Cut 2	Cushion Cut 2	Cushion Cut 2
Selvage		

2. To make the center cushion, fold the hinges in half lengthwise with wrong sides together. Press under ½″ on the short ends and sew. Baste the raw edges together and press.

Pin one hinge to an edge of one square of cushion fabric. Pin the other hinge to the second square.

Seam two boxing strip pieces on both short ends with ½″ seams to create a circle. **Staystitch** both long sides of the boxing strip ⅜″ from the raw edges.

Pin the boxing to one square with right sides together, placing the seams at the corners and clipping the boxing at the corners as needed for a smooth application.

Pin another square to the other edge of the boxing, having the hinge at the opposite end from that on the first square. Leave one side open for turning and inserting the foam form. Turn right side out and press the seams flat.

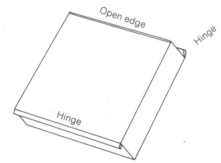

3. To make the end cushions, construct two cushions in the same manner as the center one, eliminating the hinges.

4. To attach each end cushion to the center cushion, pin and sew the open edge of the square to the hinge with right sides together. Baste under the ½″ seam allowance on the boxing at this opening.

5. Insert the foam forms. **Slip stitch** the open edges together.

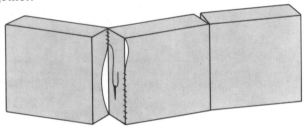

Foam Sofa and Cover

Sofa is photographed on page 42.

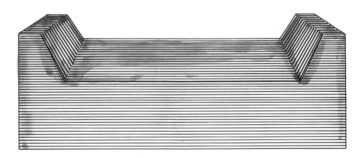

Fabric: *Cover*—10¾ yards, 36″ wide or wider; *liner* (optional)—10¾ yards muslin.

Notions: 3¾ yards self-gripping fastener tape; 8½ yards thick quilt batting; glue suitable for foam.

Foam: (two mattresses, 75″ × 30″ × 6″ each; one mattress, 75″ × 30″ × 5″; two standard wedges, 12″ × 35″ × 9″ each).

1. Glue the three foam mattresses together, one on top of the other, with the edges even. Cut each foam wedge to a 30″ length (or exact width of mattress), and glue one at each end of the foam mattresses. Let dry thoroughly.

2. Make a **template** of the foam front/back section of the sofa. Add a ½″ seam allowance all around. Cut two of these sections from the fabric and muslin, if liner is used. **Stay-stitch** the inward corners (A) on both pieces. Clip into the corner.

Note: If making muslin liner, construct first, following directions below, but **whipstitch** the bottom in place rather than closing with self-gripping fastener tape.

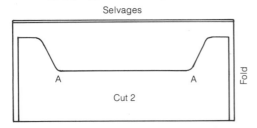

Selvages

A   A

Fold

Cut 2

3. For the sides and top of the sofa, first measure the mattress width; then measure the length, up the side, across and down the wedge, along the seat area, up and across the second wedge, and down the other side. Cut a piece of fabric according to these dimensions, plus a ½″ seam allowance all around.

4. Lay this piece over the foam and mark the location of all the corner areas on both edges of the piece. Reinforce these areas with **staystitching**.

5. Pin the front and back sections to the long piece with right sides together. Clip, as necessary, for smooth joining. Sew, press the seams, and turn right side out. Place the cover over the foam to check the fit. Make fitting adjustments as needed.

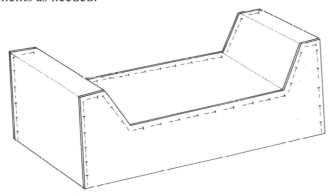

6. Cut a piece of fabric for the bottom, 76″ long × 31″ wide. Press under a ½″ seam allowance on both ends and one long edge. On these three edges, sew the loop side of the self-gripping fastener tape to the wrong side of the bottom piece, with the edge of the tape ⅛″ in from the folded edges. The tape should stop on the ends 1″ before the long raw edge.

7. Pin the long raw edge of the bottom to the lower edge of the sofa front with right sides together. Sew with a ½″ seam.

8. Sew the hook side of the tape to the right side of the other three surfaces of the sofa cover. The edge of the tape should align with the ½″ seamline, with the tape falling in the seam allowance.

9. To soften foam shape, cut pieces of batting the size cut in Steps 2 and 3, minus the seam allowances. Pin batting to the foam with T-pins and **overcast** along all the edges.

10. Place the sofa cover over the foam. Smooth the cover, pull it snugly around the lower edges, and close the bottom with self-gripping fastener tape.

Futon Pad

Futon is photographed on page 42.

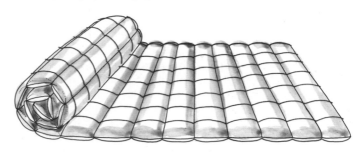

Fabric: 6⅛ yards.
Notions: 6⅛ yards batting (very thick).

1. Cut two pieces from both the fabric and the batting, each 33″ wide × 108″ long.

2. Using removable chalk or water soluble ink pen on the outside of the fabric, mark a line across the width of piece 6½″ in from each short edge. Then mark eighteen more lines between the first two, spacing them 5″ apart. (Each side of the futon pad has twenty rows of topstitching placed crosswise on the fabric.)

3. Place a piece of batting on the wrong side of the cut fabric. Pin at regular intervals across the fabric and baste the edges together. **Quilt** each piece of fabric along the twenty marked lines.

4. Pin the quilted pieces with right sides together. Sew with a ½″ seam, leaving an opening for turning.

5. To reduce bulk, trim away the batting in the seam allowance close to the stitching line. Clip the corners and press the seams open.

6. Turn the futon right side out. Press. **Slip stitch** the opening closed.

Dining Chair Cover

Covers are photographed on page 48.

Fabric: 2 yards of face fabric; ⅝ yard of lining.
Notions: 7″ self-gripping fastener tape; 2 yards of ¼″ twill tape; 2 yards of batting; 3½ yards fringe trim; 2½ yards lightweight, nonwoven fusible interfacing.

This cover is designed for a chair without vertical back slats, and with the top of seat to the bottom of the chair apron measuring no more than 3″. Adjust measurements if necessary.

1. Make a **template** of the upper portion of the chair back by tracing its outer edges. Measure the thickness of the wood chair frame. Add half that measurement to the top and sides of the template. Determine the desired length of the chair back pattern. (We suggest 8½″ to 10″ down from the top of the chair, depending on the style of chair.) Follow the design lines of the crossbars. Mark the length on your template and add a ½″ seam allowance all around to make a pattern.

2. Use the template to make a facing pattern for the bottom edge of the chair back, 2½″ deep.

3. Using the pattern, cut two chair backs from fabric, two chair backs from batting, and two facing pieces 2½″ deep from fabric. Also cut a tab piece 4″ × 3″.

4. Baste the batting to the wrong side of both chair back pieces.

5. Apply the fringe to the right side of the top and sides of one chair back piece. Sew this piece to the other back piece. Leave the seam open on one side 4″ up from the bottom edge.

6. Trim away the batting to the stitching line, and trim this seam above the opening to ¼″. Clip the curves, if needed. Overcast the seam.

7. Join the facing pieces on one short edge only. With right sides together, sew the bottom edge of the chair back to the bottom edge of the facing. Hem the raw edge of the facing.

8. Trim away the batting to the bottom stitching line. Trim the seam allowances to ¼″, clip the curves, turn, press, and overcast the seams if needed.

9. Fold the tab piece in half lengthwise and sew across the ends with ¼″ seams. Turn and press. (The finished tab should be 2″ × 3″.) Sew one end of the tab to the open side edge of the unfringed chair back.

10. **Slip stitch** the facing to the open sides and tack the hemmed edge of the facing to the batting.

11. Cut a 3½″ piece of self-gripping fastener tape in half lengthwise. Hand sew the fuzzy side of the tape to the fringed edge. The loop half can be machine stitched to the tab. Remove any basting stitches that show.

12. For the chair seat cover, make a template of the chair seat by tracing its outer edges. Add a ½″ seam allowance all around. To the back edge only, add the distance between the end of the upholstered seat and the back edge of the chair. Cut out the back corners of the pattern to fit around the chair back supports. Add ½″ seam allowances where necessary.

13. To make a pattern for the back boxing and facing, pin a piece of paper to the back edge of the seat pattern on the seamline. Fold under a ½″ seam allowance before pinning. The paper should be the width of the chair seat by 13″. Mark a "fold line" on the paper for a back flap 3½″ out from the back seamline on the chair seat pattern. Fold the paper on this line. Trim the paper to conform to the shape of the opening between the chair back supports and the back of the seat. The facing should come into the seat area at least 2½″. Unpin the paper from the chair seat pattern. Add ½″ seam allowances where necessary.

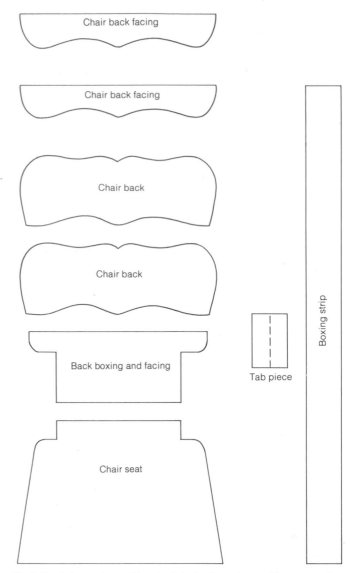

Illustration to be used as guide only. Actual pattern pieces will vary according to size of chair.

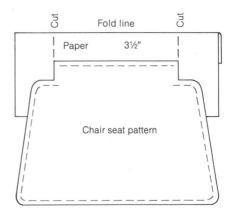

14. Cut one chair seat from fabric, lining, and batting; one back boxing from fabric and facing; and one boxing strip 8″ wide by the distance around the seat and back supports to the back flap area plus 4″.

15. If the fabric needs extra body, press the boxing strip in half lengthwise with wrong sides together. Cut interfacing and press to half of the strip (this is now the facing side). Also press interfacing to the facing side of the back boxing 3½″ from the fold line.

16. Make a narrow hem on the longest edge of the facing piece.

17. Sandwich the batting between the seat piece and the lining and pin them together.

18. Fold the boxing strip in half lengthwise with right sides together and sew across the ends with a ¼″ seam. Turn and press.

19. Apply the fringe along the raw edge of the boxing strip on the right side (the side with no interfacing), starting and stopping 1½″ from each end.

20. Apply the fringe to the back boxing strip. Seam the piece to the chair seat. Trim the batting *only* to the stitching line.

21. Sew the boxing strip to the sides and front of the chair seat, matching the center front of the chair seat to the center of the boxing strip. Make a clip in the boxing to the seamline at the point where the seaming ends.

22. Turn back the back edge facing on the fold line with right sides together. Sew along the sides of the facing and around the back corners of the seat area. Trim all the batting to the seamline. Trim the seam allowances to ¼″ and clip. Turn and press. The seams not covered by the facing can be overcast.

23. Turn in the raw edges on the boxing and **slip stitch** closed along the seamline.

24. Cut 3½″ of self-gripping fastener tape in half lengthwise. Attach it to the back flaps so that the side boxing comes underneath the back boxing.

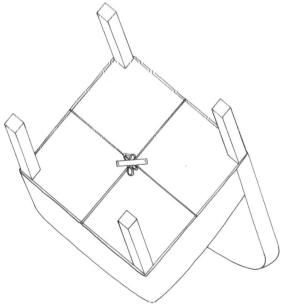

25. To secure the seat cushions to the chair, cut four 17″ pieces of twill tape. Attach the ties under the chair skirt in the seam allowance, at the center of each of the four sides. To keep the tied tapes from drooping, staple both ends of the remaining 4″ piece of twill tape to the center of the chair seat bottom. Slip tie ends through stapled tape and knot, joining side to side and front to back.

Note: To adapt pattern for armchairs, if the bar supporting the arm can be unscrewed, do so and make a buttonhole at the point of the screw hole. If the bar cannot be unscrewed, the boxing strip must be made and attached in sections with a loose flap to go around the outside of the arm support. The flap can be held in place with self-gripping fastener tape.

Folding Chair Cover
Cover is photographed on page 64.

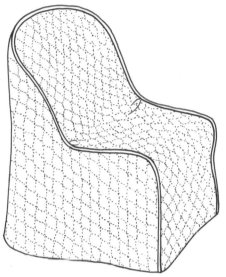

Fabric: 2½ yards prequilted fabric.
Trim: 3½ yards purchased welting.

The pattern is designed to fit a chair approximately 30½″ high × 18½″ wide × 20″ deep. If your chair is larger or smaller, adjust the pattern by increasing or decreasing all over and adjusting as in Step 5 below.

1. Enlarge the pattern.

2. Cut out the pieces according to the layout shown on the pattern diagram. Mark top, bottom, side, and front of all the pieces with water soluble ink pen.

3. Make pleats on the front section by bringing together the two solid lines, right sides together. Stitch on the line. Press the pleat toward the top. Baste in place in the seam allowance.

4. With right sides together, seam the two side pieces at the center back. Press seam open.

5. Pin the front section to the sides with a ½″ seam, right sides together. Slip the cover over the chair with the wrong side out. Fit it to your chair by repinning where necessary. Trim adjusted seam to ½″ and unpin. Adjust the paper pattern with any changes for future use.

6. Apply the **welting** to all sides of the front section except the bottom edge.

7. Stitch front section to the sides with a ½″ seam. Trim the seam allowances to ¼″. Clip and **overcast,** if desired.

8. Turn right side out. Slip the cover over the chair again and pin up the hem at the bottom edge (1″ allowed on pattern).

9. Overcast the raw edge on the bottom and sew the hem in place.

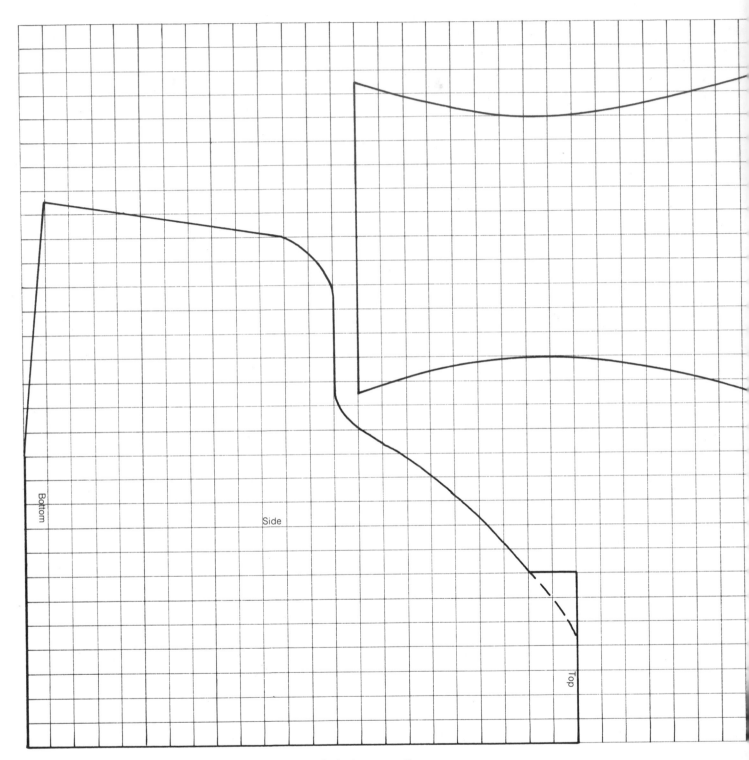

Bottom

Side

Top

Scale: 1 square = 1″

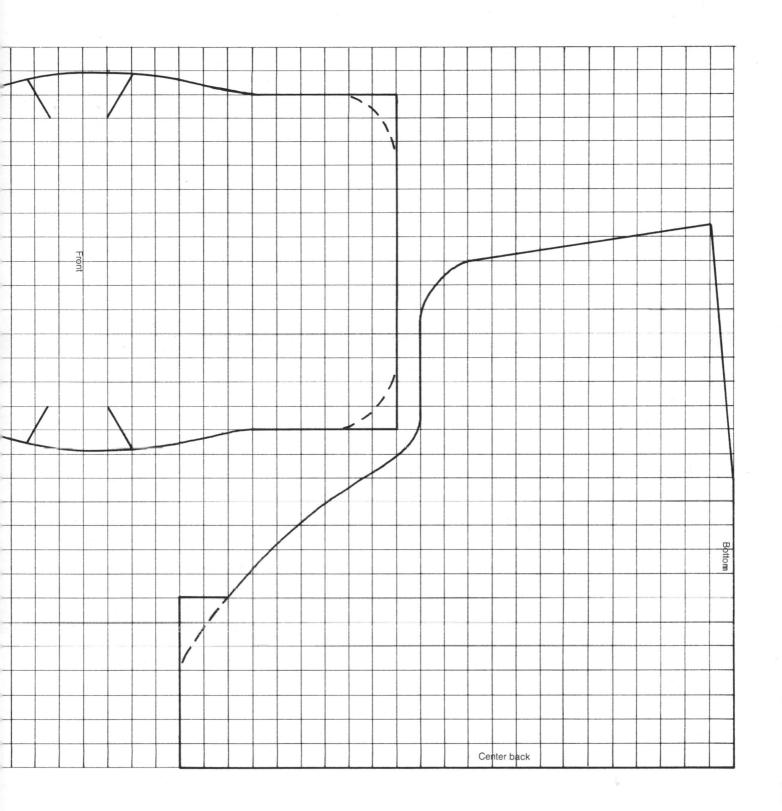

Front

Bottom

Center back

Slipcovers

Technically, slipcovers are removable or semiremovable covers for furniture. In a broader sense, however, a slipcover is a versatile and practical decorating tool that can not only hide faded or worn upholstery, but also give a new look to a room and add seasonal interest and charm. The old-fashioned practice of summer and winter covers for upholstered furniture has great practical validity, adding years to the life of your investment pieces as well as sparkle and change.

In the interest of space and clarity, our general slipcovering directions will deal with a fully upholstered armchair. The principles and techniques, however, are easily applied to the slipcovering of a sofa or any other upholstered piece.

There are many fabric types that are suitable for slipcovers. Crisp cottons, damask, linen, and medium-weight upholstery cloths are just a few. If you have a particular fabric in mind for a slipcovering project, check the list of suitable fabrics on page 16. The following guidelines are important to keep in mind when selecting fabrics for slipcovers:

- The fabric should be easy to sew and closely woven so that it will not ravel or stretch.
- The fabric should be **preshrunk.** If the selvage doesn't say "preshrunk," be sure to have it done before cutting.
- If you've never made a slipcover, try a plain fabric, one with an allover design, or one with an even stripe for your first attempt. Fabrics with a predominant design motif, a cluster of stripes, or plaids require a considerable amount of time and work in planning and matching.
- Check the weight of the fabric. Will your sewing machine stitch through at least four layers of the fabric?
- Is the fabric colorfast? Soil resistant? Easy to clean?

In addition to fabric, there are several notions and tools that are needed to make a good slipcover:

- Sewing machine needles, size 16 (100).
- Heavy duty slipcover zipper, snap tape, or self-gripping fastener tape.
- Cording, usually ⁶⁄₃₂″ to ¼″.
- T-pins (big straight pins with a T-shaped head). Heavier and longer than standard sewing pins, they can be easier to use for most of the pinning required in the construction process.
- Zipper foot for your sewing machine.
- Curved upholstery needle (optional) to whipstitch the polyester batting to the channels or crevices, or, when making foam furniture pieces, to hold the batting to the foam.

Measuring and Estimating Yardage

Yardage can be figured in either of two ways. The more accurate way is to measure carefully the piece to be slipcovered as described below. Or you can estimate by using the following chart, which is an approximate guide and allows for maximum yardages. The chart can also be used as a check to make certain you measured, added, divided, etc., correctly.

Fabric Estimate Chart

Yds of 45″–54″ Wide Fabric—Plain						
Type	# of Cushions	No Skirt	Tailored Skirt	Other Skirt	Added Yardage Welting	Amt of Welting or Trim
Arm, Club, or Lounge	1	5¾	7½	11¼	1	18
Wing Chair Low or High Back	1	5¾–9	7½–11	11¼–15	1	18–20
Sofa 6–7 ft.	2	16¼	19½	26	1¾	36
	3	17	20¼	26¾	1¾	41
Love Seat	2	12	14¼	19	1½	24
Sofa Bed (to 84″ wide)	2	16¼	19½	26	1¾	40
	3	17	20¼	26¾	1¾	45
Extra Cushions		1½	1½	1½	¼	5
Arm Protectors		½	½	½		

To use the Fabric Estimate Chart, remember that:

- These yardages are based on 44″ to 54″ plain or solid fabrics. Extra yardage must be allowed for fabric repeat. If the repeat is 3″ to 12″, add ¾ yard for a chair, 1 yard for a loveseat, and 1½ yards for a sofa. If the repeat is over 12″,

double these yardage amounts. You should also consider adding extra yardage for insurance against later damage; ½ yard for a chair or 1 yard for a sofa should be enough.
- These amounts include yardages only for the number of cushions indicated. Add the number of yards for each cushion over and above the number noted on the chart. If you will be covering additional cushions, add 1½ yards for each cushion to the total.
- The estimates assume that the skirt of the slipcover is self-lined.

Taking Measurements for Yardage

The best way to make an accurate estimate of yardage requirements is to measure the actual piece or pieces of furniture to be covered. The three basic measurements illustrated below will give you the yardage figure for a simple cover; extra yardage is needed for matching a print, for making the welting, and for an attached skirt.

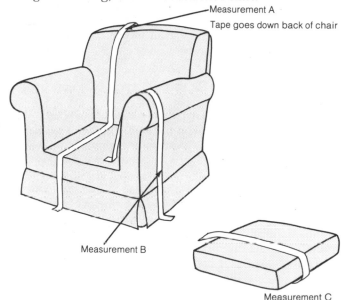

Measurement A
Tape goes down back of chair

Measurement B

Measurement C

Measurement A (back and front) Take off the cushion. Measure up from the bottom back of the chair or sofa, up and over the top, and down to the bottom front. To this total, add 12″ for the "tuck-in" at the back of the seat platform, 2″ for each seam you crossed, and a 4″ allowance for attaching a skirt. If no skirt is planned, add 11″ for facings. Multiply this total amount by the number of fabric widths needed to cover the width of the piece.

Measurement B (arms and sides) Measure from the bottom of the chair or sofa, up over the arm and down the inside arm to the seat. To this total, add 6″ for the "tuck-in," 2″ for each seam you crossed, and a 2″ allowance for attaching the skirt. If no skirt is planned, add 5½″ for facings. Double this amount to get the total for the two arms.

Measurement C (cushions) Measure around the whole cushion. Add 2″ for each seam you crossed as you measured. Multiply this total by the number of cushions this size and shape. Measure any cushions of a different size or shape in the same manner. Add all these measurements together.

You may find it helpful to enter your measurements on a chart like this one:

Measurements Needed for Total Yardage			In Inches
Measurement A	x	# of sections (fabric widths)	
Measurement B	x	2 (# of arms)	
Measurement C	x	# of cushions	
Allowance for Pattern Repeat			
Allowance for Welting			
Allowance for Skirt			
		Total Inches	

Note: Divide the total number of inches by 36 for the yardage total.

To use the above chart:
• Allow extra yardage for pattern repeat (see note under Fabric Estimate Chart, page 199).
• Add yardage for welting, also following the chart.
• Skirt yardage depends on the style chosen, whether tailored with corner pleats, pleated, or gathered. For any style, you will need two measurements, the skirt length and the skirt width.

To the finished skirt length (the distance from the floor to the seamline where the skirt and the slipcover meet), add a 1″ seam allowance. Then add a skirt hem allowance (minimum one inch), or for a self-faced hem (which we recommend), double the first measurement.

To the finished skirt width (the measurement around the chair at the seamline of the skirt and the slipcover), add 1″ for finishing the ends and 1″ for each seam which joins the fabric lengths. For a gathered or pleated skirt, multiply the above amount by 2 to 2½, depending on the fullness desired. For a tailored skirt with pleats or gathers at the corners only, add 12″ to 20″ plus seam allowances for each full pleat, remembering that the seams must be hidden in the pleats. (An additional 64″ for four pleats is average.)

Cutting and Fitting the Slipcover
(Also called "Blocking Out," or "Pin-Fitting")
The following points are important to keep in mind as you proceed through the instructions. They will *not* be repeated with each step.

• As you prepare to cut each section of the slipcover, pin the fabric to the center of the section (T-pins work best). Then smooth the fabric toward each side; then smooth upward; then downward.

• Each section of the slipcover should be pinned and cut on the straight, lengthwise **grain** of the fabric, even if the panel you are cutting is on a slant.

• Do not stretch or pull the fabric while pinning or cutting, but do pin it tautly to the chair or sofa before cutting to assure a smooth look to the finished slipcover.

• Large motifs, designs, stripes, or plaids should be centered on all front and back sections, each side of the arms, and the cushions. On the inside back of the chair or sofa,

center the motif a little more than halfway up from the center point. Measure with the cushion in place so that the motifs will be properly positioned on the completed piece.

• Control fullness in a curved area by the use of:
Gathers—Hand-gather along the seamline with a double thread and draw up to fit the other fabric edge.
Folds—Work from the center out, forming small, equal folds until the larger side fits the smaller fabric edge.
Darts—Follow the same procedure as for folds, making darts instead. The darts will be stitched down when the slipcover is sewn together.

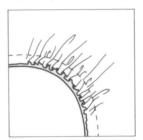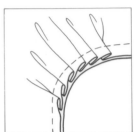

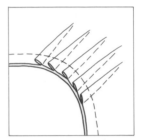

• Trim off all selvages, because they may pucker or distort the shape of the fabric.

• Plan your slipcover seams to fall exactly on top of the seams of the original upholstery in order to maintain the correct shape.

• Work with the fabric right side up during the pinning and cutting process. This method allows the exact placement of the fabric motifs, more precise matching at the seamlines, and a better fit in areas where the furniture may be slightly irregular. You will also be better able to check the placement of the design continually, and to see just how the slipcover will look when finished.

• Trim all seam allowances to ½″. (If you are more comfortable with a larger seam allowance, you can increase to ⅝″, but any more than this will make the slipcover too bulky.)

• "Tuck-ins" (extra fabric) must be allowed where movement of the slipcover occurs as the chair or sofa is actually used. Two examples of "tuck-ins" are where the seat and arms meet at the seat platform, and where the wings and the back meet on a wing chair. To prevent your finished slipcover from shifting during use, stuff the "tuck-in" areas around the seat platform with fabric remnants or rolled up newspaper.

After you have thoroughly read and understood the above points to remember, you are ready for cutting and fitting the slipcover.
1. Make the amount of **welting** you will need (see chart page 199) from bias strips and cording.
2. Remove the seat cushion and start the slipcover by draping the uncut fabric over the inside back of the chair.

Center the fabric or motif. Pin the fabric to the seamline, allowing at least a ½" seam allowance. Pin down the center, smoothing out the fabric and pinning it at the sides. If there is a boxing strip at the top connecting the inside and outside backs, it is easier to create the boxing from an extension of the inside back fabric. Starting at the front seamline, allow enough extra fabric at the top to make a 1" tuck in the fabric along the seamline. This will be cut to become the front boxing seam. You must also add enough fabric for the boxing strip and the boxing back seam allowance.

3. Bring the fabric across the seat, allowing an extra 6" to 12" of fabric for "tuck-in" between the back and the seat platform. (See A on the illustration.) The exact amount should be determined by the depth of the chair at that point.

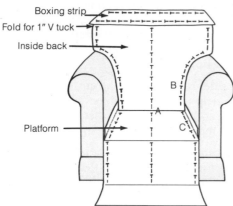

Boxing strip
Fold for 1" V tuck
Inside back
B
A
C
Platform

4. Smooth and pin the fabric across the seat platform as you did for the inside back.
5. Bring the fabric down over the front of the chair (the apron). Pin the fabric to the apron.
6. Cut away the excess fabric, allowing at least ½" where you will be making seams and 6" of tuck-in where the seat platform meets the inside arm. (See B on illustration.) Allow 1" to 2" extra fabric at the bottom of the apron. Slash and clip the fabric where necessary to make it lie smoothly.
7. Pin the welting around the inside back along all seamlines you want to trim. (Use the welt on the existing upholstery as your guide.) Clip or notch the welting where necessary to fit the curves and corners. You may want to hand-baste the welting to the fabric for your first slipcover.
8. Center the fabric over the inside arm, pinning first to the top of the arm or to the arm seam, and smoothing it down the inside of the arm to the seat. Allow for a 6" tuck-in at the seat platform and the inside arm. Trim away the excess fabric. On a chair with a curved or roll arm, you should plan the welted seam connecting the outside arm with the extension of the inside arm to meet at the fattest point on the roll. (You may need to curve the welted seam slightly from the front of the arm to meet the seam where

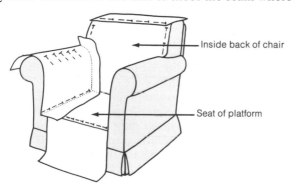

Inside back of chair

Seat of platform

the back joins the arm.) Pin on the welting at the seamlines where needed. Repeat this for the other arm. (If you are in doubt, follow the way the upholstery was done.)

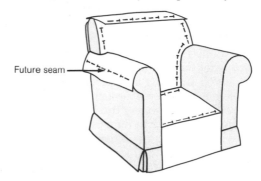

Future seam

9. Place and pin the fabric piece to the front of the arm, and trim off the extra fabric. If your fabric has a bold motif, cut the arm fronts from a background area in the print, rather than matching two large motifs that can look like headlights.

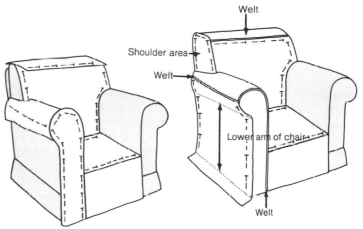

Welt
Shoulder area
Welt
Lower arm of chair
Welt

10. Now begin pin-basting the sections together. Turn under seam allowance on the side without welting and pin to the side with the welting, matching the seamlines. Also pin the other seam allowances together, joining the arm piece and inside arm to the seat. Repeat this procedure for the other arm.

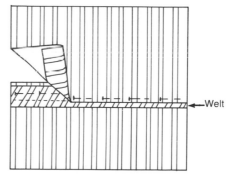

Welt

11. Finish the seat area by pinning the seat to the inside arm and/or to the lower edge of the front arm section. If the chair or sofa has a T-shaped front, cut and clip the fabric to fit.
12. Center and pin the fabric over the outside back in the same manner as you did the inside back. If you want a zipper at the center back of the chair or sofa instead of at a side, take a 1" deep tuck (2" of fabric) at the center of the back section. Trim off the excess fabric. Unpin outside back section of fabric and apply welting to the back of the

boxing strip or the edge of the inside back fabric. Pin-baste.

13. Repin the bottom edge of the slipcover, checking to see that all sides are taut.

14. Center and pin the fabric on the cushion top. Put the cushion on the chair to check the placement of the motif, if appropriate. Cut an identical piece for the other side of the cushion and pin it on. Trim off the excess fabric. Cut and fit the fabric strips for boxing, matching the motifs if necessary (especially if you are using a stripe or plaid). The boxing at the rear of the cushion will be cut separately to allow for a zipper. (See Step 8 of Sewing the Slipcover.) You can pin on the welting and pin-baste the cushion pieces together if you want to check the finished look of the slipcover; otherwise, follow the instructions for inserting the welting as you sew.

15. The skirt will be attached after the rest of the slipcover is sewn.

16. The zipper is inserted last. You may use snap tape or self-gripping fastener tape instead of a zipper.

Sewing the Slipcover

1. Remove the pins holding the fabric to the chair or sofa. Unpin one of the seams at the back of the chair or sofa to within 2″ of the top to make the zipper opening. Leave all the other seams with the pins in place. (You can also **slip-baste** the pieces together on the right side and then stitch the seams by machine on the wrong side, following the center of the basting stitch as you sew.) Carefully remove the cover from the chair. Repin the sections from the wrong side and sew along the seamline (fold line on the unwelted side). If you are more comfortable sewing the slipcover in sections instead of all at once, remove one unit at a time from the chair or sofa, sew it together, and then reposition it on the chair or sofa to check the fit and to repin it to adjoining sections. Then remove, stitch, replace, and check the next section. Make sure your final stitch lines on the welted seams are between the welted seamline and the cord so that no other stitch lines show on the right side of the cover.

Note: All sections will be sewn together in the same order in which you pinned them. Seams that will be crossed by other seams are sewn first. Wherever you must stitch across a welted seam, pull out and cut off ½″ of the cording from each end of the welt to remove bulk from the seam area. Use a zipper foot to sew all the seams with welting.

2. Start with the inside back. Make any darts, if needed. If the chair or sofa has a boxing strip at the top, sew it to the inside back.

3. Join the inside back to the inside arms, clipping the curves as necessary. Taper the tuck-in allowance to meet the seamlines.

4. Join the front arm section to the inside arm section, clipping the curves as necessary.

5. Join the outside arm section to the inside arm and front sections.

6. Stitch the seat platform section to the inside arm sections along the tuck-in allowances. (These seams have no welt.)

7. If a zipper is to be inserted in a back side seam, join the outside back to the rest of the cover, leaving the zipper seam open. Leave the seam open to within 2″ of the top, or from the widest part of the chair or sofa to the lower edge. If you prefer a center back closing, sew a seam at the center back of the outside back section from the top edge of the section to the top of the zipper opening (2″ to 3″). Leave

the rest of the seam open. Join the outside back to the rest of the slipcover.

8. To make the cushion, trim the seam allowances to ½″ on the pin-fitted cushion. Mark the corner locations on both sides of the boxing. Remove the pins. Beginning and ending at the center of the back edge, sew the welting around the top cushion piece along the seamline. See instructions under **welting** in the "Tools, Terms, and Techniques" chapter for details on how to turn the corners and finish the ends. Repeat for the bottom cushion piece.

Make a separate back section of boxing strip for the zipper, planning the strip to be long enough to go across the back of the cushion and about 2″ around each back corner. (The zipper must be at least this length.) Cut the strip the height of the boxing plus 1½″. Cut this section in half lengthwise. Sew the sections back together with a ¾″ basting seam. Press the seam open and insert a centered **zipper,** sewing several times across both ends. Join this zipper section to the rest of the boxing strip.

With the right sides together and the cushion piece on top, sew the boxing strip to the top cushion piece with the center of the zipper at the center of the back edge and the corner markings matching. Open the zipper several inches.

Stitch the unsewn side of the boxing to the cushion bottom, matching the corner markings. Trim the corners. Turn the cover right side out and insert the cushion.

9. After the slipcover is sewn, put it back on the chair or sofa and mark the seamline with pins on the cover at the lower edge of the chair or sofa in order to attach a skirt (or a facing if no skirt is planned). Use a ruler to mark an even distance from the floor all around the cover. Pin the welting to the marked seamline all around the skirt, starting and stopping at the zipper opening, with the raw edge of the welting toward the floor.

10. To finish the bottom, either make the skirt as desired or make the facings. Specific instructions follow under Finishing the Bottom Edge of the Slipcover, below.

11. Insert the zipper as described under Inserting the Zipper, page 204.

Finishing the Bottom Edge of the Slipcover

The bottom edge of the slipcover may either be faced or finished with a skirt. The faced finish is best for a chair or sofa for which you want an upholstered look, or for a piece with very pretty legs or carved feet. Skirts, which may be tailored, pleated, or gathered, can be added to any chair or sofa as long as the legs are straight enough to allow the skirt to fall smoothly.

Faced Finish

1. For each side of the slipcover, cut a facing piece 3½″ wide by the length of the side between the legs, plus 1″ for hem allowances.

2. Make narrow ½″ hems on one long and both short ends.

3. Pin the facings to the slipcover, right sides together. Stitch all around the slipcover base, including the leg areas where there is only welting.

4. In leg areas, clip into the seam allowances at each end of the facings. Turn the seam allowances in the unfaced areas to the inside and **whipstitch** them in place.

5. The facings can be held in place (anchored) on the underside of the chair in one of two ways:

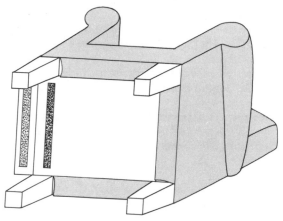

Method A:
Sew one side of snap tape or self-gripping fastener tape to the wrong side of the facing strips, and tack the other half to the wooden frame on the underside of the chair.

Method B:
Use small brads, staples, or upholstery tacks to secure the facing to the wooden frame. This method makes it more troublesome to remove the slipcover for cleaning, but is more suitable for pieces with curved bottom edges. If the chair or sofa has a curved bottom edge, fold over and tack down any excess fabric where necessary.

Skirt Finishes

When deciding on a slipcover skirt, you should choose the style most suitable for your decor as well as a style compatible with the fabric. For example, is the fabric too heavy to gather beautifully, or does it have enough body to hang properly? Most skirts are 6″ to 8″ deep and should just clear the floor or carpet.

Fabric requirements and a cutting guide for all styles are discussed in the Measurement Instructions on page 199. Remember that all seams must be hidden inside pleats or folds.

Before cutting the skirt, it will be necessary to decide on the hem finish you will use. We recommend a self-lined rather than a hemmed skirt. It hangs more successfully and is easy to make.

For a self-lined skirt, plan to cut the strips twice as wide as the finished skirt height plus 1″ (two ½″ seams). The fold will be at the bottom of the skirt. Baste the two raw edges together across the top.

In fabrics that are very heavy or that have a pattern that would show through a self-lined skirt, line the skirt with drapery lining. When the skirt is to be separately lined, cut the skirt and the lining so that the skirt fabric turns up at

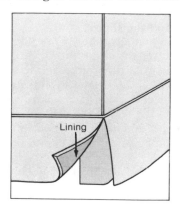

Lining

least ¼″ on the back side after they are sewn together. There will be a fold at the bottom edge. Baste the raw edges together across the top.

Tailored Skirt with Kick Pleats In this treatment, tailored, single pleats are placed at the corners of the skirt. On some furniture, especially larger pieces like sofas, you can position additional pleats along the front of the skirt.

1. Cut four lengths of fabric, one for each side of the chair or sofa. Each should be the length of the side plus 15″ to 19″ for pleat and ½″ seam allowances. The pleat allowance is a minimum of 6″ per half pleat, although 8″ is preferred. Add a ½″ seam allowance and an allowance for hiding the seam in the pleat. Allow more if matching will be necessary. If additional pleats are planned for a larger piece, add 12″ to 16″ for each additional full pleat desired.

2. With the slipcover on the chair or sofa, pin the skirt strips to the cover, starting at the zipper opening. Make a 3″- to 4″-deep pleat on each side at each corner. Repeat on each side of the chair or sofa. Plan and pin the seams at each corner area so that they fall invisibly inside the pleats.

3. Unpin the skirt from the slipcover. Seam the strips as planned. Finish the bottom edge as described above.

4. If necessary, repin the skirt to the slipcover to reposition the pleats. Pin securely or baste the pleats in place.

5. Stitch the skirt to the slipcover, right sides together. If your fabric is very heavy or you are short on yardage, separate underlay pleats can be made. Make a separate piece the exact depth of the skirt and the width desired (6″ to 8″). This underlay forms the underside of the pleat and eliminates folds, thus saving fabric and weight.

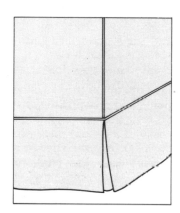

Box-Pleated Skirt Although box-pleated skirts are not photographed in this book, this is a technique that clearly merits a technical explanation in this section. Box-pleated skirts can be made with two styles of pleats: spaced and continuous, or closed. For the fitting and sewing procedures for these two styles, follow the instructions, Steps 2 through 5 under Tailored Skirt with Kick Pleats, above.

With spaced box pleats, the distance between the pleats is identical to the width of the pleats and the folds of each pleat meet at the center. Plan an uneven number of pleats, if not all around, then at least across the front of the chair or sofa. There should be a pleat at the center of the chair or sofa front. Center the spacing between the pleats at each corner over the front legs. Arrange the pleats in between. This style requires yardage equal to twice the distance around the base of the chair or sofa.

Continuous, or closed box pleats, have no spaces between the pleats and require triple fullness. It is preferable to have the back folds of the pleats meet. Plan an uneven number of pleats, if not all around, then at least across the front of the chair or sofa. Ideally, you should place a pleat at the center front and the center back, and the edges of a pleat should meet at the corners of the piece. Arrange pleats in between. Start with 3" pleats and increase or decrease until the size is perfect.

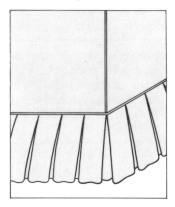

Gathered Skirt This treatment uses a continuous strip of fabric that is gathered and attached to the slipcover. Although this skirt style uses more fabric than the tailored skirt, it does not require the exact measuring and alignment of pleats to the slipcover. A gathered skirt adds softness to the furniture shape and is ideal for fabrics that gather beautifully.

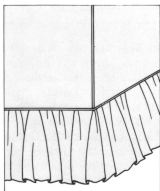

1. Cut the needed number of strips for the skirt (twice the finished skirt width is usual). Seam the short sides to make one long piece.
2. Finish the bottom edge as described on page 203.
3. **Gather** the top edge of the skirt.
4. With right sides together, pin and sew the skirt to the slipcover, distributing the fullness evenly. Begin and end at the zipper opening.

Inserting the Zipper

Slipcover zippers are available in a wide range of lengths from 12" to 72", with many sizes in between. The most commonly used lengths are 24", 27", 30", and 36", the most appropriate lengths for the zipper seams in most slipcovers. The longer 72" length is ideal for mattress and lounge pad slipcovers.

Slipcover zippers have metal teeth and are available with white and beige tapes. Although it is possible to have zipper tapes custom dyed, it is rarely worth the time and expense.

Side Closing These instructions assume that you have placed the zipper opening on the right side of the slipcover as you face the back of the chair or sofa.
1. At the zipper opening, trim the raw edges of the skirt until they are even with the raw edges of the slipcover. Pull out and trim ¾" of the cording from the welting in the seam between the cover and the skirt on both sides of the opening. Do this even if the cover does not have a skirt.
2. Turn under and baste the seam allowance of the opening on the outside back (the edge without a welt).
3. On the other side of the slipcover opening (the edge with the welt), position the closed **zipper.** The tab end of the zipper should fall ½" above the bottom edge of the skirt, if one is used, or at the bottom edge of the slipcover where there is no skirt. (Fold back the zipper tapes.) With the right sides together, pin the slipcover to the closed zipper so that the welt stitching line is ⅛" to the left of the zipper teeth. (The welt will cover the teeth.) Use the zipper foot to sew up the length of the zipper to the topmost point, sewing along the welt stitching line.
4. Place the folded edge of the other side of the opening next to the welting, covering the zipper teeth. Stitch the other zipper half to this side, ½" to ⅝" in from the folded edge, stitching several times across the zipper at the top edge. ·

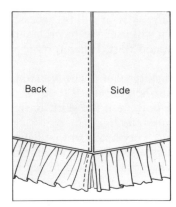

Center Back Closing
1. At the zipper opening, trim the raw edges of the skirt even with the raw edges of the slipcover. Pull out and trim ¾" of the cording from the welting in the seam between the cover and the skirt on both sides of the opening. Do this even if the slipcover doesn't have a skirt.
2. Machine-baste the rest of the center back seam down through the skirt. Press the seam open.
3. Insert the center zipper in the basted seam with the tab end of the zipper ½" above the bottom edge of the skirt or the bottom edge of the slipcover if you have not used a skirt.

Slipcovering a Sofabed

Sofabeds are slipcovered in the same manner as regular sofas, with one difference. In order to allow the bed to open without completely removing the slipcover, insert two zippers in the front, extending up the skirt and apron, across the seat platform on each side as it joins the inside arm, so that you can unzip the seat. Allow a normal tuck-in between the arms and inside back and between the inside back and the seat platform. Trim the tuck-in between the inside arm and the seat platform to a ¾″ seam allowance. Plan to make the skirt so that it opens at each side of the front arms.

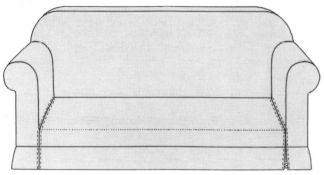

Club Chair with Tailored Skirt and Side Pocket

Slipcover is photographed on page 40.

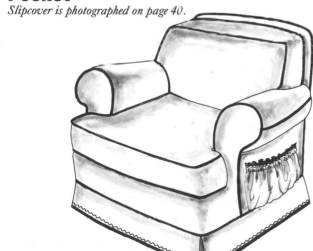

Fabric: Amount needed for slipcover with tailored skirt; contrast fabric for welting, pocket lining, and trim—amount needed for welting, page 199, plus ¾ yard.

Trims and Notions: Cording in an amount needed for slipcover welt; ½ yard of ⅜″ to ½″ elastic; jumbo rick rack in an amount equal to the distance around the skirt hem plus ¾ yard; heavy duty zipper or self-gripping fastener tape or snap tape equal to length of zipper seam.

1. Make **welting** from contrast fabric.
2. Construct the slipcover according to the general instructions on page 200, up to the point of making the skirt.
3. To make the pocket, cut a piece of slipcover fabric, 24″ wide × 7″ deep. Cut a piece of contrast fabric for lining, 24″ wide and 8¾″ deep.

Sew the center of the jumbo rick rack along the top edge of the slipcover fabric ¾″ down from the raw edge.

With right sides together, sew the rick rack edge of the slipcover fabric to the long edge of the lining along the previous stitching line. Press the seam toward the lining. Fold the piece so that the jumbo rick rack and ¾″ of lining show on the right side of the pocket.

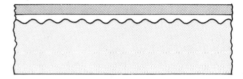

Stitch through all layers across the pocket, ¼″ below the edge of the rick rack. Stitch another row across the pocket, ½″ below the first to create a **casing.**

Insert a 16″ length of elastic through the casing, adjust the pocket fullness, and stitch across the ends of the elastic.

Gather the lower edge of the pocket until it measures 16″ across. Secure the gathers with a machine stitch.

Turn under ½″ on each side of the pocket and baste. Pin the pocket to the center of the slipcover outside arm piece (it can be sewn to either side). The raw edge of the pocket should be positioned ½″ below the stitching line where the skirt will attach to the slipcover. Stitch the pocket in place along the sides and the bottom edges.

4. Following the instructions on page 203, cut the strips for the skirt. Press them in half lengthwise. Cut 3½″-wide strips of contrast fabric equal in length to the skirt strips.
5. Sew the center of the rick rack to the right side of the skirt strips, ¾″ up from the fold.

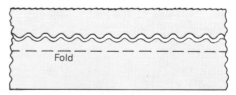

6. Place one long raw edge of the contrast fabric along the fold line of the skirt strip, right sides together. Stitch along the rick rack stitching line. Press the contrast fabric down over the fold line to the lining side so that half of the rick rack now shows. Sew the raw edge to the lining side with a zigzag stitch.
7. Re-press the skirt strips in half with ¾″ of contrast fabric showing on the right side.
8. Finish constructing the skirt and attach it to the slipcover.
9. Insert the **zipper.**

Lounge Chair or Sofa with Corner-Ruffled Skirt and Trim

Slipcovers are photographed on page 34.

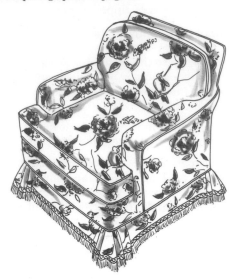

Fabric: Amount needed for slipcover with tailored skirt (be sure to include extra fabric for any loose back cushions); contrast fabric for welt (see chart, page 199).

Trims and Notions: Cording in an amount needed for slipcover welt; woven band trim (1″ to 1½″ wide) in an amount equal to the distance around the skirt hem plus 2″; heavy duty zipper or self-gripping fastener tape or snap tape the length of zipper seam.

1. Make the **welting** from contrast fabric.
2. Construct the slipcover according to the general instructions on page 200 up to the point of making the skirt.
3. To make the skirt, cut strips as you would for a tailored skirt, but **gather** the corners instead of pleating them. Allow 16″ for each corner (the strip should measure the distance around the base of the sofa plus 64″); at 2 times fullness, the gathers will fall 4″ around each side of the corner.
4. Sew the band trim along the bottom edge of the skirt.
5. Finish constructing the skirt according to the general instructions and attach it to the slipcover.
6. Insert the **zipper.**

Wing Chair with Contrast Welt

Slipcover is photographed on page 34.

Fabric: Amount needed for slipcover with no skirt; contrast fabric for welt (see chart, page 199).

Notions: Cording in an amount needed for slipcover welt; materials needed to attach facing to the bottom of the chair (see page 202); heavy duty zipper, or self-gripping fastener tape or snap tape the length of zipper seam.

The construction of a slipcover for a wing chair is essentially the same as for a fully upholstered armchair with the exception of the wing areas. Instructions for the necessary changes follow.

1. Make **welting** from contrast fabric.
2. Block out and pin-fit the inside back, the inside arms and the outside arms as described on page 200.
3. Block out and pin-fit the inside wing, clipping the seam allowances and easing the fullness as necessary. Leave at least 3″ tuck-in allowance between the wing and the inside back.
4. Block out and pin-fit the outside wing to the inside wing. Start pin-fitting at the midpoint of the wing's outside edge and work downward. Then pin-fit across the top of the wing to the back.
5. The welting is pinned in one piece across the top back edge of the chair and down the wing seam to the arm. (See the heavy lines in the illustration.)

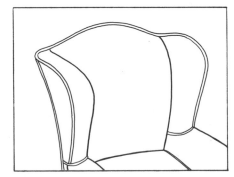

6. Continue to block out and pin-fit the rest of the slipcover as instructed in the general directions.
7. When sewing the slipcover together, sew the wing section before adding the arm sections to the inside back.
8. Complete the bottom edge of the slipcover, following instructions for the faced finish (page 202).

9. Insert the **zipper.**

10. Attach facings to the underside of the chair (see page 203 for options).

Blanket Slipcover for Foldout Foam Chair or Loveseat

Slipcovers are photographed on page 113.

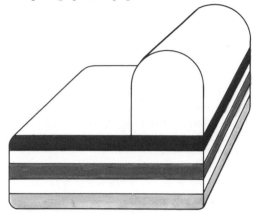

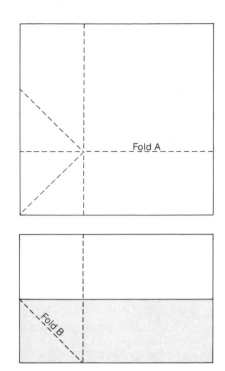

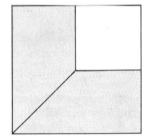

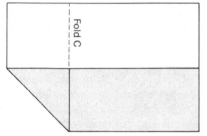

Fabric: *Chair*—one 66″ × 90″ blanket; *loveseat*—two 66″ × 90″ blankets.

Notions: *Chair*—5 yards ½″ twill tape and 10″ self-gripping fastener tape; *loveseat*—10 yards ½″ twill tape and 10″ self-gripping fastener tape.

1. Make a **template** of the side of the furniture. Add ½″ seam allowances to all sides except the bottom, where you will add 6″. Measure the width of the piece and add ½″ seam allowances to each side to determine the width of the center panel.

2. Cut the center panel from the full 90″ length of the blanket. Starting at the back bottom edge, drape the blanket over the front so that the stripes are at the ends of each strip (if you are using a Hudson's Bay trappers' blanket as shown).

3. Cut the side panels from each end of the remaining blanket. Place the center panel over the piece to determine where stripes will fall at the bottom edges. Line up the pattern for the sides on the blanket accordingly.

4. Sew the center panel, matching the stripes, to each of the side panels, right sides together; clip center and side pieces as needed to go around the corners and curves. Reinforce the corners that will be clipped closely.

5. To make the ties for the chair, cut ten pieces of twill tape, each 18″ long. For the loveseat, cut twelve pieces 18″ long and six pieces 20″ long.

6. Mark the locations on the chair for the ties, starting at a point 8½″ in from the corners. Measure the distance between these points and space the ties 7″ to 8″ apart. The chair should have three ties along each side, and two ties on each end of the center strip. The loveseat will have three 20″ ties per side and six 18″ ties across each end of the center strip.

7. Sew the ties securely to the inside of the covers along the bottom edge with about 1″ of tie attached.

8. Pull the cover over the furniture. Turn the piece over so you can work on the bottom. Tie twill tape pieces across the bottom.

9. Fold the corners to create a **miter** and pin.

10. Cut self-gripping fastener tape into four 2½″ pieces. Pin one-half of the tape to the folded edge of the miter and the other half to align with it. Remove the cover and sew tapes in place.

11. Pull the cover back over the furniture and secure with tapes and ties.

"Tie-on" Slipcover with Turkish Cushion for Chair or Sofa

Slipcovers are photographed on page 38.

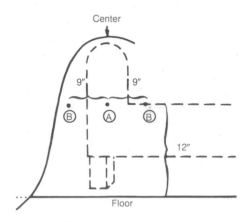

Fabric: Main fabric in an amount needed for a slipcover with a tailored skirt, plus 1 yard for self-welt; border fabric or striped fabric in an amount equal to the distance around the bottom of the slipcover (about 1½ times the length you would use in a tailored skirt).

Notions: Cording in an amount equal to the distance around all the cushions and around the bottom edge of the slipcover.

Pillow forms: Feather or down forms at least 2″ larger than desired finished size.

You will be basically following the general instructions for Cutting and Fitting the Slipcover and Sewing the Slipcover on pages 200 and 202. This cover, however, does not involve the fitting detail, the insertion of a welt in the seams, or the use of a zipper. The cover can be cut and fit with either the right or the wrong side of the fabric facing outward.

1. Following the instructions for Cutting and Fitting the Slipcover, drape the full width of fabric over the back of the piece, starting at the floor on the outside back and going up over the top, down the inside front (allowing for tuck-in), across the seat platform and down the lower front to the floor. If the fabric has large motifs, center one at the inside back with pillow cushion in place and let the rest fall where they may. Cut the fabric off across the bottom front, leaving a generous amount for any adjustments and a hem. Pin the fabric to the furniture.

2. Drape the full width of the fabric over each arm, allowing the fabric to fall to the floor at the front of the piece. Allow a tuck-in at the seat platform, and bring the fabric up over the arm and down to the floor at the outside of the arm. Cut off at the bottom, again allowing extra fabric for hem and adjustments. Pin the fabric to the furniture.

3. Pin-fit the fabric to the back of the piece where the inside back and arm meet. Pin the tuck-in allowances together where the arm and the seat platform meet, and pin the pieces together at the front (do not fit).

4. Remove the cover and sew any darts and seams you have pinned.

5. Put the cover back on the piece. Check the fit and repin at key locations to keep it from shifting.

6. Trim the fabric around the bottom of the piece, allowing ½″ for seaming the border to the slipcover.

7. To make the ties, cut four fabric pieces, 26″ long × 5″ wide. With the right sides together, fold each piece in half lengthwise and sew along the long edge and one end with a ½″ seam. Trim, turn, and press.

8. Find the center of the fabric draping over the front of the arm. Measure and mark a point, Ⓐ, about 12 ″ up from the floor. Then measure out from that point and mark a point, Ⓑ, 9″ in each direction. Vary these measurements if the ties would look better on your furniture at another location.

9. At each outer point Ⓑ, pinch a dart in the fabric, ½″ deep. Insert the raw edge of the tie on the right side of the slipcover in that dart before pinning and sewing it. (The tie is between the right sides of the fabric; the dart will be sewn from the wrong side.)

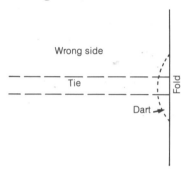

10. Cut and seam together the border fabric as needed to make a strip long enough to go around the bottom of the slipcover. Plan ½″ seam allowances.

11. Cut **bias strips** and make **welting** of main fabric to go along the border and around each Turkish corner pillow.

12. Sew the right side of the border to the wrong side of the bottom edge of the slipcover.

13. Bring the border around to the right side of the fabric, with the seam at the fold. Press under ½″ along the top raw edge of the border. Pin it in place, slipping the welting in between the border and the main fabric. Using the zipper foot, stitch the border in place as close to the folded edge as possible.

14. To make the seat cushions, follow directions for making Turkish Corner Pillows with Welt, page 142.

15. When the slipcover is on the furniture, stuff the tuck-in around the seat platform with fabric or newspaper rolls, and make bows from the ties at the front of the chair or sofa.

Loveseat or Sofa with Contrast Welt

Slipcovers are photographed on page 32.

Fabric: Amount needed for slipcover with a tailored skirt; contrast fabric for welting (see chart on page 199).
Notions: Cording in an amount needed for slipcover welt; heavy duty zipper, or self-gripping fastener tape, or snap tape the length of zipper seam.

1. Make **welting** from contrast fabric.
2. Construct the slipcover according to the general instructions on page 200 up to the point of making the skirt.
3. Plan and cut for a tailored skirt, without any pleats or gathers at the corners. Instead, allow 2″ ease for fitting each corner. Plan seams at the corners or where they will be least noticeable across the skirt front.
4. Attach the skirt to the slipcover, easing in ½″ to 1″ extra fabric at each corner to allow a smooth fit around the legs.
5. Insert the **zipper.**

Sofabed with Loose Back Cushions

Slipcover is photographed on page 40.

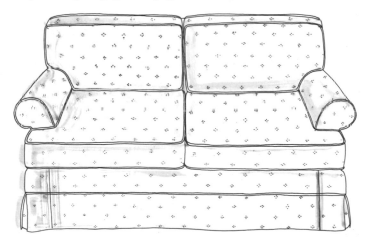

Fabric: Amount needed for slipcover with tailored skirt, self-welt, and extra cushions (see chart, page 199).
Notions: Cording in an amount needed for slipcover welt; 2 heavy duty zippers for seat platform.

1. Make self-**welting** to go in seams and twice around each seat and back cushion.

2. Construct the slipcover according to the general instructions, page 200, up to the point of making the skirt.
3. To make the skirt, start at either inside arm, where the zippers will be inserted. Plan for pleats at each corner and at the center back. Continue around the sofa to the opposite inside arm. The skirt front is cut separately with a center pleat and joins the skirt with the zippers.
4. Attach skirt to slipcover at the welted seam.
5. Insert **zippers** along each side of the seat platform (see page 205).

Sofa with Gathered Skirt

Slipcover is photographed on page 36.

Fabric: Amount needed for slipcover with gathered skirt, self-welt, and extra cushions (see chart, page 199).
Notions: Cording in an amount needed for slipcover welt; heavy duty zipper the length of zipper seam, or self-gripping fastener tape or snap tape.

1. Make **welting** from the slipcover fabric.
2. Construct the slipcover according to the general instructions, page 200.
3 Plan and construct the gathered skirt following directions on page 204.
4. Apply skirt to slipcover in a welted seam.
5. Insert **zipper.**

Wall Upholstery

Fabric can be applied to walls in many ways: by upholstering to a wood frame or directly to the wall; by gluing with wallpaper paste; by starching and applying to the walls while still wet; by shirring on rods; or by sticking the fabric against double-face tape. Of all these options, upholstering offers many advantages and is by far the most beautiful application.

By upholstering fabric onto a wall, you can successfully cover a multitude of problems such as peeling paint, cracked or uneven plaster, nail holes, and the like. Fabric-upholstered walls also provide additional insulation and offer some acoustical advantages over painted or papered walls, particularly if the fabric is applied over dense polyester batting. Fabrics can also be eased and stretched to accommodate uneven or irregular wall surfaces. Wall upholstery adds visual warmth and coziness to a room as well as a touch of luxury and old-world charm. And, when the time comes to redecorate, fabrics used in this manner can be easily removed and reused for curtain panels, pillows, and other projects.

If you are working on plasterboard walls, you can staple the fabric directly into the wall surface. However, you may want to create a wooden lattice frame at the wall edges to which the fabric can be attached. Using lattice is more costly and time-consuming, but it does provide a good, soft surface for staples, as well as raising the fabric away from the walls and adding to the custom upholstered look. And, if your walls are dense plaster or concrete, lattice or other wood strips are the *only* answer.

Upholstered walls will last beautifully for many years, especially when done in rooms with light traffic patterns such as bedrooms, dining rooms, and sitting rooms. You can successfully use wall upholstery in hallways, bathrooms, and kitchens, but because of heavy use and the chance of soil, it may need to be replaced more frequently.

Fabrics
Many different fabrics can be used successfully on walls, but it's wise to consider the following points before making a decision:

- Closely woven fabrics are always a better choice.
- Allover, small-scale patterns are easier to match and use, especially for your first wall upholstery project.
- Stripes, plaids, and strong horizontal designs accentuate uneven walls and ceilings lines. If you choose one of these designs, find a woven, rather than a printed, stripe or plaid. *Never pick a plaid or stripe for your first try. They demand experience and great patience.*
- Always choose fabric that is accurately printed on the straight grain. Uneven grainlines can cause ripples in the upholstered surface as well as make it difficult to keep a perfect pattern match along the ceiling and corner lines. Sheeting is generally not suitable for wall upholstery since it is printed with little attention to grainlines. Fabrics with light-colored backgrounds of solid colors show soil faster than those with medium or dark backgrounds.

Measuring
In planning your upholstery job, you will need to look at the room in two ways. First, determine the overall amount of space to be covered. Compute this from the perimeter of the entire room, divided by the useable width of the fabric, excluding selvages and pattern match, and multiply by the length of the panels required to go from the floor to the ceiling. Second, consider the placement of the panels on each of the walls. Although the first calculations are simple mathematics, the second require some creative judgment. You will want, for example, to center carefully any major motifs on the walls. In some cases this may mean that no two walls are upholstered exactly alike to have patterns between windows or along unbroken walls in the most pleasing way. Even with allover patterns or solid fabrics, you will want to place the seams at the most logical locations along each wall. Try to ensure the most attractive result without wasting fabric. This riddle is one of the challenges of wall upholstery!

After you have determined the number and placement of the panels along each wall, you can figure the required yardage for the whole job by multiplying the number of panels by the height of the walls *plus* the design **repeat,** *plus* 3″. Thus, on a wall measuring 8′, or 96″, using a fabric with a 12″ repeat, and allowing an additional 3″ at the bottom for pulling the panel taut as you upholster the wall, the total panel length would be 111″. This will give the total number of inches. By dividing this figure by thirty-six, you can determine the required yardage per panel. Don't subtract for doors or windows unless they are unusually large. You can plan to use any fabric remnants you cut away from openings for pillows or other small projects in the room. You may want to tack on a few additional yards for insurance before buying.

One final note about figuring fabric yardage: if you are planning to trim the unfinished edges with a self-fabric trim such as a double bias welt, you will have to allow extra fabric for this purpose. To determine the amount of yardage you will need for these finishes, refer to the section on **welting** in "Tools, Terms, and Techniques."

Materials Needed
Fabric: Enough to cover all walls (calculated as above), plus yardage, if desired, to make trim for the wall edges as discussed at the end of this chapter.

Trims and Notions: ½″ cording for double **welt**—twice the measurement of all stapled raw edges at ceiling, baseboard, in corners, around window and doors, *or* purchased trim in the same amount to cover all stapled edges; polyester batting—enough to cover all walls. Use 54″ wide, heavyweight (approximately ½″ thick) batting available by the yard, if obtainable; otherwise, you can use polyester batting sold by the piece for quilts. Select the size that most closely fits the height of your walls to keep waste to a minimum. Cotton batting is not recommended since it shreds easily both during application and after the walls are hung.

Hardware: 1″ × ¼″ wood lattice strips or similar wood strips—enough to run along ceiling and floor lines, down both sides of every corner, and to outline all windows and doors; a good quality, lightweight staple gun and ¼″ staples; a tack hammer for tapping in staples that don't enter the wood or wall entirely; a staple remover for removing badly placed staples or those which are used to anchor the fabric as you work; a plumb bob or weighted line; several nails for attaching the plumb bob; a straight edge for marking fabric for cutting and to use as a guide when trimming fabric on walls; a level, especially when using plaids, stripes, or strong horizontal patterns; long push pins for securing trim to fabric while the glue dries; fabric or white glue, or brads, to put up trim (as discussed at the end of this section); several boxes of industrial, single-edge razor blades (a utility knife to hold the razor blades while cutting is also useful); electric hot glue gun and hot glue sticks. Glue is dispensed from the gun in a bead 1⁄16″ in diameter. It bonds in sixty seconds, and is very effective in putting up lattice and finishing trim.

Instructions
These instructions may seem long, but they are very complete and easy to follow. Upholstering a room is not a small job. We've tried to anticipate your questions, based on our own experience. Read through these pages *thoroughly* before beginning the job.

1. Frame all the walls to be upholstered with lattice or other similar wood strips. Use panel adhesive or hot glue along the entire length of each strip, and nail it to the wall every three or four feet and at each end. Frame across the ceiling line (under crown molding, if any), across the top of the floor or baseboard moldings, down either side of the corners, and around all openings like doors, windows, etc. It isn't necessary to miter the lattice. Simply butt the ends together at ninety-degree angles. To repeat curves or arched doorways, cut short pieces of lattice, approximately 2″ in length, and ease them around the curves.

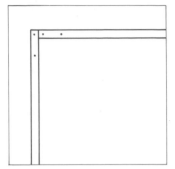
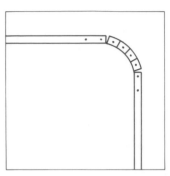

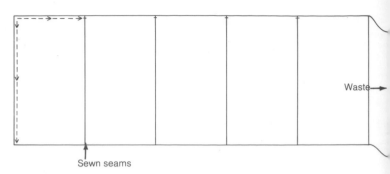

Sewn seams

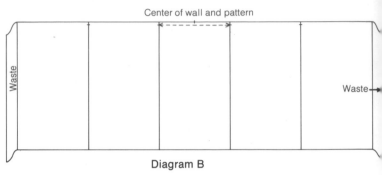

Center of wall and pattern

Waste

Waste

Diagram B

2. Remove all covers from electrical wall switches and outlets. If there are holes in the wall which you will want to use again (such as for drapery rods, shelving, etc.), mark the location with a short broken piece of matchstick placed in the hole. When the walls are completed, you will be able to slit the fabric in that spot with a razor blade just enough to pull the stick through and insert screws, nails, etc.

3. Using a staple gun and ¼" staples, attach the batting to the top and bottom lattice strips in one long piece. Staple along the outside walls, and around windows and doors, and trim away any excess. It is sometimes helpful to use one or two staples along the unsewn seams between lengths of batting to secure it before fabric is applied. Don't use too many, however, or the indentation along this line will show through the finished fabric surface. Be careful not to pull the batting too taut or it will separate.

4. Plan the fabric placement on the walls. Beginning on the "feature wall" (the one which is the most prominent in the room), place the pattern in the most attractive position, centering the predominant motifs and determining the cut line at the ceiling. It is always easier to start with a selvage edge in a corner. This gives you a straight line at the start. But let the fabric tell you what to do, and, if it is the better solution to center the pattern on the wall and work out to the left and to the right into the corners, adjust the fabric accordingly.

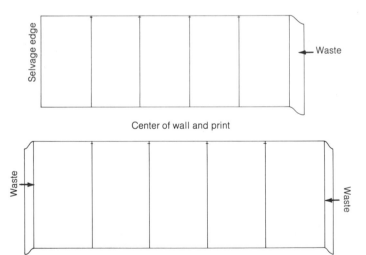

Selvage edge

Waste

Center of wall and print

Waste

Waste

Diagram A

5. After figuring the cut line at the ceiling, cut enough panels to complete the wall, allowing for repeats and leaving an extra 3" at the bottom of each panel to enable you to grip the fabric firmly to pull it taut on the wall. *Be sure to match the pattern on all the panels.* If you are using an allover design with no dominant motif, consider starting at the room's least noticeable corner so that the one place which

will not match is the least obvious. (See Diagram A.)

6. Pin or baste the panels together, carefully matching the pattern. Sew all seams with 8 to 10 stitches per inch. If your machine has a walking foot, it will prevent the matched panels from slipping during the sewing process. Trim away all selvages or clip them every inch.

7. Loosely staple the fabric "wall" to the lattice at the starting point and in one or two places along its length. This takes the weight off the cut top edge, and prevents stretching.

8. Beginning at the corner or at the center of the wall, start to staple the fabric to the ceiling line, placing the staples right next to one another. *Never pull the cut edge as you staple, since this will throw the fabric off the lengthwise grain and the seams will "bow."* Keep the top line of the fabric smooth and flat but not stretched. You may need to practice this a few times. Remember that in every step, neatness counts. Staples that are only half in the lattice will be a big problem when you are ready to trim the wall. Staples that are out of line, or too high or too low along the baseboard molding, will have to be removed, one by one, and replaced before trimming or they will show. Take the time to do the very best job you can at every step along the way. (See Diagram B.)

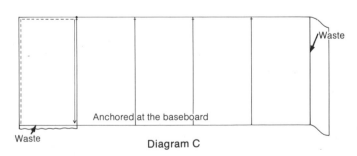

Waste

Anchored at the baseboard

Waste

Diagram C

9. If you began at a corner, after stapling across the ceiling for a yard or so, staple down the selvage along the corner, pulling the fabric down tightly as you go. Try not to pull the fabric off-grain. The selvage edge can be your straight line guide. Continue this process until you come to the first seam in the fabric "wall," and have finished the corner edge down to the floor or baseboard molding.

10. Take hold of the bottom edge of the fabric along the floor or baseboard and pull down firmly along the seam until the fabric is as taut as you can manage. Staple the seam into the lattice at the bottom to hold this tension. (See Diagram C.) Check the line of the seam with a plumb bob or weighted line. Adjust it if it is not perfectly straight. You may want to place several staples directly into the seam to hold this straight line down the length of the panel. If ¼" staples will not hold the fabric through the seam, try ⁵⁄₁₆". Put in as few staples as possible, however, since they tend to leave indentations in the seam and can be difficult to work out after the wall is finished.

11. Step back and examine the finished first panel. The pattern should be straight with no "bowing" along the seam, and the panel should look "square" and on-grain. If it doesn't, correct any problems before proceeding. (A level might prove useful here.)

12. Begin the second panel, using the plumb bob and the seam as your straight edge guide. Ease the fabric along the ceiling line as before. Anchor the bottom of the second seam. Move the bob and check the seam to make sure it is straight. Move on until you have finished the entire wall.

13. When the wall is finished, staple the bottom edge. Pull as tightly as you can without causing the pattern to pull off-grain or distort. You can check this with the level. This is the most difficult edge to do since you can't see the beginning of the baseboard and must feel it and the lattice strip with your fingers. Go slowly and remove and replace any staples that are too high or too low. Remember, neatness counts.

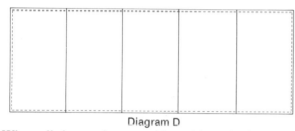

Diagram D

14 When all the staples are anchored into the lattice and the wall looks even and on-grain, cut off the excess fabric along the bottom edge and in the corner with a single-edge razor. (See Diagram D.)

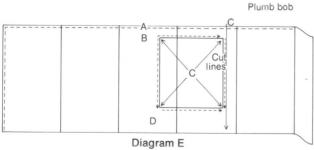

Diagram E

15. To upholster around doors and windows, staple across the top of the opening along the ceiling line so that the fabric falls over the opening, as shown in Diagram E. After the top cut edge has been securely stapled, work across the top edge of the door or window, starting at the right- or left-hand side. Work in the same direction as you are working the top edge of the fabric "wall." Feel the frame of the

opening through the fabric to determine where the lattice strip is, and, therefore, where to staple. Be careful not to miss the strip. Staple down one side.

Carefully slash through the fabric that must be eventually cut away to free it from the frame and allow it to be pulled evenly along the second side edge. Be careful to slash only as much as you need to release the tension over the opening. Staple the second side. A plumb line can be very helpful here. Drop it from the ceiling along a prominent motif and then use it as a guide to establish a straight line down the window or door edge. Ease the fabric across the bottom edge, feeling carefully for the lattice under the frame. (When working around a door, there will be no bottom edge.)

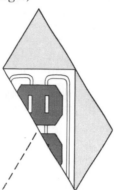 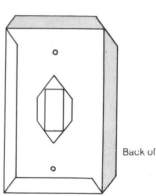

Back of plate

16. After the wall is finished, the outlets and switches must be uncovered by cutting through the fabric as described for uncovering windows and doors. To be safe, you may choose to shut off the electricity in the room before beginning to work. To uncover the electrical unit, slash the fabric over the outlet in the shape of an "X." Trim away triangles so that the fabric just covers the edges of the electrical box. The replaced switch plate will cover the raw edges. You may choose to staple the fabric around the outlet to ensure that it won't work its way out.

You can cover the switch plates with fabric by cutting a piece of fabric that matches the area on the wall. Hold the switch plate in place and align the design. Double-face tape on the switch plate will hold the fabric in place temporarily. Glue the fabric to the plate, wrapping about ¾" around to the back, as shown.

17. After completing the first wall, proceed to the second, working in the same direction, and carefully matching any pattern in the corner. If you have planned the room properly, the print should fall in the best possible way all around the room. Not every wall will be perfectly centered unless you have been able to fudge a little in the corners. When working with small, nondirectional prints, centering is not so crucial, but with large, demanding prints, it is sometimes better to center the motif on each wall, letting the corners fall as they will. Only you, the room, and the choice of fabric can determine this decision. Even if all the corners match at the beginning, there will undoubtedly be one at the end where there is a mismatch. Obviously, this last corner should be in the least visible place in the room. Do the best matching job you can, and don't worry about the places where a match is impossible. A well-positioned mirror or piece of art can distract the eye from any awkward corner.

Trimming the Walls

Trimming the walls is the final step. Even before deciding what sort of trimming method you will use, you need to determine the quantity of trim needed to finish the room. To do this, first measure across the ceiling and floor lines. Add the heights in each corner, allowing for a double line of trim to cover the double line of staples in the corners. Then measure around all the openings. You'll find that you need a surprisingly large amount of trim.

If your room does not yet have a crown or baseboard molding, you may choose to upholster the walls first and then install painted moldings over the staple lines. This will eliminate the need for trim in these areas, leaving just doors, windows, and corners to do. (This technique was used in the breakfast room photographed on page 53.)

There are many choices for fabric wall trims:

Double Bias Welting. Generally available only through upholstery workrooms with a commercial machine. It is often possible to pay a shop to produce the amount you need. If they request that you cut the bias strips of fabric for them, follow the instructions for cutting continuous **bias strips,** page 122, in "Tools, Terms, and Techniques." To figure the amount of additional fabric you will need, consult the chart on the same page.

Making your own double bias welt is a time-consuming process, but the techniques are easy to master:

1. Purchase twice the amount of trim needed in ¼" cording.

2. Cut 1¾"-wide **bias strips** in an amount equal to the length of trim needed. Be generous!

3. Wrap one side of the bias strip around one cord. With a zipper foot, stitch close to the cord along the entire length of the bias strip with a ⅛" to ¼" seam allowance along one edge.

4. Place the second cord next to the first on the wrong side of the fabric. Then bring the fabric over the second cord as illustrated.

5. Turn the welting piece to the front side. Change to a regular presser foot. Stitch over the first stitching line, being sure to hold the fabric firmly over the second cord as you sew. Keep the cords close together.

6. Trim away all excess fabric from the back side of the welt.

7. Apply the welt with small brads or glue (see page 211).

Purchased Trims. Trim companies offer many flat braid or gimp trims which can be used effectively on upholstered walls. Even grosgrain ribbon can be used. A classic, color-coordinated trim is usually a better choice than a demanding or jazzy one. Contrasting trims can give a room a special quality, of course, but you may tire of them more easily or they may compete with later additions to the room. Considering that the investment in trim yardage will be a large one, it's generally better to make a more conservative selection. Purchased trims can be applied with brads or glue.

Flat Bias Strips. This technique was used to finish the plaid bedroom on page 70.

1. To make your own, cut 1"-wide **bias strips** in sufficient quantity to cover all raw edges in the room except for the corners. Cut 2"-wide strips for the corners. Fabric can be cut on the straight grain, but you will have to miter trim at the corners, which can be bulky, instead of easing trim around them.

2. With the wrong sides together, press over the long edges of the strips so that they meet in the center of the strip. (1" then becomes ½"; 2" becomes 1".)

3. Cut strips of fusible web the finished width of the bias strips. Insert it between the layers of fabric and fuse.

4. Glue these strips in place over the staples. A hot glue gun is the faster method, but a thin layer of craft glue is adequate. Before gluing the corner strips in place, crease them down the center to make them fit perfectly.

Fabric Borders. Where a border motif can be successfully cut from a fabric, it can be used to cover staples at the ceiling line and/or along the baseboard. This technique was used in the breakfast room on page 53.

1. Cut border strips from the fabric about 2" wider than the desired finished width (allowing 1" excess on either side of the border). Cut strips of fusible web slightly narrower than the border strips. Seam the fabric strips together if necessary.

2. To adhere fusible web to the wrong side of the border fabric, place strip of fusible web on a piece of tempered glass (e.g., the bottom of a glass baking dish). Place the strip of fabric on top of the fusible web. Fuse with a dry iron, on cotton setting. Peel the fabric away from the glass. The fusible web adheres to the fabric, but not to the glass.

3. Trim the border to the desired finished width. Fuse it to the wall upholstery with a hot, dry iron on cotton setting. If you are working with a synthetic or blend, be sure to test a remnant first to ensure that the fabric won't scorch. A small travel iron works well in tight places. If you do not want to go around the corners, stop just beyond each corner and cut the border. Turn the next strip under 1" at the end and put a small piece of fusible web underneath. Fuse into place. The border can also be applied with a thin layer of craft glue or spray adhesive. Test a piece first to determine that the glue won't bleed through the border fabric.

Combination of Flat Fabric Strips and Welt. This technique was used to finish the batik bathroom shown on page 88.

1. Make flat, straight-grain or **bias strips** from contrast or coordinating fabric as described above. Apply with glue.

2. Make **welting** from bias strips of wall fabric. Trim away seam allowance from welting to the stitching line. Apply over 1"-wide flat strips with glue, placing the raw edges toward wall.

Beds, Bedding, and Bedroom Accessories

The bedroom offers more opportunities for projects that can be sewn from or covered with fabric than any other room in your home. The projects featured here cover many different styles and tastes. Since bedrooms are often shared by two people whose design preferences differ, a combination of styles is frequently the preferred decorating direction. Bold tartan plaids can be softened by the addition of bias ruffles. (See page 71.) Simply tailored designs can be enhanced by the use of luxurious silk. (See page 76.)

No matter what style you choose, it's important to keep in mind that correct measurements here, as in all project areas, are crucial, and that bed measurements can vary from manufacturer to manufacturer. Always check before cutting to ensure a perfect fit. These standard measurements can, however, be used as a guide:

Twin—39″ wide x 75″ long
Double—54″ wide x 75″ long
Queen—60″ wide x 80″ long
King—78″ wide x 80″ long

Since the bedroom is a private rather than a public space in your home, it's the perfect place to stretch your skills and imagination and to tackle decorating options that are more experimental and aesthetically challenging.

Canopy Beds

A canopy bed is the focal point of a bedroom, lending charm, luxury, and scale to the room. It can be simple or elaborate, tailored or feminine, depending upon your choice of fabric and the style of bed fittings. As you plan a canopy bed, keep the following information in mind:

• The instructions in this section are generally written for a queen-size bed. Notes for adjusting to smaller or larger sizes will appear at the beginning of each project, but you will need to consider the specific size adjustments to fit your bed as you proceed through the instructions.

• The bed parts are constructed and installed in the following order: (1) ceiling panel; (2) rods for the back and side panels, where needed; (3) back panel; (4) curtain panels; and (5) valance.

• In canopy bed and headboard designs that require some carpentry work, we've included basic information, diagrams, and instructions to complete the projects. It's wise to complete any carpentry work needed to build the bed frame before beginning the sewing portion of the project. We recommend that all canopy bed frames be attached to the ceiling by a professional carpenter for reasons of safety. If a canopy bed is planned for a child's room, considerable care should be exercised in attaching the frame to the ceiling securely; undue stress on the fabric side panels could loosen the frame.

• Fabric yardages required for each section of the canopy bed project are listed separately by item. Add these together for the total amount of fabric you will need to complete the whole canopy bed. We chose this method because it gives you more flexibility when selecting matching or contrasting fabrics for linings, pillows, dust ruffles, and the like.

• Read through the instructions for all parts of the project before beginning.

Canopy Bed with Unlined Panels and Valance

Canopy bed is photographed on page 71.

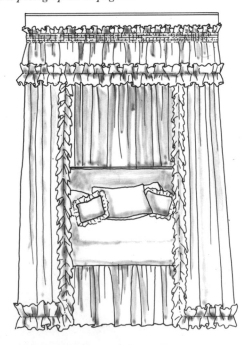

Canopy Frame and Ceiling Panel Frame

Plan the canopy frame 5″ wider and 5″ longer than the bed to allow for the folds in the fabric panels.

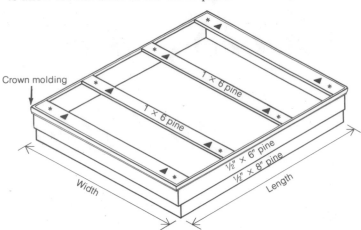

Wood: Pine boards for the canopy frame (Diagram A): (1″ × 6″ by 4 times the width of the frame; ½″ × 6″ by the perimeter of the frame; ½″ × 8″ by the perimeter of the frame; crown molding the width desired by the length needed to go around the sides and bottom end of the frame); pine boards for the ceiling panel frame—1″ × 3″ by the length needed to construct the frame as illustrated in Diagram B.

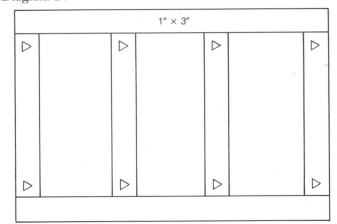

Hardware: 8 lag bolts or butterfly bolts (4″); 8 screws.

Have a professional carpenter build the frames according to Diagrams A and B. The ceiling panel frame will fit inside the canopy frame, allowing ¼″ all around for ceiling fabric. Make matching screw holes in both frames before applying the fabric. The ½″ × 8″ and the ½″ × 6″ boards, as well as the crown molding on the canopy frame, will show when the bed is completed, so be sure to put a finish on these boards or paint them.

Bed Ceiling Panel

Fabric:

Mattress Size	45″ Fabric	54″ Fabric
Twin	7½ yards	6 yards
Double	8¾ yards	7 yards
Queen	10 yards	8 yards
King	12½ yards	10 yards

Tools: Staple gun and staples.

1. Cut five equal panels from 45" fabric or four from 54" fabric. The length of each fabric panel should be equal to the width of the ceiling panel frame plus 8" to 10" for wrapping around the frame.

2. **Gather** the panels at all cut ends of the pieces to 2½ times fullness. (A 45" panel will gather to 18", a 54" panel will gather to 21".)

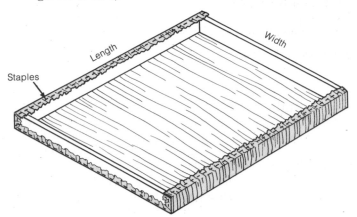

3. Staple the gathered panels along one long side of the ceiling frame piece. Space the panels evenly along the length. The panels do not need to be seamed together.

4. Bring the panels over the frame to the opposite side. Pull them taut and staple them securely. Adjust the folds.

5. At each end of the bed (the head- and footboards), pull the fabric just over the frame edge and staple it in place.

6. Push the ceiling frame into the inside of the canopy and screw it in place.

Bed Back Panel

Fabric: For twin bed, 3 times the distance from the top of the canopy to 8" to 10" below the top of the mattress; for double/queen, 4 times this distance; for king, 5 times the distance.

Hardware and Tools: ⅜" brass rod equal in length to the inside width of the bed, and mounting hardware; staples and staple gun.

1. Cut the number of panels of fabric needed as indicated above, and seam them together along the lengthwise edges, right sides together.

2. Turn under 1¼" at the top edge to the wrong side of the fabric for the **casing**. Turn raw edge under ¼" and stitch the hem in place, leaving both ends open. Make a narrow hem in the bottom edges of the panel.

3. **Gather** the bottom edge to the length of the brass rod.

4. Install the brass rod on the inside of the canopy bed frame as close to the ceiling panel and the corners as possible. Slip the panel over the installed brass rod. (See Step 9 of Bed Curtain Panels, following, for details.)

5. Screw a board into the wall behind the bed, 6" to 8" below the top of the mattress.

6. Pull the panels down firmly, being careful not to distort any pattern or plaid. Staple the panel to the board. Adjust the folds of the gathers.

Bed Curtain Panels

Fabric: Six panels, each the distance from the floor to the ceiling panel less ¾". Also 5 to 7½ yards of 54" fabric for ruffle (add 1 yard for 45" fabric). If using 54" fabric for a twin bed, consider five panels: 1½ panels at each bottom corner and ¾ panel at each side of the headboard.

Hardware: Six ⅜" brass rods plus mounting hardware. For twin size, use 15"-long rods or less; for double, 17" or less; for queen, 18"; for king, 20".

1. The bed has a single panel on each side of the headboard and two panels at each of the footboard corners. Seam the panels together for the foot of the bed to within 6" of the top edges with an **enclosed seam.**

2. Cut the bottom corners of the panels into a curved shape, except for the corners at the back edge of the headboard panels (see diagram).

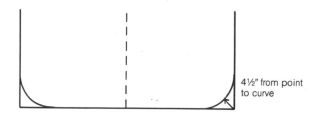

4½" from point to curve

3. Make a narrow hem on the sides and bottom of all the panels.

4. Turn under 1¼" at the top edge to the right side of the fabric for a **casing.** Turn the raw edge under ¼" and stitch the hem in place, leaving it open at both ends.

5. To make **ruffles,** cut enough 6½" wide **bias strips** to create 30 to 37 yards of bias, depending on the fullness desired. If you are using 54" fabric, fifteen strips of double fullness are needed, and eighteen for 2½ times fullness; add two or three strips for narrower fabric.

6. Seam the bias strips together. Make a narrow hem on both long edges.

7. **Gather** the bias strips through the center of the strip. You can gather by hand as you sew, or zigzag over a string. If you do the latter, sew about 2 yards, stop, and pull up the ruffles; continue sewing 2 yards at a time and pulling up the ruffles to the end of the fabric. The yield is about 15 yards of ruffles.

8. Sew the ruffles to the sides and the bottoms of the panels, beginning and ending just below the casing. On the headboard panels, apply them only to the front side edge and the bottom. Place the center of the ruffles on or near the narrow hem of the panel.

9. Install the brass rods on the inside of the bed canopy frame as close to the ceiling panel and the corners as possible. The panels go on the rods with the back of the casing toward the wood frame. Be sure the ceiling frame is in place before installing the hardware for the rods.

Bed Valance

Fabric:

Mattress Size	45" Fabric	# of Strips	54" Fabric	# of Strips
Twin	5 yards	11	4 yards	9
Double	5½ yards	12	4½ yards	10
Queen	6 yards	13	5 yards	11
King	6½ yards	14	5 yards	11

plus 4½ yards of 54" fabric, or 5½ yards of 45" fabric for ruffles.

Notions and Hardware: 4-string shirring tape—13¼ yards for twin-size; 14¼ yards for double; 15¼ yards for queen; 16½ yards for king; brads.

1. Using the chart above as your guide, cut the number of 16" panels required for your bed size and fabric.
2. Seam the panels together on the short edges to create one strip. Make a narrow hem along the bottom and side edges.
3. Press under ½" to the wrong side along the upper edge. Sew the shirring tape to this edge on the wrong side of the valance, starting the tape ⅛" down from the folded edge. Sew along the top and bottom edges of the tape and on each side of all strings (eight rows).
4. Make bias **ruffles** as directed in Steps 5 through 7 of Bed Curtain Panels, preceding.
5. Sew the ruffle to the bottom edge of the valance with the center of the ruffle on or near the hem of the valance.
6. Pull the strings till valance is 6" to 8" longer than the canopy measurement. (The valance covers only three sides of the bed.) Adjust the gathers evenly and tack the valance with brads to the outside of the canopy frame, allowing extra fullness at the corners and bringing the valance around the back corners about 2" to 3". Adjust the gathers to cover the brads.

Canopy Bed with Lined Panels and Valance

Canopy bed is photographed on page 69.

Canopy Frame and Ceiling Panel

Build the frames following the instructions for Canopy Bed with Unlined Panels and Valance, page 216, eliminating the crown molding and the ½" × 6" boards. Instead of ½" × 8" boards, use 1" × 3" boards, covered or painted to match the bed lining fabric.

Bed Ceiling Panel

Use the same materials and instructions as in Canopy Bed with Unlined Panels and Valance.

Bed Back Panel

Use the same materials and instructions as in Canopy Bed with Unlined Panels and Valance.

Bed Curtain Panels

Fabric: Six panels of face fabric, each the distance from the floor to the ceiling panel plus 7¾". If using 54" fabric for a twin bed, consider 5 panels: 1½ panels at each bottom corner and ¾ panel at each side of the headboard. Lining fabric in the same amount.
Hardware: Six ⅜" brass rods plus mounting hardware. For twin-size, use 15"-long rods or less; for double, 17" or less; for queen, 18", and for king, 20".

1. The bed has a single panel on each side of the headboard and two panels at each of the footboard corners. Seam the panels for the foot of the bed to within 6" of the top edges. Do this for both face fabric and lining.
2. Put a 3" double hem in the bottom of the face fabric and a 3¼" double hem in the lining panels.
3. Pin the linings to the face fabric panels, right sides together, along the side edges only, aligning them at the top edges; the lining should be ½" above the bottom edge of the face fabric. Stitch to within 6" of the top edge.
4. Press the seams open. Turn the panels right side out. Press the panels flat with the seams at the outside edges.
5. At the top edge of the panel, turn 1¼" of the fabric and the lining together to the right side of the fabric for a casing. (The lining will be on the outside.) Turn the raw edges under ¼" and stitch in place, leaving it open at both ends. The panels at the footboard corners have two separate casings (one for each side of the corner), where the seam was left open. On a twin-size, where one and one-half panels per corner are used, split the panel for 6" in the center of the top and finish off the raw edges.
6. Install the brass rods on the inside of the bed canopy frame as close to the ceiling panel and corners as possible. Panels go on the rods with the back of the casing toward the wood frame. Be sure the ceiling frame is in place before installing the hardware for the rods.

Bed Valance

Fabric: See the valance fabric chart under Canopy Bed with Unlined Panels and Valance, page 216; lining fabric in the same amount.
Notions and Hardware: 4-string shirring tape—13¼ yards for twin-size; 14¼ yards for double; 15¼ yards for queen; 16½ yards for king; brads.

1. Cut 16"-long panels for the valance from the face and lining fabrics. Seam the panels together to create one strip of face fabric and one of lining.
2. Sew the face fabric strip and the lining strip, right sides together, along the side and bottom edges with a ½" seam allowance.

3. Press the seams open. Turn right side out and press. Baste the raw edges together ¼″ from the top.

4. Press under ½″ to the lining side along the upper edge. Sew the shirring tape to this edge on the wrong side of the valance, starting the tape ⅛″ down from the folded edge. Sew along the top and bottom edges of the tape, and on each side of all strings (eight rows).

5. Pull up the strings till the valance is 6″ to 8″ longer than the canopy measurement. (The valance covers only three sides of the bed.) Adjust the gathers evenly and tack them with brads to the outside of the canopy, allowing extra fullness at the corners and bringing the valance 2″ to 3″ around the back corners. Adjust the gathers to cover brads.

Canopy Bed with Eyelet-trimmed Panels, Valance, and Tie Backs

Canopy bed is photographed on page 102.

In order to use tie backs, the canopy bed must have tall posts at the head and foot of the bed.

Canopy Frame and Ceiling Panel

Fabric: Muslin or lining fabric (optional) to cover the frames.

Wood: Pine board, 1″ × 6″ by the length needed to construct a frame as illustrated below. Plan the frame to be 5″ longer and 5″ wider than the bed. Pine board, 1″ × 3″ by the perimeter of the frame.

Hardware: Four 6″ lengths of sturdy chain; eight large cup hooks; four toggle bolts.

1. Cut the boards to the specified lengths and construct the frame as illustrated. Cover the frame with muslin or lining fabric, if desired.

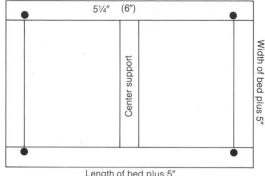

2. Attach the cup hooks at each dot (●) on the illustration.

3. Position the toggle bolts in the ceiling to correspond to the location of the cup hooks on the frame. Attach one of the four lengths of chain to each of the bolts. Suspend the frame by hooking the chain with the cup hooks.

4. Make and attach the bed ceiling panel to the frame as described under Canopy Bed with Unlined Panels and Valance, page 216, eliminating Step 6.

5. Cut the 1″ × 3″ board into the lengths needed to go around the perimeter of the frame. Cover the boards with muslin or lining fabric, if desired. Nail or screw the boards to the sides of the frame over the fabric, so that the top of the board is flush with the top of the frame and creates a "lip" on the frame.

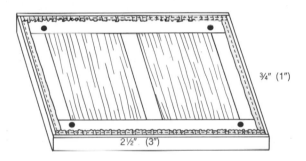

6. Before the final hanging of the frame, cover the chains with fabric, if desired, as described later in these instructions.

Bed Back Panel

Use the same materials and instructions as in Canopy Bed with Unlined Panel and Valance, page 216, except hang the brass rod from large cup hooks screwed into the underside of the lip on the canopy frame. Cup hooks will probably be necessary at each end and at two to four positions in between, depending on the width of the bed.

Bed Curtain Panels

Fabric: Six panels the height of the bed from the floor to the bottom of the canopy frame lip. Fabric width of each panel should allow about 2½ times fullness on rods specified below. Lining fabric in the same amount.

Trim: 60 yards of 3″-wide flat eyelet.

Hardware: Six ⅜″ brass rods plus mounting hardware. For twin-size, use 15″-long rods or less; double, 17″ or less; queen, 18″; king, 20″; twelve large cup hooks.

1. The bed has a single panel on each side of the headboard and two panels at each of the footboard corners. Seam the panels of both the face and lining fabrics for the foot of the bed to within 6″ of the top edges. If the fabric has a lengthwise border stripe, as photographed, plan so that the border is positioned at the side seam edge of all the panels.

2. **Gather** the eyelet to 2½ times fullness. (60 yards will yield approximately 24 yards of ruffled eyelet.)

3. Sew the eyelet to the side and bottom edges of the face fabric, right sides together, with a ⅜″ seam. On the headboard panels, apply the eyelet only to the front edge and the bottom. End the eyelet 4″ from the top raw edge of the panel.

4. Sew the lining to each face fabric panel with a ½″ seam, right sides together, along the side and bottom edges only. Turn the panels right side out and press.

5. At the top edge of the panel, turn under 2″ of the fabric and the lining together. Turn under ½″ along the raw edges and stitch in place, leaving it open at both ends. The panels at the footboard corners have two separate **casings** (one for each side of the corner) where the seam was left open.

6. Screw the cup hooks into the underside of the canopy frame lip, spacing them evenly 16″ to 20″ apart. Hang the curtain panels on the brass rods held up by these hooks.

7. To make tiebacks, cut a 3-yard length of fabric into four 11″-wide strips. If the fabric has a border stripe, plan so that the stripe will be centered on the front of the tie. Also, adjust the width of the tie based on the width of the stripe. The ties should be 4″ to 6″ wide.

Fold each tie in half lengthwise, right sides together. Trim the ends on a diagonal. Stitch across the ends and along the lengthwise raw edge with ½″ seams, leaving an opening along the lengthwise edge for turning. Trim the seam allowances to ¼″ and press open. Turn right side out. Press again with the seam at an edge. Close the opening with a **slip stitch.**

Fold the tie in half vertically. Stitch across the tie vertically about 3″ from the fold creating a **casing** to slip over the bedpost. Adjust the casing depth so that the tie will slip easily but firmly over the post.

Slip the tie over the post. Bring the ends to the outside of the bed and tie them in a large bow.

Bed Valances

This bed hanging uses two valances—one of the main fabric on the outside of the canopy frame, and a second of contrast fabric, matching the bed ceiling panels and lining of bed panels, that is installed inside the frame.

Fabric: Outside valance (amount of fabric indicated in chart plus enough extra fabric to cut border strips the length around the valance before shirring); inside valance (amount of fabric indicated in chart).

Mattress Size	45″ Fabric	# of Strips	54″ Fabric	# of Strips
Twin	10 yards	11	8 yards	9
Double	11 yards	12	9 yards	10
Queen	12 yards	13	10 yards	11
King	13 yards	14	10 yards	11

Trims and Notions: 3″ wide flat eyelet 2½ times the length of the outside valance; self-gripping fastener tape (for the outside valance, the length of both sides and the bottom of the bed plus 10″; for the inside valance, the length of all four sides of the bed); 4-string shirring tape in an amount equal to the ungathered length of each valance; glue, nails, or staples for fastening self-gripping fastener tape to canopy frame.

1. Using the chart above as a guide, cut the number of 25″-long panels required for your bed size and fabric width, and seam the strips together on the short ends.

2. **Gather** the eyelet to 2½ times fullness.

3. Sew the eyelet to the bottom edge of the valance, right sides together, with a ⅜″ seam.

4. Fold the valance in half lengthwise, right sides together. Sew the raw edges together with a ½″ seam. Turn right side out. Press. Fold in ½″ at each end of the valance and stitch in place.

5. Cut and seam the strips for the border. Plan the finished border to be a minimum of 4½″ in width.

6. Press under seam allowances on the top and bottom edges of the border strip. Place along the upper edge of the valance, matching the fold of the valance to the top edge of the border. Topstitch along both edges of the border strip.

7. To make top shirring, place shirring tape on the wrong side of the valance, starting ½″ down from the top edge. Sew along the top and bottom edges of the tape and on both sides of each string (eight rows).

Stitch securely across one end of the tape to hold the strings, or tie the strings together. Pull shirring tape to the desired finished size (length of both sides and bottom plus 10″). Stitch across the tape securely at the second side. Adjust the gathers evenly.

8. Sew the fuzzy side of self-gripping fastener tape to the top edge of the valance, with the top of the fastener tape ¾″ down from the top edge.

9. Glue, nail, or staple the loop side of the self-gripping fastener tape to the outside lip of the canopy frame at the same distance on the frame as the tape is positioned on the valance. The tape should continue 5″ around to the back side of the frame at each headboard corner.

10. Cut and construct the inside valance in the same manner, eliminating the eyelet and positioning the seam at the top, instead of the bottom, of the valance. The loop side of the self-gripping fastener tape is attached to the inside lip of the canopy frame, so that the top of the inside valance will meet the ceiling panel.

Ruched Chain Cover

Fabric: Two strips of fabric, each 2½ times the length of the chain by 3″ wide.

1. Gather up both long edges of both strips of fabric to the length of the chain plus 1″.
2. Sew the two strips together along the gathered edges. Turn right side out.
3. Turn in ½″ at both open ends. Sew in place without closing the tunnel.
4. Slip the casing over the chain. Tack the cover to the chain at the top and bottom edges to hold in place.

Canopy Bed with Scallop Edged Panels and Valance

Canopy bed is photographed on page 72.

Fabric: 10 yards of main fabric for twin-, double, and queen-size beds (add ¾ yard for king-size); 10 yards of lining fabric for twin-, double, and queen-size beds (add ¾ yard for king-size), plus enough to cut four panels 8″ to 10″ longer than the space between the canopy frame and the headboard (for double and queen; for twin, cut three panels, and five for king); 10 yards of underlining if dark fabric is used on one side of valance (optional).
Notions: 16 yards single-fold bias tape (add 1 yard for king); 11 yards seam binding (add 1 yard for king), (optional); 1″-wide cardboard strips to attach valance to three sides of canopy frame.

1. To make the back panel, cut the necessary number of panels from the lining fabric. Each panel should be 8″ to 10″ longer than the opening between the canopy frame and the headboard.

2. Seam the panels together along the selvages. Clip the selvages and press the seams open.
3. Make narrow hems at the top and bottom raw edges.
4. Gather the panels about 1″ in from the hemmed edges on the top and bottom to 2½ times fullness.
5. Divide and mark the canopy frame and the headboard below it into as many sections as the number of panels needed for your bed size. Staple the seams of the panels to the marks about 1″ down from the top edge. Adjust the gathers and staple between the seams. Pull down firmly and staple the bottom edge in the same manner.
6. To make the curtain panels, cut two panels the width of the fabric by the height of the bed plus 2″ from both main and lining fabrics (and underlining if used).
7. Lay out the panels on a large flat surface with lining fabric on the bottom and main fabric on the top, wrong sides together. If underlining is used, it should be slipped in between the main and lining fabric.
8. Enlarge the scallop design and make a pattern **template.** Lay the template over the main fabric panel. Use the selvage as the back edge of each panel and be sure you make a right and left panel. Starting at the front bottom corner, working up to the top edge and out to the back corner, trace the scallop design, placed 1″ in from the bottom and front edge, with a pencil. Pin the layers together along all the edges just inside the scallop design. With fabrics sandwiched together, cut out the scallop design.

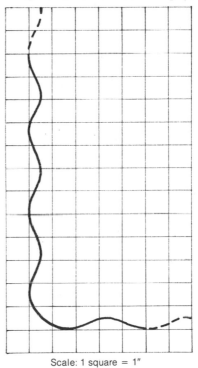

Scale: 1 square = 1″

9. Seam together all lengths of single-fold bias tape across their short ends to total the bias yardage needed for your bed size. One folded edge of binding can be pressed if desired.
10. Apply the bias to the scallop design along the front and bottom edge of each panel, right side of the bias to the right side of the main fabric. The raw edge of the bias should line up with the raw edge of the main fabric along the scallop design. Stitch along the fold line of the bias with a ¼″ seam, leaving ½″ of extra tape at the edges.
11. Trim allowances to ⅛″. Clipping curves is not necessary.

12. Press from the right side to flatten the seam, pressing the seam allowance toward the tape.

13. Bring the bias around to the lining fabric side of the panel and pin it in place so that the bias falls beyond the previous stitching line.

14. From the main fabric side of the panel, "stitch in the ditch," catching the bias on the other side (see "Tools, Terms, and Techniques," page 123). Turn in the extra bias at the edges before stitching the ends. Use the tape color for the bobbin thread and the main fabric background color for the top thread.

15. Sew the back selvage and top edges together through all layers with an **overcast** or straight stitch. The top edge can be bound with seam tape pressed in half, if desired.

16. **Gather** the panels to approximately double fullness, allowing 3″ to go around to the back of the bed frame. Staple the panels to the canopy frame about 1″ down from the top edge. The panels should just clear the floor.

17. Using the remaining fabric for the valance, cut enough strips 19″ wide to equal the length of the sides and bottom of the canopy frame plus 6″ to 8″. If the fabric has an overall two-way design, the valance pieces can be **railroaded** with seams placed at the corners, if possible. If fabric has a one-way design, cut matching strips on a crosswise grain.

18. Seam the valance pieces as needed and make narrow hems at each end.

19. Follow the directions for the curtain panels, Steps 7 through 15, preceding. Use the same scallop template, at the bottom edge of the valance only, starting at the center of the valance and working out to each end.

20. Staple the valance to the canopy frame. The top 2″ of the valance is stapled to the frame with the main fabric side of the valance against the frame. The lining fabric side is facing you. Start at the center of the bottom of the canopy frame and work out in each direction. Staple in place every 5″ to 6″. Do not pull taut. Ease a bit of extra fabric into the corners. Bring the extra around to the back of the bed. Flip the valance down to check its fit.

21. Flip the valance back up as in Step 20. For a straight top edge on the valance, align the edge of the 1″ cardboard strips close to the top of the canopy frame. Staple closely around the canopy top, adding strips of cardboard as needed. Flip the valance down over the cardboard.

Tie-on Bed Curtain

Bed is photographed on page 116.

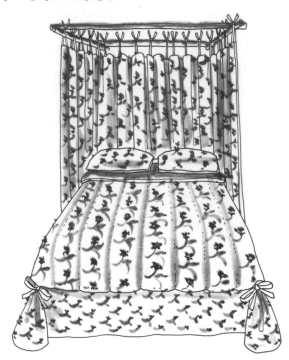

Fabric: Three twin-size sheets (use full-size sheets for king-size bed).

Wood: Four tree branches—Two branches equal the outside width of the bed, and two are the width of the canopy, approximately 20″.

Hardware: Wire, chain, or heavy fishing line; four cup hooks; four toggle bolts.

1. Seam two twin sheets together for the back panel. Split the third sheet in half lengthwise for the side panels.

2. Use the wide, hemmed edge of the sheet for the bottom of the panels. Determine panel length, allowing for a 1¼″ double hem, and cut. (The cutoff will be used for ties.) Make 1″ hems on the side edges of the back and side panels.

3. To make ties, cut thirty-three strips, each 23″ long × 1½″ wide. Seam the long edges of each strip with a ¼″ seam. Turn, press, and close the ends.

4. Fold the ties in half. Along the top edge of the panels, place a tie at each end, and space the others in between about 6″ apart. (Twenty-one ties are for the back panel and six are for each side panel.) Sew the ties to the panels at the fold.

5. To hang the tree branches from the ceiling, lash the ends of the branches together and suspend them with chain, wire, or heavy fishing line from cup hooks which have been positioned in the ceiling on toggle bolts.

6. Tie the curtains to the tree branches.

Headboards

Without a headboard, no bed is truly complete. Fabric-covered headboards, whether used alone or in combination with a curtained or canopied bed, add comfort and elegance to a bedroom. If you have chosen to use a shirred back panel in your bed design, a headboard will keep your pillows from resting against the backdrop and wrinkling it.

Upholstered Headboard
Headboards are photographed on pages 71 and 76.

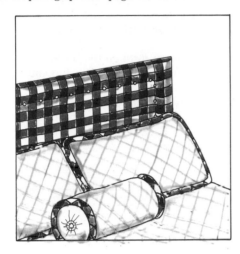

Fabric:

Bed Size	45" Fabric		54" Fabric		Railroaded Fabric (45"–54")	
	Front	Back*	Front	Back*	Front	Back*
Twin	3 yards	1¼ yards	1½ yards	1¼ yards	1½ yards	1¼ yards
Double/ Queen	3 yards	2½ yards	3 yards	2½ yards	2 yards	2 yards
King	4½ yards	3 yards	3 yards	2½ yards	2¾ yards	2½ yards

*Muslin or Lining Fabric Suitable

Wood: Four pine boards, ⁵⁄₄" × 4" for base frame; ¼" plywood for front (see illustrations for details).
Notions: Polyester batting to cover frame in double thickness.
Hardware and Tools: Six corner braces (angle irons), 3" × 3"; two 4"-long flat braces; nails; wood glue; ½"-diameter brass nailheads; staples and staple gun or brads.

1. Cut two pine boards for the sides of the frame, each the height of the bed to the top of the mattress plus 26". Cut two pine boards for the cross pieces, each the desired width of the frame minus 7" (which is the total width of the end boards).

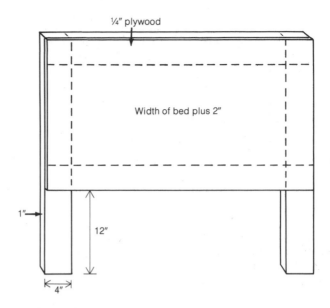

2. Glue the frame together and support the joints with the corner braces and the top ends with the flat braces as shown.

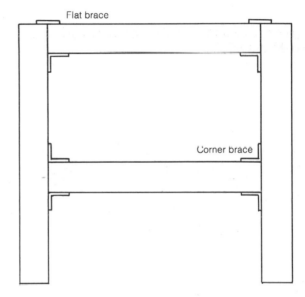

3. Cut the plywood to cover the front of the frame above the legs. Glue plywood and nail securely to frame all around.
4. Cover the frame with a double layer of batting. Pull the batting around to the back side and staple it to the frame.
5. Piece the fabric, if necessary, to obtain the needed width by cutting it into 1½-yard lengths. Split one piece lengthwise and sew one-half to each side of the other full panel.
6. Center the fabric panel on the headboard and staple it to the frame in the same manner as the batting, pulling the fabric firmly around the frame. At the corners of the headboard, fold in on the diagonal line (A) so that lines B and C meet to form a sharp corner (see diagram).

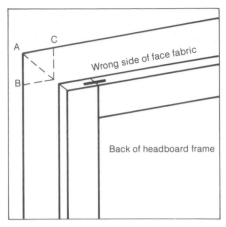

Wrong side of face fabric

Back of headboard frame

7. Cut a piece of fabric the size of the headboard frame. Press under the raw edges 1″ to 2″. Center the fabric on the back of the headboard and use brads, staples, or brass upholstery tacks to secure it in place. Cover the legs of the headboard frame with matching fabric. Staple the fabric to the frame in the least conspicuous spot.

8. To create a decorative or tufted look, use brass nailheads appropriately spaced on the headboard.

Ruffled Headrest Panel for Open Headboard

Headrest is photographed on page 69.

Fabric and Foam:

Mattress Size	Fabric Yardage	Foam Size
Twin	3 yards, 45″ or 54″	38″W x 18″L x 2″D
Double	4½ yards, 45″ or 54″	53″W x 18″L x 2″D
Queen	5½ yards, 45″ 4½ yards, 54″	59″W x 18″L x 2″D
King	6½ yards, 45″ 5½ yards, 54″	77″W x 18″L x 2″D

Notions: Polyester batting to wrap around the foam piece (optional). The dimensions and measurements given in the instructions are for a queen-size bed. Adjust accordingly for a smaller or larger bed.

1. To piece the fabric for the headrest, cut three lengths of fabric 22″ by the width of the fabric. Split one piece into four sections lengthwise. Apply a section to each side of both full-width panels. Trim the width of the seamed pieces to 62″ and round off the top corners slightly.

2. To make the **ruffle,** cut the remaining fabric into 11″-wide **bias strips.** Piece the strips to make a 6½-yard length. Press the pieced strip in half lengthwise, wrong sides together. Baste the raw edges together by machine, ¼″ from the raw edge. **Gather** the 6½-yard length to about 106″. Square off the ends, turning in ½″ to finish both ends and sew closed.

3. Apply the ruffle to the right side of the sides and top of one seamed panel. Begin and end the ruffle 2″ from the bottom edge of the panel.

4. Stitch the panels, right sides together, around the top and sides only, with a ½″ seam. Turn right side out and press.

5. If desired, wrap the batting around the foam piece to create a softer look. Sew the batting to the foam by hand to hold it in place. A curved upholstery needle is helpful for this.

6. Insert the foam form through the bottom opening. Turn in the extra fabric on the bottom. Pin and **slip stitch** to close.

7. Make ½″-wide ties from either bias or straight strips of fabric. (The number of ties will depend on the size and style of headboard.) Tack ties to the back of the panel and attach it to the headboard.

Duvet Covers

A duvet cover is really a giant pillowcase, cut slightly larger than the duvet (also called a continental quilt or comforter) and left open at one end. It can be closed with a zipper, snap tape, or self-gripping fastener tape.

In Europe, duvets have traditionally been a favored wedding gift to the bride from her family. In recent years, the duvet (now available with down, feather, or wool filling) has also gained popularity in the United States, both for its practicality in a time of high heating bills and for ease of bed-making. Duvet covers keep the duvet clean and in good condition, thus protecting an often sizable investment, and offer an economical way to have a wardrobe of bed coverings. To maintain the duvet's inherent appeal of maximum warmth with minimum weight, keep in mind that a lightweight cover fabric is your best choice.

The yardage requirements for the three duvet covers that follow are based on the approximate standard sizes given in the chart below. Be sure to measure the duvet to be covered and adjust the yardage requirements, if necessary, based on actual size.

Simple Duvet Cover

Duvet cover is photographed on page 103.

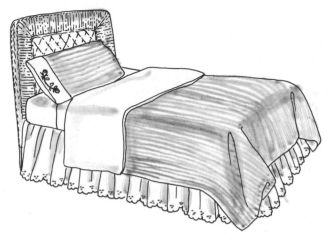

Fabric:

Mattress Size	Approximate Finished Size	44"–45" Fabric* for Each Side	Lengths	54" Fabric* for Each Side	Lengths
Twin	70"W x 88"L	5 yards	2	5 yards	2
Double	78"W x 88"L	5 yards	2	5 yards	2
Queen	88"W x 88"L	7½ yards	3	5 yards	2
King	104"W x 88"L	7½ yards	3	5 yards	2

*Yardage is given for one side of the duvet cover only. You will need this amount for *each side*.

Notions: 1¼ yards self-gripping fastener tape or snap tape, or 40" zipper (shorter for twin-size); 1½ yards of ½" twill tape.

1. Cut the face fabric into the number of 2½-yard lengths needed. Split one length in half lengthwise. Sew half to each side of a full length. (If using narrow fabric for a queen- or king-size cover, piece the three lengths together.) Repeat this process for the lining fabric. Cut the seamed sections to the exact length and width needed plus ½" seam allowances.

2. Sew the face fabric section to the lining fabric section, right sides together, leaving an opening at one end between the two inside seams as illustrated on the diagram (about 44").

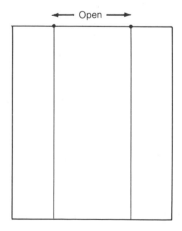

← Open →

3. Coming to within 1" of the opening, trim the seam allowances to ¼" and finish the edges with a zigzag stitch.
4. Cut the twill tape into eight equal pieces. Sew four tapes to the inside of the duvet cover, one in each corner on the seam allowance.
5. Turn the duvet cover right side out.
6. Sew snap tape or self-gripping fastener tape to the inside of each side of the opening, covering the seam allowance, or insert a **zipper.**
7. Sew the remaining four twill tapes to the corners of the duvet.
8. Slip the duvet inside the cover, tying the twill tapes. Shake out to distribute the duvet evenly.

Duvet Cover with Welting

Duvet cover is photographed on pages 72 and 74.

Fabric: See the chart for Simple Duvet Cover, preceding; ½ yard contrast fabric for welting (if making bias).
Notions: 1"-wide bias tape (if you are not making bias strips for welting)—9 yards for twin, 9½ yards for double, 10 yards for queen, 11 yards for king; ⁶⁄₃₂" cording in the same amount as the bias tape; 1¼ yards self-gripping fastener tape or snap tape, or 36" to 40" zipper; 1½ yards of ½" twill tape.

1. Cut the face fabric into the number of 2½-yard lengths indicated on the chart. Split one length in half lengthwise. Sew a half to each side of a full length. (If using narrow fabric for a queen- or king-size cover, piece the three lengths together.) Repeat this process for the lining fabric. Cut the seamed sections to the exact length and width needed plus ½" seam allowances.
2. Cover cording with 1" fabric **bias strips** or purchased bias tape to make the **welting.**
3. Apply welting around all edges to the right side of the face fabric.
4. Continue as in Simple Duvet Cover, preceding, Steps 2 through 8.

Duvet Cover with Ruffle

Duvet cover is photographed on page 68.

Fabric: See the chart under Simple Duvet Cover, page 225; *ruffle fabric*—3½ yards 45″ fabric or 3 yards 54″ fabric. (Yardage is given for double/queen; adjust accordingly for twin or king.)

Notions: 1¼ yards self-gripping fastener tape or snap tape; or 40″ zipper (shorter for twin); 1½ yards of ½″ twill tape.

1. Cut the face fabric into the number of 2½-yard lengths indicated on the yardage chart. Split one length in half lengthwise. Sew a half to each side of a full length. (If using narrow fabric for a queen- or king-size cover, piece the three lengths together.) Repeat this process for the lining fabric. Cut the seamed sections to the exact length and width needed plus ½″ seam allowances.

2. To make the **ruffle,** cut the additional fabric into 6″-wide **bias strips.** Piece the strips until they measure 25 yards in length, or 2½ times the distance around the duvet cover. Press the bias strip in half lengthwise, wrong sides together. Baste the strip together ¼″ from the raw edges.

3. **Gather** the 25-yard length to about 10 yards, or 2½ times fullness. Apply the ruffle around all edges to the right side of the face fabric. Where the ends of the ruffle meet, open out the ruffle. Seam the ends together.

4. Continue as in Simple Duvet Cover, preceding, Steps 2 through 8.

Blanket Covers, Coverlets, and Comforters

Blanket covers, coverlets, and comforters are all the same size and are constructed in basically the same way. They are all short bed covers that end 3″ to 6″ below the bottom of the mattress. They are commonly used in combination with a separate dust ruffle and pillow shams.

Blanket covers, designed as lightweight, protective covering for bed linens and blankets, are made with a single layer of fabric and end at the top of the mattress or headboard. Generally, the top edge of a blanket cover is covered by the hem fold-back of the top sheet. Coverlets are lined or made from pre-quilted fabrics. They usually end at the top of the mattress or headboard, but are sometimes cut long enough to cover the pillows, especially in children's rooms. The bottom edges of blanket covers and coverlets are generally rounded. Comforters, on the other hand, have square corners and are more plump than coverlets because they are made with loftier batting or filling. Comforters can also be used with duvet covers.

Most fabrics can be used for all bed covers (including duvet covers), but obviously some fabrics will withstand more wear than others. If your cover is primarily decorative and will be removed at night, less practical fabrics may be selected. If, however, you will sleep under the cover, sturdy, washable fabrics are preferable.

The following chart provides the yardages and panel cutting guides for a standard blanket cover, coverlet, and comforter. The chart allows for a **drop** of up to 14 inches. Adjust the width of the side panels, if necessary, for the drop you desire.

Lace-Trimmed Blanket Cover

Blanket cover is photographed on page 68.

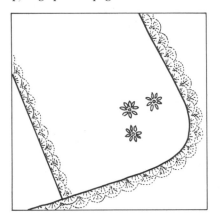

Fabric: See chart on next page.
Trim: ¾″ lace trim—12¼ yards for twin, 12¾ yards for double, 13¼ yards for queen, 14¼ yards for king; 22 flower motifs; six-strand green embroidery floss.

1. Use the chart as a guide for cutting the panels. (Remember to cut two side panels.)

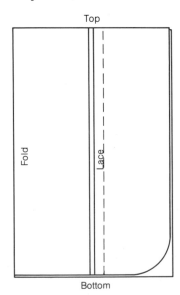

Top

Fold

Lace

Bottom

Blanket Cover Yardage

Mattress Size	Approximate Cover Size	Fabric Required 45"	Fabric Required 54"	Cut Width of Center Panel	Cut Width of Side Panel	Length of Cut Panel
Twin	69"W x 90"L	5 yards	5 yards	23"	24"	91"
Double	84"W x 90"L	5 yards	5 yards	38"	24"	91"
Queen	90"W x 95"L	8¼ yards	5½ yards	42"	24½"	96"
King	106"W x 95"L	8¼ yards	5½ yards	45" (45" fabric) 54" (54" fabric)	32½" (45" fabric) 27" (54" fabric)	96"

2. Seam the side panels to the center one, inserting the lace trim in the seam. Press the trim toward the outside edges. Trim the seam allowances to ¼" and **overcast** by machine or by hand.

3. To trim the bottom corners of the blanket cover to a curved shape, mark out a square as illustrated. Measure out the length of the desired **drop** from the inner corner to make an arc. Cut along the arc line.

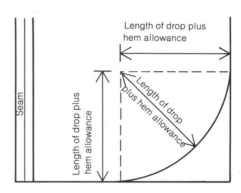

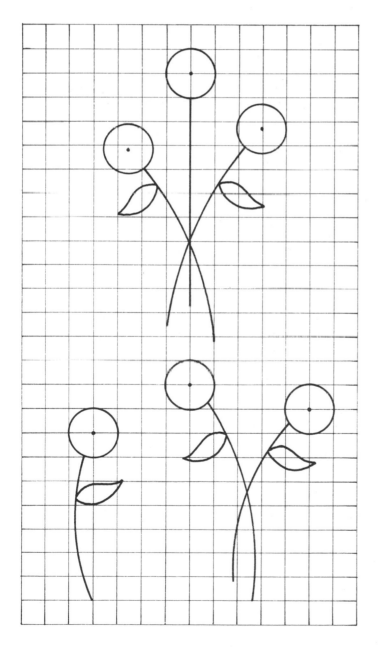

4. Finish all outer edges with a ½" hem.

5. Apply the lace trim to the sides and bottom of the blanket cover with the straight edge of the lace on the wrong side, stitching close to the edge of the cover.

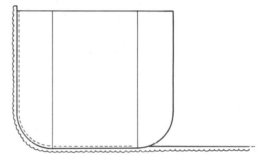

6. Apply the flower motifs, and, using three strands of embroidery floss, **chain stitch** the stems and leaves. Place the triple bouquet at each cover corner, a double bouquet at the center of each side not far from the hemmed edge, and the rest of the flowers in the center panel.

Blanket Cover with Self-Binding

Blanket cover is photographed on page 71.

Fabric: See the chart above, plus ¾ yard for a binding around the outside edge.

1. Use the chart as a guide for cutting the panels.
2. Seam the side panels to the center panel and make **enclosed seams,** if desired.
3. Trim the bottom corners to a curved shape as shown in the diagram on page 227.
4. To finish off all outside edges, cut 2½"-wide **bias strips** from the remaining fabric. (You will need 10 yards of bias for a twin-size, 10½ yards for a double, 11 yards for a queen, and 12 yards for a king.) **Bind** the edges so that the binding is about ⅝" wide when finished.

Quilted Coverlet with Contrast Binding

Coverlet is photographed on page 76.

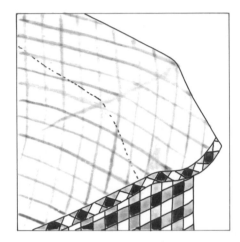

Fabric: Prequilted fabric per the chart, page 227; ¾ yard of contrast fabric for binding.

1. Use the chart as a guide for cutting the panels.
2. Seam the side panels to the center panel.
3. Trim off the batting in the seam allowances. Finish the seams in one of the following ways: trim the seams to ¼" and **overcast** them together by machine; make a **flat-felled seam** or trim the seams to ¼" and **bind** with bias binding.
4. To finish off the outside edges, cut **bias strips** 3" wide from the contrast fabric. Bind the edges so that the binding is about ¾" wide when finished.

Coverlet with Fitted Corners

Coverlet is photographed on page 102.

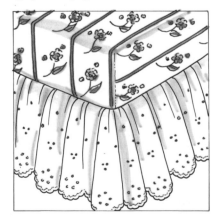

Fabric: Prequilted fabric per the chart on page 227, plus 30" on each panel length; ¾ yard of contrast fabric for binding.

1. Follow Steps 1 through 3 for Quilted Coverlet with Contrast Binding, preceding. Be sure to add 30" on each panel length to fold over the pillows.
2. To fit the bottom corners, fold the coverlet diagonally, right sides together, so that the side raw edge meets the bottom raw edge. Find the point where the distance between the fold and the raw edges is equal to the length of the desired drop of the coverlet. Stitch a seam along that line. Trim away the triangle to ¼" from the seam and **overcast** the edges together by machine.

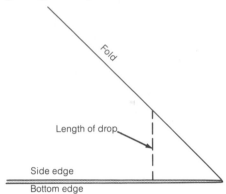

3. To finish off all the outside edges, cut **bias strips** 3" wide from the contrast fabric. **Bind** the edges so that the binding is about ¾" wide when finished.

Bedspreads

Bedspreads (also called throws or throw-covers) are simple, flat bed covers that fall to the floor. They can be cut long enough to cover pillows or not, as you prefer.

Bedspreads can be sewn from a single layer of fabric or from prequilted material. The corners at the foot of the bed are usually rounded in order to keep the excess fabric off the floor. Edges around the bedspread can be finished with a simple hem, a welt or other trim, or bound off with purchased or self-made binding.

The following chart provides yardages for a standard bedspread with a 20" **drop;** our two projects are variations. You should allow about 30" extra fabric on each panel if the spread is to fold over the pillows. If you are planning a twin bedspread, consider reducing the width of the center section to the width of the bed. The chart on page 227 will give you a guide for the panel widths for all sizes. Adjust the width of the side panels so that they will go to the floor and make similar adjustments to the length of the panels. Instructions for cutting the curved corners at the foot of the bed are on page 227.

Bedspread Yardage

Mattress Size	Approximate Throw Size	Fabric	
		45"	54"
Twin	79"W x 100"L	6 yards	6 yards
Double	94"W x 100"L	9 yards	6 yards
Queen	100"W x 110"L	9½ yards	6 yards
King	118"W x 110"L	9½ yards	9½ yards

Bedspread with Ties

Bedspread is photographed on page 116.

Fabric: One king-size or two twin-size sheets, or see the preceding chart for cut yardage.

1. If using twin sheets, split one sheet lengthwise and seam to both sides of the other sheet. Trim to the width needed plus a ½″ hem allowance. (King-size sheet is treated as one piece.) If using cut yardage, cut one length for center section, attaching additional yardage on either side.
2. Trim the bottom corners to a rounded shape (see diagram, page 227).
3. Finish all the outer edges with a narrow hem.
4. To make the ties, cut four pieces 3½″ wide by 20″ long out of cutoff from the sides. Fold the pieces in half lengthwise, right sides together, and sew along the long edge and one end with a ½″ seam. Trim, turn, and press.
5. At each side of the corners of the spread, measure and mark a point 12″ up from the floor. (If the drop is more than 20″, adjust the point upward from 12″.) At each point, pinch a tuck in the fabric, ½″ deep. Insert the raw edge of the tie on the right side of the spread in that tuck before pinning and sewing from the wrong side of the fabric.

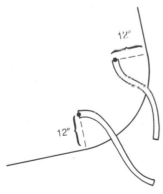

6. Make a bow at each corner after the spread is positioned on the bed.

Daybed Throw

Throw is photographed on page 114.

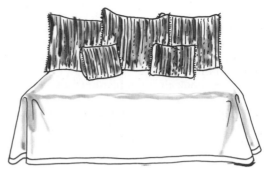

Fabric: 7 yards or one queen-size sheet; ¾ yard of contrast fabric for binding.
Notions: 1 yard twill tape (optional).

1. If using cut yardage, split the fabric into two equal lengths. If the fabric is 45″ wide, split one length lengthwise and seam each half to either side of the second one. If the fabric is 54″ wide, seam it with only one seam. When the whole piece is trimmed to the correct width, this seam should fall across the length of the daybed, toward the back so that the pillows will cover it. (Queen-size sheet is treated as one piece.)
2. Trim the length and width to the exact measurements of the bed. Shape the corners to a curve (see diagram, page 227).
3. If a fitted back edge is desired to help keep the throw from shifting forward, fold each back corner diagonally, right sides together, with the side and bottom edges matching. Locate the point where the distance between the fold and the raw edges is equal to the length of the **drop** of the throw. Stitch a seam along that line. Trim away the triangle to ¼″ from the seam and overcast the edges together by machine.
4. Bind the edges with **bias strips,** cut 3″ wide. The finished width of the binding will be 1″.
5. To keep the throw more securely in place, sew twill tape ties to the back corner seam allowances and tie them around the bed legs.

Fringed Blanket

Blanket photographed on page 113 is 66″ x 90″.

Fabric: Purchased blanket.
Notions: Four-ply knitting worsted in desired colors (see directions to determine amount necessary); large crochet hook.

1. To finish the ends of the blanket with 5″ knotted fringe, cut a cardboard piece 6″ long. Wrap yarn around cardboard (allow five strands per knotted fringe), then cut through yarn at one end only.
2. Insert crochet hook through blanket from wrong side about ⅝″ from the edge. Center five strands of yarn on the hook and bring the loop through the blanket about 1½″.
3. Bring all strands of yard from the right side of the blanket through the loop and pull to tighten. Repeat this process for each loop, spacing each fringe ¾″ apart, or as desired.

Dust Ruffles

Dust ruffles are skirts for the bed designed to hide the box spring and bed legs. They are usually used in combination with a covered duvet, blanket cover, coverlet, comforter, or short bedspread. There are three different styles with their variations: tailored (usually with pleats at the corners), gathered, and box-pleated.

Most fabrics are suitable for dust ruffles. Sheers and lightweight fabrics look best when gathered; heavy fabrics are better suited to a more tailored treatment. Dust ruffles can be self-lined, lined with a coordinating fabric, or unlined. To reduce the amount of fabric needed to line a gathered skirt, make the lining following instructions for a tailored dust ruffle on page 232. All may be finished with either simple or decorative hem treatments.

The skirt of the dust ruffle can be attached to an inexpensive piece of fabric that fits fully under the mattress (an economical twin-size sheet is an inexpensive top piece for twin, double, and queen-size beds; a king-size bed can use a double sheet); or it can be sewn to a band of the dust ruffle fabric and attached directly to the box spring.

If the dust ruffle and the fabric to which it is attached are different, topstitch a 3″ strip of the dust ruffle fabric, which will probably be left over as cutoff, at the seam that joins the dust ruffle and the top piece, mitering at the two bottom corners. This will give the appearance of a decorator fabric top piece without the expense. Another alternative for gathered dust ruffles *only* is to lengthen the skirt so that it extends between the box spring and mattress. To do this, add up to 1″ to the dust ruffle panels and subtract up to 2″ from the side measurement of the box spring top piece.

If the bed has bedposts at the bottom corners, the dust ruffle must be split to fit. Construct the ruffle as one long piece, and then cut it into the lengths you need for the sides and bottom of the bed. Make narrow hems on the cut edges. Adjust the gathers so that the pieces overlap slightly at the corners.

On beds that have heavy posts at the corners, even corner-split dust ruffles may not fit. In this case, the ruffles should be made with casings at the top and hung from ⅜″ brass rods which are attached to the bedposts. This method can be used if you want to expose the side rails of the bed.

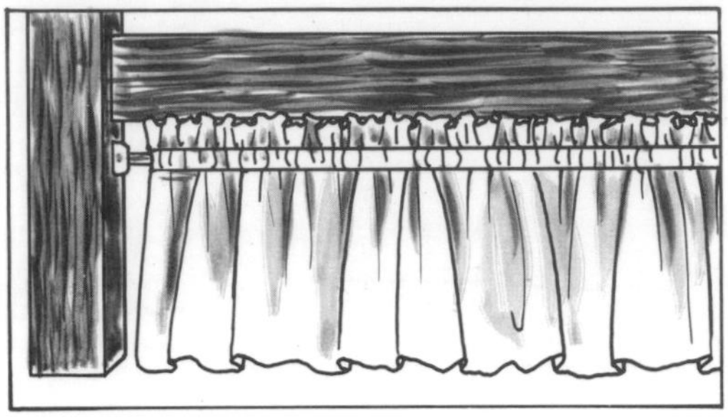

Gathered Dust Ruffle

Dust ruffle is photographed on page 68.

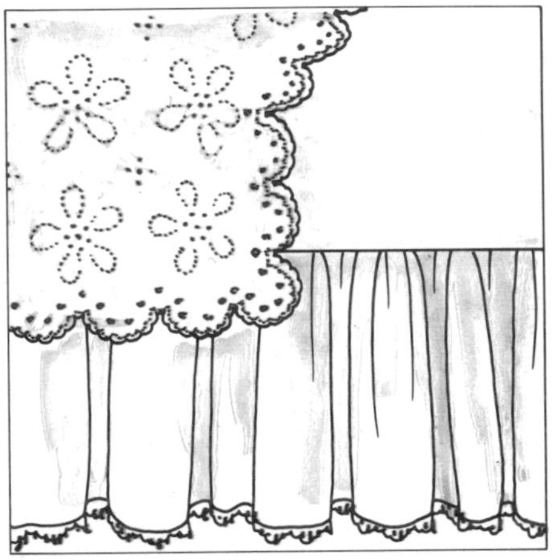

Fabric: See chart for yardage requirements.
1. Cut 15¼″-deep ruffle panels from the fabric. If lace or trim is to be sewn to the bottom of the dust ruffle, subtract from 15¼″ the amount the trim will add to the length. Seam the panels together, matching the pattern, if necessary, to create one long strip.
2. Make a ½″ hem along the bottom and ends.
3. Sew lace trim to the bottom edge of the dust ruffle, if desired.
4. Gather the top edge of the ruffle about ⅜″ in from the raw edge to 2½ times fullness.
5. If you are attaching the ruffle to a top piece, either use a sheet, or cut the appropriate yardage into two equal

Gathered Dust Ruffle Yardage

Mattress Size	Drop	45″ Fabric	# of Strips	54″ Fabric	# of Strips	45″ Fabric for Top Piece	or	45″ Fabric for Band	Trim (Optional)
Twin	14″	4¾ yards	11	4 yards	9	2¼ yards		1½ yards	13¾ yards
Double	14″	5½ yards	12	4½ yards	10	3½ yards		2 yards	15 yards
Queen	14″	5¾ yards	13	5 yards	11	3½ yards		2 yards	16½ yards
King	14″	6¼ yards	14	5 yards	11	4½ yards		2¼ yards	17½ yards

Note: Flat sheets may be used instead of seaming yardage: twin size sheet for twin, double, and queen top; full sheet for king top.

lengths. Seam along the selvages and trim. Press the seam open. From this fabric, cut the top piece to the measurement of the box spring plus ½″ seam allowances and 4″ to 8″ in length for the headboard end flap. (It is a good idea to measure your box spring as it may vary from standard size.) Trim to this shape, slightly rounding the corners as shown in the diagram.

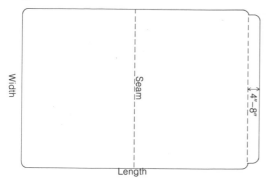

Sew the ruffle around the top piece, right sides together, with a ½″ seam allowance, bringing the ruffle around the top corners to the edge of the flap. Allow extra fullness in the corners. Make a narrow hem around the flap piece.
6. If you are attaching the ruffle to a band, cut strips 13″ wide from the required yardage. Seam together on the short ends. Press the strip in half lengthwise (6½″) and trim to 2 times the side measurement, plus the bottom measurement, plus 7″. Sew the ruffle to one side of the band, right side of the band to the wrong side of the ruffle, with a ½″ seam. Start and stop the ruffle 1″ from the ends. Bring the band to the right side of the ruffle. Turn in the raw edge and topstitch the band in place. Attach the band to the box spring with safety pins.

Gathered Eyelet Dust Ruffle with Lining
Dust ruffle is photographed on page 103.

Fabric: Eyelet fabric 15″ or 22″ wide × 2½ times the distance around both sides and the bottom of the bed; fabric for top piece or band per chart under Gathered Dust Ruffle, preceding; fabric for lining per chart under Gathered Dust Ruffle, preceding.

1. Cut eyelet, if necessary, to desired length plus ½″ seam allowance. (Remember, you need not allow for a hem.)
2. To make dust ruffle lining, cut the lining fabric following the preceding directions for Gathered Dust Ruffle, page 230 (the lining should be cut shorter than the eyelet), and baste top raw edges together.
3. Gather the basted top about ⅜″ in from the edge to 2½ times fullness.
4. Attach the skirt to either a top piece or band following the directions above.

Dust Ruffle with Stand-up Ruff and Contrast Hem
Dust ruffle is photographed on page 74.

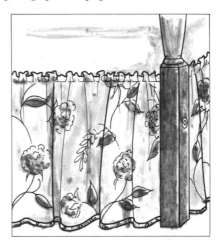

Fabric: Skirt fabric per preceding chart. (Yardage given is for a standard 14″ drop; for a longer dust ruffle, such as the one pictured, allow additional yardage); top piece or band per chart; ¾ yard of contrast hem fabric.

1. Cut 15½″ deep ruffle panels from main skirt fabric. Seam the panels together to create one long strip 2½ times the distance around both sides and the bottom of the bed. Mark a narrow hem at each short end.
2. Cut and sew together 2″-wide **bias strips** from the contrast fabric to go around the skirt, a length equal to the trim yardage given in the chart. **Bind** the bottom edge of the ruffle with the bias.
3. Make a narrow hem at the top edge of the skirt.
4. Gather the dust ruffle ¾″ down from the top edge. When it is gathered, the dust ruffle should be the length of the three sides of the bed plus 6″.
5. Apply the ruffled section to the right side of the top piece or band, according to the preceding instructions under Gathered Dust Ruffle, with the following adjustments:
For a top piece—Follow Step 5 except cut the top piece with ¾″ seam allowances. Sew the ruffle to the top piece, placing the stitching line of the ruffle ¼″ from the edge of the top piece.
For a band—Follow Step 6. Turn under ½″ on all the raw edges and topstitch the edges together. Sew the ruffle to the right side of the band, placing the stitching line of the ruffle ¼″ from the edge of the band.

Beds, Bedding, and Bedroom Accessories/231

Tailored Dust Ruffle with Pleats

Dust ruffle is photographed on page 76.

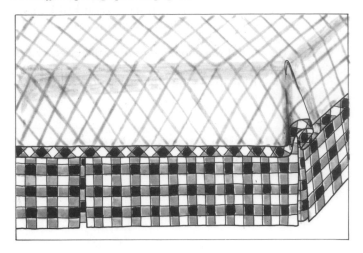

Mattress Size	Drop	45″ Fabric	# of Strips	54″ Fabric	# of Strips	Lining 45″	Lining 54″
Twin	14″	3 yards	6	2½ yards	5	2½ yds.	2 yds.
Double	14″	3 yards	6	2½ yards	5	2½ yds.	2 yds.
Queen	14″	3½ yards	7	3 yards	6	3 yds.	2½ yds.
King	14″	3½ yards	7	3 yards	6	3 yds.	2½ yds.

Fabric: Fabric for top piece or band per chart under Gathered Dust Ruffle, page 230.

1. From the face fabric, cut strips 17½″ long by the width of the fabric. From the lining fabric, cut the panels 14½″ long by the width of the fabric. Seam the face fabric panels together on the short ends. Plan so that the seams will come inside the pleats; do the same for the lining panels.

2. Press up a 3″ hem on the face fabric. Press the hem allowance in half, creating a 1½″ double hem.

3. Lay out the face fabric wrong side up. Place the lining fabric, right side up, on top of the face fabric, tucking the bottom edge of the lining into the hem area so that the raw edge of the lining is at the bottom fold of the hem.

4. Pin the hem and top edges so the lining will stay in place. Sew the hem with a **blind stitch** by machine or by hand. Sew along the top edge of the dust ruffle ¾″ from the raw edge.

5. Cut the dust ruffle strip into the following lengths: two the length of the bed plus 18″; one the width of the bed plus 15″; and two 9″ long for the corner flaps, if the bed has posts at the bottom.

6. On the ends of the side and bottom pieces, press under 1½″ for hems; turn under ¼″ at the raw edge and blind stitch in place. On the flap pieces, turn in ½″ on the lining and face fabrics. Stitch in place.

7. To make the center pleats, fold the side and bottom pieces in half crosswise, right sides together, and stitch a basting line 6″ from the fold.

8. Press the pleat and baste it in place. The fold line should align with the basting stitches.

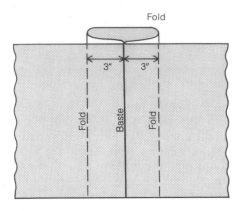

9. Pin the dust ruffle panels to the top piece or band, following the preceding directions under Gathered Dust Ruffle. The side and bottom pieces should butt at the bottom front corners. Center the flap pieces at each front corner and pin them in place. Sew the tailored ruffle strips and top piece or band together with a ½″ seam allowance. Remove basting stitches and overcast the raw edges of the seam with a machine zigzag, if desired.

Decorated Sheets and Pillowcases

Sheets and pillowcases can be easily embellished to add a personal touch to your linens. The use of monograms, embroidery, and other decorative details is an old-world practice that can be accomplished with purchased trims, commercially done monograms, or a bit of handwork.

In the bedrooms photographed on pages 74 and 102, we've threaded ⅛″ satin ribbons through the holes in an eyelet sheet hem and pillowcase trim to enhance the detailing of the sheets and coordinate them with the rest of the

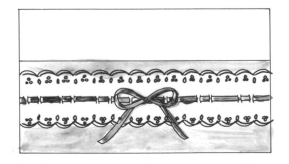

bed coverings. You can adjust the width of the ribbon and the spacing according to the requirements of the trim on your linens. If your sheets and pillowcases don't have an attached decorative hem trim, you can, of course, add one of your own.

To personalize your bed linens, as in the bedroom on page 102, you can write your name or initials on them with a water soluble ink pen and then embroider them with a **chainstitch,** using three strands of embroidery floss.

Bed Pillows

Bed pillows can be decorative as well as functional. They can take many shapes and sizes, but the two we deal with here are pillow shams and neckrolls. For additional pillow ideas, see the chapter on "Pillows," page 136.

Pillow shams are designed to cover the bed pillows and dress up the bed. They are somewhat loose-fitting with ruffles, or lace-, welt-, or braid-trimmed borders. Shams are usually combined with a bed covering that does not fold over the pillows. The back of the sham has a lapped opening that permits the pillows to be slipped in and out easily. In the interest of practicality, however, you may choose to have a separate set of sleeping pillows for your bed and to keep your sham-covered pillows as a decorative daytime accent.

Neckrolls are handy little pillows for reading or simply lounging in bed. Done with coordinating fabrics and decorative trims, they are delightful additions to a collection of bed pillows.

Sham with Lace Trim
Sham is photographed on page 69.

Fabric: 1¼ yards for standard and queen, and for king in 54″ fabric only; 2 yards of 45″ fabric for king.
Trims and Notions: 3 yards lace edge trim for standard and queen; 4 yards for king; 14 flower motifs; green 6-strand embroidery floss; 2⅜″ buttons or self-gripping fastener tape spots.

1. Cut the sham pieces following the chart.

Pillow Size	Front (A)	Back	
		(B)	(C)
Standard (20″ x 26″)	21″ x 27″	21″ x 20¼″	21″ x 10½″
Queen (20″ x 30″)	21″ x 31″	21″ x 23½″	21″ x 11½″
King (20″ x 38″)	21″ x 39″	21″ x 29½″	21″ x 13¾″

2. Make narrow hems on one 21″ edge of back pieces B and C.
3. Apply lace trim to the right side of front A, slightly rounding the lace as you go around the corners. Apply the flower motifs and embroider the stems and leaves with **chain stitch** (see page 227 for flower diagram).
4. Right sides up, lap the back piece C over the back piece B so that their combined width equals the width of the front piece. Baste the two back pieces together.

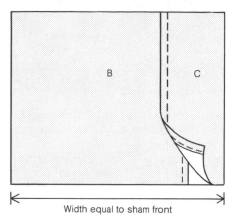

Width equal to sham front

5. Pin and sew the back to the front, right sides together.
6. Remove the basting stitches from the back and turn the pillow right side out through the back opening and press.
7. To close the sham back, either make two buttonholes near the hemmed edge of back piece C and sew the buttons underneath on piece B, or apply self-gripping fastener tape spots.

Sham with Jumbo Welting
Sham is photographed on page 76.

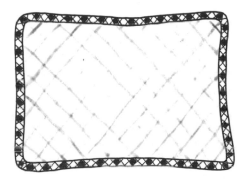

Fabric: 1¼ yards for standard and queen, and for king in 54″ fabric only; 2 yards of 45″ fabric for king; ½ yard of contrast fabric for welting.
Trims and Notions: 3 yards of ½″ cording for standard and queen. 3½ yards for king; two ⅜″ buttons or self-gripping fastener tape spots.

1. Follow the preceding instructions for Sham with Lace Trim, but delete Step 3 and instead make **welting** from contrast fabric. Sew the welting to the right side of the front piece.
2. Continue with Sham with Lace Trim Steps 4 through 9.

Ruffled Sham

Sham is photographed on page 74.

Fabric: 2¼ yards for standard and queen, and for king in 54″ fabric only; 3¼ yards of 45″ fabric for king; ½ yard of contrast fabric.
Notions: Two ⅜″ buttons or self-gripping fastener tape spots.

1. Cut the sham pieces following the chart under Sham with Lace Trim, page 233.
2. Make narrow hems on one 21″ edge of sham back pieces B and C.
3. To make **ruffle,** cut five ¾″-wide **bias strips** from the remaining fabric. Sew them together with **enclosed seams** to make a 7-yard circle.
4. Cut 2″-wide **bias strips** from contrast fabric, sew them together to make a 7-yard length, and use it to **bind** the bottom edges of the ruffle.
5. Make a narrow hem at the top edge of the ruffle.
6. Gather the ruffle ¾″ down from the top edge. Adjust to fit around the pillow and sew the wrong side of the ruffle to the right side of the sham, placing the gathering line of the ruffle about ¼″ from the edge of the sham.
7. Finish the sham following Steps 4 through 7 under Sham with Lace Trim.

Tie-On Sham

Sham is photographed on page 116.

Fabric: 1½ yards.

1. Cut a piece of fabric 2½″ wider than the pillow and 49″ long.
2. Finish all the edges with a ½″ hem.
3. To make ties, cut six strips, each 12″ long × 2″ wide. Seam the long edges of each strip with a ¼″ seam. Turn and press. Close the ends.
4. Sew the ties to the right side of the pillow piece as shown:

5. Wrap the pillow piece around the pillow and make bows with the ties, tucking in the 8″ flap.

Boudoir Sham with Lace Trim

Sham is photographed on page 69.

Fabric: ⅜ yard.
Trims and Notions: 1¼ yards ¾″ lace edge trim; 3 flower motifs; green six-strand embroidery floss; ⅜″ button (optional).
Pillow Form: 12″ × 16″ boudoir.

1. Cut one piece for front 13″ × 17″, and two for back: 13″ × 12½″ and 13″ × 8½″.
2. Make narrow hems on one 13″ edge of sham back pieces B and C.
3. Finish by following Steps 4 through 7 under Sham with Lace Trim, page 233.

Boudoir Sham with Contrast Welting

Sham is photographed on page 71.

Fabric: ⅜ yard each of main and contrast fabrics.
Notions: 1¼ yards of ½″ cording; ⅜″ button (optional).
Pillow Form: 12″ × 16″ boudoir.

1. From main fabric, cut one piece for front 13" × 17", and two for back: 13" × 12½" and 13" × 8½".
2. Make narrow hems on one 13" edge of sham back pieces B and C.
3. Monogram pillow front, if desired.
4. From contrast fabric, make 1¼ yards of **welting** and apply to sham front A.
5. Finish by following Steps 4 through 7 under Sham with Lace Trim, page 233, substituting the welting for the lace trim.

One-Piece Neckroll

Neckroll is photographed on page 43.

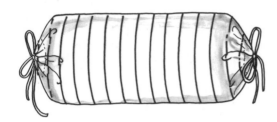

Fabric: ⅝ yard.
Notions: 1½ yards cord or ribbon.
Neckroll Form: 13" × 5".

1. Cut a fabric piece 20" wide by 20¾" long.
2. Stitch the 20" edges, right sides together, with a ½" seam to make a tube.
3. To make a casing, turn under ¾" at each end of the tube. Turn under ¼" at the raw edge and stitch. Tack securely at the casing seamline and at the folded edge of the neckroll seam.
4. Open up the neckroll seam on the outside or inside of the casing, depending on whether or not you want the bow to show.
5. Insert cording in each casing, and knot all ends of the cord. Insert the neckroll form, pull up the cord, and tie.

Neckroll with Lace Trim

Neckroll is photographed on page 69.

Fabric: ⅝ yard.
Trims and Notions: 1¼ yards ¾" lace edge trim; 3 flower motifs; green six-strand embroidery floss; 1½ yards of ⅜" ribbon for ties.
Neckroll Form: 13" × 5".

1. Cut the main neckroll piece 20½" long by 14" wide.
2. Cut two end strips 20½" long by 3¾" wide.
3. Apply the flower motifs and embroider the stems and leaves with **chain stitch,** to the center of the main piece. (See page 227 for flower diagram.)
4. With right sides together, stitch the 14" edges of the main piece. Stitch the end pieces along the 3¾" edges.

5. Sew the lace to each end of the main neckroll piece, right sides together, matching the seamlines of the lace and the neckroll.
6. To make a casing on the two end pieces, turn under ¾" on one edge of each, and turn under ¼" at the raw edge. Stitch to form the casing. Tack securely at the seam area and at the folded edge of the casing in the seam area. Clip the stitches in the casing area on the outside and thread the ribbon ties.
7. Sew the ends to the neckroll, matching seams. Press the seams toward the pillow.
8. Insert the form and pull up the ties.

Neckroll with Welting

Neckroll is photographed on pages 71 and 76.

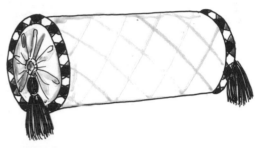

Fabric: ⅝ yard of main fabric; ⅜ yard of contrast welting fabric.
Trims and Notions: 1½ yards of ⅜" ribbon for ties; 1¼ yards of ½" cording; 2 purchased tassels (optional).
Neckroll Form: 13" × 5".

1. Cut the main neckroll piece 20½" long by 14" wide.
2. Cut two end strips 20½" long by 3¾" wide.
3. With right sides together, stitch the 14" edges of the main piece. Stitch the end pieces along the 3¾" edges.
4. From contrast fabric, make 1¼ yards **welting** and sew to each end of the main neckroll piece, matching the seams of the welting and neckroll.
5. Finish by following Steps 6 through 8 for Neckroll with Lace Trim, preceding. Tack the tassels to each end, if desired.

Neckroll with Eyelet and Trim

Neckroll is photographed on page 93.

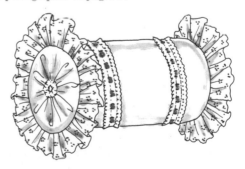

Fabric: ⅝ yard.
Trims and Notions: 3½ yards of 3½" flat eyelet trim; 1¼ yards of band trim; 1½ yards of ⅜" ribbon for ties.
Neckroll Form: 13" × 5".

1. Cut the main neckroll piece 20½" long by 14" wide.
2. Cut two end strips 20½" long by 3¾" wide.

3. Apply the band trim to the main neckroll piece, centering it over a line about 2¾" in from the seamline on each side.

4. **Gather** eyelet to 1¼ yards. Cut in half.

5. With right sides together, stitch the 14" edges of the main piece. Stitch the end pieces along the 3¾" edges.

6. Sew the gathered eyelet to each end of the main neckroll piece, right sides together, matching the seamlines of the eyelet and the neckroll.

7. Finish by following Steps 6 through 8 for Neckroll with Lace Trim, preceding.

Miscellaneous Bedroom Accessories

Reading pillows, bed caddies, and vanity skirts are additions that can make any bedroom a more luxurious place. Since we all spend considerable time in this room, these little projects seem well worth the extra time and effort.

Vanity skirts in particular deserve special mention here. After many years out of fashion, the vanity, or dressing table, has begun to reappear. Vanities can be created from simple tables with skirts or, if you are fortunate enough to have one, from the old-fashioned type with swing arms, which allow access to drawers hidden beneath the skirt. In either case, they make a very desirable bedroom accessory.

Shirred Vanity Skirt
Vanity skirt is photographed on page 73.

Fabric: 4½ yards of 45" fabric for the skirt; ¾ yard of 45" fabric for top piece.

Trims and Notions: 7 yards single-fold bias tape or ribbon; 5 yards two-string shirring tape; self-gripping fastener tape in the amount needed to go across the front and along both sides of the skirt, plus 2" to 3"; ¾ yard fusible interfacing for top piece.

Glass top.

1. Measure the height of the vanity table. Add 5¾" to that amount. Cut four panels of fabric in that length by the full width of the fabric. Trim the selvages.

2. Seam the four panels lengthwise with **enclosed seams,** making two vanity skirt pieces.

3. Make a 1" finished hem along the side edges of the vanity skirt pieces.

4. Make a ½" hem at the upper edge of the vanity skirt. Make a 2½" double hem at the bottom edge.

5. Apply the bias tape or ribbon as trim on the lead and bottom edges of the skirt. The front edge of the bias should be ⅞" from the lead edge of the skirt and 2" from the bottom edge. **Miter** the front corners. Be sure to make a left and right panel.

6. Determine how far down from the top of the vanity table you wish to attach the skirt. On the inside of the skirt, pin the shirring tape that distance down from the top edge. Stitch close to the upper and lower edges of the tape in between the two strings and across the ends. Keep the strings free.

7. Pull the strings up until the vanity skirt covers half the distance around the table. Knot the ends. Repeat with the other panel.

8. Sew the fuzzy side of the self-gripping fastener tape to the center of the gathered shirring tape. Glue, nail, or staple the loop side of the self-gripping fastener tape to the vanity table. Attach the skirt.

9. To make the vanity top piece, cut the remaining fabric into a shape 1" larger all around than the top. Fuse interfacing to the wrong side of the fabric. Trim the fabric to the exact size of the top and place on the vanity. Cover with the glass top.

Pleated Vanity Skirt
Vanity skirt is photographed on page 76.

Fabric: 3½ yards of 45" fabric for skirt; ¾ yard or 45" fabric for top piece; ¾ yard of contrast fabric for bias trim.

Notions: Self-gripping fastener tape as needed to go around the front and along both sides of the skirt, plus 2" to 3"; ¾ yard fusible interfacing for top piece.

Glass top.

1. Measure the height of the vanity table. Add 1¼" to the amount and cut four panels in that length by the full width of the fabric. Trim the selvages.

2. Seam the four panels lengthwise with **enclosed seams,** making two vanity skirt pieces.

3. Press a 1¼" hem on the lead edge of each panel. Be sure to make both a left and right panel.

4. On each panel, start the pleats ½″ in from the fold line. Mark the top edge at ½″ intervals across the full width of the vanity skirt. Each pleat uses ½″ of fabric (¼″ pleat) with ½″ of fabric between pleats. Sew the pleats down 3″ from the top edge and continue making pleats until each piece measures half the distance around the front and sides of the vanity plus 1″ to wrap around to the back.

5. Cut off the excess fabric on the side and make a narrow hem. Press the pleats flat.

6. Finish the hem at the lead edge of the vanity skirt by turning under ¼″ on the raw edge and **blind stitching** by machine or hand.

7. Press down 1″ to the wrong side along the top pleated edge. Sew the fuzzy side of the self-gripping fastener tape to the wrong side of the skirt ½″ down from the folded edge. (Adjust the distance if needed. The skirt should be even with the top of the vanity or just barely above it.)

8. From contrast fabric, cut enough **bias strips** 3″ wide to make 5 yards. **Bind** the bottom edge of the vanity skirt with the bias strips.

9. Glue, nail, or staple the loop side of the self-gripping fastener tape to the vanity table. Attach the skirt.

10. To make the vanity top piece, make a **template** of the top surface. Trace a shape 1″ larger all around than the top and cut from the remaining fabric. Fuse interfacing to the wrong side of the fabric. Trim the fabric to the exact size of the top and place on the vanity. Cover with the glass top.

Gathered Vanity Skirt with Attached Top Piece

Vanity skirt is photographed on page 88.

Fabric: 4¼ yards of 45″ or 54″ fabric, or 5½ yards of narrower fabric; 5½ yards of border strip.
Glass top (optional).

1. Cut four lengths of 45″ or 54″ fabric, or five lengths of narrower fabric, each the height of the vanity plus ½″ to accommodate a border seam. Stitch them together on the lengthwise edges. Make narrow hems at the back edges.
2. Sew the right side of the border strip to the wrong side of the bottom edge of the vanity skirt with a ½″ seam, leaving a ½″ excess at each end. Press the seam toward the border.
3. Bring the border strip to the front of the skirt with the seam at the bottom edge and pin. Turn under a ½″ seam

allowance on the top and side raw edges of the border. Topstitch in place.

4. Make a **template** of the vanity top by tracing around the top onto a piece of paper. Add a ½″ seam allowance on the front and sides and add 8″ to the back edge. Cut out the pattern from the fabric. Mark the seamline on the back edge of the top, 5″ in from the sides.

5. **Gather** the top edge of the skirt to fit the front and sides of the vanity plus 6″. Pin the gathered piece to the vanity top piece at the front and side edges, bringing it around 3″ to the back side at each end. Match the seamlines of the vanity top and the vanity skirt at the back edge. Sew together.

Bed Caddy

Bed caddy is photographed on page 68.

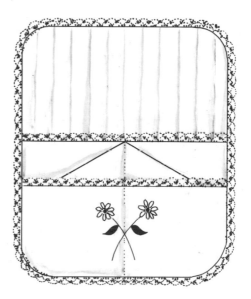

Fabric: 1¾ yards.
Trims and Notions: 4 yards of ¾″ lace edge trim; 2 flower motifs; green six-strand embroidery floss; 20″ × 15″ piece of batting; 8″ × 13″ piece of cardboard.

1. **Enlarge** the pattern pieces from the diagram and cut the fabric as directed on each piece *except* the bed caddy base.
2. Apply the flower motif to the center of the top pocket. Embroider the leaves and stems in a **chain stitch** (see page 227 for flower diagram).
3. Cut two pieces of fabric and one piece of batting, each 15″ wide × 20″ long. Sandwich the batting between the fabric pieces, right sides out, and pin.
4. **Quilt** this section, making vertical rows of machine stitching 1½″ apart. Cut one bed caddy base from this section.
5. Make a narrow hem on the straight edge of the bed caddy flap. To create a pocket for the cardboard, pin the wrong side of the flap to the top back side of the bed caddy base.
6. Press on the fold line on both Pocket A and Pocket B, as shown. Sew the lace to the back side of each pocket so that the lace shows from the front.
7. Sew the Pocket C with a ½″ seam allowance, right sides together, at the upper slanted edges only. Trim, turn, and press.

8. Pin the three pockets together, with Pocket A on the bottom. The raw edges at the sides and bottom should align. Stitch through the center of all the pockets on the dotted vertical line.

9. Pin the pocket section to the bottom front side of the bed caddy base.

10. Bind the outer edges of the bed caddy with a 2"-wide self-fabric **bias strip.** Apply the bias 2" in from the raw

edges on the front side. After stitching, turn the bias to the back side, turning under the raw edge. Pin this just over the previous stitching line, and **slip stitch** in place.

11. Sew the lace trim to the outer edges of the binding.

12. Cut cardboard slightly smaller than the bed caddy flap without the seam allowances. Slip it into the back flap.

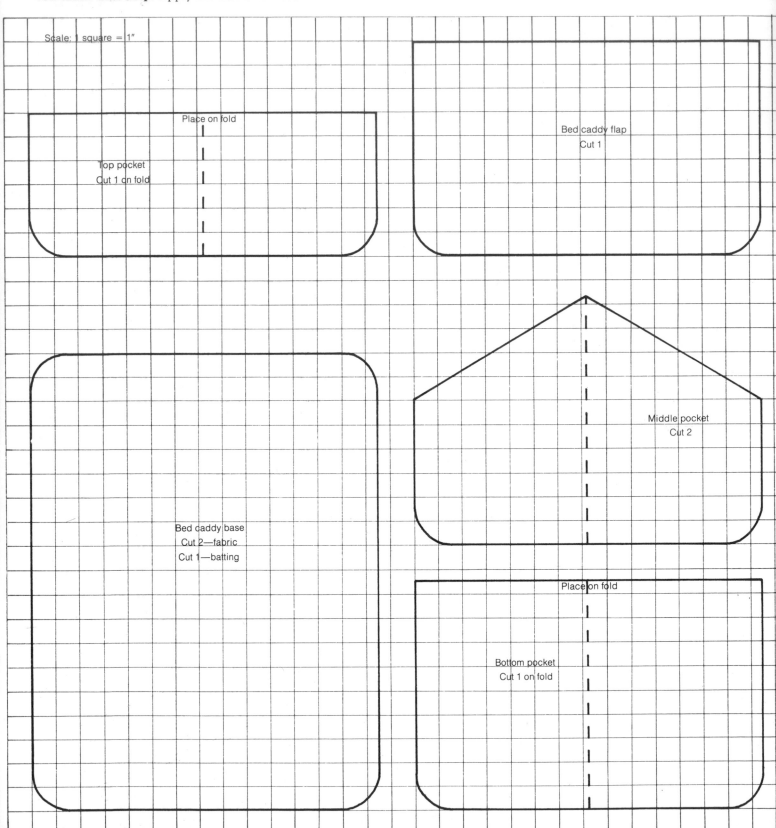

Scale: 1 square = 1"

Place on fold

Top pocket
Cut 1 on fold

Bed caddy flap
Cut 1

Bed caddy base
Cut 2—fabric
Cut 1—batting

Middle pocket
Cut 2

Place on fold

Bottom pocket
Cut 1 on fold

Kitchen Accessories

In general, in the kitchen, function dictates aesthetics. It is of the utmost importance that fabrics used for kitchen accessories have excellent maintenance qualities. This doesn't imply by any means that only vinyl-coated fabrics or those made of never-iron blends will do, but it is necessary to accept the inevitability of frequent laundering as part of the selection process. Sometimes the style of a particular fabric makes its less than easy care requirements acceptable, such as the charming linen towels used in the kitchen photographed on page 58, but these fabrics should be used for accessories that are more decorative than those in constant use. Sewing for the kitchen is a rewarding experience, and even the most functional space will benefit from the addition of cheerful fabric accessories.

Appliance Covers

Although we've specifically included covers for three appliances—a toaster, a blender, and a mixer/food processor—the sizes and designs can be adapted for any appliance you might own. We do suggest that you carefully measure your appliance (length, depth, and height) and compare the measurements to those of our patterns before cutting the fabric. If you need to alter the patterns, first adjust the measurements on the front and back pieces, and then make the necessary changes on the long inset strip.

Note that the patchwork appliance covers would be the most difficult to alter, but it is possible by changing the size of the strips that border the patchwork squares. Trace the pattern for the back piece from the front.

Appliance Covers with Border

Appliance covers are photographed on page 62.

Two-Slice Toaster Cover

Fabric: ⅞ yard main fabric; ⅞ yard backing fabric; 1⅛ yards border strip.
Notions: ⅞ yard polyester batting.

1. Quilt main fabric, batting, and backing. If you have a walking foot for your machine, use it for this step. **Enlarge** pattern pieces as shown on the diagram and cut two out from the quilted fabric. Cut one inset strip 7″ wide × 25⅞″ long.
2. With right sides together, pin and sew the front and back pieces to each side of the inset strip, using ½″ seams.
3. Trim the seam allowances to ¼″. Finish the raw edges with a zigzag stitch, if desired. Turn right side out; press the seams.
4. Center a border strip motif on the front cover and seam the border to make a continuous strip along the bottom edge of the cover. With wrong side of the border to right side of the cover, line up raw edges and pin.
5. Turn under raw edges on the upper edge of the border fabric and pin. Stitch close to the folded edge. (If border design suggests additional stitching lines, as the one we used does, quilt following the motif lines.)
6. Stitch around the cover close to, but not into the edge of, the border print. Trim the batting and backing fabric to ⅛″ less than the finished length of the cover.

7. Fold the bottom edge of the cover to the inside along the bottom line of the border print. Turn under the raw edge and pin. Stitch from the right side on the previous stitching line, catching the hem on the inside.

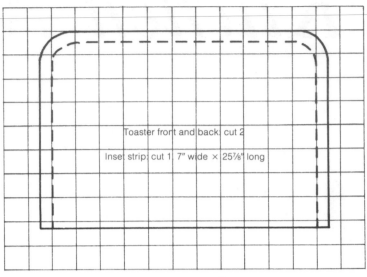

Toaster front and back: cut 2

Inset strip: cut 1 7″ wide × 25⅞″ long

Scale: 1 square = 1″

Blender Cover

Fabric: 1⅛ yards main fabric for outside; 1⅛ yards backing fabric; 1 yard border strip.
Notions: 1⅛ yards polyester batting.

Follow instructions for the Two-Slice Toaster Cover immediately preceding.

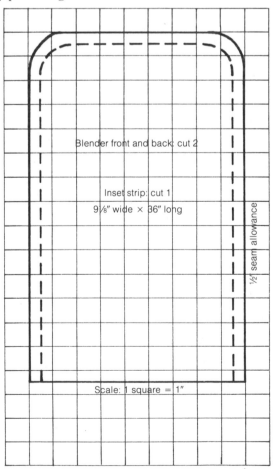

Blender front and back: cut 2

Inset strip: cut 1
9⅛″ wide × 36″ long

½″ seam allowance

Scale: 1 square = 1″

Mixer/Food Processor Cover

Fabric: 1⅛ yards main fabric; 1⅛ yards backing fabric; 1¼ yards border strip.
Notions: 1⅛ yards polyester batting.

Follow the preceding instructions for the Two-Slice Toaster Cover.

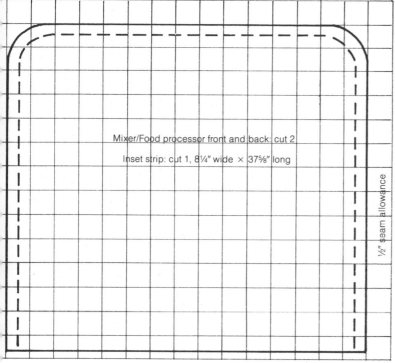

Patchwork Appliance Covers

Appliance covers are photographed on page 60.

These appliance covers for two-slice toaster, four-slice toaster, blender, and mixer/food processor can be made in either the star design or the churn dash design. The yardage requirements and directions for making the star design patchwork are on page 151, and for the churn dash on page 156. The number of patchwork squares you need for each cover is noted in the individual instructions.

We chose a prequilted fabric for the backing and inset strip on these covers. Since, however, prequilted coordinated fabrics are not always available, we have included references to **quilting** techniques, whenever pertinent. If you are using prequilted fabric, skip these referenced steps. In addition, if you are using a pre-quilted coordinate print, be sure to purchase a small amount of the same print unquilted to use in the construction of the patchwork squares.

Two-Slice Toaster Cover

Fabric: ½ yard main fabric; ½ yard lining; 8″ × 9″ contrast fabric.
Notions: ½ yard polyester batting; 2¾ yards extrawide double-fold bias tape.

1. Make one patchwork square following the instructions on pages 151 or 156.
2. Enlarge the patterns from the diagram. Cut out the side patches, the top patch, and insert strip (6¾″ by 24¾″) from the main fabric. From the lining fabric, cut the toaster cover back.

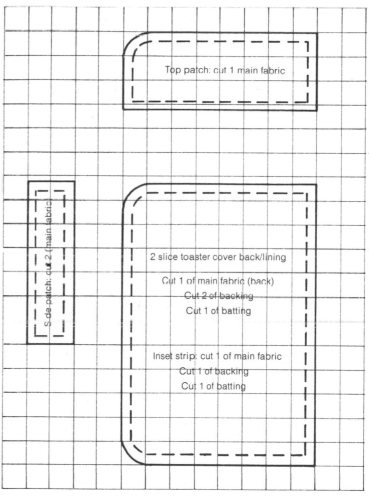

3. To construct the front of the cover, stitch the top patch to the upper edge of the patchwork square, and then stitch the side patches to each side with the rounded edge at the top, allowing ⅜″ seams.

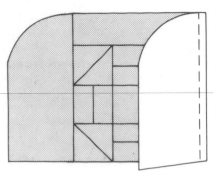

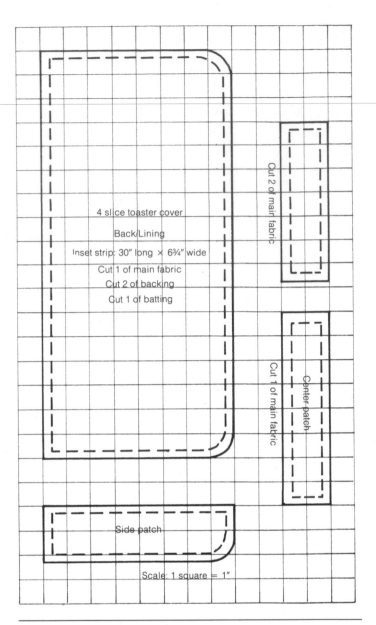

4. With the wrong sides together, pin the patchwork front to the lining piece. Baste the raw edges together.

5. Cut the fabric pieces to be quilted approximately 1″ larger all around than the pattern size to allow for take-up in the quilting process. **Quilt** the main fabric, batting, and lining for the cover back and the inset strip. If you have a walking foot for your machine, use it when quilting to make the job easier. After quilting, cut the pieces to the exact pattern size.

6. With the lining sides together, pin and sew the cover front and back pieces to each side of the inset strip, allowing ⅜″ seams. Ease fabrics as needed in curved areas.

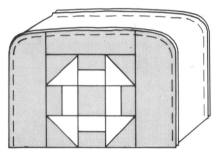

7. Bind the raw edges with double-fold bias tape with the fold line of the tape just covering the stitching lines. Do the side and top seams first and the lower edge of the cover last. (Because of the bulk of the fabrics, we recommend that you use Method B for the application of bias tape, described on page 123. If you sew the bias tape on in one operation or machine-stitch the second side, the tape tends to ripple.)

Four-Slice Toaster Cover

Fabric: ½ yard main fabric; ½ yard lining; 8″ × 18″ contrast fabric.
Notions: ½ yard polyester batting; 3¼ yards extrawide double-fold bias tape.

1. Make two patchwork squares following the instructions on pages 151 or 156.

2. Enlarge patterns from the diagram. Cut out side, top, and center patches from the main fabric. Cut one cover and one inset strip 30″ × 6¾″ from the lining fabric.

3. To construct the front of the cover, stitch a top patch to the upper edge of each patchwork square. Stitch the center patch to one side of each square, thus joining the two squares. Sew side patches to each side of this rectangle with the rounded edges at the top. (⅜″ seam allowances are included.) Press seams open.

4. Finish the construction following Steps 4 to 7 for the Two-Slice Toaster Cover, preceding.

Blender Cover

Fabric: ⅞ yard main fabric; ⅞ yard lining; 14″ × 22″ contrast fabric.
Notions: ½ yard polyester batting; 3¼ yards extrawide double-fold bias tape.

1. Make four patchwork squares following the instructions on pages 151 or 156.

2. Enlarge the patterns from the diagram. Cut the border strips, border patches, and center top patch from the main fabric, and the inset strip from the lining fabric.

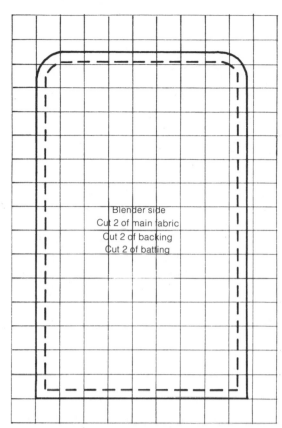

Blender side
Cut 2 of main fabric
Cut 2 of backing
Cut 2 of batting

Inset strip: 34½″ long × 8¾″ wide
Border strip: 34½″ long × 1¾″ wide

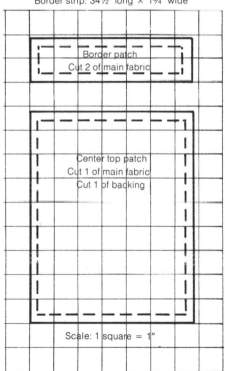

Border patch
Cut 2 of main fabric

Center top patch
Cut 1 of main fabric
Cut 1 of backing

Scale: 1 square = 1″

3. To construct the front of the cover, stitch the border patch between two patchwork squares. Press the seams open. Repeat this with the two remaining squares for the back of the cover.
4. Join the above two sections to the center top patch. Press seams open.
5. Sew a border strip to each side of the patchwork strip.

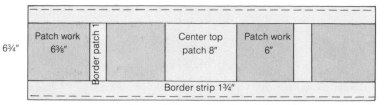

Patch work 6⅜″	Border patch 1	Center top patch 8″	Patch work 6″	

6¾″

Border strip 1¾″

6. With the wrong sides together, pin the patchwork strip to the inset strip (in lining fabric). Baste the raw edges together.
7. Finish the construction following Steps 5 to 7 for the Two-Slice Toaster in this chapter, **quilting** the sides only.

Mixer/Food Processor Cover

Fabric: ¾ yard main fabric; ¾ yard lining; ¼ yard contrast fabric.
Notions: ¾ yard polyester batting; 3½ yards extrawide double-fold bias tape; 1 yard single-fold bias tape.

1. Make four patchwork squares following the instructions on pages 151 or 156.
2. **Enlarge** the patterns from the diagram. Cut out one mixer/food processor cover from the lining fabric.

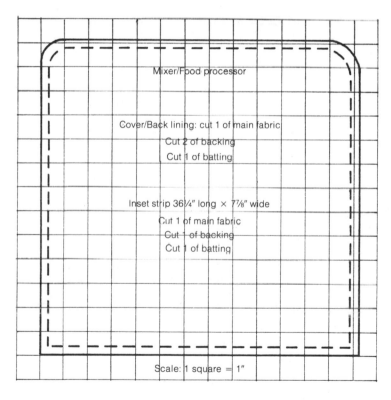

Mixer/Food processor

Cover/Back lining: cut 1 of main fabric
Cut 2 of backing
Cut 1 of batting

Inset strip 36¼″ long × 7⅞″ wide
Cut 1 of main fabric
Cut 1 of backing
Cut 1 of batting

Scale: 1 square = 1″

3. To construct the front of the cover, cut two pieces of single-fold bias tape, each 7″ long. With the right sides together, pin the bias tape to the lower edge of two patchwork squares, lining up the fold line of the tape with the ⅜″ seamline of the square. Stitch along the fold line of the tape. Trim the seam allowances even with the tape edge and press them toward the tape. Stitch the remaining patchwork squares to the other edge of the bias tape in the same manner.
4. To make one large square, cut another piece of single-fold bias tape 13½″ long and stitch the tape to the two rectangles at the center, following the same procedure.

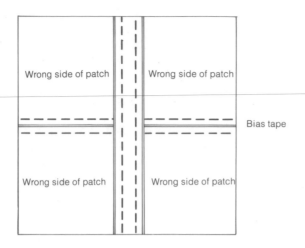

5. Finish the construction following Steps 4 to 7 for the Two-Slice Toaster Cover in this chapter. Round off the top corners on the patchwork front so that they are even with the corners on the lining piece.

Potholders

There are no rules about the size of potholders, so one of the advantages of sewing your own is that you can make them as large as you find comfortable. Also note that there is no consideration given here to using fabrics that are flame or heat resistant, and that potholders constructed from fabrics like the ones suggested in this book should be used with care on hot cooking utensils.

Tea Toweling Potholder with Appliqué

Potholders are photographed on page 59.

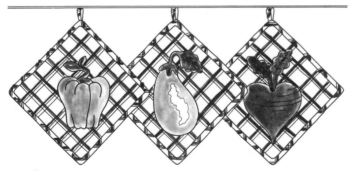

Fabric: 1 yard tea toweling or ⅓ yard 44″ to 45″ fabric; remnants for appliqué.
Notions: 10″ square polyester batting; ⁶⁄₃₂″ cording—1¼ yards.

1. Preshrink tea toweling.
2. Cut two 10″ squares from toweling, centering each on the fabric design, if appropriate. Cut enough **bias strips** ½″ wide to cover the cording and to make a loop for hanging.
3. Baste batting to wrong side of one square.
4. Enlarge the appliqué design and cut it from fabric scraps. **Appliqué** the pieces to the 10″ square of toweling backed with batting. (Use a fine zigzag stitch for detail lines within the motifs.)

Scale: 1 square = ½″

5. Make **welting** and sew it to the right side of the appliquéd square with a ½″ seam allowance.
6. Make a 3″ long tube for the loop from the bias strip, and baste it into the seam allowance in the appropriate corner.
7. Using a ½″ seam allowance, sew the other square to the appliquéd piece, right sides together, leaving a 4″ opening on one side for turning.
8. Trim the batting to the stitching line. Trim the seam allowances to ¼″, clip the curves, turn, and press. Stitch by hand to close the opening.

Patchwork Potholders

Potholders are photographed on page 60.

Following the materials needed and instructions, Steps 3 to 8, for patchwork squares found under Tabletop Accessories on page 151, construct patchwork squares in the star design. For churn dash design, refer to page 156, Steps 1 to 6. Please note that instructions for border patches are given only in the star design directions. In addition, you will need the following:

Fabric: 10″ square for backing.

Notions: 10″ square polyester batting; 1¼ yards extrawide double-fold bias tape; ½″ diameter ring.

1. With the wrong sides together, pin the patchwork square to a backing square of equal size for the back of the potholder. Slip batting between the two pieces.

2. Bind the outer edges of the potholder with bias tape.

3. Sew the ring in one corner.

Tea Toweling Oven Mitt with Appliqué

Mitt is photographed on page 58.

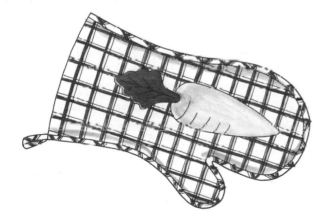

Fabric: ¾ yard tea toweling or ½ yard 44″ to 45″ fabric; remnants for appliqué.

Notions: ⁶⁄₃₂″ cording—1⅛ yards; purchased mitt liner.

1. Preshrink tea toweling fabric.

2. To make the pattern, trace around the mitt liner. Add ¾″ all around the mitt except at the open edge. Make a straight line for the open edge.

3. Cut two mitt pattern pieces from fabric, placing the open edge of the pattern along the stripe of the tea toweling closest to the **selvage.** The fabric between the stripe and the selvage is the hem allowance.

4. Cut the appliqué shapes from the fabric scraps. Center and **appliqué** the design to one mitt piece.

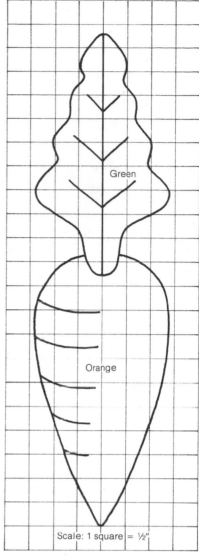

Green

Orange

Scale: 1 square = ½″

5. From the remaining fabric, cut 1½″-wide **bias strips** to cover the cording and to make a loop for hanging the mitt.

6. Make **welting** and sew around the appliquéd mitt piece except along the open edge, using a ½″ seam allowance.

7. Make a 3″ long tube for the loop from the bias strip and baste it in the seam allowance at the bottom of the mitt's thumb edge.

8. Sew the other mitt piece to the appliquéd piece, right sides together, with a ½″ seam allowance. Trim, clip, turn, and press. The seams can be **overcast** if desired.

9. At the open edge, turn in the hem allowance along the stripe. Hand- or machine-stitch hem in place.

Appliquéd Tea Towel with Crochet Lace Trim

Tea towel photographed on page 58 is 16" × 34".

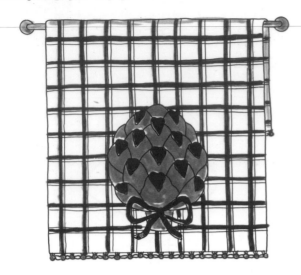

Fabric: 1 yard tea toweling or purchased tea towel; remnants for appliqué.
Notions: 1 yard crochet lace trim.

1. Preshrink tea toweling fabric.
2. If toweling yardage is used, make a narrow hem on both raw edges.
3. Sew the crochet lace trim to both short ends of the towel.
4. Cut the appliqué design from fabric scraps and **appliqué** to the towel.

Scale: 1 square = ½"

Apron with Patchwork Bib and Pockets

Apron is photographed on page 56.

The patchwork squares for this apron can be made in either the star design or the churn dash design. Directions for the star are on page 151. The churn dash design is found on page 156.
Fabric: 2⅝ yards main fabric; ⅜ yard contrast fabric.
Notions: 2¼ yards extrawide double-fold bias tape; two ½" buttons.

1. Make three potholder patchwork squares according to the directions in this chapter, eliminating the polyester batting and ring.
2. Cut the apron pieces as follows:
Skirt: Cut one piece, 53" wide × 32" long.
Bib: Cut two pieces, 9¾" × 9¾".
Strap: Cut two pieces, 29½" long × 4½" wide.
Waistband: Cut two pieces, 26½" long × 3" wide.
Tie: Cut two pieces, 18½" long × 5" wide.
(½" seams are allowed on all pieces.)
3. Shape one end of each tie and strap as illustrated:

Fold line

4. Fold the straps in half lengthwise, right sides together. Stitch, leaving one straight, short end open. Turn right side out; press. Make the ties in the same way.
5. On the right side of one bib piece, baste the straps to the top edge, raw edges together. The outside seamed

edge of the strap should be ¾″ from the side edge of the bib.

6. Pin the other bib piece over the one with the straps, right sides together. Stitch, leaving the bottom edge open. Turn right side out and press.

7. Pin a long edge of one waistband piece to the bottom edge of the bib, right sides together, matching the center of the waistband to the center of the bib. Baste.

8. Baste the raw edge of one tie to each end of the waist-band piece, right sides together.

9. Press under ½″ on one long edge of the other waist-band piece. Pin the other long edge to the waistband piece right sides together over ties and bib. Stitch along the top edge where bib is attached and across both ends. Turn waistband right side out and press.

10. Make narrow hems on both 32″ edges of the apron skirt. On the bottom edge, turn up a 2⅝″ hem. Turn under ¼″ on the raw edge and hand- or machine-stitch the hem in place.

11. Pin two potholder patchwork squares to the skirt for pockets. Each should be positioned 6″ down from the top raw edge of the skirt and 12¼″ in from each hemmed side edge. Stitch them in place close to the inner edges of the bias tape and along the side and bottom edges only.

12. Gather the upper edge of the apron. Pin, then sew, the skirt to the waistband, right sides together, with the center of the skirt matching the center of the waistband. Press the seam allowances toward the waistband. By hand, **stitch** the folded facing side of the waistband over the seam.

13. Sew the buttons to the inside of the waistband, 3½″ in from the seam for the ties and close to the bottom edge of the waistband.

14. Try on the apron, crossing the straps in the back. Mark the desired location for the buttonholes on the straps. Make the buttonholes.

15. Pin the remaining potholder patchwork square over the bib. Stitch it in place close to the inner edges of the bias tape.

Decorative Shelf Trim

Trim is photographed on page 16.

Fabric: 1½″- to 2½″-wide decorative edge trim in an amount equal to the length of the shelf plus 2″ to finish the ends for each shelf.
Notions: Glue or small brads.

1. Measure the shelf to be trimmed. Cut the trim this length plus 2″ and hem the ends.
2. Allowing 1″ at each end, apply trim to the shelf edge with glue or small brads.

Bathroom Accessories

This chapter offers some simple technical information to help you personalize an existing bath or glamorize a new one. Anyone who has ever shopped for ready-made bathroom accessories knows how very frustrating and boring that search can be. What's available is generally undistinguished, tasteless, or worse, and special sizes or styles are impossible to find. Sewing for your bathroom, on the other hand, offers infinite options in custom sizes and designs and is simple and easily managed for minimal expense. The only rule here is that washable fabrics function best in the bath because they are far more easily maintained than those which require drycleaning.

Shower Curtains

As most of us know, ready-made shower curtains are 72″ × 72″. If your shower or tub enclosure requires a curtain that is larger or smaller than this dimension, you're out of luck unless you choose to make your own. Sewing a custom shower curtain is not only practical and simple, but also very rewarding. You can shirr to any fullness: split the curtain into two panels for a window curtain effect, or add a trim that extends beyond the traditional finished measurements of the curtain to ensure that the plastic liner will not show.

Since most fabrics aren't 72″ wide, you will probably need to piece your fabric for a full tub-width curtain. In most cases, it's best to plan an enclosed seam at the center of the curtain and to trim away any excess at the sides.

Remember that most decorative shower curtains need to have a plastic liner curtain hung behind. If you can't hang both the curtain and the liner from the same shower curtain hooks, you will need two rods; one in the front for the decorative curtain, and one behind for the liner. (See the bathroom photographed on page 86 where the shower curtain remains stationary while the plastic liner moves on its own rod.)

Shower Curtain with Attached Valance
Shower curtain photographed on page 81.

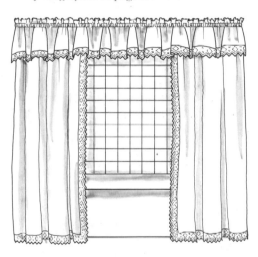

Measurements used are for a 6′-wide tub area with an 89″ finished length for the curtain. Trim width, after application to the curtain, is 1⅞″. Make appropriate measurement adjustments based on your needs.
Fabric: 7 yards 45″ to 54″ wide.
Notions: 12 yards lace trim (1½″ to 2″).
Hardware: 1⅝″-diameter wooden pole and mounting hardware.

1. Cut two curtain panels 85″ long × 42″ wide. Cut three valance strips, 21½″ deep by the width of the fabric.
2. On each curtain panel, press a 1½″ hem on the sides and bottom edge. Turn under ¼″ on the raw edges and sew the hems in place. Apply the trim to the inside, or lead, edge and the bottom of each panel, **mitering** the corners. Be sure the trim is applied to the correct edges for making a pair of panels.
3. Sew the shorter sides of the valance sections together.

Make narrow hems at each end. Hem the bottom edge in the same manner as with the curtain panels. Apply the lace trim to the bottom edge of the valance.
4. Press under ¼″ along the top edge of the valance. (If you are using terry cloth, as shown in the photograph, we suggest that you zigzag over this edge rather than turning under the ¼″ hem to eliminate bulk.) Turn down an additional 4½″. Press. Stitch across the valance 2″ down from the top folded edge for the header.
5. On a large flat surface, lay out the valance, wrong side up. Pin the panels on top of the valance at each end so that the top raw edge of the panel is about 1″ into the **casing** area of the valance. Allowing 2½″ for the casing, pin the casing in place through all thicknesses. Check the finished measurements. Sew down the casing through the panels and the valance.
6. Slip the wooden pole through the casing and mount it in the tub/shower enclosure in front of the standard liner curtain rod.

Shower Curtain with Border
Shower curtain is photographed on page 88.

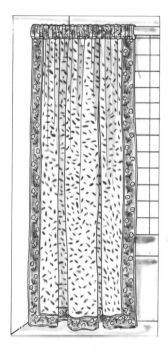

Fabric: 4 yards of main fabric for standard-size curtain; 2 yards of border fabric.
Hardware: Bamboo pole; shower curtain mounting hardware.

1. Cut two lengths of main fabric, each 70″ long, and join them with an **enclosed seam.** Trim the sides away so that the seam is centered on the curtain and the piece is 68″ wide.
2. From the border, cut and seam enough strips 7″ wide to go down both sides and across the bottom of the curtain. Cut enough strips 8″ wide to go across the top.
3. Sew the right side of the 7″ strips to the wrong side of the curtain, down the side and across the bottom edges, using a ½″ seam and **mitering** at the bottom corners only. Press the seams toward the border.
4. Bring the border strip around to the front of the shower curtain. Turn under a ½″ seam allowance on the raw edge

of the border and pin the border to the front so that the folded hem edge is just over the previous stitching line. The finished strip should be about 3″ wide. Topstitch the strip in place.

5. Repeat this procedure for sewing the 8″-wide strip to the top edge. Turn under and stitch narrow hems at each end of the border strip before sewing the strip to the shower curtain. Do *not* stitch across the ends.

6. Slip the rod through the **casing** created by the top border strip. The bamboo pole should be mounted in front of the regular shower curtain rod.

Shower Curtain with Border and Valance

Shower curtain is photographed on page 86.

Fabric: 6½ yards for floor length shower curtain and valance; 2 yards for borders and tiebacks; lining fabric to cover mounting board (optional).
Notions: 12 large eyelets; 2 small rings; 4-string shirring tape—2½ times the finished length of the valance; self-gripping fastener tape in an amount equal to the finished length of the valance.
Hardware: 2 cup hooks; wooden board—¾″ to 1″ deep × 2″ to 2½″ wide × length of tub enclosure; angle irons for mounting board; brads or glue; paint (optional).

1. Cut two lengths of fabric, each the desired finished length plus 6″. Join with an **enclosed seam.**

2. Cut enough border fabric to go along the lead edge of the shower curtain, planning ½″ seams on either side of the border. Join the border pieces, if needed.

3. Sew the right side of the border to the wrong side of the shower curtain along the front edge with a ½″ seam.

4. Bring the border around to the right side of the curtain with the seam at the edge; pin. Turn under ½″ on the raw edge of the border. Sew in place.

5. Make a 1″ double hem at the wall edge of the shower curtain. At the top and the bottom edges, make 1¼″ double hems.

6. Beginning 1½″ in from each side edging, insert the eyelets, spacing them evenly across the top. Center the eyelets in the top hem allowance.

7. To make the tieback, cut a fabric piece 37″ long by 2 times the width of the border plus ½″ seam allowances. If the border is narrow (less than 2″), use 2 stripes. Cut so that the lengthwise seam will be at the center back of the tie, and the stripe will be centered on the front.

Seam the tieback lengthwise and press the seam open. Turn and press again.

At each end, turn in ½″ and stitch closed. Attach a ring to the center of each end.

Screw the two cup hooks into the wall at the desired heights for the tieback, spacing them about ½″ apart. Hook an end of the tieback on each.

8. To make the valance, cut enough sections of fabric, 14½″ deep, to make a strip 2½ times the width of the tub enclosure. Join the sections together with an **enclosed seam.**

9. Cut enough border fabric to go along the bottom edge, planning ½″ seams on both long edges. Seam as needed. Sew the right side of the border to the wrong side of the valance along the bottom edge, using a ½″ seam.

10. Bring the border around to the right side of the fabric with the seam at the bottom edge and pin. Turn under ½″ along the raw edge of the border. Sew in place. Make narrow hems at each end of the valance.

11. At the top of the valance, press ½″ to the wrong side. Apply shirring tape, placing it ¼″ down from the top edge. Pull up the strings until the valance is the same width as the tub enclosure. Adjust the gathers evenly.

Sew the fuzzy side of self-gripping fastener tape to the valance over the shirring tape ½″ down from the top edge.

12. Mount the wooden board on the side walls of the tub enclosure with the narrow edge facing into the room. When planning the height, keep in mind that the valance must cover the shower curtain rod by several inches. Cover the board with lining fabric, if desired, or paint it to match the ground color of the print.

13. Attach the loop side of the self-gripping fastener tape to the front edge of the board with glue and/or brads. Mount the valance.

Shower Curtain Liner

Liner is photographed on page 86.

Fabric: Two vinyl tablecloths to fit your size needs. (We suggest machine washable and dryable heavyweight vinyl cloths. In the photograph, the liner was 78″ × 78″ and used two standard 60″ × 90″ cloths.)
Notions: 12 large eyelets.

1. Determine the size you will need for the liner. Cut the tablecloths, being careful first to align the motifs and scallops. Allow ⅝″ for the seam that joins the two cloths and 4½″ for the top hem.
2. Join the two cloths on the lengthwise cut edges with an **enclosed seam.** It will help to use paper clips to hold the edges together for the first seam.
3. At the top edge, turn down 1½″ three times for eyelet support. Sew down the hem.
4. Beginning 1½″ in from the side edge, insert the eyelets, spacing them evenly across the top edge. Eyelets should be centered in the hem allowance along the top.
5. Press out the wrinkles with a warm (not hot) iron, using a pressing cloth. Test a remnant of the vinyl first.

Sink Skirts

Sink skirts add a special touch to wall-hung or pedestal sinks, and in the process also provide extra storage space while hiding unsightly plumbing. Sink skirts can be mounted either on the outside porcelain or from underneath the apron of the sink. Use snap tape or self-gripping fastener tape to attach the skirt to the sink. Contact cement or molding and emblem adhesive from the auto supply store are the best glues for attaching the tape to the sink surface.

To calculate the yardage for a sink skirt, first measure the desired finished length of the skirt and add 6″ (5″ for a 2½″ bottom double hem and 1″ for the top turn-under) to that measurement for the cut size of the panel. Then measure the distance around the sink, adding 4″ because the skirt should come around the two back corners for 2″. Multiply this measurement by 2½ to determine the width of the skirt before gathering. Divide this last number by the useable width of the fabric (discounting selvages) to determine the number of panels you will need. Multiply the number of panels by the length of each panel, and then divide by 36 for the correct yardage figure.

Under-Mounted Sink Skirt with Border

Sink skirt is photographed on page 89.

Fabric: Main fabric in an amount calculated as described above, adding only 1½″ instead of 6″ to the finished height; border strip sufficient to go around the bottom of the skirt.
Notions: 2-string shirring tape in an amount equal to the width of the skirt before gathering; self-gripping fastener tape or snap tape equal in length to the distance around the sink; contact cement.

1. Cut from main fabric the number of panels needed for the skirt and seam them together.
2. Sew the right side of the border strip to the wrong side of the bottom edge of the sink skirt with a ½″ seam. Press the seam toward the border.
3. Bring the border strip around to the front of the skirt with the seam at the bottom edge and pin. Turn under a ½″ seam allowance along the raw edge of the border. Topstitch in place.
4. Make narrow hems on the side edges of the skirt.
5. At the top edge of the skirt, turn under 1″ to the wrong side. Sew shirring tape over this seam allowance, placing the tape ¼″ down from the top edge. Pull up the strings until the skirt is the desired finished width. Adjust the gathers evenly.
6. Sew the fuzzy side of the self-gripping fastener tape to the top right side of the skirt over the gathers, placing the tape ½″ down from the top edge.
7. Glue the loop side of the self-gripping fastener tape to the underside of the sink apron. Attach the sink skirt.

Top-Mounted Sink Skirt with Border

Sink skirt is photographed on page 87.

Fabric: Main fabric in an amount calculated as described above, minus 4½″ in length per panel; border strip sufficient to go around the bottom of the skirt.

Notions: 2-string shirring tape in an amount equal to the width of the skirt before gathering; self-gripping fastener tape or snap tape equal in length to the distance around the sink; glue.

1. Cut the number of panels needed for the skirt and seam them together. Cut the border strip long enough to go around the bottom edge of the skirt, planning ½″ seams on both long edges of the strip.

2. Sew the right side of the border to the wrong side of the skirt along the bottom edge with a ½″ seam. Bring the border around to the right side with the seam at the bottom edge and pin. Turn under ½″ on the border's raw edge. Sew in place.

3. At the top edge of the sink skirt, turn under 1″ to the wrong side. Apply shirring tape, placing it ½″ down from the top edge. Pull up the strings until the skirt is equal to the distance around the sink. Adjust the gathers evenly.

4. Sew the fuzzy side of the self-gripping fastener tape to the wrong side of the sink skirt, centering it over the shirring tape.

5. Glue the loop side of the self-gripping fastener tape to the outside of the sink. Attach the sink skirt.

Miscellaneous Bathroom Accessories

Towels and toweling by the yard, as well as other practical and washable fabrics, can be used for a myriad of bathroom accessories. Bath mats can be quilted, trimmed, monogrammed, appliquéd with a motif that fits your decorating scheme, or sewn from washable fabrics. Specialty items, such as towel holders, bath mats, laundry bags, and even bags for bath salts are useful and attractive additions to any bathroom. Just remember that washability is crucial to your fabric choice.

Towel Holder

Towel holder is photographed on page 85.

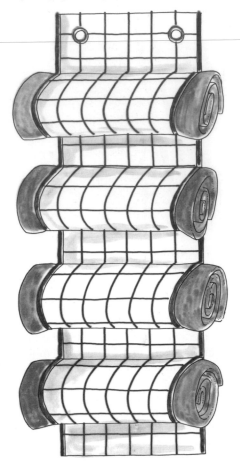

Fabric: 2¼ yards.

Notions: 2¼ yards heavy, iron-on interfacing; 8 yards 1″ bias tape; 2 large eyelets.

1. Cut two panels from both the fabric and the interfacing, one 10″ × 48″, the other 10″ × 74″.

2. Fuse the interfacing to the wrong side of both pieces. Trim the panels to 8¼″ widths, and 46″ and 72¾″ lengths, respectively.

3. Press the bias tape in half lengthwise. Bind the long, raw edges on both panels.

4. Place the two panels together with the longer one on top, wrong side of top panel to right side of bottom panel. Zigzag the two pieces together at both the top and bottom raw edges.

5. Stitch across through both panels, 1¾″ down from the top and 1″ up from the bottom.

6. Measure down 6″ from the top raw edge and stitch across through both panels.

7. To create pockets, measure 5¼″ down from the line made above on the back panel and mark. Measure down 12″ on the front panel and mark. Match up the marks and sew across through both panels. Measure down 4″ from that line and sew across through both strips.

8. Repeat Step 7 to create three more pockets.

9. Turn under 2″ at the top edge and 1¼″ at the bottom edge and stitch in place.

10. Insert the eyelets at the top edge.

Quilted Bath Mat with Crochet Lace and Monogram

Bath mat is photographed on page 80.

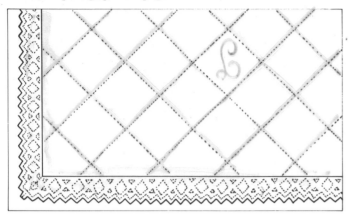

Fabric: 1½ yards of main fabric; muslin—40″ × 27″ (optional).

Trims and Notions: 4 yards crochet lace trim about 2″ wide; polyester batting—40″ × 27″.

1. Cut a piece of main fabric 40″ × 27″. Back with the batting and muslin and **quilt.** For a diamond pattern as shown, mark the center of the bath mat piece and extend the point to make perpendicular lines. Measure out and mark 3″ from the center point on each line. Draw a diamond by connecting the points. Extend the lines to the edge of the fabric. Make additional parallel lines 4¼″ apart.

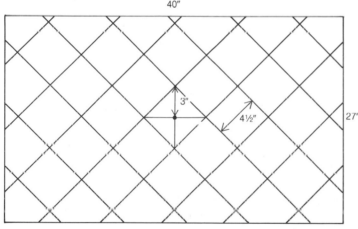

40″

3″

4½″

27″

● = center of the mat

2. Have the center of this piece professionally monogrammed, if desired.

3. Trim the quilted piece to 36″ × 24″. Cut another piece from the unquilted main fabric in the same size. Sew these two pieces, right sides together, leaving an opening on one side for turning.

4. Trim away the batting in the seam allowance to the seamline. Press the seams open; clip corners; turn and press. **Slip stitch** the opening closed.

5. Place the lace trim around the bath mat. **Miter** the corners, matching the lace pattern to best advantage. If the lace border is larger than the mat, ease the lace to fit. Sew the lace to the mat.

6. If desired, you can stitch over the quilt lines again through the mat back.

Panel Print Bath Rug

Bath rug is photographed on page 89.

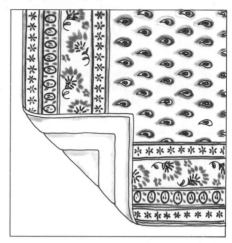

Fabric: Panel print fabric; backing fabric the size of the panel print fabric.

Notions: Polyester batting the size of the finished rug.

1. Sandwich the batting between the panel fabric and the backing fabric with the wrong sides together. **Diagonal baste** through all layers.

2. On the top side, starting at the center and working toward the edges, **quilt** the layers by stitching around motifs as desired.

3. Trim only the batting and the backing fabric to the finished size.

4. Turn the raw edges of the panel fabric twice and bring them around to the back of the rug. Pin. (Only the printed design of the fabric should be visible from the front.) Stitch the turned-under hem in place from the right side, using the print as a guide.

Quilted Toilet Seat Cover with Monogram

Seat cover is photographed on page 80.

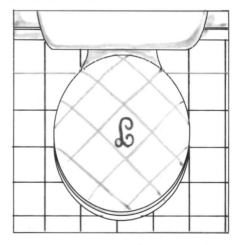

Fabric: ⅝ yard of main fabric; muslin—22″ × 22″.

Notions: 1¾ yards of single-fold bias tape; 2 yards of strong cord or string; polyester batting—22″ × 22″.

1. Make a **template** of your toilet seat. Add 2¼″ all around the template except for the back edge, where only 1″ is added.

2. Cut one 22″ × 22″ piece from the main fabric. Back it with the batting and muslin. **Quilt** as desired. For the diamond pattern, mark the center of the seat pattern and extend the point to make perpendicular lines as shown. Measure out and mark 3″ from the center point on each line. Draw lines connecting these points. Extend the lines to the edge of the fabric. Make additional parallel lines 4¼″ apart.

3. Center the toilet seat pattern on the quilted fabric. Cut out the seat.

4. Press open one folded edge of bias tape. Pin, right sides together, to the edge of the cover, matching raw edges. Turn under the ends of the bias, beginning and ending on the back edge about 1″ in from the corners.

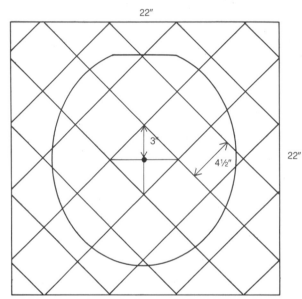

22″

3″

4½″

22″

● = center of the seat pattern

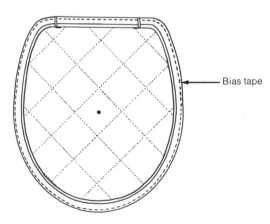

Bias tape

5. Cut a piece of bias long enough to go across the back edge, allowing ¾″ at each end for overlapping the other piece of bias. Pin the bias to the back edge of the cover, right sides together.

6. Stitch along the fold line of the bias (about ¼″ from the raw edge) all around the cover through all thicknesses.

7. Turn the bias tape to the inside of the cover. Pin and stitch close to the free edge of the bias tape.

8. Insert the string through the openings in the bias casing.

9. Have the monogram embroidered in the center of the cover, if desired.

10. Put the cover on the toilet seat and pull up the strings to fit; tie. Do *not* cut off the extra string; you'll need the extra length to release the gathers for laundering. Simply tuck the string into the toilet seat cover.

Bath Salts Bag with Trim

Bath salts bag is photographed on page 82.

Fabric: 21″ × 7″.
Trims and Notions: ½ yard of ¼″ cable cord; 7″ of lace trim, about 2″ wide.

1. Cut two pieces of fabric 10½″ long × 6¼″ wide.

2. Apply the lace trim to one piece so that the top edge of the trim is 3″ above the bottom raw edge.

3. Zigzag over the top raw edges of each piece.

4. Pin the two pieces, right sides together. Sew down the sides and across the bottom allowing a ½″ seam allowance, beginning and ending 3½″ from the top edge.

5. At the top edge, turn down 1¾″. Turn in ½″ at the unsewn side edges. Stitch across the top, ¾″ down from the folded edge. Make another row of stitching ⅝″ down from there to create a **casing.**

6. Thread the cable cord through the casing. Make knots at the ends of the cord.

Bath Mitt with Lace Trim

Bath mitt is photographed on page 82.

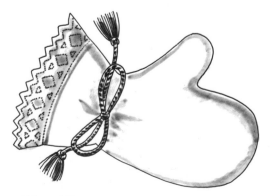

Fabric: 13″ × 18″.
Trims and Notions: ½ yard of ¼″ cable cord; ½ yard of 1″ bias tape; 10″ of ¼″ elastic; ½ yard of lace trim about 2″ wide.

1. **Enlarge** bath mitt pattern and cut two pieces from the fabric.

2. Pin the two pieces, right sides together, and sew around the mitt, leaving the bottom edge open. Trim the seams to ¼″ and clip the curves. **Overcast** the edges, if desired.

3. At the bottom edge, turn up a ¼″ hem to the right side. Stitch in place.

4. Place the top edge of the trim over the hem and stitch in place, overlapping trim ends where they meet.

5. On the inside of the mitt, center the bias tape over the **casing** line beginning and ending at a seam. Fold under the ends of the tape, and stitch in place on the long edges.

6. Insert elastic through the bias tape casing. Adjust to the desired size and sew the ends of the elastic together.

7. Make a bow from cable cord and stitch it to the mitt at the dot.

Fabric: ¾ yard.

Trims and Notions: 1¼ yards crochet lace trim about 2″ wide; ¾ yard single-fold bias tape; 16″ zipper; plastic hanger.

1. **Enlarge** laundry bag pattern and cut two pieces from the fabric; ½″ seams are allowed.

2. Cut out the opening of one piece (front). Press open one folded edge of bias tape. Sew the bias, right sides together, around the opening. Turn the bias to the inside and stitch in place to **bind** the opening. Embroider "Laundry" above the opening, if desired.

3. To form an opening for the hanger, turn down ½″ at the top edge of the front and back pieces of the bag. Stitch ¼″ from the folded edge and again ⅛″ from that.

4. With right sides together, sew front to back along the bottom edge. For zipper seam, change from a standard machine stitch to a basting stitch for the center 16″. Insert the **zipper.**

5. Stitch trim to the front of the bag as illustrated.

6. Pin the remainder of the bag front to back, right sides together. Stitch, leaving the top open for a hanger.

7. Turn the bag right side out, press, and insert hanger.

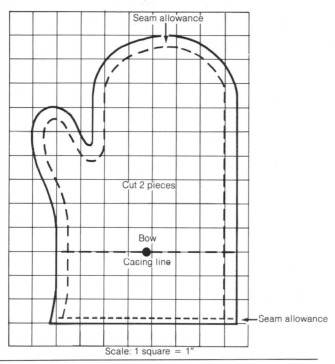

Scale: 1 square = 1″

Laundry Bag

Laundry bag is photographed on page 82.

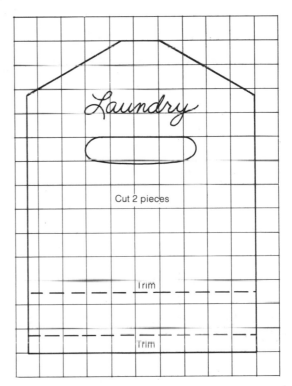

Scale: 1 square = 2″

Decorated and Embellished Towels

Decorating and embellishing purchased towels are wonderful ways to personalize your bathroom. You can use the three basic techniques we've illustrated here to create your own customized projects.

Appliquéd Towels with Monogram

Towels are photographed on page 87.

Fabric: Purchased towel; motifs cut from printed fabric.

1. Cut the motifs from the printed fabric. Allow a margin of approximately ⅛″ of background fabric when cutting.
2. Arrange the motifs as desired, reserving a place for a monogram, if one is to be used. **Appliqué** the motifs to the towel. When appliquéing, use a ⅛″ zigzag stitch and a thread color to match the towel. In this way, the thread color does not have to change as the motif color changes, and the pattern lines do not have to be followed exactly.

Towels Trimmed with Eyelet and Fabric Border

Towels are photographed on page 86.

Fabric: Purchased towels; border fabric or stripe motif cut from fabric, in an amount equal to the width of the towel plus 1½″ to finish the ends. (Any width can be used but 3″ to 4″ is best.)
Trim: Flat eyelet trim about 4″ wide in an amount equal to the width of the towel plus 1½″.

1. If you are cutting a stripe motif from fabric, allow ½″ at each long edge of the design for the seam allowance and ¾″ at each end.
2. Press under the seam allowances on the long edges of the border fabric or the stripe motif.
3. Pin and sew the flat eyelet trim to the bottom of the towel.
4. Pin the fabric strip just over the top edge of the eyelet and stitch close to the folded edges. Turn under the extra fabric at the ends of the strip and stitch to secure.

Towels Trimmed with Crochet Lace and Monogram

Towels are photographed on page 81.

Fabric: Purchased towels.
Trim: Crochet lace trim about 2″ wide in an amount equal to the width of the towel plus 1½″ to finish the ends.

1. Sew the lace to the towel with the top edge of the lace trim placed next to the bottom edge of the flat woven "stripe" found on most towels. Turn under the raw edges at each end of the trim and stitch down the folded edge.
2. Have the towel professionally monogrammed. The bottom edge of the monogram should be positioned about 3½″ up from the "stripe" on a bath towel. Adjust for smaller or larger towels.

Nursery and Children's Accessories

Sewing for kids' spaces requires some purely pragmatic considerations before any aesthetic decisions can be made. It is critical, for example, that accessory items sewn for a newborn or very young child be safe, free from any possible hazards (such as buttons that might be swallowed or exposed zippers), and thoroughly washable. The older child still imposes easy-care requirements on fabrics, and nonbleeding, preshrunk, or minimum wrinkling types are usually preferable. Fabrics designed for rugged use are the best for kids, whatever their age. Yet, within these practical guidelines, you can exercise a great deal of creativity by choosing from fabrics such as washable cottons and blends, serviceable velours, and sturdy canvas.

Baby Door Pillow

Door pillow is photographed on page 90.

Fabric: Remnant 8″ long by 18″ wide; contrast strip 32″ long × 1″ wide.

Trims and Notions: 2½ yards flat eyelet, 2″ to 2½″ wide; narrow ribbon—½ yard in each of three colors; 6-strand embroidery floss; polyester fiberfill.

1. Cut two pieces of fabric, each 8″ wide × 6¾″ long with a ½″ seam allowance.
2. **Enlarge** design and **transfer** to the right side of one piece. Using the picture as your guide, embroider it with **chain stitch,** satin stitch, and french knots.
3. Press the contrast strip in half lengthwise. Sew it to the embroidered piece so that a generous ⅛″ will show when the pillow is finished. Because the strip is not cut on the bias, it will be necessary to cut the strip at the corners and overlap the pieces there.
4. **Gather** the eyelet and sew it to the pillow front, right sides together.
5. Sew the back to the pillow front, leaving an opening for turning.
6. Turn and press. Stuff with fiberfill, and **slip stitch** the opening.
7. Braid the ribbons, tie a bow, and tack the ends to the top edge on the back of the pillow.

Scale: 1 square = ½″

Crib Canopy

Crib is photographed on page 92.

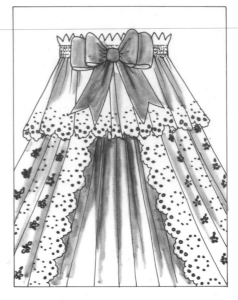

Fabric: 11 yards of eyelet with decorative border on one edge; 4 yards of eyelet with an overall pattern or other decorative fabric for the back panel.

Trims and Notions: 2½ yards of 1″-wide eyelet trim (optional); 3 yards of 4″-wide ribbon for the bow; 2 yards of 4-string shirring tape.

Mounting Board and Hardware: Wood semicircle—16″ in diameter; 42″ length of 3″-wide thin wood; 3 plastic anchors or molly bolts; 3 angle irons; 15½″ and 27″ brass or metal rods (⅜″) and hardware; paint.

1. To construct the canopy board, cut a semicircle of wood with a 16″ diameter. To make the lip, attach the 3″-wide strip of wood around the curved edge only. (You may need to have a woodworking shop shape and attach the lip piece.) Paint the wood to match the color of the canopy panels and the valance.
2. Using plastic anchors or molly bolts, attach the canopy to the wall (we suggest 6′ above the floor) with angle irons. Plan the angles at the outside at least 1″ in from the sides.
3. Mount the 15½″ rod on the wall ½″ underneath the canopy. The other rod will be mounted on the wall near the baseboard, but make the back panel before deciding on the exact spot.
4. To make the back panel, cut the 4-yard eyelet piece into two 2-yard pieces. Seam them together lengthwise. At the top edge turn under 2″ to the wrong side. Make a ½″ heading and a 1″ **casing.** Repeat at the bottom edge.
5. Install the back panel on the top rod. Locate the proper position for the lower rod and mount it on the wall.
6. Cut two 3-yard lengths from the longer eyelet yardage for panels. Use the remaining eyelet to continue the design along the bottom edge of the panels, **mitering** the eyelet at the front corners. An eyelet trim can be stitched over the horizontal seam, if desired, to conceal the seam.
7. Make a narrow hem at the top raw edge of the panels. **Gather** the top edge of the panels and nail or staple the panels to the mounted semicircle.
8. Cut two yards for a valance from the remaining eyelet fabric. Trim the fabric width to 14½″. Make a narrow hem at each short side. Press under ½″ on the long raw edge to

the wrong side. Apply **shirring** tape to the wrong side of the fabric at the top edge. Pull the strings and gather to the length needed to fit around the canopy board.

9. With small brads, tack up the shirred valance over the panels.

10. Tie a bow and tack it to the center of the canopy.

Crib Dust Ruffle

Dust ruffle is photographed on page 92.

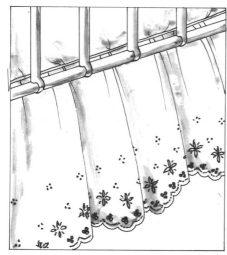

Fabric: 9½ yards of eyelet fabric (flounce widths can be purchased, 14″ to 22″ wide); 1¾ yards for the top piece.

1. Cut the fabric for the top piece to the crib mattress measurements plus seam allowances, plus 8″ in length for an end flap.

2. Trim the top piece to the shape in the diagram, slightly rounding the corners.

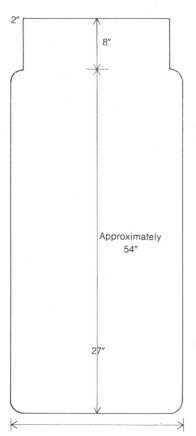

3. **Gather** the eyelet to 2½ times fullness and sew it to the top piece, bringing the eyelet around the corners about 2″ at the flap end. Finish off the raw edges of the flap end with a narrow hem.

Crib Comforter

Comforter is photographed on page 92.

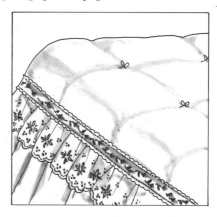

Fabric: 3 yards.

Trims and Notions: 15 yards of 4″- to 4½″-wide flat eyelet; 6 yards of 2″-wide flat eyelet; 6 yards of ¼″-wide ribbon; polyester batting—54″ × 45″.

1. Cut the fabric in half to yield two pieces, 54″ × 44″ each.

2. **Gather** the eyelet to 196″ and seam the ends together.

3. Stitch the gathered eyelet to one piece of the comforter fabric, right sides and edges together.

4. Pin the second piece of comforter fabric on the first with right sides together. Pin the batting on the bottom side of the comforter.

5. Sew around the comforter with a ½″ seam allowance, leaving a 10″ opening on one side.

6. Trim the batting *only* as close to the stitching line as possible. Turn and press. **Slip stitch** the opening.

7. Apply the trim to the comforter at the edges, **mitering** at the corners. The trim should just cover the seam between the fabric and eyelet.

8. Cut the ribbon into twenty 10″ pieces. Mark the positions for the ribbons with pins. Space them evenly four across and five down. Tack the ribbons to each point using a straight or zigzag stitch. Tie them into bows.

Crib Dust Ruffle with Alphabet

Dust ruffle is photographed on page 94.

Fabric: 5 yards of main fabric for skirt; ⅝ yard of contrast fabric for alphabet appliqués; 1¾ yards for top piece.
Notions: 10 yards wide double-fold bias tape or ¾ yard of contrast fabric for binding.

1. **Enlarge** the alphabet pattern on pages 265–67 to 3¾" high. Cut out the letters from the appliqué fabric.
2. Follow Steps 1 and 2 under Crib Dust Ruffle, preceding, to cut the top piece.
3. Cut the skirt fabric into eight panels, each the height from the top of the crib springs to the floor plus 1". Seam the panels together.
4. Divide the skirt length into five equal sections, marking the divisions with pins. Cut the skirt into three pieces: two pieces with two sections each for the sides, and one piece equal to one section for the bottom end.
5. Arrange the letters A–M evenly along the bottom edge on one side section. The letters N–Z should be placed on the other side section. The base of the letters should be 2" up from the raw edge. **Appliqué** the letters to the skirt. There should be no letters on the bottom end section.
6. Make a narrow hem on the side edges of each skirt section.
7. **Bind** the bottom edge of the skirt with bias tape or with **bias strips** that you make yourself.
8. **Gather** the skirt pieces at the top edge to the sizes needed, about 54" for each side and 27" on the end. Sew these pieces to the top piece, right sides together, bringing the skirt around the corners about 2" at the flap end. Finish off the raw edges of the flap end with a narrow hem.

Crib Spread
Spread is photographed on page 95.

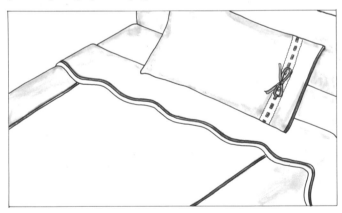

Fabric: 1¾ yards.
Trim: 10 yards of double-fold bias tape.

1. Cut two pieces from the fabric, one 45" wide × 56" long, and the other 45" wide × 6" long.
2. Cut two pieces of bias tape, each 60" long. Sew these bias strips to the right side of the spread 12½" in from each side edge to create a "welted" look.
3. **Enlarge** the pattern and cut a scallop edge along one long side of the narrow strip of fabric. **Bind** the bottom edge and two sides with bias tape. This is your "hem."
4. **Bind** the outside edges of the large spread piece with bias tape. The bottom corners of the spread can be rounded to make application easier.
5. Placing the right side of the "hem" to the wrong side of the spread, sew the "hem" strip to the top edge of the spread with a ½" seam. Trim the seam allowance to ¼".

Overcast with a zigzag stitch.
6. Bring the "hem" around to the front of the spread and press.

Pillowcase for Baby Pillow
Pillowcase is photographed on page 95.

Fabric: ¾ yard.
Trims and Notions: ¾ yard double-fold bias tape; ¾ yard eyelet beading; 1 yard of ¼" ribbon.
Pillow Form: baby boudoir pillow—12" × 16".

1. Cut the fabric 18" wide × 25" long.
2. **Bind** one long edge with bias tape.
3. Thread the ribbon through the eyelet and apply the trim to the pillowcase 2½" from the biasbound edge. Tie the two ends of the ribbon into a bow.
4. Fold the pillowcase in half crosswise with right sides together (piece now measures 18" × 12½"). Sew the raw edges together with ½" seams. Trim the seam allowances to ¼" and overcast with a zigzag stitch.
5. Turn the case right side out, and press.

Crib Bumper Guard
Guard is photographed on page 94.

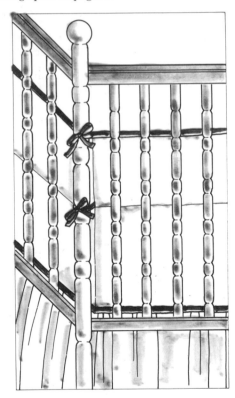

Fabric: 1⅝ yards of 54" fabric, if it can be **railroaded,** or 3⅛ yards for 45" width, or fabric with a one-way design.
Trims and Notions: 11 yards of wide double-fold bias tape; six 27" × 8" pieces of foam, 1-inch thick (layers of batting basted together can also be used).

1. For the end guard sections, cut four rectangles measuring 28" × 9" from the fabric. For the side guard sections, cut four rectangles measuring 55" × 9". If the fabric has a one-way design, you will have to make a seam down the middle for a 55" width; i.e., you will need two rectangles 28" × 9".

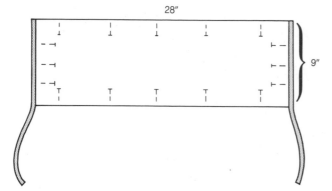

2. Pin rectangles of equal size wrong sides together. Turn under ½" on both bottom long edges of each of the resulting four rectangles and pin. Sew down the center of each 55" rectangle to create two pockets for foam.
3. Apply one 17" piece of bias tape to each short end of the four rectangles so that 8½" extends beyond the bottom edge. Sew the binding close to the turned-under edge of the bias and continue stitching down the length of the tie, turning in the raw edges at the end of the ties.

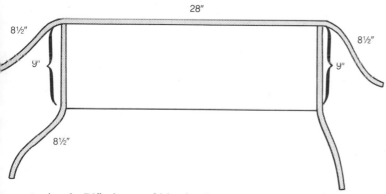

4. Apply 72" pieces of bias in the same manner to the top edges leaving 8½" ties at each end of the bumper guard sections.
5. Insert the foam pieces from the open bottom edges, one piece for each end and two pieces for each side section, and close by hand or machine.
6. To create ties for the center of each side section, cut a 17" piece of bias tape. Topstitch the edges together, turning under the raw edges at the ends. Sew ties to the bias binding at the center of each side section.

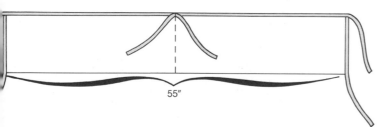

7. Place the guard sections in the crib at the appropriate positions. Join the end and side section ties at the corners, and tie to the crib to secure. Tie the center ties on each side section to a crib rung.

Changing Table Cover
Cover is photographed on page 96.

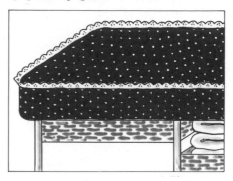

Fabric: 1¼ yards face fabric; ½ yard backing fabric.
Trims and Notions: 3¼ yards preruffled eyelet, ¾" to 1" wide; polyester batting—½ yard or piece 18" × 36" (or 1" larger all around than the tabletop).

1. Quilt ½ yard of the face, batting, and backing fabric together. Cut the piece to the size of the tabletop plus a ½" seam allowance all around.
2. Sew the eyelet around all sides of the top of the quilted piece, right sides and raw edges together.
3. From the remaining face fabric, cut three strips, each the width of the fabric × 7". Seam them together on the short ends.
4. Press the strip in half lengthwise, wrong sides together.
5. Sew the strip around the quilted piece, right sides together, with a ½" seam. Make a seam where the ends of the strip meet.
6. Trim the seam allowances to ¼". **Overcast** with a zigzag stitch.

Wreath from Quilt Remnants
Wreath is photographed on page 94.

The wreath photographed has a 16" diameter, but can be made in any size you desire. Alter your fabric needs accordingly.
Fabric: 18" square of backing fabric; eight pieces of quilt remnants, each approximately 9" square.
Trims and Notions: 2 yards of ribbon for the bow, 1" wide; yarn for tufting ties; bone ring for hanging; polyester fiberfill.

1. To make a pattern, draw a paper circle 16" in diameter. Add a ½" seam allowance to the outside edge. Centered inside the larger circle, draw a smaller circle, 7" in diameter. Add a ½" seam allowance to the inside of that circle. Cut out the center of the circle along the innermost line.

2. From the backing fabric, cut out the whole circle. **Stay-stitch** along the inner seamline.

3. Fold the pattern into eight equal parts. Cut out one of the eight sections. Add a ½" seam allowance to each straight side of that section. Using this section as your pattern, cut 8 pieces from the quilt remnants.

4. Sew the quilt remnants together to form a circle. Stay-stitch along the inner seamline.

5. Sew the front and back pieces together along the outer seamline. Trim the seam allowance to ¼". Turn right side out and press.

6. Lay the wreath flat. On the inner circle, make marks in the seam allowance of the backing fabric at the front seam points. **Slip stitch** or **whipstitch** the inner edges of the front and back pieces together, stuffing the wreath firmly with fiberfill as you go.

7. In the center of each seam on the front piece, make a **tufting** tie.

8. Make twelve 3" loops from the ribbon and join for the bow. Tack to the wreath.

9. Sew a bone ring to the back for hanging.

Decorated Sheets and Pillowcases

We've already discussed decorated sheets and pillowcases on page 232 in the "Beds, Bedding, and Bedroom Accessories" chapter. It seems relevant to mention them again here, however, since the use of decorated or embellished bed linens in children's rooms has a special importance. Children love this sort of detail and, if you take the time and make the extra effort, a child will notice and appreciate the gesture. For a tot, the sheep appliqué with its charming little numbers done in **chain stitch** (photographed on page 95) is particularly appropriate for bedtime learning games. The rosebud appliquéd bed linens (photographed on page 103) are perfect for a little girl. Decorated sheets and pillowcases make wonderful children's gifts in their own right, as well as contributing to the magic in a newly decorated child's bedroom.

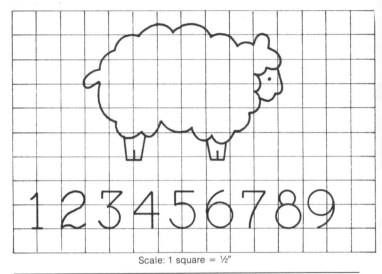

Scale: 1 square = ½"

Blanket with Name Appliqués
Blanket is photographed on page 100.

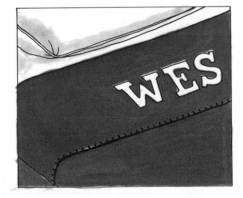

Fabric: Remnant for appliqué; purchased blanket of desired size.
Trim: 4-ply yarn for blanket stitching.

1. Remove any binding from the blanket and steam out any markings from the stitching.

2. Do a **blanket stitch** in yarn around the entire blanket.

3. **Enlarge** the alphabet letters, pages 265–67, to a 2½" height.

4. Cut the desired letters from the fabric remnant. Adhere them to the blanket about 6" up from the edge. (A fabric glue stick works well here.)
5. Appliqué the letters to the blanket with a close machine zigzag stitch.

Sack Neckroll
Neckroll is photographed on page 100.

Fabric: ½ yard; contrast remnant to cover cord.
Notions: ½ yard of ½" cord; fusible web strip—½" × 32".
Neckroll Form: 13" × 5".

1. Cut a piece of fabric 32" wide × 21" long, and a fabric circle 7" in diameter.
2. Join the 32" edges with a ½" seam.
3. Sew the circle to one end of the tube just created, right sides together, with a ½" seam.
4. At the open end, turn down 11" to the inside of the tube. Hold the raw edge in place with a narrow strip of fusible web.
5. With the contrast remnant, make a tube of fabric to accommodate the cording, following the directions for Napkin Ring of Bias-Covered Welt, page 159.
6. Insert the neckroll form into the "sack" and tie with the cording.

Neckroll with Appliqué
Neckroll is photographed on page 103.

Fabric: ⅜ yard for ends, cut crosswise (⅔ yard if cut lengthwise, as in the photograph); ⅜ yard for center; remnants for appliqué.
Trims and Notions: 1½ yards narrow ribbon.
Neckroll Form: 13" × 5".

1. Cut two ends, each 20¾" long × 5¾" wide, and one center, 20¾" long × 9½" wide.
2. Cut out the rosebud design and **appliqué** to the center of the center piece.

Actual size ———— Pattern must be reversed to complete motif

3. Stitch the end pieces to the center section along the long edge with ½" seams. Press the seams toward the center unless they will show through the center section.
4. Stitch the center bottom seam of the cover with a ½" seam.
5. Press under ¾" at each end to make **casings.** Turn under ¼" along the raw edge and stitch in place. Tack it securely at the stitching line and the folded edge of the casing in the seam area. Clip a few stitches of the seam in the casing area on either the inside or outside for inserting ribbons.
6. Insert the pillow form, pull up the ribbons, and tie.

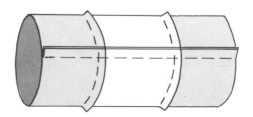

Appliquéd Children's Towels

Towels are photographed on page 99.

Fabric: Remnants for appliqués; purchased towels.

1. Cut appliqué designs from fabric remnants. The five crayons on this towel are 3½", 4½", 5", 4¾", and 4¼" tall; adjust the pattern pieces accordingly.

2. Appliqué the pieces to the center of the towel above the flat or colored "stripe" on the towel. To make the strings and bow of the balloon, use a wide, close machine zigzag stitch. For the crayons, zigzag across the dotted lines with a medium-width, close machine stitch. Create "smoke" lines from the cars with a medium-width, close, machine zigzag stitch.

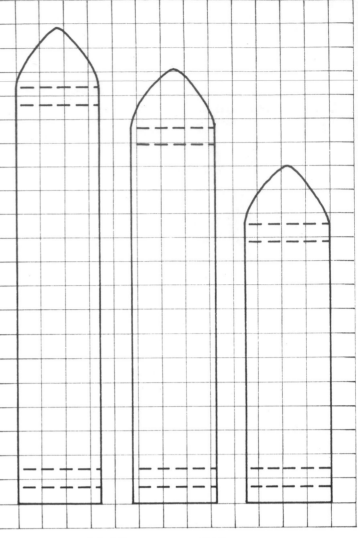

Actual size   Cut 5 crayons

Actual size   Cut 3 cars

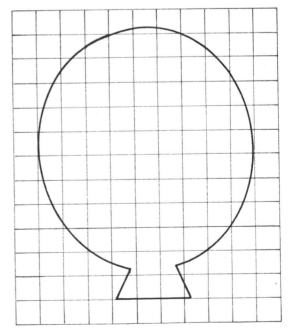

Actual size   Cut 3 balloons

A B C Quilt
Quilt is photographed on page 97.

Fabric: 3¾ yards white fabric; 1½ yards backing fabric; ⅝ yard each of green, blue, and yellow fabrics; ¼ yard red fabric.

Notions: 27″ yellow shoelace; 7″ red zipper; 6 large eyelets; 2⅝″ white snaps; ½ yard of ¼″ blue grosgrain ribbon; twin-size batting; fusible web (optional); remnants of interfacing (optional); clear nylon thread.

1. From white fabric, cut four strips, each 7″ × 72″ for quilt edging and thirty squares 10″ × 10″. From colored fabrics, cut thirty 10″ squares: eight red, seven yellow, seven green, and eight blue.

2. **Enlarge** the letters on pages 265–67 to a 5″ height. Enlarge the patterns for the four corner learning squares.

3. For the colored square "frames," make a **template** 6″ square with slightly rounded corners. Center the template on the wrong side of each colored square cut in Step 2. Trace around the template with a pencil. Cut out the centers and *save*.

4. Cut out the appropriately colored letters from the centers of the colored frames using the photograph on page 97 as a guide. Lay the right side of the letter pattern on the wrong side of the fabric. Trace around with a pencil and cut out. Cut out the corner pattern pieces, except for the red train wheels, using the centers and leftover pieces.

5. Place each colored frame on a square of white fabric. Baste or adhere it with fusible web. Stitch close to the inner edge of the frame with a medium-width, satin zigzag stitch.

6. **Appliqué** the letters in the center of the squares in the same manner.

7. To make the Turtle/Lacing learning square, appliqué the yellow circle and the whole turtle to the center of the green square. Fold the two green circles in half on the fold line. (Apply interfacing to half of each circle if more body is desired.) Insert eyelets according to the package directions. Appliqué the two halves over the whole turtle. Embroider the eye and mouth by hand or machine. Insert a shoelace.

8. To make the Apple/Zipper learning square, fold the apple pieces in half on the fold line. Apply interfacing if desired. Stitch a half to each side of the zipper, leaving the zipper teeth exposed. Do *not* cut off the excess zipper yet. Appliqué the apple and stem to the center of the red square. Do not attach the apple except at the outside edges. When stitching, stop at the top and bottom of the zipper. Cut off excess; satin stitch well across the ends.

9. To make the Engine/Snaps learning square, appliqué the blue train to the blue square, placing the red trims where shown, except for the wheels. On the right side of the red fabric, trace around the wheel twice. Back with another piece of red fabric, wrong sides together, and put a small piece of batting between them. Stitch around both wheels on the pencil lines with a very close satin stitch. Cut away the fabric outside the stitching lines. Apply snaps to the wheels and square according to the manufacturer's directions.

10. To make the Flowers/Tying learning square, appliqué the flowers and stems to the yellow square. Center the ribbon under the stem before completing the appliqué. Tie a bow.

11. Lay out the thirty squares using the photograph as a guide. Sew the squares together in horizontal rows with ½″ seams. Press the seams open. Pin and sew the rows together in the correct order, carefully matching the intersecting seams. Press the seams open.

12. Cut the batting 12″ wider and 12″ longer than the quilt top. Sandwich the batting between the top and backing, centering each on the batting. There should be 6″ of batting beyond all of the edges of the quilt when the right sides of the top and back are facing out. Baste them together with **diagonal stitches.**

13. Sew all three layers together by machine, stitching in the seams between the squares with clear nylon thread.

14. Sew two white strips to the sides of the quilt with ½″ seams, the right side of the white fabric to the right side of the quilt top. Leave 3″ extra beyond the top and bottom of the quilt.

15. Press under ½″ on the raw edge of the white fabric. Fold the polyester batting so that it will "stuff" the white quilt edging. Bring the strips around to the back of the quilt and **whipstitch** in place just over the previous stitching line.

16. Sew the other white strips to the top and bottom edges of the quilt in the same manner. Stop the stitching at the point where the strip meets the side border. Leave 6″ to 7″ of fabric beyond this point. **Miter** the corners and whipstitch them in place.

17. Bring the strip around to the back and finish it in the same way that the sides were done.

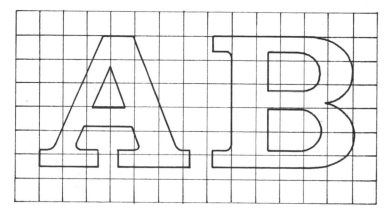

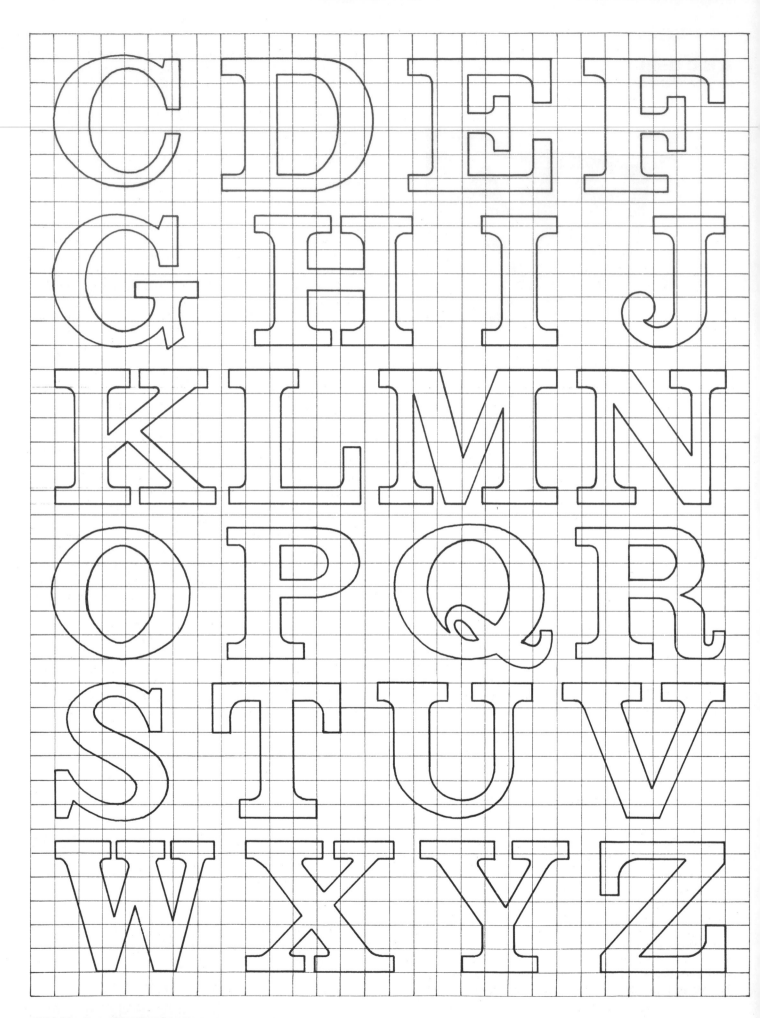

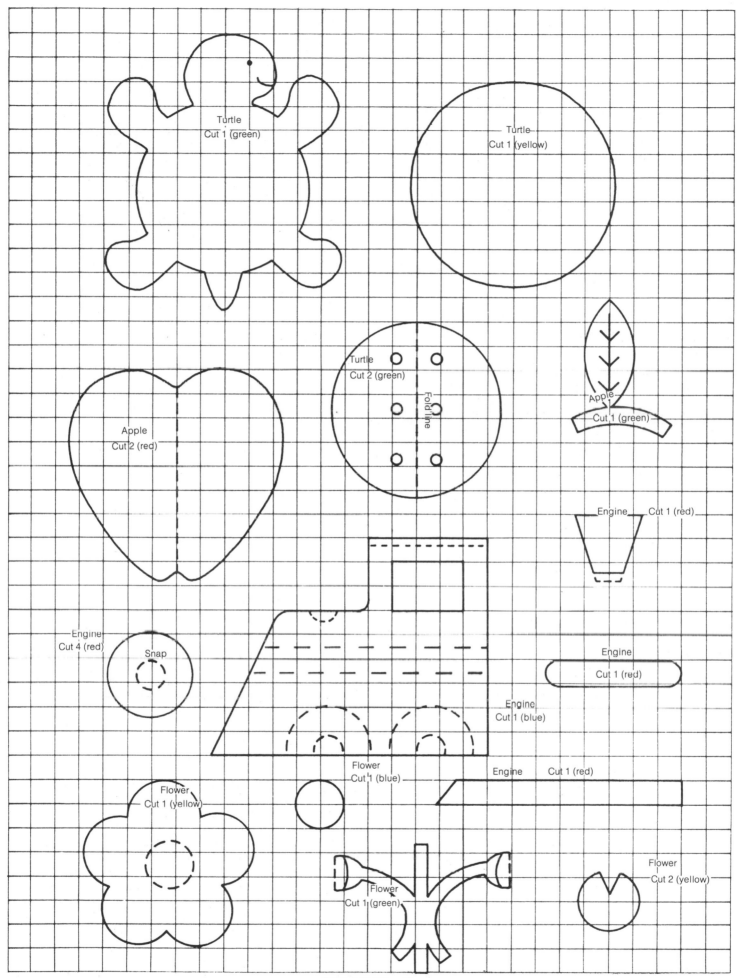

Turtle
Cut 1 (green)

Turtle
Cut 1 (yellow)

Turtle
Cut 2 (green)

Fold line

Apple
Cut 2 (red)

Apple
Cut 1 (green)

Engine   Cut 1 (red)

Engine
Cut 4 (red)

Snap

Engine
Cut 1 (red)

Engine
Cut 1 (blue)

Flower
Cut 1 (blue)

Engine   Cut 1 (red)

Flower
Cut 1 (yellow)

Flower
Cut 2 (yellow)

Flower
Cut 1 (green)

Scale: 1 square = 1"

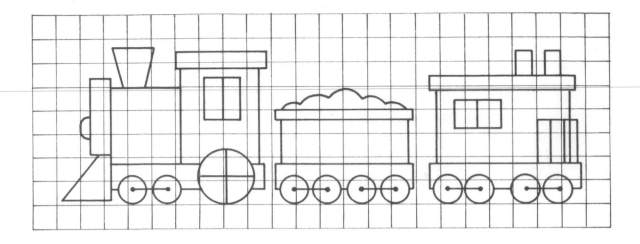

Scale: 1 square = 1"

Bath Mat with Train Appliqué
Bath mat is photographed on page 99.

Fabric: Remnants for appliqué; purchased bath mat or towel.

1. **Enlarge** the appliqué design and cut the pieces from fabric remnants.
2. **Appliqué** the pieces to the bath mat with a close, medium-width zigzag stitch.

Reading Pillow
Pillow is photographed on page 100.

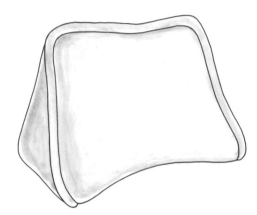

Fabric: 1½ yards; 1⅜ yards of muslin.
Notions: 1¾ yards jumbo cording (1" diameter); 16" zipper; polyester fiberfill—about 5 pounds.

1. **Enlarge** and cut the pattern pieces from the muslin.
2. Sew the center seam on the bottom pieces.
3. Sew the bottom to the lower edge of the back, matching the large dots and the center back bottom. Start and stop sewing at the X's. Clip at the large dot on the back. Leave about 8" open between the large dots for stuffing.
4. Sew the back to the front, starting and ending the stitching at X. Clip as needed and ease the back onto the front at the upper edges. Match the center front and center back to the center bottom seam.
5. Clip the curves and corners. Turn and press. Stuff with fiberfill and close the opening.
6. From fabric, cut out the pattern pieces and use the left-over fabric to make 1¾ yards of **bias strips.**
7. Make **welting** with cording and bias strips. Baste the welting to the sides and upper edge of the front.
8. Proceed as in Steps 2 through 4, except in Step 3, use a basting stitch between the large dots and insert the **zipper** in that area. Open the zipper before sewing the front to the back.
9. Trim the seams. Clip the curves and corners. Turn and press. Insert the muslin form.

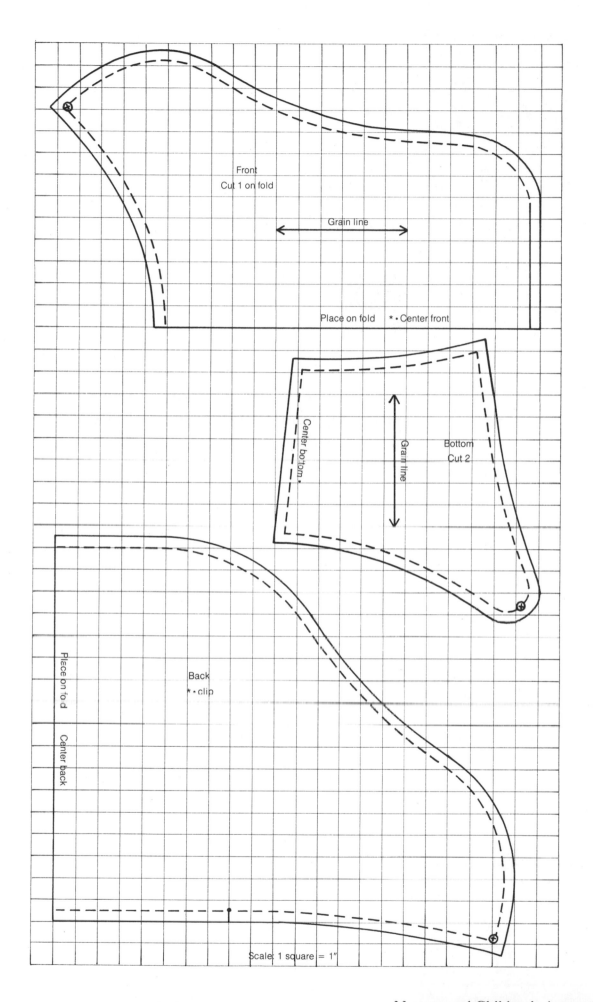

Front
Cut 1 on fold

Grain line

Place on fold   * • Center front

Center bottom.

Grain line

Bottom
Cut 2

Back
* • clip

Place on fold

Center back

Scale: 1 square = 1"

Outdoor Accessories

Nearly anything that can be sewn for indoors can be adapted to outdoor use. Once again, the choice of fabric is key to an item's success in outdoor or partially enclosed spaces. Choose a fabric that resists sun-fading and rotting, and that is mildew resistant. Acrylics, cotton/polyester blends, and cottons all fare well. Wools and silks should be avoided. You may decide to have a particular fabric professionally vinylized before using it outdoors. A local upholsterer can usually have your fabric processed before it is cut. Another helpful tip is to choose rust resistant hardware for outdoor projects. Marine stores are a good source for heavy duty hardware that can hold up to any weather.

Beach Tote

Tote is photographed on page 109.

Fabric: ⅝ yard of 54″ fabric, or 1 yard of 44″ to 45″ fabric; remnants for appliqué.

Notions: 3⅓ yards of webbing (1⅛″ wide); 7″ zipper; 18″ narrow cord.

1. Cut the piece for the tote 22″ wide × 36″ long. Cut the pocket 9″ wide × 10½″ long.
2. Zigzag over the raw edges on the 22″ sides and along one 9″ edge of the pocket.
3. Turn down a 1″ hem on both 22″ edges and on the zigzagged edge of the pocket. Stitch in place.
4. Cut the appliqué design from fabric remnants. **Appliqué** the pieces to the pocket.
5. Turn under ½″ at the bottom edge of the pocket. Center the pocket on one side of the bag with the top edge of the pocket 4″ down from the top of the bag.

6. Pin the webbing to the tote, allowing 8″ between the inside edges of the webbing and 25″ for each handle. On the back side of the tote, starting 5″ down from the edge of the tote, leave 7″ of the strap on each side unstitched for insertion of newspaper, umbrella, etc. The sides of the pocket should be ½″ under each of the straps.

7. Sew the webbing strap to the canvas, stitching close to both edges. At each point where the stitching stops or starts, reinforce with box stitching.
8. Sew across the bottom of the pocket close to the folded edge.
9. Sew the side seams with a ½″ seam and trim the seam allowance to ¼″. Zigzag over the raw edges.

10. To box the corners of the tote, fold each bottom corner into a triangle. Measure 3″ in from the apex and stitch across where the bottom of the triangle equals 6″.
11. To make the inside zipper bag, cut a piece 8½″ × 11″ from a fabric remnant. Seam the 8½″ edges together with a ½″ seam, using a machine basting stitch for the center 7″ to allow the insertion of a zipper. Press seam open. Insert the **zipper.**
12. Seam the sides of the zipper bag, catching the narrow cording in the seam near the zipper seam. Be sure to leave the zipper open before completing this step. Sew the other end of the cord to the seam allowance in the tote.

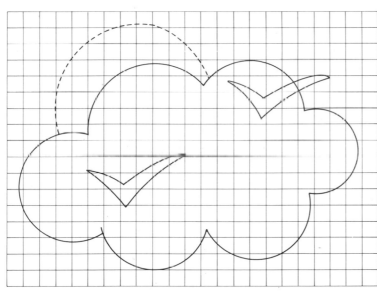

Tote: 1 square = 1″   Towel: 1 square = 1½″

Duffle Bag

Bag is photographed on pages 104 and 108.

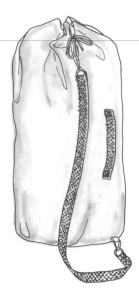

Fabric: 1⅝ yards, 54″ wide.

Notions: 2 yards of rope or heavy cord; 2¼ yards of webbing, 1⅛″ wide; 2 metal rings, 1½″ in diameter; 2 metal snap hooks; 12 large grommets.

1. Cut an 18″ circle and a rectangular piece, 39″ long × 54″ wide, from the fabric.

2. Cut two pieces of webbing 7½″ long for tabs. Put a ring on each and fold one piece of webbing in half. Baste the ends together; pin the raw edges of this tab to the center of one 54″ edge of the fabric (now the bottom edge).

3. Cut a 17½″ piece of webbing for a hand strap. Pin to 8″ in the middle of the duffle (see diagram). Turn under 1¼″ at each end of the strap. Sew it in place with a boxing stitch as described on page 271. After stitching, trim away any excess webbing.

4. Fold the other ring tab so that one end of the webbing is 1″ longer than the other. Fold the extra over the raw edge of the shorter end. Position it on the bag in line with the other tab and handle, with the "extra" side down, 5″ from the top end. Sew with boxing stitch.

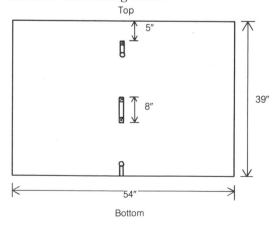

5. With right sides together, seam the lengthwise edges with a ½″ seam. Press open.

6. Sew the bottom edge of the duffle to the circle, right sides together, with a ½″ seam.

7. Press down 2½″ at the top of the duffle to the inside. Turn under ½″ on the raw edge and stitch in place.

8. Insert twelve grommets evenly spaced in the top edge of the duffle. Thread the cord through the holes and knot the ends.

9. Cut a 42″ piece of webbing for the shoulder strap. Thread a snap hook onto each end of the strap, allowing 3″ at each end to turn back. Turn under 1¼″ at each raw edge and sew down to the main strap with a boxing stitch. Attach a snap hook to each of the rings on the duffle.

Beach Blanket

Blanket is photographed on page 109.

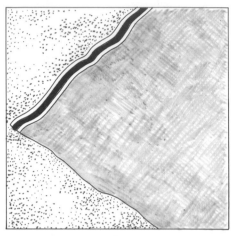

Fabric: Purchased blanket.

Notions: 1½″-wide ribbon in a length twice the width of the blanket plus 2″; narrower ribbon in the same length.

1. To create your own stripe ribbon, center the narrower ribbon on the 1½″ ribbon and stitch along both edges.

2. Sew the ribbon to the hem edges of the blanket, turning under ½″ inch on each end.

Beach Towel

Towel is photographed on page 109.

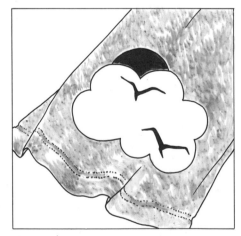

Fabric: Purchased beach towel; fabric remnants for appliqué; fabric glue stick (optional).

1. **Enlarge** the appliqué design on page 271 so that one square = ½″, and cut out from fabric remnants.

2. **Appliqué** to the towel. (A fabric glue stick will help hold the appliqué in place for stitching.)

Beach Mat

Mat is photographed on page 109.

Fabric: 2½ yards, 60″ wide (5 yards if less than 60″). 48 ounces of polyester fiberfill.
Notions: 1¼ yards of webbing, 1⅛″ wide; 1 metal ring, 1½″ in diameter; 1 metal snap hook; water soluble ink pen.

1. Cut the fabric length to 89″. Split the fabric lengthwise to get two pieces, 89″ × 30″ each.
2. Fold one end of the webbing as follows:

Thread a metal ring onto the webbing and position it at A. Pin.

3. Pin the folded end of the webbing B to the center of the 30″ edge on one of the fabric pieces.
4. With right sides together, seam the two pieces along the short ends and one long side with a ½″ seam.
5. Press the seams open. Turn and press again.
6. Press under ½″ seam allowances on the open long side.
7. Topstitch ³⁄₁₆″ from the edge around the three seamed sides. Pin the open edges together.
8. Section the mat by dividing it lengthwise into eleven equal sections of 8″ each. Use the water soluble ink pen to draw lines. Stitch the sections, making sure that the edges meet on the open end.
9. Stuff each section with fiberfill. Pin closed.
10. Sew along the open end ³⁄₁₆″ from the edge.
11. Sew a snap hook to the end of the long piece of webbing. There is 3″ allowed to turn back with a 1″ turn-under where the webbing is sewn down at C.
12. Roll up the mat. Bring the webbing strap around the mat and clip it to the ring.

Flatware Holder

Flatware holder is photographed on page 111.

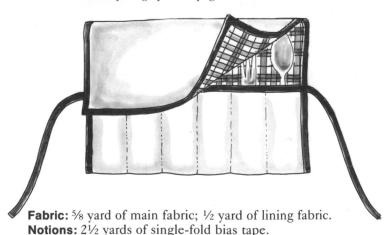

Fabric: ⅝ yard of main fabric; ½ yard of lining fabric.
Notions: 2½ yards of single-fold bias tape.

1. From main fabric, cut a piece 12¾″ × 20¼″. From lining fabric, cut a piece 12¾″ × 15½″.

2. With wrong sides together, lay lining fabric on top of main fabric, aligning the fabrics at the sides and Edge D (see diagram). Lining fabric should meet Fold A.
3. Bind Edge C with bias tape on main fabric only.

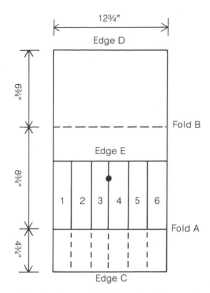

4. Turn up main fabric on Fold A. Stitch pocket lines, making six 2⅛″ pockets.
5. **Bind** remaining raw edges, following the directions for Binding Outward Corners on page 123.
6. Press a 27″ piece of single-fold bias tape in half lengthwise; stitch, finishing the ends. Attach the center of the tie to the main fabric at the large dot on the diagram.

Wine Glass Holder

Wine glass holder is photographed on page 111.

Fabric: ⅝ yard of main fabric; ½ yard of lining fabric.
Notions: 3 yards of single-fold bias tape.

1. From main fabric, cut a piece 12¾" wide × 21" long. From lining fabric, cut a piece 12¾" wide × 14" long.

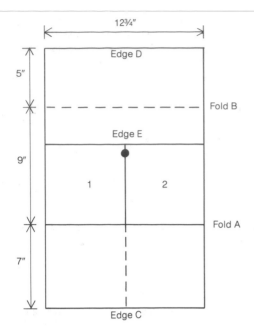

2. Lay lining fabric on top of main fabric, wrong sides together, aligning the fabrics at the sides and at Edge D. (Lining fabric should meet Fold A.)
3. Bind Edge C with bias tape on main fabric only.
4. Turn up main fabric on Fold A. Stitch pocket lines, making two 6⅜" pockets.
5. Bind remaining raw edges, following the directions for Binding Outward Corners on page 123.
6. Press a 40" piece of single-fold bias tape in half lengthwise; stitch, finishing the ends. Attach this tie to the main fabric at the large dot on the diagram.

Wine Bottle Holder
Wine bottle holder is photographed on page 111.

Fabric: ½ yard of main fabric; ½ yard of lining fabric.
Notions: 1 yard of single-fold bias tape.

1. Cut two pieces from each fabric, each piece 6¾" wide × 16" long (½" seam allowance is included).
2. With the right sides together, sew the two pieces of main fabric on the sides and the bottom with a ½" seam, starting and stopping at Points A (see illustration). Repeat for lining fabric, but leave a 3" opening in the bottom seam. Press the seams open on the sides.

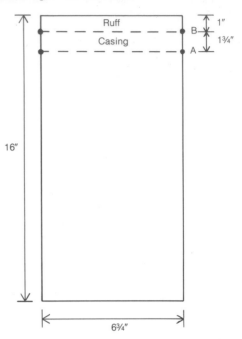

3. Place the lining section inside the main section with the right sides together. Align the side seams and sew the sections together across the top, beginning and ending at Points B (see illustration). Trim the seams and the corners and turn the holder right side out through the opening in the lining. Stitch by hand to close the lining.
4. Sew the casing lines 1" down from the top and again 1¾" below that. These should align with the opening along the sides between Points A and B.
5. To box the bottom of the holder, fold the bottom corners, catching both the outside and lining fabrics to create a triangle. Measure 1" in from the apex and sew across through all layers where the bottom edge of the triangle equals 2".

6. To make the ties, press the bias in half lengthwise. Stitch. Cut the tie in half. To create the drawstring, insert one tie at one side opening and thread it through both sides of the bag. Knot the ends. Repeat this procedure for the second tie, but start at the opposite side. Finish off the ends of the ties.

Basket Liner

Basket liner is photographed on page 111. (Basket photographed is 10" × 16" × 9".)

Yardage requirements may vary with basket size. Yardage given is for basket as shown.
Fabric: 1 yard of main fabric; 1 yard of backing fabric.
Notions: 4 yards of 1"-wide single-fold bias tape; ¼" elastic (optional).

1. Make the pattern pieces according to your basket measurement, using the diagram as a guide. You may have to make separate pattern pieces for the sides and bottom if your basket has a unique shape. Cut one pattern from each fabric.

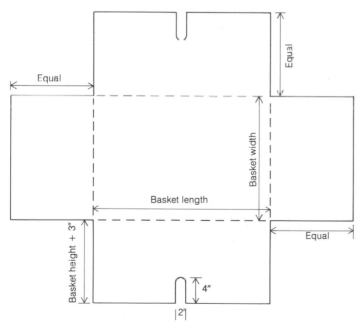

2. Sew the cut-out corners together, right sides together, on both fabrics. Press seams open.
3. Pin the main fabric to the backing, wrong sides together. Baste the top and handle slot edges.
4. Bind the U-shaped handle slot with bias tape.
5. Bind the top edges with bias tape, leaving 12" free at each edge of both U-shaped slots to make ties.
6. If your basket has a unique shape, elastic can be inserted through the bias tape to draw up the liner and help it to fit more snugly. Fasten the elastic at each edge of the handle slot.
7. Fold each 12" length of the ties in half lengthwise and stitch.
8. Insert the liner into the basket and tie bows around the handle.

Picnic Tablecloth with Napkins

Tablecloth is photographed on page 110.

Fabric: Tablecloth—a square of fabric in desired size (if the square is to be larger than the width of the fabric, use the chart under Basic Round Tableskirt or Cloth, page 146, to determine yardage); napkins—squares of fabric cut to desired size, or purchased napkins.
Notions: 1"-wide single-fold bias tape in an amount equal to the perimeter of the cloth plus 10"; single-fold bias tape — amount equal to the perimeter of the napkin plus 3" (per napkin); monogram (optional).

1. Cut a square the desired size from the fabric. If piecing is necessary because of the width of the fabric, consult instructions for a Basic Round Tableskirt or Cloth, page 146, for directions.
2. Bind the edges with the wide bias tape, following instructions for Binding Outward Corners on page 123. When the bias is folded in Step 2 of these instructions, allow the folded edge to extend approximately ¼" beyond the top raw edge. This accommodates the greater width of bias used on this cloth.
3. Have corner professionally monogrammed, or apply purchased monogram letters by hand.
4. To make napkins, bind each square of fabric with bias tape. If you prefer, you can round the corners slightly, to make the application of bias tape easier, or proceed as for picnic cloth, above.

R·E·SO·U·RC·E·S

Glossaries

Source Directory

Index

Fabric Glossary

Names and technical terms used in referring to fabrics, fibers, and weaves are often confusing. This glossary is intended as a handy reference guide, offering brief descriptions of some of the more common such terms, and, in addition, a helpful suitability code to assist you in matching up fabric and project. **U** indicates that a particular fabric is suitable for upholstery; **C** fabrics are fine for curtains; **D** materials are good for drapery treatments; and **S** is a yes for slipcovers. Please note that no indications have been listed for such accessory items as tableskirts, pillows, kitchen and bath accessories, bed linens, and the like. This is because nearly any fabric can be made into these items, and they would therefore appear in nearly every case. Some lighter weight fabrics can be successfully backed or quilted to make them suitable for heavier use.

In some instances, fabric types are woven in many different fibers, creating a variety of weights and fabric personalities under the same generic name. Broadcloth is such a type. For these, you should use your own judgment based on the fiber you've chosen. In any case, there are always exceptions to the rules, and once you have some experience sewing for your home, you'll see that virtually any fabric can be adapted to *any* project. When you want to experiment with a fabric, buy a length and try it to check its suitability before sewing up an entire room. The glossary, while far from exhaustive (there are literally thousands of fabrics) should provide you with the basic information and prepare you to make intelligent fabric choices for any project in your home.

A

Acetate: A man-made fiber derived from cellulose acetate. Fabrics made with acetate fibers have a luxurious soft feel, a silklike appearance, and excellent draping qualities. Acetate is used in such fabrics as taffeta, faille, lace, satin, and crepe, where it may be combined with other fibers. Acetate fabrics may wrinkle, but they are resistant to stretch and shrinkage. The fiber takes color well, but some dyes are subject to atmospheric fading. Acetate fabrics are usually dry-cleaned.

Acrylic: The generic term for the synthetic textile fiber that resembles wool. Acrylic fabrics are available in a variety of weights, from sheer, wool-like voiles and medium-weight flannels to heavy canvas constructions and pile fabrics. Acrylic fabric is resistant to wrinkles, lightweight, and quick drying; it is strong, colorfast, holds its shape well, and has excellent resistance to mildew and sunlight. Acrylic fabric is mothproof and can often be washed following the fabric-care labels. It dries quickly and requires little or no ironing.

Antique Satin: A dull-faced, heavy-weight satin weave fabric. **D,U**

Antique Taffeta: A crisp taffeta woven with uneven or slubbed yarns. **D**

Argyle Plaid: A fabric with large diamond-shaped motifs that have contrasting diagonal overstripes to create a plaid design.

B

Bagherra: A fine knitted or woven velvet with an uncut pile. **D,U**

Barkcloth: A woven drapery fabric with a rough or barklike appearance. **C,D**

Basket Weave: A plain weave fabric woven with paired or multiple threads to produce the effect of a basket. This weave is available in a wide variety of fibers in fabrics such as hopsacking, oxford cloth, and monk's cloth.

Batik: A fabric that has the design dyed into the cloth; removable wax is applied to the surface, so that only the exposed areas take the dye. The process can be repeated to create complex designs. Originally developed as a hand process in Java, the technique can be adapted to machine printing.

Batiste: A soft, sheer, plain weave fabric, usually in white and a pastel color range. It can be woven of cotton, silk, linen, wool, or synthetic fibers and blends. **C**

Bedford Cord: A sturdy, ribbed fabric with a raised lengthwise cord. It may be woven of cotton, silk, wool, or synthetic fibers. **C,D,S,U**

Bengaline: A finely woven fabric with a pronounced horizontal rib, similar to, but heavier than, poplin or faille. **D,U**

Bobbinet: A fine, machine-made net with hexagonal mesh used as a base for embroidered and appliquéd laces.

Bouclé: A woven or knitted fabric with a loopy, knotted surface and a springy, spongy hand. Bouclé yarns may be used to add novelty and textural interest to fabrics.

Broadcloth: A densely textured cloth with a plain or twill weave and a lustrous finish. It may be woven in cotton, silk, wool, or synthetic fibers. **C,D,S,U**

Brocade: A heavy jacquard woven fabric with a rich, raised design that gives an embossed effect because of contrasting surfaces and colors. **D,U**

Brocatelle: A very heavy jacquard weave fabric resembling brocade, but with a more highly raised design. **U**

Burlap: A coarsely woven cloth made of jute, flax, or hemp fibers. **C,D**

Burn-out: A sheer patterned curtain weight fabric created by the chemical "burning out" of a design, leaving more dense areas floating in a less dense ground. **C**

Butcher's linen: A coarse, homespun linen weave cloth originally used for French butchers' smocks and now imitated in many man-made fiber fabrics. **C,D,S,U**

C

Calico: A plain weave, lightweight fabric, similar to percale, that is printed with small figured patterns. Originally woven in all cotton, calicos now are often blends of polyester and cotton. **C**

Cambric: A fine, closely woven white or solid color cotton fabric with a glazed or glossy appearance on the right side. **C**

Canvas: A heavy, strong, firmly woven cotton, linen, or synthetic fabric that may be either soft-finished or highly sized. **C,D,S,U**

Cashmere: The soft, glossy hair of the Kashmir goat, which is spun and then knitted or woven (often in combination with silk, cotton, or wool) into very soft fabrics.

Challis: A soft, supple, lightweight fabric that is usually printed with a delicate cravat floral or Persian pattern. It may be woven of wool, rayon, cotton, or a blend. **C**

Chambray: A fine quality plain weave fabric with a linenlike finish, combining a colored warp and white filling yarns. Chambray is woven in solids, stripes, and checks. **C**

Chenille: A fabric woven with tufted, velvety pile yarns similar in appearance to fuzzy caterpillars.

China silk: A plain weave silk fabric of various weights. **C**

Chino: A coarse cotton fabric woven of combed yarns in a twill weave that is usually preshrunk. **C,D,S,U**

Chintz: A plain weave cotton fabric with a glazed surface in solid colors or printed with birds, flowers, figures, etc. **C,D,S,U**

Ciré: A shiny patent leather effect produced on fabrics and laces by the application of wax, heat, and pressure.

Cloqué: A fabric with an irregularly raised or "blistered" surface, similar to matelassé. **U**

Corduroy: A cut-pile fabric woven in either a plain or twill weave with lengthwise wales, cords, or ribs of varying widths, as in pinwale and wide wale. **D,S,U**

Cotton: A fibrous, downy, soft substance obtained from the seed pods of the cotton plant, which is spun into yarn and then woven into textiles. Cotton is used in weaving such cloths as organdy, broadcloth, poplin, and corduroy. **Combed cotton** is a more expensive fabric made from yarn that has been cleaned with wire brushes and roller cards to remove all short fibers and impurities. Fabrics of cotton are strong, comfortable, and absorbent, are free from static electricity, and have a good affinity for dyes. They do, however, have a tendency to wrinkle, deteriorate from mildew, and shrink badly if untreated.

Covert Cloth: A durable, hard- or soft-finished fabric of medium- to heavyweight, woven in a diagonal twill. It is made of tightly twisted two-ply yarns, one woolen or worsted, the other contrasting wool, cotton, silk, or synthetic, giving the finished cloth a finely speckled surface. **D,U**

Crash: A coarsely woven, lightweight, rough-textured fabric of cotton or linen. **C**

Crepon: A fabric with lengthwise crinkles or "tree bark" texture, resembling crepe, but with a thicker, firmer texture. It is sometimes patterned with jacquard designs. **C**

Cretonne: A medium- to heavyweight unglazed cotton or linen fabric in a variety of weaves that is colorfully printed with large floral designs. **C,D,S,U**

Damask: A fabric woven on the jacquard loom which produces a figured design by combining a number of different weave patterns. Damask patterns often utilize a satin weave in areas of pattern against a plain or twill background so that light will be reflected from the fabric. **C,D,S,U**

Denim: A strong, coarse, washable, twill-weave fabric of cotton or cotton blend, with a colored warp and white filling yarns. Denims may be woven in solids, stripes, and plaids. **C,D,S,U**

Dimity: A sheer fabric, usually woven of combed cotton, with fine lengthwise cords, stripes, or checks. **C**

Dobby: A fabric woven on a machine with an attachment that permits weaving of small geometric patterns beyond the range of simple looms. Piqué is an example of a dobby weave.

Dotted Swiss: A fine, sheer cotton fabric with an embroidered dot pattern and a crisp, stiff finish. Nylon and polyester/cotton blends imitate the look of dotted swiss. **C**

Double Knit: A fabric knitted on a special machine that uses a double set of needles to produce a double thickness of fabric. It has excellent body and stability. **S**

Dupion: A fabric woven of slubbed, uneven, double silk threads produced when two cocoons have nested together. **C,D**

Drill: A strong, twilled cotton fabric similar to denim. When dyed olive drab, it is called khaki. **C,D,S,U**

Duck: See Sailcloth.

Duvetyn: A smooth, close-napped twill weave fabric that has been sheared and brushed for a velvety or suedelike appearance. It may be woven of wool, cotton, rayon, or silk. **U**

Eyelet Embroidery: A lightweight fabric characterized by small cutout areas with decorative stitching around them to form a design. Also called *broderie anglaise.* **C**

Faille: One of the grosgrain family of cross-rib fabrics, characterized by light, flat cords that are usually soft and somewhat glossy. Often woven of silk, cotton, or synthetic fibers. **D,U.**

Felt: A nonwoven fabric produced by processing a mat of fibers with heat, moisture, and pressure. It is best made of wool, fur, or mohair, since these fibers possess natural felting properties, but it may contain cotton or rayon. Felt of the finest quality may be supported with a sheer nylon core. **U**

Fiberglass: A fabric constructed from glass in its fibrous form. It is inherently flame retardant. **C**

Fibranne (Fibrene): The generic French term for viscose rayon and spun rayon yarns.

Flannel: A soft fabric of plain or twill weave with a slightly napped surface on one or both sides. It may be yarn-dyed, piece-dyed, or cross-dyed. **D,S,U**

Flannelette: A soft, plain weave fabric, usually of cotton, with a brushed nap on one side.

Flax: Soft, silky fiber obtained from the bark of the flax plant. It is processed and used in the manufacture of linen.

Flocked Fabric: A fabric with a design formed by the application of short, fibrous particles or short hairs. A common method for flocking is to print the motif or design on the cloth with an adhesive substance and then dust with the flocks, which adhere only to the printed areas. **C,D**

Foulard: A lightweight twill or plain weave fabric, often woven of silk or rayon, that is printed with small cravat designs.

Frieze (Frise): A thick, heavyweight fabric with a rough, raised surface usually made by an uncut loop. **U**

Gabardine: A firm, tightly woven fabric with a close diagonal twill weave surface and flat back. It may be woven of wool, cotton, or synthetic blends and is usually piece-dyed and finished with a high sheen. **D,S,U**

Galloon: A lace or embroidered fabric that has both sides finished with a decorative edge design. **C**

Gauze: A sheer, thin, open weave fabric similar to cheesecloth that is sometimes finished with a stiff sizing. **C**

Georgette: A sheer, dull-textured fabric with a pebbled or crinkly crepe surface that is heavier than chiffon. **C**

Gingham: A firm, plain weave fabric of light- to medium-weight, woven into checks, plaids, or stripes. It was originally made of yarn-dyed cotton, but now is often woven from a blend of polyester and cotton. Also refers to the traditional check pattern woven of wool, silk, or other fibers. **C,D,S,U**

Glen Check: Small, many-lined, even check design originating in Scotland. Authentic fabrics are of wool, but the design is interpreted in other fibers.

Grosgrain: A closely woven fabric of dull luster with a pronounced crosswise rib or cord, usually woven of silk or rayon with a cotton filling. **D,U**

Habutai: A soft, light, smooth, plain weave fabric of silk, originally hand-woven in Japan. **C**

Haircloth: A wiry, stiff fabric woven with a cotton, linen, or worsted warp and a horsehair filling. **U**

Harris Tweed: Handwoven narrow-width woolens loomed on the Outer Hebrides, off the northern coast of Scotland. **D,U**

Herringbone: A broken, irregular twill weave that creates a zigzag effect like the backbone of a herring by alternating the direction of the twill.

Homespun: Cloth which was originally handwoven at home instead of at a mill. Early American settlers wove linsey-woolsey, butternut, and coarse flannels. Also refers to coarse fabric of jute, silk, linen, cotton, or blends. **C,D,U**

Honan: A fine-quality pongee-type fabric made from Chinese wild silk. It originated in the province of Honan, but is now imitated elsewhere. The wild silk is less uniform in diameter and is coarser than cultivated silk and adds interesting textures to the cloth. **C,D**

Hopsacking: A rough-surfaced cotton, linen, or rayon fabric characterized by

a plain basket weave pattern. **C,D,S,U**

Houndstooth Check: A four-pointed star check design woven in a broken twill weave.

Huck: A heavy linen or cotton fabric with a honeycomb effect that is used for toweling or as a base cloth for hand embroidery.

Ikat: Any of the various China silk fabrics made in Java. Characterized by soft geometric patterns created by colored warp yarns.

Irish Tweed: A tweed fabric that is usually made with white warp and colored filling yarns. **D,U**

Jacquard: A complex loom with a versatile pattern-making mechanism that permits the weaving of very elaborate designs. It was named for J. K. Jacquard, the French weaver who invented the loom. Damask and brocade are woven on the jacquard loom.

Jaspé: A heavy, closely woven, durable cotton or cotton blend fabric made with narrow warp stripes of several colors or shades of the same color to create a shadow effect. **D,S,U**

Khaki: A sturdy cloth of cotton or wool, often used in military or safari garments. Also refers to a light olive drab color. **C,D,S,U**

Knits: Fabrics constructed by interlocking a series of loops of one or more yarns. The three classes of knits are warp knit, circular or tubular knit, and flat knit.

Lace: A fine, openwork fabric with patterns of knotted, twisted, or looped threads on a ground of net or mesh. Lace made by needle is called point lace; Alençon and Venise are both point laces. Lace made on a pillow by means of bobbins is called pillow lace and these include Chantilly, Cluny, and Valenciennes (or Val) laces. Other types of lace include Irish lace, a heavy crocheted fabric; Renaissance lace, made with woven tape motifs; Brussels lace, in which designs are appliqued to the net ground; and Filet

lace, which has square patterns woven or darned on a mesh ground. **C**

Lawn: A lightweight, sheer cloth of combed or carded cotton, linen, or cotton blend with a crisp finish. It may be woven with plissé effect or satin-stripe designs. **C**

Leatherette: Imitation leather, made of vinyl material and embossed to copy the texture and grain of real leather. **U**

Leno: A strong, stable fabric weave in which the warp yarns are paired and twisted, as in marquisette. Leno may also refer to a family of lightweight cottons and blends that have decorative weaves combined with a plain weave ground to create interesting patterns. **C**

Linen: A natural fiber that is removed from the stem of the flax plant. Linen is strong, naturally lustrous, and absorbent. It is woven into fabrics from sheer handkerchief weights to heavy, coarse weaves. No longer produced in the United States, most linen is imported from Ireland or Belgium. **C,D,S,U**

Linsey-Woolsey: A coarse fabric originally made in Lindsey, England, of wool combined with cotton or flax. **D,U**

Loden: A thick, coarse woolen cloth of Tyrolean origin, in a characteristic loden green color. Because it is made from wool of coarser grades that retains some grease, it is naturally wind and water resistant. **U**

Madras: A fine, hand-loomed cotton fabric from India, woven in a natural color, or colored with vegetable dyes and woven into plaids and stripes that are meant to "bleed." **C**

Malimo: Fabric constructed on a machine from East Germany which produces fabric very rapidly from three sets of yarns—warp yarns, filling yarns laid across the warp, and a third system of yarns that stitches them together. The fabric is technically neither woven nor knitted, but is said to be more stable than either.

Marquisette: A lightweight, transparent, open mesh leno weave fabric. It can be made from cotton, rayon, nylon, polyester, silk, or glass fiber. **C**

Matelassé: A patterned fabric with raised woven designs, loomed on a jac-

quard machine. The surface appears to be quilted or puckered. U

Melton: A flat-napped, nonlustrous, heavy woolen material finished without glossing or pressing. **U**

Modacrylic: A synthetic fiber formed by a long-chain polymer. Wrinkle resistant, resilient, with a pleasing hand, but sensitive to heat.

Mohair: A fabric of cut or uncut loops with cotton or wool back and mohair pile. **U**

Moiré: Fabric with an irregular water ripple finish on a corded or ribbed weave that is produced by engraved rollers, steam, heat, or chemicals. It is usually made of silk, cotton, or rayon. **C,D,U**

Mousseline: A lightweight, muslinlike cotton with a crisp finish that is closely woven of highly twisted yarns. The name is ordinarily used in combination with fiber names, as in *mousseline de soie.* **C**

Muslin: Wide variety of plain weave cotton fabrics ranging from sheer to heavy sheeting. It can be unbleached, bleached, dyed in solid colors, or printed. **C**

Nacré Velvet: Velvet with an iridescent, changeable appearance produced by weaving the back of one color and the pile of another color. **D,U**

Nainsook: A lightweight, soft, cotton cloth of plain weave mercerized cotton with a lustrous finish. It is slightly heavier than batiste or lawn. **C**

Ninon: A sheer, crisp, smooth, good quality fabric of hand-twisted yarns in plain or open weaves, with a clear, transparent surface. It may also be called *triple voile.* **C**

Nun's Veiling: A good quality, plain weave soft cloth, similar to challis, that is usually made of cotton, silk, or worsted. **C**

Nylon: Generic name for man-made polyamide yarns or fibers. Several different types of nylon produce a wide variety of fabric textures, from smooth and crisp to soft and bulky. Nylon is often blended with other fibers. It is very strong, elastic, and resilient, and has high resistance to mildew and moths. It does not soil easily, but it may pill. Nylon washes easily and

requries little if any ironing with a cool iron.

Nytril: A synthetic fiber related to acrylic. It is soft, resilient, easy to care for, and wrinkle resistant.

Oatmeal Cloth: A soft, durable fabric with a pebbled surface. It is made of wool, linen, cotton, or synthetics with fine warp threads and coarse filling yarns. **C**

Oilcloth: A waterproof fabric made of heavy cotton muslin, coated on one side with a glossy finish of oil, clay, and pigments. It is available plain or printed.

Olefin: Generic name for a paraffin-based, man-made fiber. It has a waxy luster and holds dyes easily; it is strong and tough and wears very well. Olefin is adaptable to bulky, textured yarns and deep pile fabrics. It is usually machine washed in lukewarm water. Stains generally blot away with absorbent cloth. Olefin fibers cannot be dry-cleaned if perchloroethylene is the solvent used.

Organdy: A very fine, sheer, transparent cotton cloth with a crisp finish. It is woven of tightly twisted yarns. **C**

Organza: A fine, crisp, transparent silk organdy. **C**

Osnaburg: A rough, coarse fabric originally made of flax and named after a town in Germany. Now it is a plain weave, coarse cotton of loose but durable construction that can be medium- to heavyweight. It is often used in the unbleached state. **C,D**

Ottoman: A heavyweight fabric with pronounced crosswise rounded ribs that are often padded. It is similar to faille or bengaline but has heavier ribs. **D,U**

Oxford Cloth: A cotton fabric in plain or basket weave, with two fine warp yarns and a heavier filling yarn. It has a lustrous, soft finish. **C**

P

Paisley: Decorative multicolored design, woven or printed, originally taken from the genuine cashmere shawls of India by shawl weavers in Paisley, Scotland. The designs have typical Indian palm or cone figures and elaborate symmetrical detail.

Panne: A very lustrous velvet fabric with the pile pressed flat in one direction.

Peau de Soie: French term (meaning "skin of silk") for a soft, closely woven satin with a mellow luster. Originally made of silk, it may now be made of synthetic fibers. **C,D**

Percale: A fine, lightweight, plain weave cotton or cotton blend fabric with a firm, balanced construction caused by an equal number of threads per inch in warp and weft. **C**

Percaline: A plain weave, lightweight cotton that is sized and calendered to give it a glossy, moiré finish. **C**

Pile Fabric: Fabric with cut or uncut loops which stand up to form a soft, thick, deep surface. Pile fabrics are not to be confused with napped fabrics that have a brushed surface. Velvets, velveteens, and corduroys are pile fabrics.

Pima Cotton: A high quality, long staple cotton fiber developed from the Egyptian cotton seed and originally grown in Pima, Arizona. Now also grown in other western states, it is used for fine combed cottons and is often mercerized.

Pinstripe: A fabric with a fine slender parallel stripe design.

Piqué: A dobby weave fabric that has raised, lengthwise cords, welts, or wales in a variety of plain or patterned effects. Piqué textures include fine, medium, and heavy wales, honeycomb, waffle, diamond, as well as bird's eye and bull's eye piqué, which are woven with diamonds and center dots of varying sizes. **C,D,S,U**

Plaid: Pattern of colored stripes or bars crossing each other at right angles; from the Scottish term for a shawl-like garment woven in a traditional tartan or clan plaid pattern.

Plissé: A thin cotton fabric, soft or crisp, with puckered stripes or patterns in allover blister effect. The texture is obtained either by weaving with yarns having different degrees of shrinkage in finishing, or by chemical treatment. **C**

Plush: A warp pile fabric with a silk, wool, or mohair pile that is longer than that of velvet, but not as densely woven. **U**

Point d'Esprit: A type of cotton bobbin net that has square dots scattered all over the surface. **C**

Polished Cotton: A cotton fabric that has a shiny surface achieved either through a satin weave or a waxed finish. **C,D,S,U**

Polyester: Generic term for a synthetic fiber with superior properties of wrinkle resistance and ease of care. It is available in many weights, textures, and weaves, and is often used in blends for minimum care and durable press fabrics. Polyester is produced in larger quantities than any other man-made fiber. It is generally washable, quick drying, and resistant to stretching, shrinking, mildew, and moths. Polyester may yellow, but it is otherwise colorfast. It may pill and pick up lint.

Pongee: A plain weave, light- to medium-weight fabric made from wild silk. It is usually natural, pale, or dark tan. **C,D**

Poplin: A plain weave fabric that has a fine rib running from selvage to selvage. It is similar to cotton or rayon broadcloth, but has a slightly heavier rib. It may be woven of silk, cotton, rayon, wool, or blends. **C,D,S,U**

Popline: A fabric resembling poplin, with a silk or rayon warp and a wool filling. **S,D,U**

R

Ratiné: A rough, nubby, plain weave fabric made with ratiné yarns in the warp and/or the weft. Ratiné yarns are textured by twisting a thick and a thin fiber under uneven tension. The fabric may also be called eponge, frisé or spongecloth. **U**

Raw Silk: Silk fibers as they are taken from the cocoon, before the natural gum has been removed.

Rayon: Generic term for man-made fibers, monofilaments, and continuous filaments made from modified cellulose (i.e., wood pulp or cotton fibers that are too short to spin into yarns). Rayon is used in a wide range of qualities, from lightweight to heavy construction. It can be made to resemble natural fibers, has a soft hand, and drapes well. It has a good affinity for dyes and is usually colorfast. It has low resistance to mildew, and relatively low strength. It is even weaker when wet. Rayon wrinkles unless it is specially finished, and may shrink or stretch if not treated. It is usually dry-

cleaned because of its low tolerance for moisture.

Rep (Repp): Fabric woven of cotton, wool, or silk with well-defined, round padded ribs running from selvage to selvage. **D,U**

S

Sailcloth: A heavy, strong, extremely durable plain weave canvas fabric woven of cotton, linen, synthetics, or blends. It is woven in plain or rib weaves in various weights. Also called *duck*. **C,D,S,U**

Saran: A man-made generic fiber that is weather resistant, flame retardant, and moth- and mildew-proof. It may be combined with modacrylics for flame resistant fabrics.

Sateen: A cotton fabric characterized by a satin weave; it is usually mercerized and is often treated with high luster and crease resistant finishes. **C,D,S,U**

Satin: A smooth fabric of silk, cotton, rayon, acetate, or wool with warp threads floated to the surface to give a lustrous face finish. **D,U**

Schiffli: A type of shuttle embroidery done on a sheer fabric ground by a machine that can be hand-guided to create patterns of great complexity. After the embroidery design is done, the open areas may be burned out. Venise lace can be made on Schiffli machines.

Seersucker: A lightweight cotton or cotton blend fabric with crinkled stripes woven in the warp direction by holding some yarns under tighter, and others under looser, tension. **C**

Serge: A crisp, flat, twill weave fabric with a prominent diagonal on both sides of the cloth. **D,U**

Shantung: A plain silk weave, originally made in the Shantung Province of China on hand looms from wild silk. It is characterized by a rough, slubbed surface caused by knots and slubs in the filling yarns. Today, shantung is made of silk, cotton, wool, or man-made fibers. **C,D**

Sharkskin: Term used to describe two different types of fabric: 1) a fine, even twill weave fabric of wool with warp and filling yarns that alternate white with a color (usually black, brown or blue), to create a mottled effect, and 2) a plain weave fabric with

a smooth, almost shiny surface, made of dull luster rayon acetate or triacetate.

Silk: Continuous protein filament produced by the larvae of the silkworm when they are building their cocoons. The filament is reeled off and boiled to remove the stiff natural glue, and woven into strong fabrics with a soft luster and luxurious hand. Silk is available in a variety of weights and weaves, from sheer chiffon to pongee, heavy tweeds, and brocades. It has good wrinkle resistance and is exceptionally strong for its fineness. Silk has an excellent affinity for dyes, but it may bleed. It is weakened by sunlight. It has excellent resistance to mildew and moths. Silk is usually dry-cleaned.

Slipper Satin: A strong, compact satin weave fabric of silk, rayon, acetate, or blends, often with a cotton back. **D,U**

Suede Cloth: A woven or knitted fabric of cotton, synthetics, wool, or blends, finished to resemble suede leather. **U**

Surah: A soft, lustrous, fine twilled fabric, often woven of silk or man-made fibers. Surah is available in plaids, stripes, and prints as well as solids. **C,D**

T

Taffeta: Basic group of plain weave fabrics that are smooth on both sides, crisp, and usually lustrous. Taffeta may be plain, woven with a fine rib, woven in checks, stripes, or plaids, printed, or woven with uneven threads to create antique taffeta. Weights may vary from paper-thin to heavy. **C,D**

Tartan: A woolen or worsted twill fabric woven with varicolored lines or stripes at right angles to form a plaid design. Authentic tartans were woven for Scottish Highlanders in specific colorings and patterns to designate particular clans. **C,D,S,U**

Terry Cloth: An absorbent toweling fabric, woven or knitted with loop pile that projects on one or both sides of the cloth. It is woven of cotton or cotton and polyester blends. **C,S**

Thai Silk: A plain weave silk fabric made in Thailand, often in large, brightly colored, yarn-dyed plaid designs. **C,D**

Ticking: A strong, durable, closely woven twill fabric with distinctive narrow warp stripes in traditional blue or red alternating with a white ground. Ticking may be woven of cotton, linen, or blends. **C,D,S,U**

Toile de Jouy: An elaborate floral or scenic design printed on cotton or linen from a finely engraved copper plate. It is usually one color on a white or natural ground. **C,D,S,U**

Triacetate: Generic name for cellulose triacetate, a man-made fiber. It is similar to acetate, but has higher heat resistance and improved ease-of-care characteristics. Triacetate knits and wovens can be hand- or machine-laundered and pressed with the rayon setting on the iron.

Tricot: A warp knit fabric made from two sets of threads. It is characterized by vertical wales on the face and horizontal ribs on the back. Tricot has very little lengthwise stretch and a high resistance to runs. It is used as a backing on bonded knits, among other things.

Tussah: A silk fabric made from the cocoons of wild silkworms. Tussah silk fibers are short, less even, and stiffer than cultivated silk fibers. Natural tussah is brownish in color. **C,D**

Tweed: A wide range of rough-textured fabrics with a multicolored effect achieved by using yarns of mixed fibers, colors, and textures.

Twill: A basic textile weave characterized by a diagonal rib that generally runs upward from left to right. The ribs may be set at sharp or blunt angles and may be imbedded in, or raised from, the fabric surface. Flannel, serge, gabardine, and surah are all twill weaves.

U

Uncut Velvet: A kind of velvet made with a terry-type pile with the loops left uncut. **D,U**

V

Velour (Velours): The French word for velvet, velour is a soft, closely woven smooth fabric with a close, dense, even, short pile, providing a soft hand and velvety appearance. Originally made of wool, it is now made in other fibers. Also, a knitted fabric with the same soft hand, dense pile, and velvetlike surface. **U**

Velvet: A warp pile fabric with short, closely woven cut pile producing a smooth, rich surface that is soft and luxurious to the touch. Originally made of silk, it is now woven of rayon, cotton, or synthetic fibers. **D,U**

Velveteen: A cotton or rayon fabric with a short, close filling loop that is cut by sharp knives to create an erect, velvety pile. Unlike velvet, it is woven as a single cloth; the velveteen backing may be a plain weave or a twill weave which holds the pile more firmly. **D,U**

Venise: A fine damask table linen with large floral designs, made in France and the Netherlands. See also Lace. **C**

Vicuña: The finest of all animal fibers, vicuña is taken from a wild relative of the llama in Peru. It is expensive and scarce, with sales regulated by the Peruvian government.

Vinyl (Vinal): Thermoplastic fibers of varying chemical composition. Vinyl is available in monofilament yarn, staple, and film form.

Viscose: One of the three types of rayon, made of regenerated cellulose, most commonly obtained from wood pulp.

Voile: A fine, lightweight, sheer fabric with a crisp hand. Woven of cotton, silk, wool, or rayon, it is like heavy veiling. **C**

W

Whipcord: A rugged twill weave fabric, similar to gabardine, but with a more defined diagonal rib on the right side. It is usually woven of cotton or worsted. **D,U**

Wool: The soft, fine fleece covering the sheep, also known as *laine* in French. It also includes the hair of the Angora or Kashmir goats, as well as the specialty fibers from the hair of the camel, alpaca, and vicuña. (**Virgin wool** refers to new wool that has never undergone any manufacturing process. The term is no guarantee of quality because any grade of wool can be virgin wool.) Wool has minute scales which give it its unique felting and insulation properties. It is versatile in weight, texture, weave, and color. Because of its unique properties, it can be woven in constructions not possible in any other fiber, from sheer challis to medium-weight gabardines to heavy-weight upholstery cloths. The wool fibers trap air and provide great natural warmth. Wool has excellent elasticity and wrinkle resistance, and is exceptionally absorbent, holding a large amount of moisture before it feels damp; however, it may be attacked by mildew if soiled or damp. When wet, wool weakens and stretches. It is susceptible to shrinking and pilling, and must be treated to repel moths. Wool fabrics are generally dry-cleaned and brushed between cleanings. Some wools may be handwashed and gently pressed at low heat setting with a steam iron or damp press cloth. Wool may be combined with polyester to add washability.

Woolen: Fabric made from wool fibers that are carded and spun directly into yarn without combing. Woolen fibers are less tightly twisted than worsted yarns and are used in bulky, heavy, fulled, or napped wools.

Worsted: Fabric made from yarn spun from the hard "tops" of raw wool that have been combed. The yarn is fine and strong and can be made into fabrics with a smooth, tight weave and a crisp hand.

Decorative Trims and Notions Glossary

This glossary functions like a dictionary, listing alphabetically all of the most common styles and types of decorative trims and notions. Trims that are usually sold by the yard, such as braids, bands, laces, and ribbons, are defined here, as well as the prepackaged varieties like bias tape and rick rack. In addition to trims, the most common sewing notions are listed, including all the shade tapes, welt, drapery heading tapes, and so forth, that we've used to sew the projects in this book. Use this glossary as a handy reference guide when you're planning the construction of particular projects and as you determine the final decorative trims.

Alençon: A trimming with net background and floral design that is outlined with a heavy thread. It was originally made by hand in Alençon, France.

Appliqué: A cutout decoration of lace or fabric that can be applied to another material. Commercially available appliqués either have adhesive backing or require sewing in place.

Austrian Ring Tape: Shirring tape with plastic rings attached that is used in making Austrian curtains. It is usually available in white or cream.

Ball Fringe: A decorative trim constructed of cut yarn ends that are fastened together and then steamed to form a ball which is then hung from a header by a loop. Available in ½" to 1" diameter balls in a variety of colors.

Band Trim: A wide variety of embroidered, beaded, sequined, fringed, or braided ribbons and trims which are finished on both edges.

Batting: Originally layers or sheets of raw cotton or wool used for backing quilts, batting is now usually made of polyester or a polyester/cotton blend,

and is available by the yard or in prepackaged quilt sizes.

Beading: An edging, insertion, or galloon with a parallel openwork design through which a ribbon may be worked.

Bias Tape: Prepackaged fabric cut on the bias with both raw edges folded under; it is used for casings, facings, and decorative trimming. Bias tape is available in a wide range of colors and in the following specifications:
single-fold bias—½" wide
wide single-fold bias—⅞" wide
double-fold bias—¼" wide when folded
wide double-fold bias—½" wide when folded
2" hem facing—2" wide, with the raw edges turned under

Blanket Binding: A 2" folded fabric, usually of nylon, that is folded evenly to edge blankets, coverlets, and quilts.

Border: A decorative design printed on fabric and cut into strips that can be applied to a ground cloth as trim.

Box Pleating: A fabric made by folding pleats in opposite directions so that they meet in the middle; it is bound together at the top edge.

Braid: Decorative trim with three or more component strands that are plaited to form a regular diagonal pattern along the length of the piece.

Brush Fringe: A trim made of short pieces of cut yarn fastened together along one edge to create a brush effect. May also be called *moss fringe*.

Buckram: A stiff-finished, heavily sized fabric that may be made from layers of open weave cloth glued together. Strips of buckram may be used for interlining drapery headings.

Bullion Fringe: Tightly twisted yarn that is attached to a header, creating a spiraling or rope effect.

Butterfly Pleating: Fabric pleated in a series of varying widths held together with a stitching line through the center.

Cable Cord: A white, ropelike, all-purpose cord made of cotton or polyester. It is available in several sizes (diameters) and may be premeasured and packaged or sold by the yard. Cable cord, unlike piping cord, may be used uncovered.

Chainette Fringe: A shimmering, cascading fringe that falls from a header; it is usually made of rayon, silk, or polyester.

Chantilly: A delicate lace with floral or scroll designs and thread outlines on a mesh ground. Originated in Chantilly, France.

Cluny: A crochet type lace, usually in a wheel or paddle design, made of heavy thread. Named for the Cluny Museum in France.

Cording: Tubular braid or bias fabric strips covering twisted strands of yarn. Also refers to the roping used to raise and lower Roman shades, balloon shades, and Austrian curtains.

Crochet: Method of interlocking loops or stitches with a hook to create plain or fancy designs for lace trimming.

Crystal Pleating: A fabric that is permanently pressed into accordion folds.

Edging: A narrow trimming, flat or ruffled, with scallops on one side and a straight edge on the other.

Elastic: A narrow fabric woven of yarns that contain rubber or synthetic spandex.

Eyelet: A lightweight fabric in which holes have been cut and then satin stitched to form decorative designs. Eyelet is available as flat or ruffled edging, galloon, flounce style, or beading.

Eyelet Ruffling: A gathered edging of narrow eyelet fabric that is stitched into a fabric strip called a header.

Eyelets: Metal hole reinforcements. Fastener tools are available for inserting eyelets into fabric.

F

Fagoting: A border in which horizontal threads are removed and the cross-threads stitched together, creating a ladder effect. Also called *entredeux*.

Fiberfill: Stuffing material made of polyester and used to fill pillows, cushions, stuffed animals, etc.

Flounce: A flat or gathered edging with a border design that measures 12" or more in width.

Fold-over Braid: A decorative trim that is prefolded in half to be used for encasing raw edges; it is available in a range of colors, fibers, and widths.

Fringe: A decorative trim constructed of loose hanging strands of thread or yarn that are knotted and fastened to a band.

Frog: A decorative closing or fastener usually made of braid in an ornamental design with a loop on one side and a thick knot or button on the other.

Fusible Web: A lightweight, non-woven polyester fiber mesh that will melt when heated to fuse two surfaces. It is available prepackaged as narrow strips or sold by the yard.

Galloon: A narrow lace or embroidery fabric with a scalloped edge on both sides.

Grenadine: Silk cords made of several twisted strands braided together.

Grommet: A metal hole reinforcement similar to, but larger than, an eyelet.

Grosgrain Ribbon: A closely woven, corded, narrow fabric usually made of cotton, polyester, rayon, or silk. It is available in a wide range of solids, as well as woven stripes and prints, and is readily obtained in widths from ⅛″ to 2¼″; larger widths are available from specialty resources.

Guimpe (Gimp): A narrow ornamental braid trim often made with a loop or scroll design; it may use two or more weights, textures, or colors of yarn.

I

Insertion: A narrow lace, binding, or embroidery with a plain edge on both sides. It can be inserted between two pieces of fabric to create a see-through effect.

Invisible thread: Monofilament thread that is clear so that it can be used on any color fabric.

J

Jacquard Ribbon: A narrow fabric woven on a jacquard loom capable of weaving intricate designs. Typical designs are multicolored florals, reversible patterns, and metallic accented scroll or paisley designs.

L

Lace: A delicate open-work fabric of threads woven together to form intricate, decorative designs. Lace is available in very narrow to very wide widths, and from delicate sheers to heavy crochet type weights. It also appears in flat edging, galloon, and ruffled styles.

Loop Fringe: Any fringe made with continuous or uncut loops that often hang from a header which may be plain or designed.

Macrame: A fringe, lace, or trimming created by knotting thread or yarns together in a decorative pattern.

Middy Braid: A narrow flat braid made in several widths.

Motif: An individual lace medallion which can be separated from the lace background. It may be sold individually or in a row. It is held together by delicate threads that can easily be clipped to produce the desired length.

Pailette: French term for a sequin; actually, it is somewhat larger than a sequin, with a hole off-center so that the pailette hangs freely.

Passementerie: Generic French term for edgings and trimmings usually made from beads, cord, guimpe, braid, or metallic thread.

Pearl (Perle) Cotton: Mercerized cotton thread or yarn used for embroidery and other needlework, available in an extensive range of colors and in light or heavy weights.

Picot: An ornamental woven edge consisting of tiny loops on the selvages of lace or ribbon. May also be called *feather edge*.

Piping: A narrow piece of fabric folded on the bias and stitched over piping cord. It is designed for stitching into a seam or creating a raised edge accent. May also be referred to as welt, welting, or cording.

Piping Cord: Cotton fibers that are held together with an open tubular cotton covering to be used as the base for making welt or piping. It is available in widths from ⁴⁄₃₂″ to 1″ in diameter.

Plaiting: The braiding or interlacing of three or more strands of rope, yarn, thread, fabric, etc.

Pleater Tape: Stiffened fabric woven with evenly spaced pockets and used to make curtains or draperies. By inserting pleater hooks into the pockets, the look of pinch pleats is created.

Point d'Esprit: A delicate net lace covered with small dots.

Pompon Fringe: Cut yarn ends that are fastened together and agitated or steamed to form balls, and then strung together in a continuous line.

Rattail: A narrow, rounded soutache braid.

Reticella: A form of needlepoint lace that has geometric designs connected by picoted bars.

Ribbon: A narrow woven fabric with a cord finish or simple selvage along both edges, used for trimming or decoration. Ribbons are available in a wide range of fibers, weaves, and widths from ¹⁄₁₆″. Readily available widths may be referred to by the following numbers:

¼″—#1	⅞″—#5
⅜″—#1½	1½″—#9
½″—#2	2¼″—#16
⅝″—#3	3″—#40

Larger widths are available from ribbon importers and specialists. (See separate entries under Grosgrain Ribbon, Picot, Velvet Ribbon, etc.)

Rick Rack: A decorative flat braid with a uniform zigzag form. It is readily available prepackaged in a wide range of colors and in several widths, from ¼″, baby, to a ⅝″ jumbo width. Wider varieties are available in limited colors by the yard.

Ring: A circlet made of bone, ivory, plastic, or metal in sizes that range from ½″ to 3″ in diameter. Plastic rings are generaly available in white, but some larger decorative sizes may come in tortoise, black, and other colors. Metal rings may be plain or decoratively twisted.

Roman Shade Tape: Twill tape with plastic rings attached every 5″ to 6″; used in making Roman shades.

Ruche: A pleated, fluted, or gathered strip of fabric used as a trim.

Ruffling: A strip of lace or fabric that is gathered into a heading along one edge.

Satin Ribbon: Narrow woven fabric with a satin weave construction on one (single-face), or both (double-face) sides, used for decorative trims, bows, drawstrings, etc. Satin ribbon may be made of silk, rayon, or polyester.

Seam Binding: Narrow woven fabric used for finishing hems or staying seams.

Self-gripping Fastener Tape: Two-piece nylon tape made with a hook construction on one side and a fuzzy loop construction on the other; when pressed together, the hook and loop grip firmly to each other. It is available in several widths sold by the inch and in precut shapes (small circles, squares, and rectangles).

Sequin: A small plastic or metal disc with a center hole used as trimming; also called *pailette* or *spangle*.

Shirring Tape: Woven fabric with cording placed in horizontal rows. The tape is sewn to the inside of fabric, so that when the cords are pulled, the fabric is gently gathered. Shirring tape is available with one, two, and four rows of cording.

Snap Tape: A fastener that consists of two pieces of twill tape with spaced balls and corresponding sockets on the opposing tapes.

Soutache: A very narrow, flat decorative braid woven in a herringbone pattern with an indentation in the center for stitching.

Swag Fringe: A decorative fringe with a scalloped effect, often made of tubular rayon or silk cords that attach to the header, creating a swag design. It may also be called *rattail fringe*.

Taffeta Ribbon: A narrow fabric with a crisp, shiny surface woven of silk, rayon, nylon, or polyester. Taffeta ribbon may be plain, checked, plaid, or moiréd for a lustrous ripple appearance.

Tassel: A pendant ornament consisting of a tuft of loosely hanging threads or cords.

Tassel Fringe: Tufts of cut yarn ends that are fastened together to form a tassel and then attached to dangle from a band or header.

Tatting: Originally a knotted lace worked with fingers and shuttle, creating clover leaf and wheel or circle designs; today, it is an imitation lace design simulating hand tatting.

Teneriffe: A delicate lace with little wheel or cobweb designs, originally developed in Teneriffe, France.

Tieback: Decorative twisted or braided cord used to pull back and secure curtains or draperies to the side of a window; often, the cords end with a tassel.

Twill Tape: Exceptionally strong tape with a diagonal rib that is used for casings, ties, drawstrings, and decorative trims. It is available in four widths from ¼" to 1" and in several colors.

U

Upholstery Zipper: Heavy duty zipper with a sturdy white or beige tape and metal teeth in lengths from 12" to 72"; used in making slipcovers.

V

Val: A narrow bobbin lace with mesh ground and a dainty floral or scroll design outlined by open work. It was originally made by hand in Valenciennes, France, but is now usually machine-made.

Velvet Ribbon: A narrow fabric with a low, dense pile on one side; made of silk, rayon, nylon, or polyester and readily available in a variety of widths from ³⁄₁₆" to 2¼".

Venise Lace: A heavily designed lace created by a multitude of close stitches on a ground fabric that is eliminated during the finishing process. It leaves a bold string of motifs such as flowers, leaves, or medallions that may be used in a row or cut apart for the individual motifs.

W

Weights: Used to encourage curtains and draperies to hang evenly, weights are available individually in a wide variety of sizes and shapes, or as weighted tape or covered chain.

Welting: Cording that has been covered with bias-cut fabric and sewn into seams for a decorative or finishing touch.

Woven Bands: Decorative trims with straight edges that usually measure over 1½" in width. They may be woven on jacquard looms for intricate designs, or on dobby looms for simple, often geometric designs.

Source Listing

This chapter is a systematic listing of all the firms and manufacturers whose products are featured in this book, along with their complete addresses. Please do remember that even though a particular fabric, trim, notion, antique, or accessory was available at the time of writing this book, it may not be at the time you read it. It does help, however, to know who manufactured or sold something you are intrigued by, because even though that product might be discontinued or sold, something in stock or in a current collection might be even more suitable.

Fabrics

Manufacturers and Distributors

A. E. Nathan Co., Inc.
108 West 39th Street
New York, NY 10018
    pages 66, 68, 69, 90, 94, 96, and 97

Anglo Fabrics
1407 Broadway
New York, NY 10018
    page 27

Bloomcraft
295 Fifth Avenue
New York, NY 10016
    pages 10, 11, 22, 51, 53, 86, 87, 102, 106, 107, 127, 210, and 257

Boussac of France, Inc.
1412 Broadway
New York, NY 10018
    jacket and pages 36, 37, 50, and 98

Blue Ridge Winkler
119 West 40th Street
New York, NY 10018
    pages 100 and 101

Cohama Riverdale Decorative Fabrics
200 Madison Avenue
New York, NY 10016
    title page and pages 23, 28, 29, 30, 31, 32, 33, 38, 39, 74, 75, and 144

Cyrus Clark Co., Inc.
267 Fifth Avenue
New York, NY 10016
    pages 6, 34, 35, 40, 41, and 178

Dan River, Inc.
111 West 40th Street
New York, NY 10018
    pages 103 and 116

Fabriyaz
41 Madison Avenue
New York, NY 10010
    jacket and pages 9, 36, 74, and 75

Hamilton Adams Imports, Ltd.
104 West 40th Street
New York, NY 10018
    pages 35, 48, and 49

J. P. Stevens & Co., Inc.
1185 Avenue of the Americas
New York, NY 10036
    pages 7, 70, 71, 110, and 111

Liberty Fabrics of New York, Inc.
2 Park Avenue
New York, NY 10016
    pages 52, 53, and 116

V. I. P. Fabrics
1412 Broadway
New York, NY 10018
    pages 56, 57, 60, 61, 64 and 65

Waverly Fabrics, Inc.
58 West 40th Street
New York, NY 10018
    pages 25, 68, and 69

Wyla Fabrics
295 Fifth Avenue
New York, NY 10016
    pages 92, 93, and 103

Retailers

B & J Fabrics
263 West 40th Street
New York, NY 10018
    pages 54 and 55

Laura Ashley
714 Madison Avenue
New York, NY 10021
    pages 72, 73, and 215

Fabricville
122 Watchung Avenue
Upper Montclair, NJ 07043
    pages 58 and 59

Far Eastern Fabrics
171 Madison Avenue
New York, NY 10016
    pages 26, 34, 35, 76, 88, and 89

Jensen-Lewis
89 Seventh Avenue
New York, NY 10011
    pages 104, 108, and 109

Pierre Deux
879 Madison Avenue
New York, NY 10021
    pages 62 and 63

Poli Fabrics, Inc.
132 West 57th Street
New York, NY 10019
    pages 32, 33, 44, 48, and 49

Silk Surplus
223 East 58th Street
New York, NY 10022
    page 34

The Vermont Country Store
Weston, VT 05761
catalog free
    pages 78, 80, 81, 82, and 83

Decorative Trims and Notions

Manufacturers and Distributors

B. Blumenthal & Co., Inc.
1372 Broadway
New York, NY 10018
    page 90

C. M. Offray and Sons, Inc.
261 Madison Avenue
New York, NY 10016
    pages 90 and 95

Coats and Clark, Inc.
Department CS
P.O. Box 1010
Toccoa, GA 30577
    pages 106 and 107

Conso Products Company
Division of Springs Industries
Union, SC 29379
    pages 27, 30, and 82

The D.M.C. Corporation
107 Trumbull Street
Elizabeth, NJ 07206
    pages 26 and 90

Hamilton Web Co.
24 West 40th Street
New York, NY 10018
    pages 80, 81, 82, and 83

St. Louis Trimming Co.
1119–1127 Washington Avenue
St. Louis, MO 63101
    pages 66, 68, and 69

Talon, Inc.
1350 Broadway
New York, NY 10018
    pages 51 and 85

William E. Wright
One Penn Plaza
New York, NY 10119
     pages 48, 49, 58, 59, 64, 65, 68, 69, 72,
     73, 78, 91, 92, 93, and 102

Retailers and Mail Order
Greentex
236 West 26th Street
New York, NY 10001

Newark Dressmaker Supply
6473 Ruch Road
P.O. Box 2448
Lehigh Valley, PA 18001
     catalog free

New York Notion Co. of Chicago
2040 North Janice Avenue
Melrose Park, IL 60160
     catalog free

Total Sewing, Inc.
P.O. Box 438
3729 Grand Blvd.
Brookfield, IL 60513
     catalog free

Sheets, Towels, and Blankets

Dan River/Marimekko
111 West 40th Street
New York, NY 10018
     page 95

L.L. Bean, Inc.
9935 Spruce Street
Freeport, ME 04102
     page 113

Martex Division of West Point-
Pepperell, Inc.
1221 Avenue of the Americas
New York, NY 10020
     pages 80, 81, 84, 85, and 116

Stevens-Utica
1185 Avenue of the Americas
New York, NY 10036
     page 114

Wamsutta Home Products
111 West 40th St.
New York, NY 10018
     pages 74, 75, and 102

Antiques and Accessories

Art Acquisition–Jacqueline Stamato
22 Douglas Road
Essex Fells, NJ 07021
     page 68

Catherine Blair Antiques
83 Summit Avenue
Summit, NJ 07901
     pages 70 and 71

The Browser's Nook
322 Orange Road
Montclair, NJ 07042
     page 26

Cherchez
864 Lexington Avenue
New York, NY 10021
     pages 68, 69, 70, 71, and 115

Cherishables
1816 Jefferson Place, N.W.
Washington, DC 20036
     page 76

Dexterity Limited
26 Church Street
Montclair, NJ 07042
     pages 61 and 102

Dulken & Derrick, Inc.
12 West 21st Street
New York, NY 10010
     pages 34 and 75

Emily de Nemethy
Longview Road
Far Hills, NJ 07931
     pages 70 and 71

Gerard Lindner Antiques
223 Glenridge Avenue
Montclair, NJ 07042
     pages 74 and 75

John Rosselli Antiques
255 East 72nd Street
New York, NY 10021
     pages 34 and 35

Poster Originals
924 Madison Avenue
New York, NY 10021
     pages 42 and 43

Scottish Products, Inc.
133 East 55th Street
New York, NY 10022
     pages 70 and 71

Vito Giallo Antiques
966 Madison Avenue
New York, NY 10021
     pages 38, 70, and 71

Woolworks Inc.
838 Madison Avenue
New York, NY 10021
     pages 70 and 71

Flowers, Plants, and Fruit Arrangements

J&M Plant and Wicker
201 Main Street
Madison, NJ 07940
     pages 34, 36, 47, 58, 76, 77, 81, 83, 84,
     and 94

Royal Gifts
1 Mount Prospect Avenue
Verona, NJ 07044
     pages 54 and 55

Carpets

Carpet Showrooms, Inc.
979 Third Avenue
New York, NY 10022
     pages 42 and 43

Phoenix Carpets
979 Third Avenue
New York, NY 10022
     page 27

Stark Carpet Corporation
979 Third Avenue
New York, NY 10022
     pages 34 and 35

Furniture

Conran's
160 East 54th Street
New York, NY 10022
     page 42

Kay-Lyn, Inc.
P.O. Box 2366
High Point, NC 27261
     pages 40, 41, and 70

Leaves, Ltd.
57 Church Street
Montclair, NJ 07042
    pages 34, 76, and 77

Wickerland
43-A Church Street
Montclair, NJ 07042
    page 92

Services

Computer-blended Paint
Janovic/Plaza
1150 Third Avenue
New York, NY 10021

Custom-covered Buttons
Reliable Button Works
65 West 37th Street
New York, NY 10018
    page 22

Custom-cut Foam
Foam Firm
Main Street
Gladstone, NJ 07934
    page 98

Custom Umbrellas
Uncle Sam Umbrella Shop
161 West 57th Street
New York, NY 10019
    pages 104 and 109

Fabric Protection
Fiber-Seal International, Inc.
10755 Sanden Drive
Dallas, TX 75238

Monogramming
Carriage House Monograms
Betty Shelby
7 Knollwood Road
Short Hills, NJ 07078
    pages 70, 71, 80, 81, 86, 87, and 110

Pleating
Gaspare Cannizzaro Pleating Co., Inc.
660 Newbridge Road
East Meadow, NY 11554
    pages 28 and 29

Index

W

Z